WRITINGS ON EMPIRE AND SLAVERY

Writings on
Empire and Slavery

ALEXIS DE TOCQUEVILLE

Edited and Translated by

Jennifer Pitts

THE JOHNS HOPKINS UNIVERSITY PRESS
Baltimore & London

*This book was brought to publication with the generous assistance of
the Karl and Edith Pribram Fund.*

The Johns Hopkins University Press
2715 North Charles Street
Baltimore, Maryland 21218-4363
www.press.jhu.edu

Library of Congress Cataloging-in-Publication Data will be found at the end
of this book.
A catalog record for this book is available from the British Library.

ISBN 0-8018-6509-3

CONTENTS

ACKNOWLEDGMENTS

I am indebted to Gallimard for kind permission to make use of their edition and editorial notes, and to the editors of the 1962 Gallimard edition of Tocqueville's writings on empire (*Œuvres complètes*, volume 3, part 1), André Jardin and Jean-Jacques Chevallier, for their thoroughness and care in creating that excellent volume, without which this translation would not exist. I am grateful also to J.-P. Mayer, editor of the Gallimard *Œuvres complètes*, volume 5, part 2, where Tocqueville's notes on his 1841 trip to Algeria were first published in full.

For many illuminating conversations about Tocqueville and the history of political thought, and for thoughtful comments on various drafts of this project, I am grateful to Stanley Hoffmann (who first suggested that I examine Tocqueville's writings on Algeria), Pratap Mehta, Richard Tuck, and Melvin Richter, whose own learned and creative work on Tocqueville has been an inspiration for me. I am grateful to Robert and Elborg Forster for their careful reading of the introduction and the translation. Christopher Brooke, Michaele Ferguson, Gerard James Livesey, Patchen Markell, Anthony Pagden, and Karen Shelby offered helpful responses to earlier versions of the introduction. For five years, Sankar Muthu has been my most treasured critic and companion; he has read countless drafts with sensitivity and keen intelligence and has been steadfast in his support throughout this project.

I am deeply indebted to Marie-Laure Neulat, who read the entire translation and, with her fine grasp of nuance in both French and English, suggested many valuable improvements. I should also like to thank Arthur Goldhammer, Patrice Higgonet, Mary Pitts, and Toni Wagner for help with certain terms and passages.

The Minda de Gunzburg Center for European Studies at Harvard University brought together a superb community of scholars in my time there and provided me with an unparalleled research environment. I am grateful to the Charlotte Newcombe foundation for a dissertation completion grant that freed me from teaching duties for a year and enabled me to devote some time to this translation. I am grateful as well to my editors at the Johns Hopkins University Press, Douglas Armato, Henry Tom, and especially Peter Dreyer, whose keen eye and command of French language and history have improved every page of this book.

Any remaining errors in the translation or the introduction are mine alone.

INTRODUCTION

LIFE

Alexis de Tocqueville was born in Paris in 1805 to a noble family badly scarred by the French Revolution.[1] His mother's grandfather, Lamoignon de Malesherbes, had defended Louis XVI before the Convention and was guillotined in 1794. His parents, Hervé de Tocqueville and Louise de Rosanbo, imprisoned in their early twenties, had escaped execution but emerged weak and anxious. Alexis, their third son, was educated at home by the abbé Lesueur, a nonjuring priest who had been Hervé's tutor and had returned to the family after his revolutionary exile. At sixteen, Tocqueville entered the collège de Metz, where he excelled, despite his father's fears that the abbé's instruction had been excessively lax. After studying law in Paris, Tocqueville was appointed to a prestigious post as a magistrate in Versailles, apparently as a favor to his father. His colleague there, Gustave Auguste de Beaumont de La Bonninière (1802–66), a former schoolmate who was also of an aristocratic family, would become his close friend and traveling companion. Their political careers, like so many, were disrupted by the July Revolution of 1830, when the right-wing Bourbon monarchy of Charles X was overthrown and replaced by the constitutional "bourgeois" monarchy of Louis-Philippe. Tocqueville reluctantly swore allegiance to the new regime, although his father, a legitimist, or supporter of the deposed Bourbons, refused to take the oath.[2] Tocqueville himself would have to fight imputations that he was a legitimist for much of his political career.

Tocqueville and Beaumont resolved to leave the country for a year to avoid the personal compromises that they felt involvement in the new regime would demand. They received permission to travel to America as official representatives of the French state (though they paid their own way), in order to study the progressive penitentiary system of the United States. Although their *Système pénitentiaire*, published in 1833, received a prize from the Institut de France, far more ambitious goals had always inspired their journey. As Tocqueville wrote to a friend in 1830, "For a long time now, I have had a very strong desire to visit North America. I will go there and see what a great republic is."[3] They planned to write a book together describing Europe's democratic future as it appeared in America, and thus "separate ourselves from the crowd" and open the way to political careers. In the event, their projects diverged. Tocqueville wrote the political work, and Beaumont wrote *Marie, ou, l'esclavage aux Etats-Unis (Marie, or, Slavery in the United States)*, a novel about a romance between a young Frenchman and a mixed-race American woman, and a social commentary that reflected his discouragement and pessimism about the state of race relations in America.[4]

The first volume of *Democracy in America* was published in 1835, winning Tocqueville immediate celebrity and critical praise. Although there are no records of the number of books in each printing, we know that sales far outpaced the publisher's expectations, so that by 1840 (when the second volume was published) *Democracy in America* had gone into its eighth printing.[5] Also in 1835, Tocqueville married an Englishwoman, Mary Mottley, against the wishes of his family. After having failed to win election to the Chamber of Deputies in 1837, Tocqueville entered the Chamber in March 1839 as the representative for Valognes, the Norman district that included the family seat and town of Tocqueville. He had fought to maintain his independence during the campaign, and to fight off insinuations that he was a legitimist. As he would insist to his constituency again in June 1842, "I am a liberal and nothing more. I was one before 1830; I am still one."[6]

Throughout his parliamentary career (1839–51), and despite his constituents' apparent enthusiasm, Tocqueville was plagued by self-doubt. He considered himself a mediocre public speaker, and he believed that his resolute independence of any faction was politically crippling. After publishing the second volume of *Democracy in America* in 1840, Tocqueville devoted particular energy to France's foreign and colonial policy, for he believed that it was on this neglected terrain that France's stability and international reputation might be built. Despite his refusal to join a side in the divisions leading to the revolution of 1848, which again led to suspicions on the left that he was a reactionary, Tocqueville was elected to the National Assembly, the body that replaced the Chamber of Deputies, which first met in May 1848. He reports these events in an engaging and highly personal account in his *Recollections* (1851). Tocqueville served as foreign minister in the short-lived Barrot ministry (from June to October 1849), during which time he was preoccupied mostly with the republican rebellion in Rome against Pope Pius IX.

The 1851 coup of Louis-Napoleon Bonaparte, who declared himself Emperor Napoleon III in December 1852, brought Tocqueville's political life to an end, for although the new prince-president begged Tocqueville to join his government, he adamantly refused. He devoted the energies of his last decade to writing his history of centralization in France, *The Old Regime and the Revolution* (1856), for which he planned, but never completed, two other volumes: one to cover the revolution itself and the other to consider Napoleon Bonaparte and the first Empire.[7] Tocqueville's health, always somewhat fragile, deteriorated notably beginning in 1850, though he maintained a rigorous schedule of writing and archival research. He was in the midst of researching the second volume of the *Old Regime* when in 1858 his worsening tuberculosis forced him to move south for the winter; he died in April 1859 at Cannes.

TOCQUEVILLE AND THE FRENCH IMPERIAL PROJECT

When Tocqueville called for a new political science for a new world in his introduction to the first volume of *Democracy in America* (1835), declaring, "Il faut une science politique nouvelle à un monde tout nouveau," he had in mind the profound political transformations in "the Christian nations of our day": developments that appeared to be leading inexorably toward democracy and social equality. His statement might just as well have applied to the equally revolutionary developments in Europe's relations with the non-European world. France, having relinquished most of her New World possessions to Britain in the preceding century, had just conquered the city of Algiers in 1830 and, over the next two decades, was to consolidate a North African empire that would last, violently and precariously, until 1962. Britain, which had lost much of its own empire in the Western Hemisphere, was expanding its territories and the depth of state involvement in the east, especially in India.

Tocqueville himself felt these developments were little understood in Europe; they called for investigation and explanation by someone who appreciated their novelty and the considerable effect on European states and cultures they were bound to have. In order to write such explanations himself, shortly after his return from America, Tocqueville began to study Algerian history and culture and to read the Koran. He examined the former Ottoman administration of Algeria and accounts of the British conquest of India, in addition to dispatching a steady stream of questions about British colonial policy to his many well-placed correspondents, such as John Stuart Mill.[8] Indeed, Tocqueville planned to write a work on British India, although he abandoned the project after he became convinced that his delicate health would prevent him from ever making the journey there.[9] During his politically most active period, from 1837 to 1851, he was to visit Algeria twice and become one of parliament's foremost experts on the subject, writing the essays, articles, and exhaustive parliamentary reports included here.[10] This volume brings together Tocqueville's most important writings on empire, translated into English for the first time.[11]

Although Tocqueville never gave his thoughts on empire the systematic treatment that produced *Democracy in America* and *The Old Regime and the French Revolution,* he left an extensive body of writings on the subject of Europe's relations with the non-European world that deserve to be read by all students of Tocqueville, of empire, and of French history and nineteenth-century political thought. These writings, at once broadly reflective and immediately political, elucidate the more famous writings in which Tocqueville remained an observer and historian. They place the evolving American and French democracies in the global context in which Tocqueville himself felt they must be understood.

Tocqueville followed the French colonization of Algeria from its earliest years. In 1833, the twenty-seven-year-old Tocqueville and his cousin Louis de Kergorlay (who had participated as an officer in the 1830 conquest of Algiers) began to consider purchasing land in Algeria and becoming settlers. In 1841, the same year that the French began the total conquest and deliberate colonization of Algeria, Tocqueville made the first of his two visits there (the second came in 1846). Although he had by this time abandoned his plans to settle in Algeria, he considered firsthand observation crucial for an understanding of the colonial project. He remained firmly convinced that colonization of Algeria was essential to France's interests.

Tocqueville's writings on Algeria are an invaluable source of information about how French liberal thinkers treated the political, military, and moral aspects of a vast colonization project in its early days. Perhaps the most perceptive observer of politics and society of his day, he sought to grasp what was known as the "Algerian question" with as much attention as he had devoted to understanding American democracy. He was quick to appreciate the novelty of colonial warfare and administration, and he devoted careful and sometimes chillingly dispassionate study to questions about the means of colonization: how could France bring down the cost of its colonial military and make conquest more efficient? How much violence against the indigenous population was necessary in order to establish security for the colonists? Was intermarriage between settlers and native Algerians possible and desirable? The remarkable mixture of cruelty and sensibility we find in Tocqueville's writings on empire has led one scholar to remark that his colonial policy was "on the one hand quite unethical and on the other rather enlightened."[12] Tocqueville consistently rejected the arguments of critics of the French imperial project who claimed it was immoral, illegitimate, or imprudent, although he was critical of aspects of the French military regime in Algeria and advocated certain reforms.

Given his own belief in the signal importance of imperialism to the politics of his day, we cannot thoroughly understand Tocqueville's thought without considering his writings on empire. Tocqueville spent a considerable portion of his most active years engaged in the study and defense of French colonialism, and he saw imperial expansion as a kind of salvation for the crises of French domestic politics in his day. Tocqueville's readers have often been shocked at the ruthlessness of many of his recommendations for imperial conquest. Many have found it difficult to reconcile his imperialism with his often avowedly moralist politics and with his liberalism — that is to say, with his defense of individual liberty and his efforts to describe a political regime that would balance people's desire for equality with a respect for liberty and the rights of humanity. Regarding Tocqueville's belief that the apathy and individualism that plagued France might be remedied by the "great task" of imperial expansion, Melvin Richter comments, "The amount of self-delusion in this point of view is too obvious to need any elaborate analysis. But its presence in a man of Tocqueville's abilities is surely an indication of how deeply rooted was the European sense of superiority to the rest of the world."[13]

Do Tocqueville's writings on Algeria belie the commitment to liberty and human equality that we observe in *Democracy in America*? Richter has argued that "Tocqueville's stand on Algeria was inconsistent with the *Democracy*.

When this issue forced him to choose, he placed nationalism above liberalism; the interests of 'progressive' Christian countries above the rights of those that were not."[14] It should be noted, however, that Tocqueville's statements in the *Democracy* deploring the European settlers' violence toward Amerindians and slaves never amounted to a critique of expansion and conquest. Indeed, Tocqueville considered America a model for French Algeria. Tocqueville argued repeatedly that France's power and reputation within Europe would rely, increasingly, on its colonial possessions; a wide range of colonial actions were justified, he believed, by this patent need. The imperatives of nineteenth-century nation building were deeply felt by theorists like Tocqueville and Mill, and every one of Tocqueville's works attests to his fear that French liberty was fragile, far more vulnerable than the liberty of America or Great Britain.

Far from contradicting *Democracy in America,* Tocqueville's writings on Algeria may lead us to read that work in a somewhat different light and draw our attention to tensions within it. In America, Tocqueville had noted repeatedly the troubled relations among European settlers, slaves, and Amerindians. He pointed in particular to the hypocrisy of the Anglo-Americans, whose expansion was, he believed, just as violent as the notorious Spanish conquests, but who shrouded this violence in the language of rights, law, and civilization. The Americans, he wrote, had exterminated the indigenous people "with singular felicity, tranquilly, legally, philanthropically, without shedding blood, and without violating a single great principle of morality in the eyes of the world. It is impossible to destroy men with more respect for the laws of humanity."[15] On Christmas Day 1831, Tocqueville shared a riverboat down the Mississippi with a Choctaw tribe being expelled from its lands by the United States government. "The poor Indians take their old parents in their arms; the women load their children on their backs; the nation finally sets out, carrying with it its most precious possessions," he wrote that day in a letter to his mother. "It abandons for ever the soil on which, for a thousand years perhaps, its fathers have lived, to go establish itself in a wilderness where the whites will not leave them ten years in peace. Do you note the results of a high civilization?"[16] Such sentiments have led some prominent thinkers to conclude that Tocqueville was a resolute anti-imperialist. Isaiah Berlin, for instance, has remarked that Tocqueville upheld "an opposition to paternalism and colonialism, every form of rule by outsiders no matter how benevolent." Berlin's claim that Tocqueville opposed colonialism, apparently an extrapolation from pluralist arguments in *Democracy in America,* suggests, however, that to ignore Tocqueville's writings on empire is to misunderstand quite profoundly the implications of his writings on Western democracies.[17]

For Tocqueville's writings on European expansion in North America are tinged with the same ambivalence that would permeate his writings on Algeria. His protests at the cruelty of the American settlers and his laments over the extermination of noble cultures were heartfelt. Still, he could not help admiring the energy and perseverance of the English settlers in North America, who continued to push forward the frontier of settlement with tiny clearings and primitive log cabins, while preserving a keen interest in the events and ideas of New York and Europe. Tocqueville noted, in an early essay reproduced in this volume, that whereas French settlers in the same territory had failed to plant the roots of civilization, becoming only isolated, half-savage trappers and traders, the English were founding vibrant, self-governing towns, as well as frontier cities like Cincinnati, whose industry and dynamism struck Tocqueville forcefully.[18]

Although he regretted the injuries and indignities that indigenous peoples and slaves had suffered at the hands of Europeans, Tocqueville suggested as well that both Amerindians, whom he classed among "savage nations," and slaves were incapable of participating in a democratic order and thus destined to remain excluded: expelled from the territory, killed off, degraded beneath notice, or shunted into a state of permanent enmity with American democracy. The two groups together represented the extremes of liberty and servitude. They thus figured symmetrically in the landscape of democracy—or, rather, stood outside democracy entirely, marking its fixed limits. Both, in Tocqueville's view, had participated in their own exclusion from democratic politics. American slaves had had the misfortune to grow accustomed to servitude and accept it; Amerindians, lying "on the uttermost verge of liberty," could have chosen civilization but disdained to do so, and their extreme love of liberty had facilitated the corruption of their society.[19] The vices of both extremes thus demonstrated, by negative example, the qualities needed to sustain democracy. Tocqueville believed that by the time he arrived in America, the Amerindians were already condemned to extinction. "It is the misfortune of Indians," he wrote, "to be brought into contact with a civilized people who are also (it must be owned) the most grasping nation on the globe," a people whose apparent regard for the language of rights, liberty, and international law masked very poorly their ruthless expansionism.[20] As it was too late to improve the tribes' fortunes, in his judgment, Tocqueville believed that one could only express nostalgia for their uncorrupted past and lament the Americans' failure to improve the European record in the New World. Tocqueville's account of Amerindians and slaves in this work is, as a result, a highly aestheticized one, more tableau than argument.

If Tocqueville was not already convinced that relations with non-Europeans would become an inextricable element of modern democracy, his examinations of empire shortly after his return soon persuaded him of this. Only in the writings on Algeria and slavery did Tocqueville develop the notion, implicit in *Democracy*, that imperial expansion might be more than an arbitrary fact about the modern democratic state. He had seen the frontier as an essential element of the American experience and as a breeding-ground for the self-reliance that characterized American citizens, and he believed American industrialization relied on slave labor. Still, he had declared indigenous peoples and blacks tangential to his subject in *Democracy in America*, calling them "American without being democratic."[21] As a result, in his writing on America, he never directly confronted the deep entanglement of American democracy in the exploitation of those living on its margins. Tocqueville would write in 1841 that "Africa has henceforth entered into the movement of the civilized world and will never leave it," in part as justification for the claim that France should not abandon its conquest. His study of America, and especially Algeria, were to persuade him that, however asymmetric the relationship between Europeans and colonized peoples, European liberalism and democracy were stamped, just as the colonies were, with the mark of European imperialism.

This intertwining of democracy and imperialism took on special urgency in France in the 1830s. Despite what Tocqueville believed to be a general trend in modern Europe toward greater freedom and equality, the twin threats of anarchy and despotism meant that France was in no way assured a gentle transition from the old regime to a stable democratic government. With the conquest of Algiers, men across the political spectrum who earlier had shunned imperial conquest — from François Guizot on the right to Louis Blanc on the left — developed a new appetite for empire, believing that the weak and divided French polity would find strength in national glory.[22]

Tocqueville himself came to believe that the instability of French domestic politics since the Revolution could not be righted through domestic politics alone. France, he believed, was a nation lurching toward modern democracy. The country's past was dominated by a powerful central government, which the Revolution, contrary to appearances, had only consolidated. The memory of the Eighteenth Brumaire, and the prospect, which he anticipated long before his parliamentary colleagues, of another revolution and another dictatorial coup, drove Tocqueville to seek means of consolidating the moderate republican government at home. With weak leaders capable only of petty quibbling, and a divided and apathetic public, France, in Tocqueville's view, required new occasions for virtuous or glorious action.[23] The conquest of Algeria, and in the 1840s the debate over the abolition of slavery in the French Antilles, provided precisely such occasions. The abolition of slavery would be a noble, moral act and would regain for France some of the luster of her humanitarian reputation, which had passed over to Britain when that country abolished slavery in its colonies in 1833. Conquering and settling Algeria would constitute a national project: it would capture the public's attention, unify the fractured political scene, and gain Europe's respect.[24]

THE "LETTERS ON ALGERIA"

From the beginning of his political life, Tocqueville placed French colonialism at the center of his agenda.[25] During his first effort to win a seat in the Chamber of Deputies, in 1837, Tocqueville published two "Letters on Algeria," the first product of his several years of study of Algeria and of the past seven years of French activity there.[26] "I have no doubt," he declared, "that we shall be able to raise on the coast of Africa a great monument to the glory of our country." The first "Letter" consisted of a summary of the available ethnography on the peoples of Algeria and an account of the former Ottoman government there. Here Tocqueville experimented with a theory of social development that recalled theories of social stages — savage, barbarian, civilized, and commercial — popularized in the eighteenth century by thinkers such as Montesquieu, Adam Smith, and Adam Ferguson. He wrote of the "half-savage" coastal Arabs, for instance, noting that the contours of their society "are not peculiar to them but belong to the period of civilization at which they find themselves." Although Tocqueville occasionally used the notion of social stages to account for indigenous practices or to justify European conquest, neither here nor in his later works did Tocqueville develop a thoroughgoing theory of progress, and he remained critical of such theories and justifications of empire when he encountered them among his English acquaintances.

Tocqueville was fascinated by the differences he perceived between the mostly sedentary Kabyle tribes (Berbers living in the Atlas mountains), and the more nomadic Arab population. He described the Kabyles, whom he as well as later French administrations were to favor over the Arabs,[27] as living in an early stage of society in which freedom and equality coexisted with a level of social organization. The Kabyles, he suggested, were the true "natural men" whom Rousseau had sought among Amerindian tribes. "If Rousseau had known the Kabyles," he wrote,

> he would not have uttered such nonsense about the Caribs and other Indians of America: he would have sought his models in the Atlas; there he would have found men subject to a sort of social police and nonetheless almost as free as the isolated individual who enjoys his savage independence in the heart of the woods; men who are neither rich nor poor, neither servants nor masters; who name their own leaders, and hardly notice that they have leaders, who are content with their state and preserve it.

As for the Arabs, Tocqueville was struck by their careful documentation of collective property rights and by their well-developed religious aristocracy of marabouts. Finally, he criticized the Ottoman regime as "not truly speaking a government but a continuation of conquest, a violent exploitation of the conquered by the conquerors." He believed that the Ottoman Janissaries had wrongly remained aloof from the population, disdaining even their own children by Arab women (the mixed-race population known as *coulouglis*), and that they occupied the country merely to levy taxes to be sent off to Turkey, rather than taking any interest in governing the indigenous population.

The second "Letter" constituted an informed and focused attack on the past seven years of French colonial policy in North Africa and presented Tocqueville's vision of colonial society (one that would change considerably in later years) and the means of achieving it. After their conquest of Algiers, he argued, the French had behaved with ignorance and arrogance in deporting the former Ottoman rulers and destroying their records and even their roads. Instead of being able to draw on the Turks' knowledge of the country and its inhabitants, the property system the Ottoman regime had documented, and their well-established taxation scheme, the French had found themselves forced to extort money and goods "from our unhappy subjects by means far more Turkish than those the Turks had ever used."

Knowing, in addition, nothing of the political organization developing among the local tribes, the French unwittingly were driving all the tribes into the arms of a single capable leader, the marabout emir Abd-el-Kader, and encouraging an Arab "national unity" that would make it impossible to subject the Arabs to French rule. Tocqueville believed that the Arab capacity for self-governance had merely been weakened, rather than destroyed, by centuries of Ottoman rule. The immediate result of the French conquest was to open a space for political organization, of which the Arabs, and in particular their religious aristocracy, were quick to take advantage. The French, he argued, should permit this renewed self-government but control it and put it to their own use.

Finally, not understanding the distinctions between Arabs and Kabyles, the French were attempting to conquer the entire Algerian population through a uniform policy of violence. The Kabyles were, in Tocqueville's opinion, more materialistic and less spiritual (or less fanatical) than the Arabs. The Atlas mountains in which the Kabyles lived were impenetrable to French armies, "but the soul of the Kabyles is open to us." Rather than attempting to rule the Kabyles directly, which would be costly and futile, the French could co-opt them effectively by trading with them and making them dependent on French goods and employment. Tocqueville maintained this position on French-Kabyle relations throughout his career.

At this early stage in his engagement with Algeria, Tocqueville believed firmly in what he called "amalgamating the two races," French and Arab, a process that entailed both intermarriage and a gradual progression toward common towns and laws for both groups (the Arabs, if persuaded not to fear the French, would, he believed, come to prefer settled life to nomadism). The amalgamation would be achieved through religious toleration and legal pluralism, each community living under laws it could respect; this meant, above all, that the French would have to recognize and tolerate the centrality of the Koran to Arab civil law. The subject of the role played by religious law in Arab life had preoccupied Tocqueville since his reading of the Koran in the early 1830s; his notes on the Koran, which are included in this volume, offer a sense of his early understanding of Islam and its relation to Arab social and political life. In these early writings on Algeria, we see evidence of the respect for local diversity and the hostility to centralization and uniformity for which *Democracy in America* is justly famous. "We must take care in Algeria to give up this taste for uniformity that torments us and to realize that it would be as dangerous as it is absurd to apply the same laws to different beings," he wrote in the second "Letter." Tocqueville's affection for cultural pluralism was limited, however, and he was convinced that such pluralism would be necessary only for a transitional period. Later, the two peoples would "refound themselves as a single whole," under largely European laws.

Such is Tocqueville's initial vision of French Algeria: at first, a colony of many populations living under different laws, and with different degrees of autonomy, but all firmly under French rule. Eventually, a single population would emerge, living under French laws and French governors, "a great monument to the glory of our country." Two aspects of Tocqueville's early colonial writings are most striking: first, his interest in Arab forms of political organization and self-governance, and second, his desire to see the integration of French settlers and Algerians through a policy of toleration and pluralism. Both would largely disappear in his later works as he became convinced that integration was impossible and turned increasingly to strategies of military domination.

JOURNEY TO ALGERIA AND THE "ESSAY" OF 1841

After a year in the Chamber of Deputies (he won the seat for Valognes in 1839), and after a thorough study of government reports on the colony, Tocqueville made his first trip to Algeria in the company of his brother Hippolyte and Gustave de Beaumont.[28] Fascinated by the new colonial society even more than by the Algerians whose society and religion he had been studying, Tocqueville interviewed a number of military and colonial officials and kept a revealing journal of his trip, included in this volume. In his journal he noted the dynamism of the city of Algiers, with its multiethnic population and the great burst of building projects that had begun under the French. Although charmed by the traditional architecture of the city, he concluded that it supported the idea, derived from his reading, that Muslims lacked a real public political life.

Tocqueville's earliest letters and diary entries from the trip emphasized the country's exotic appearance. For all his desire to focus his study of the country on bureaucratic records, Tocqueville's early impressions recall the more Romantic responses to North Africa of Gustave Flaubert and Eugène Delacroix. "I hope this voyage will be useful to us and to the country," he wrote in a letter to his father. "You couldn't make a more curious one. Never in my life have I seen anything more bizarre than the first sight of Algiers. It is a tale out of the *Thousand and One Nights*. . . . It's an enchanted country farmed by savages."[29]

Several weeks in the country, however, allowed him to develop a sense of familiarity and only increased his desire to possess the country. The chaos he saw in the streets of Algiers and Philippeville reminded Tocqueville of the American frontier, and he hoped the disarray might be evidence of an American vitality and promise. "At the first sight of Philippeville," he wrote to his brother Edouard, "I thought I was in America."

> Two years ago it was a deserted beach. Today, the city already has five thousand civilian inhabitants. I leave you to judge of the disorder that accompanies such a rapid creation. Everything is happening at once. Streets are laid; houses are built; debris of all kinds lies everywhere. And everything has that appearance of feverish activity that I have not encountered anywhere since the United States.[30]

In America, Tocqueville had observed the brutalizing effects of colonial rule on both the indigenous people and their occupiers. Here, too, he recognized the pervasive violence characteristic of colonial warfare: the French would be fighting, not a professional army, but rather the entire society. It was impossible to establish a secure border, so wars at the frontier would continue indefinitely. Still, Tocqueville's 1841 visit only served to convince him that the imperial goal justified the means, and that the French must be prepared to use violence against civilians in ways that would be unconscionable in Europe — to "burn harvests, empty silos, and capture unarmed men, women, and children," as he wrote later that year in his "Essay on Algeria," which offers the most brutal judgments of his writings on Algeria. Another European nation would seize Algeria immediately if France were to pull out. In the interest of France's glory and reputation in Europe, the French must accept the violence and expense necessary to establish a permanent French presence in North Africa.

Tocqueville contracted dysentery in Algeria and had to skip part of his planned journey around the country; he wrote the "Essay on Algeria" while recuperating in France.[31] Although Tocqueville did not intend the work for publication (it remained unpublished until 1962), the *Essay* was his first extended effort to produce a colonial policy, and served as a working draft for many of his later, more public, reflections, and for these reasons it is significant.[32] Although it was written only four years after the "Letters on Algeria," the "Essay" reveals a dramatic shift in Tocqueville's position on colonization.

He had become far more concerned with the role Algeria would play in securing France's international reputation, and less interested in the contours of the new society for that society's own sake. Seeing Algeria for himself had caused Tocqueville to abandon his early hopes for integration of the French and Algerian populations into a single "new civilization." Only people who have never been to Africa, he now wrote, could entertain the "chimera" of a fusion of the two peoples. Tocqueville's use of such terms as ignorant, savage, and half-civilized to describe the indigenous population became far more frequent, and his military recommendations increasingly harsh. His earlier respect for Abd-el-Kader as an emerging "national" leader had essentially disappeared: now he saw the marabout as a "Muslim Cromwell," a clever but unprincipled man who would manipulate the religious passions of his followers, and adopt European strategies of warfare, to unite his countrymen and expel the French. Tocqueville also compared Abd-el-Kader to a medieval European king who sought to consolidate his own power by crushing the feudal lords: Arab society was, he suggested, at the very stage Europe had passed through hundreds of years earlier. Rather than simply trying to crush him, the Europeans should seek to dissolve Abd-el-Kader's power by bribing his allies and offering them real protection if they deserted. As it was, throughout the world the French had repeatedly abandoned their own indigenous allies and proven that French friendship was fatal. "Isn't it finally time," Tocqueville wrote, "to show, even if only in a tiny corner of the desert, that people can attach themselves with France without losing their fortunes or their lives?" Even so, he now believed that such alliances must be temporary and that Algerians, no matter how accommodating to their French invaders, must always be treated as a separate and subject population.

After his firsthand investigation of the country, Tocqueville had concluded that military domination without colonization was a futile strategy. As the Arab population would be unrelentingly hostile to the expropriation of land necessary for widespread European settlement, the French would have to adopt uncompromising strategies for defeating the inevitable Arab resistance. In addition to halting all trade with indigenous tribes, the strategy entailed *razzias* (violent raids on villages), imprisoning unarmed civilians, including women and children, and destroying any towns the Arabs might try to establish. This position, Tocqueville believed, was the moderate one: he rejected both the summary execution of civilian prisoners advocated by many in the military, and he scorned as soft and idealistic those few Frenchmen who protested against *razzias* and crop-burning. "[I]n order for us to colonize to any extent, we must necessarily use not only violent measures, but visibly iniquitous ones," Tocqueville wrote. "The quarrel is no longer between governments, but between races . . . the day a European plow touches the soil."

As a result of his tour, Tocqueville's interests had shifted decisively in the direction of the European settlers and their laws and away from relations between the French and indigenous peoples. Having decided that colonization was the primary purpose of military domination, and that relations with Algerians would consist largely of violence, Tocqueville set about devising an ideal legal and administrative structure for the European colonists. Current conditions were, he believed, intolerable. Settlers must encounter a "perfect image of their homeland" in Algeria, or they would never stay and the colony would fail. With conditions in Algeria as bad as they appeared to Tocqueville and his companions, only the settlers' "ignorance and misery" in Europe could explain their decision to emigrate there. The fundamental rights of modern society — respected in even the most despotic European countries — were security of persons and property, and these were violated regularly and wantonly by the colonial authorities. Europeans could be arrested and summarily deported without any legal guarantees or appeal process, and the authorities could, and often did, seize property for "public purposes" without indemnifying the owners. Thus, he had discovered, "a man who has left Algiers to spend eight days in Toulon could find his house razed on his return."

What the colonial governors failed to understand was that Europeans would leave the comforts and protections of European societies only if they had good reason to expect to get rich in Algeria: property rights were far more important to them than political participation or freedom of speech.[33] Tocqueville argued that speculators with no intention of cultivating had snapped up all the land, boundaries were in dispute everywhere, and many plots had been sold to several buyers. Forced expropriations, disastrous in principle, were necessary here to sort out the mess and place property on a firm footing; otherwise cultivation would cease and the colony would fail.

Tocqueville also proposed detailed institutional reforms: Algeria suffered from both too little centralization and too much. Responsibility for Algerian affairs was scattered among a slew of ministries in Paris and Algiers, so that nobody was accountable, and at the same time communities in Algeria were prevented from taking charge of their own affairs by scores of centralizing, bureaucratic regulations.[34] The Paris bureaucrats must give up their aesthetically pleasing, uniform designs and allow authorities on the spot to tailor policies to local conditions: as it was, a town had to apply to the Paris ministries for funds to fix the church roof. The dangers of centralization had preoccupied Tocqueville from the time of his earliest writings on France and America. Here, for the first time, he outlined his ideas for a new society in the face of France's tendency to centralization. When he applied his historical research to institutional design in his own day, however, the result was a far less radical critique of centralization than his other works would suggest. For despite his pleas for greater local autonomy, for municipal councils and settlers' active participation in government, on the American model, Tocqueville did not want the colonists to develop too great a sense of independence: as he would write in his first parliamentary report, "We should set out to create not a colony properly speaking in Algeria, but rather the extension of France itself across the Mediterranean."

The "Essay" is the most uncompromising of Tocqueville's writings on Algeria. He wrote it fresh from his tour of the country, and with most of his parliamentary career ahead of him, and we should read it as the blueprint for a colonial society by a powerful, prominent, and widely respected expert on the subject. His scorn for the idea of a rapprochement between French and Algerians, as well as his new disdain for critics of empire who had never visited the country (such as the leftist deputy Amédée Desjobert) give his writings of this period a haughty and even cruel edge. Indeed, as his friends Beaumont and Nassau Senior reported after his death, Tocqueville believed that the small group of anti-imperialist leftists in the Chamber of Deputies, such as Desjobert, were wrong "on everything to do with Algeria," and he voted against them every time.[35] Over the course of the next decade, although Tocqueville remained a staunch and prominent supporter of the French colony in Algeria, the ambivalence about colonial violence that he had demonstrated in his earlier writings about America would creep back into his thoughts on North Africa. The "Essay" itself, however, shows little evidence of such uneasiness or self-doubt.

PARLIAMENTARY REPORTS

After his second trip to Algeria in 1846, Tocqueville was appointed to draft two reports by a parliamentary commission convened for the purpose of examining military requests for additional funds for their operations in

Algeria, and for evaluating the military colonies proposed by General Bugeaud.[36] The first report, whose ostensible concern was whether the fast-growing military force in Algeria could be reduced, ranged far more broadly to discuss the security of French possession of the colony, relations between France and the indigenous Algerians, and what Tocqueville saw as the administration's misgovernment of French settlers. The second report considered and rejected a plan for military colonization, which had been one of General Bugeaud's pet projects and was proposed by the subsequent administration.[37] It was more narrowly focused than the first report, but in treating various means of settling the new country, Tocqueville found a way to address the question of the foundation of new societies that had occupied him from the time of his visit to America. While he necessarily included a great many technical details absent from his earlier writings, Tocqueville took a broad and relatively philosophical view of his mandate as commission reporter. Although the reports are more assured and imperious in tone than Tocqueville's often troubled and ambivalent private letters, the positions he advocated in the report accord with his other statements on empire, and it is reasonable to read the report as presenting Tocqueville's own views.

The reports argued that, thanks to General Bugeaud, colonial war had become a science. Knowledge, power, and peace had been mutually reinforcing. Domination of the tribes and establishment of a tenuous peace had allowed the French to study them, for "you can study barbarous people only with arms in hand." Algerian society had become transparent — "indigenous society no longer wears a veil for us" — and domination simpler. The report's many references to the importance of knowledge for domination suggest that Tocqueville and his colleagues viewed investigations in Algeria such as his own as instrumental to French rule there. Thanks to research into the Arabs' and Kabyles' history and social institutions, the conquerors could now determine the "true and natural limits of our domination" and thus devote resources to achievable ends.

In contrast to Tocqueville's earlier writings, which actively advocated conquest in the face of official indecision and general indifference, these reports spoke of the conquest and settlement of Algeria as a fait accompli. The task now was to rule securely without having to continue the dramatic troop escalations of the past decade, to develop a proper legal system for the existing European population and to promote its growth, and to govern the Arabs, now seen as a society apart, with strict justice, encouraging them to adopt certain aspects of Western civilization while keeping them in their place. Tocqueville preserved a hope that European rule over the indigenous Algerians would become regularized, sustained through custom and a recognition of French authority rather than remaining "accepted only as the work of victory and the daily product of force."

As the two reports illustrate, by 1847, Tocqueville had been chastened by the wanton violence of the French army and had concluded that the government in Algeria was disorderly and tyrannical. As a result of his 1846 trip to Algeria (when he managed to escape from his Potemkin-style tour and meet some of the indigenous leaders), Tocqueville came to see that the very means he had countenanced five years before had sown disaster among the native population and produced a society of settlers more violent and oppressive than the army itself.[38] Indigenous farmers had been dispossessed of their land and then hired by lazy settlers at paltry wages to do the same work they had once done as small landowners. Muslim society, although "backward and imperfect," had been far from uncivilized; the French had made it barbaric. As Tocqueville's direct involvement in the Algerian question drew to a close in the late 1840s, then, he seems to have become more sensitive to the moral problems of empire, without relinquishing any of his earlier faith that a French colony could and should be maintained in Algeria. In a letter of 10 October 1846, he wrote, "How can we manage to create in Africa a French population with our laws, our mores, our civilization, while still preserving vis-à-vis the indigenous people all the regard that justice, humanity, our interest well understood, and, as you have said, our honor strictly oblige us to preserve? The question has these two sides. One cannot usefully imagine the first without seeing the second."[39]

Tocqueville argued that France could attempt to promote such acceptance of her rule by respecting the Algerians' laws and customs and demonstrating the extent to which their interests matched French interests, although he did not elaborate much in these later reports on the mechanisms of rule that would replace violence. At the same time, Tocqueville believed that the Algerians' nomadism — what he termed their *mobility* — meant that French rule must be aggressive and harsh. (He was careful not to claim, as his friend J. S. Mill was arguing for India, that despotism was necessary because of the indigenous peoples' barbarous customs or backwardness.) In order to govern, the French had not only to seize the administrative apparatus from the Ottomans but also to "subjugate the population." Tocqueville had questioned his British correspondents about British means of governing the populations of India, New Zealand, and the African Cape. He learned from their method of indirect governance through indigenous notables, and advocated the same for Algeria.[40] The "art of the conqueror" required controlling the natives' disposition toward their European governors: Tocqueville believed that until the French had established some moral authority among the population, they could rule only by co-opting indigenous leaders and governing through them. France must neither "forget its position as conqueror" nor "allow our Muslim subjects exaggerated ideas of their own importance." He held that Muslims were not fellow citizens or equals; moreover, it was just to treat them as inferiors, since that was what they expected from French domination. Still, while it would be wrong to leave the best land for the Arabs, the French must be scrupulous about indemnifying indigenous property holders for the property they took.

In his early studies of Algerian society, Tocqueville had found much support for his belief in the importance of religion to social order, and he now criticized the French administration for having made havoc, not just of property rights, but more destructively of indigenous legal and religious institutions and education. The French had encountered a society that had been poor and nomadic, but also well ordered, with extensive networks of religious schools and charities; they had demolished these, leaving "Muslim society much more miserable, more disordered, more ignorant, and more barbarous than it had been before knowing us." Fanaticism would always find leaders; to suppress the religious schools and charitable foundations in the name of enlightening or abolishing Islam would only be to cede power to impostors and demagogues. In the interest of stability, the French should resurrect Algeria's once flourishing educational network, from the primary schools through Koranic legal training.[41] In sum, the French owed the Arabs good government and "exact, but rigorous, justice." Plans for the assimilation of Arabs, such as Tocqueville earlier had supported, and efforts to transplant "European civilization" to North Africa, were, he now believed, futile and misguided. At best the French could hope to weaken indigenous hostility to French rule and win the population's support not through ideas or integration but by demonstrating their common interests through effective imperial governance.

Having dismissed the hope for an assimilation of Algerians and Frenchmen, the reports proposed a vision of a separate European society in Algeria, again drawing frequently on Tocqueville's knowledge of the British experi-

ence. The French should professionalize colonial administration by establishing a school like the East India Company's college at Haileybury.[42] They
should make property sales simple and quick to encourage settlement, as Lord
Durham's famous report about Canada had instructed. As it was, the sale or
rental of the smallest plot had to be approved by the minister of war: at that
rate, the new society was bound to be stillborn. Centralization in Paris and an
insistence on the letter of the bureaucratic law had led to a breakdown of the
rule of law. Denied liberty, the colonial authorities took license, surreptitiously
and irregularly.

Moments of caution in the reports indicate a retreat from the harshness of
Tocqueville's 1941 "Essay on Algeria." The intervening years had been those of
Bugeaud's governor-generalship in Algeria: an era that Tocqueville had come
to see as characterized by increasing military arrogance and intransigence, of
growing hostility between soldiers and civilian settlers, and of the brutal *razzias* that had terrorized the Arab population without subduing them. Tocqueville, along with many in Paris, had by this point turned against Bugeaud and
his tactics:

> And if on the contrary—without saying so, for these things are often done
> but never admitted—we act in a manner that shows that in our eyes the old
> inhabitants of Algeria are but an obstacle to be crushed or trampled under
> foot, if we surround their populations, not for lifting them in our arms
> toward well-being and enlightenment but to destroy and suffocate them, the
> question of life or death will pose itself between the two races. Algeria will
> become, sooner or later, a closed field, a walled arena, where the two peoples
> will have to fight without mercy, and where one of the two must die. God
> save us, gentlemen, from such a destiny! Let us not, in the middle of the
> nineteenth century, begin the history of the conquest of America over again.

The humanity of this passage should not be exaggerated, for it was inspired
largely by the new confidence that Tocqueville expressed at the beginning of
the first report, when he asserted that France's "domination" over Algeria had
never been more secure. Perhaps, as Melvin Richter has suggested, Tocqueville preserved many of the earlier essay's ideas but chose to soften its harsh
tone when he wrote for public consumption.[43] Still, in both reports, the last
extended treatment Tocqueville would give to the question of empire, we
glimpse as well his increasing disillusionment with the colonial experiment.

The next few years, the last of his political career (1848–51), would be almost wholly occupied with France's domestic crisis.[44] Tocqueville would devote his final decade, as a private citizen, to the study of French history, in his lifelong effort to craft a historical vision and a political order for France that could bear the weight of modern democracy.

SLAVERY IN THE FRENCH EMPIRE

Tocqueville devoted considerable energy in and out of parliament to the question of the abolition of slavery in France's colonies.[45] In 1835, Tocqueville, along with other prominent liberals, joined the Société française pour l'abolition de l'esclavage (French society for the abolition of slavery), a moderate abolitionist society founded the previous year by the duc de Broglie.[46] In 1839, just months after his election to the Chamber of Deputies, Tocqueville was appointed rapporteur for a committee to study the question of emancipation. The Chamber shelved the bill proposed in his report and convened another parliamentary commission, led by Broglie, also a moderate abolitionist, to study the question. Tocqueville's report for the committee proposed that the Chamber should fix a date for the simultaneous emancipation of all slaves, after which the freedmen would serve as apprentices under the guardianship of the state; that it should determine the indemnity to be paid slaveholders, for which the state would be reimbursed through deductions from the freed slaves' wages; and that the state should continue to regulate labor and oversee the "education and moralization" of the freed slaves.[47]

In 1843, Tocqueville took his case for abolition to the public in a series of essays for the journal *Le Siècle,* included in this volume (although they were published anonymously, the articles' authorship was widely known). The Broglie commission, to which Tocqueville had also been appointed, had just published its report on the abolition of slavery. The majority of the Broglie commission had recommended a ten-year preparatory period before complete emancipation, during which the slaves would receive education and training to prepare them for freedom. Although, as André Jardin and J.-J. Chevallier note,[48] Tocqueville had failed to persuade the commission to recommend immediate emancipation followed by state supervision of the freed slaves, he commended the report in his articles and praised its author's "true love of humanity." In contrast to stauncher abolitionists, Tocqueville and Broglie agreed that the state owed the masters indemnification.

In the *Siècle* articles, Tocqueville argues that, for the sake of France's interests and honor, the Chamber must immediately develop a plan for abolition. France must abolish slavery (and indemnify the slave owners) if she wished to keep her Caribbean possessions and her reputation as the world's defender of human equality. Tocqueville's interest in abolition was tied closely to his ardent desire to preserve and strengthen the French colonies: he believed that history was marching toward abolition and that French resistance to abolition would only result in a loss of the colonies. He had noted repeatedly in the Chamber that it was no longer a question of whether to abolish slavery, but only of when. Britain, having banned the slave trade in 1808, had emancipated slaves in all British colonies in 1833. Tocqueville believed that Britain's example had proven the economic wisdom of abolition, and, more important, that France must not leave it to Britain to be the primary representative of what he called *French* principles (the principles of the Revolution) in the world. In addition, he feared that regiments of freed slaves from the British colonies, some of which were only a few dozen miles from French islands, would storm the French colonies to free their slaves.

The *Siècle* articles display the wide range of timbres in which Tocqueville was capable of writing about contemporary moral and political issues. They progress from the righteous tone of the first article, a general consideration of the grandeur of the current drive to emancipate slaves in the French colonies, to the flinty pragmatism of the last two articles, which consider the means by which to emancipate slaves without destroying colonial economies.[49] Tocqueville's national pride and liberal sentiment combined to produce an unequivocal celebration of emancipation: justice, interest, and the national character — and even competition with Britain — together showed emancipation to be the only possible route for France. The mediocrity and pettiness of French politics under the July Monarchy meant that there were few possibilities for great action: like colonial expansion, abolition of slavery was one. Only the selfish, though self-defeating, shortsightedness of the colonists prevented emancipation: "it is the *status quo* that will lose the colonies; every impartial observer recognizes this without trouble. And if there is a means for France to maintain the colonies, only the abolition of slavery can provide it."

British emancipation, in Tocqueville's view, vindicated his belief in the equality of races, while demonstrating the dangers of a total, unregulated emancipation. Freed slaves had proven themselves to be interested in education and material improvement. Allowed to buy land, they had promptly bought what they could and set up small farms, depleting the labor force and causing wages to skyrocket, he argued.[50] Tocqueville claimed that the only remedy for what he saw as an intolerable consequence of emancipation was to prohibit freed slaves from buying land; such a measure would suppress wages and save the colonial economy. Immediate emancipation had also raised slaves' expectations for their political status and for material well-being; a better course would be slowly to improve slaves' living conditions and only later to emancipate them, remaining a step ahead of their expectations in order to forestall rebellion. In the event, some minor measures were taken to alleviate the slaves' suffering (in 1843, the whipping of female slaves was banned), but the administration never acted on Tocqueville and Broglie's proposals. By 1848, gradual emancipation had become impossible. Word of the February revolution in Paris spread quickly to the colonies, and unrest among the slaves so worried the planters that the municipal councils of Guadeloupe and Martinique decided to enact immediate emancipation themselves, rather than wait for a decree from Paris.

If the tone of Tocqueville's anti-slavery articles suggests the posture of a crusader, then, his position on the question of abolition was representative of the moderate liberal position. The articles are a striking illustration of Tocqueville's lifelong effort to marry what he saw as progressive humanitarianism with hard-headed attention to the details of social relations and social policy. They offer an important perspective on the passages on slavery in *Democracy in America,* for like his writings on Algeria, these show Tocqueville confronting issues like those he faced in America, but with the responsibilities of a leading policy maker rather than with the luxury of the unaccountable observer. The articles are also essential for an understanding of Tocqueville's colonial policy, for they attest to his belief in the vital importance of France's colonies for the nation's international status, despite their political or economic costs, and they demonstrate what Tocqueville took to be France's moral duties in the world. "As the persevering enemy of despotism everywhere and under all its forms," Tocqueville wrote in an open letter in 1855,

I am pained and astonished by the fact that the freest people in the world is, at the present time, almost the only one among civilized and Christian nations which yet maintains personal servitude. . . . As a man, too, I am moved at the spectacle of man's degradation by man, and I hope to see the day when the law will grant equal civil liberty to all the inhabitants of the same empire, as

God accords the freedom of the will, without distinction, to the dwellers upon earth.[51]

The writings collected here should help Tocqueville's English-speaking readers to examine both the extent and the limits of such humanitarian claims.

TOCQUEVILLE AND LIBERAL IMPERIALISM

Tocqueville has been called one of the "artisans of [France's] colonial renaissance."[52] Not only was he personally a central figure in the development of parliamentary interest in and policies on Algeria, but he was also representative of mainstream thought on empire in mid-nineteenth-century France. Only a few voices to his left kept up the call for free trade and extrication from the colonies; the most notable anti-imperialist, Amédée Desjobert, although a deputy of long standing and an author of many books on colonial policy, never achieved anything like the support Tocqueville had on the Algerian question.[53] Most Frenchmen of the mid nineteenth century believed that imperial expansion was essential to the domestic and foreign politics of their turbulent age. As the country ousted first the extreme rightist government of Charles X in 1830 and then the constitutional monarchy of Louis-Philippe in 1848, these regimes and their successors attempted to use conquest to save themselves.[54] The French in Algeria, bent on catching up with British imperial successes, eager to appropriate the best land for themselves and to establish large settlement colonies, and determined to use violence to impose centralization and uniformity, engendered a dynamic of violence and repression that has continued to plague Algerian society throughout the twentieth century.

Tocqueville, who had used all his eloquence to defend such violent methods in the early 1840s, could not persuade his country to practice restraint when, by 1847, he came to believe that only a more reformed, moderate rule could preserve French Algeria, which he remained determined to save. There is a certain tragedy in the development of Tocqueville's understanding of Algeria between 1830 and 1850. He began, filled with optimism and national pride, by imagining a French bastion in North Africa that would be the envy of all Europe. He stopped writing about Algeria more than a decade before his death, dismayed by many of the consequences of the French presence in North Africa, but unwilling to reject the colonial project.

Tocqueville's support for French imperialism belonged to a more general shift in liberal views on empire in the early and mid nineteenth century. In the late eighteenth century, a broad consensus had emerged for the first time among political thinkers that the European project of unlimited imperial expansion was unwise and immoral. From Edmund Burke to Jeremy Bentham, Immanuel Kant to Adam Smith, prominent thinkers of many political stripes denounced European imperialism, invoking a wide range of arguments — the rights of man, popular self-determination, the economic wisdom of free trade and foolishness of conquest, the corruption of natural man by a degenerate civilization, the impossibility of sustaining freedom at home while practicing despotism abroad. European explorers, wrote Denis Diderot in 1780,

> arrive in a region of the New World unoccupied by anyone from the Old World, and immediately bury a small strip of metal on which they have engraved these words: *This country belongs to us*. And why does it belong to you? . . . You have no right to the natural products of the country where you land, and you claim a right over your fellow men. Instead of recognizing this man as a brother, you only see him as a slave, a beast of burden. Oh my fellow citizens![55]

While Diderot's anti-imperialism was among the most radical and thoroughgoing, skepticism about both particular imperial ventures and the general project of unlimited expansion was, by the 1780s, received wisdom among liberal intellectuals. Just fifty years later, however, we find no prominent thinkers in Europe criticizing the European imperial project. Indeed, the greatest liberals of the nineteenth century, including Tocqueville and J. S. Mill, were avid imperialists. "Despotism," wrote Mill in a typical passage, "is a legitimate mode of government in dealing with barbarians, provided the end be their improvement."[56]

How are we to account for this dramatic shift in liberal opinions on empire in this short period? One could claim that liberalism has always contained an imperialist core: that a liberal insistence on progress and establishing the rule of law at any cost has led liberals over and over again to support imperialist projects. On this view, nineteenth-century Britain and the French *mission civilisatrice* serve as typical examples of the imperialist logic of liberal political thought. A contrasting argument could claim that liberalism is inherently anti-imperialist, given its commitment to human equality and self-government: on this account, otherwise liberal thinkers who support empire merely reveal an illiberal side or smuggle illiberal ideas into their arguments. But the first view cannot explain the wide range of thinkers rightly considered liberals who strongly opposed European imperialism, particularly in the eighteenth century. And the second disregards the fact that many of the staple concepts of liberal political thinking have indeed been mobilized in favor of the European imperial enterprise, and that European liberalism from Grotius onward was forged alongside, and deeply affected by, imperial expansion. Liberals, in different times and under diverse circumstances in the history of the liberal tradition, have been among imperialism's most prominent defenders and its sharpest critics. No explanation that rests on some set of basic theoretical assumptions in the liberal tradition can possibly explain such flexibility on the question of empire: liberalism does not lead ineluctably either to imperialism or anti-imperialism. Rather, we must turn to the pressures and anxieties of certain historical moments to understand how thinkers whom we understand to exist within a broad but identifiable tradition could have disagreed so thoroughly about one of the most important political developments of the late eighteenth and nineteenth centuries: the expansion of European colonial empires.[57]

Postrevolutionary France offers a particularly stark example of anti-imperialism's retreat to the margins of political debate. The nation's unstable and unsettling domestic regime for much of the nineteenth century led liberals, including Tocqueville, to embrace imperialism as a kind of national salvation. This rather desperate grasp at imperialism at a crucial moment of nation-building left its mark not only on the French nation — whose subsequent century and more of colonial rule and fight against decolonization would be considerably more violent than Britain's — but on French liberalism as well. The dominant strand of liberalism that was forged during this period was to be exclusionary and nationalist; and it would sit uneasily with the Revolution's apparent legacy of universal human equality and liberty.

Tocqueville's turn to Algerian colonization as a kind of solution for France's domestic political crisis — a solution he clung to with sometimes desperate hope in spite of its clear moral and practical flaws — demonstrates his sense of crisis during the 1840s. It also illustrates certain ill-known contours of his liberalism: its susceptibility to the notion of national glory as a substitute for political virtue; its willing exclusion of unfamiliar peoples from moral consideration for the sake of national consolidation. Tocqueville's commitment to the colonial project, though unusual in the quantity and level of scholarship it inspired, was typical of the period and was shared across an astonishingly broad political spectrum. Given the similarly widespread *hostility* to empire among political thinkers and actors of the previous generation, this new support for conquest and empire demands an explanation sensitive to historical context.

Efforts to reconcile Tocqueville's divergent statements on politics and morality in the context of imperialism must ultimately fail.[58] To dismiss his writings on empire as a mere anomaly in the context of his work as a whole, however, is to ignore important implications of his struggle, as a liberal political thinker, with one of the key questions of nineteenth-century politics. How were European societies to make the transition from the old autocratic regimes to republics without succumbing to anarchy or state terror? Tocqueville's writings on Algeria imply that this transition required the exploitation of non-European societies, that nation-building legitimated the suspension of principles of human equality and self-determination, and that French glory justified any aggression the nation could muster. His writings on empire show, as no other aspect of his work does, the tremendous pressure French liberals found themselves under as they tried to carry out the work of refounding the nation in the postrevolutionary age.

A BRIEF HISTORY OF NINETEENTH-CENTURY FRENCH ALGERIA

The Ottoman Empire had dominated the Maghreb since the sixteenth century, ruling the regions around Algiers, Tunis, and Tripoli through fairly independent *deys* chosen by the corps of Janissaries (an elite corps of soldiers) and advised by a small council of Ottoman officials.[59] In the regency of Algiers, the population consisted mostly of rural Arabs, whose ancestors had migrated west in the age of Muhammad, and Berber tribes, who lived in the mountains (the largest group of whom were called Kabyles, from *qabā'il*, Arabic for tribe).[60] It also came to include *coulouglis* (or *koulouglis*), the descendants of Turkish soldiers and Arab women, who were shunned for the most part by the Turks and prohibited from living in Turkey, but who also proved useful intermediaries between the Ottoman rulers and their Arab subjects. European powers carried on a lively trade in the Maghreb, and although they often protested that their ships were vulnerable to raids by the notorious Barbary coast privateers, such raids had diminished considerably by the nineteenth century.[61]

According to the classic if somewhat improbable account of France's conquest of Algiers in 1830, the precipitating event had occurred three years earlier, when the *dey,* enraged by French dithering about the repayment of some loans, slapped the French consul with a fly swatter.[62] The French responded first with a naval blockade; then, in 1829, a bombardment of Algiers; and finally, in May 1830, the seizure of the city's qasba, or fort. Whatever the initial catalyst may have been, by 1830, Charles X's conservative and unpopular Polignac ministry had decided to capture Algiers outright, a move dictated both by the regime's desire for international consequence and by its hopes of distracting a restive French public. The attack, although a military and popular success, failed to keep the regime in power.

Having inherited Algiers, the July Monarchy (1831–48) held the territory without making any definite plans to keep it, until a parliamentary commission, convened in 1834, declared it essential to France's "honor and interest" to rule over the North African coast. By an ordinance of King Louis-Philippe, Algeria was annexed to France in July of that year.[63] Thereafter, Algeria saw a regular escalation of French troops and the development of plans for domination that culminated in the appointment, in 1840, of General Thomas-Robert Bugeaud as governor-general.

Bugeaud's first task in Algeria had been to come to terms with Abd-el-Kader, an Arab leader of great military and political skill who controlled the western part of the country around the town of Oran. The son of a marabout as well as a member of a *sherif* family (one descended from the Prophet), Abd-el-Kader was named *Emir el-mouminin* (defender of the faithful) at age twenty-four.[64] His position was strengthened by two treaties with the French. The Desmichels Treaty of 1834 recognized his sovereignty in western Algeria (apart from Oran, Arzeu, and Mostaganem, which were held by the French), and the Tafna Treaty of 1837, negotiated with Bugeaud, extended the area of Abd-el-Kader's sovereignty.[65] The other prominent Muslim leader in Algeria, Ahmad Bey, dominated the eastern part of the country around Constantine. After years of warring and treaty-making, both leaders surrendered to the French in 1847 and were imprisoned or exiled, ending hopes for the expulsion of the French and the establishment of an Islamic state.[66]

Bugeaud, once a parochial landowner preoccupied with agricultural development in his native Périgord and ardently opposed to colonization, had undergone a conversion during the 1830s and declared that total subjugation of Algeria was France's only option. He fought and governed brutally until his resignation of the governor-generalship in 1847. He managed to earn the animosity not only of the local population—who watched Bugeaud's troops burn their crops, destroy their villages (in the deadly raids known as *razzias*), and suffocate hundreds of their members in caves—but also of the French settlers, who found his rule despotic.

The 1848 constitution of the Second Republic declared Algeria "an inte- gral part of France," paving the way for the eventual incorporation of the colony into the metropolitan administrative structure. A decree of December 1848 divided the limited civil regions of the country into three *départements,* Oran (western Algeria), Algiers (central), and Constantine (eastern), al- though much of the country remained under direct military rule.[67] These departments were granted representation in the Chamber of Deputies, but the franchise was limited to Europeans and to a small minority of indigenous Algerians, who were required to renounce Islam in order to obtain French citizenship.[68] Tocqueville himself had sought such an incorporation when, in his 1847 report, he described the goal that would guide France's elusive, destructive, and ultimately failed project in Algeria:

> We should set out to create not a colony properly speaking in Algeria, but rather the extension of France itself across the Mediterranean. It is not a matter of creating a new people, with its own laws, its customs, its interests, and sooner or later its separate nationality, but of implanting in Africa a population that resembles us in everything. If this goal cannot be attained immediately, it is at least the only one for which we should constantly and actively strive.

This ostensible goal of total assimilation was belied by the exclusion of the vast majority of Algerians from economic prosperity and democratic participation, and an Algerian nationalist movement began to emerge in the early twentieth century. Early Algerian nationalist leaders tended to be French-educated, and French citizens; their demands at first were restricted to legal equality for Algerians rather than independence. Several years under the Vichy regime, however, radicalized Algerian opposition to French rule. A series of episodes of nationalist violence and French repression beginning in May 1945 led to the outbreak of war on 1 November 1954, led on the Algerian side by the National Liberation Front (FLN). The bloody conflict, made more intractable by the presence of a large population of European settlers who opposed granting any concessions to the indigenous Algerians, continued for eight years. It led to the collapse of the Fourth Republic in France, the reelection of Charles de Gaulle, and the declaration of the Fifth Republic.

A cease-fire was signed in March 1962, and in a referendum of 1 July 1962, nearly 6 million Algerians voted in favor of (and 16,000 against) President de Gaulle's proposal for independence. Independence was declared two days later, and a constitution was ratified in September 1963, with Ahmed ben Bella as the new country's first president.[69]

WRITINGS ON EMPIRE AND SLAVERY

SOME IDEAS ABOUT WHAT PREVENTS
THE FRENCH FROM HAVING
GOOD COLONIES (1833)

Even supposing that the territory that is to contain the colony has been discovered and that it combines the conditions necessary for the success of the
enterprise, there still remain the difficulties of execution. These were great for
England; they seem insurmountable for France.[1]

The foremost of all, it must be said, is found in the French genius, which
does not appear very favorable to colonization.*

France, by its geographic position, the extent of its territory, its fertility,
has always been in the first rank of continental powers. The land is the natural
theater of her power and glory. Maritime commerce is but an appendage to
her existence; the sea has never excited, nor will it ever excite, those national
sympathies and that sort of filial respect that navigating or commercial peoples
have for it. Maritime enterprises will never attract attention in France nor gain
the help of wealth or talent. In general, the only men one sees engaging in such
enterprises are those whose mediocre talents, declining fortunes, or memories
of a former life forbid the hope of a promising future in their country.

Besides, our national character displays a singular mix of domestic tendencies and passion for adventure, two things that are equally bad for colonization. The Frenchman has a natural taste for quiet pleasures; he loves the
domestic hearth, he rejoices at the sight of his native parish, he cares about

---

* [Variant: *génie de la nation qui paraît invariablement opposé à* (the nation's genius,
which seems invariably opposed to).]

family joys like no other man in the world. Snug in the modest fortune into which he was born, he feels less tormented than anyone else by the thirst for gold. He is rarely absorbed by love of wealth, and his life plays out comfortably in his birthplace.

Uproot him from these quiet habits, strike his imagination with new scenes, transplant him under another sky, and this same man is suddenly possessed by an insatiable need for action, for violent emotions, for vicissitudes and dangers. The most civilized European becomes a passionate lover of the savage life. He prefers savannahs to city streets, hunting to farming; existence holds no worries for him, he lives without a care for the future. "The whites of France," say the savages of Canada, "are as good hunters as we are; like us, they despise the comforts of life and brave the terrors of death. The Great Spirit created them to make their home in the Indian's cabin and to live in the wilderness."[2]

These two opposite dispositions, which are joined together in the French character, are singularly unfavorable for the establishment of a colony.

It is almost impossible to convince the poor and honest population of our countryside to leave their homeland to seek their fortune. The peasant is less afraid of misery in his birthplace than of the risks and rigors of distant exile. But it is only with men of that sort that the core of a good colony can be formed.

Once you have taken great pains to send him to another shore, it is difficult to make him settle there. He never shows that ardent and obstinate desire to make his fortune that stimulates the Englishman's daily efforts and seems to lead all his energies together toward a single end. The French colonist only gradually improves the land entrusted to him and makes slow progress in every respect; his needs are easily satisfied; he is constantly ensnared by the charms of an idle and vagabond life.

This first obstacle, created by our national character, is joined by those created by our political habits and our laws.

For several centuries, the central government in France has worked constantly to control every decision itself; today, we can say that it does not just govern but administers all the separate parts of the realm. It would be beyond the scope of our subject to study what might be useful or dangerous in this state of affairs; we limit ourselves to noting that it is so.

The resulting legal obligations and political habits are not very favorable to the foundation, let alone the development, of a colony. If the central government often finds it impossible to judge soundly and to resolve in good time the difficulties that arise in a province near the seat of empire, this will be even more the case when it has to concern itself with interests stirring three thousand leagues away.

To provide the means of execution, to choose able officers, to impose certain general laws that no one is allowed to break: these are the obligations that the mother country must take on when she sends some of her children to seek their fortune in another hemisphere. As for the daily concerns of public administration, the individual efforts of the colonists, the metropole neither can nor should try to control them.

All the great colonizing nations exercise this minimal control. But we should note that none of them has centralized the government at home.

It was never that way with us: on the contrary, we have seen France constantly try to transport abroad principles of government and administrative habits that resist the very nature of things.

We have noted that in France it has been hard to find talented men to run colonial enterprises, while in other countries they have come forward in droves. Whether lack of confidence in those it employed, or rather jealousy of the power and rule of habit, the French government has always made extraordinary efforts to keep the same place at the head of the colony that it holds at the center of the realm. We have seen it try to judge what it could not know, to regulate a society different from the one at hand, to provide for needs it knew nothing about, and to suspend all rights for the sake of justice. It wanted to predict everything in advance, it feared relying on the zeal or, even more, on the self-interest of the colonists, it demanded to examine everything, direct everything, oversee everything, do everything itself. It undertook an immense task, and it exhausted itself in futile efforts.

Besides, the political education that the French colonist received in his country left him almost unable to do without a guardian. Left in a place where he has to take charge of himself in order to prosper, he has proven uneasy in the exercise of his new rights. If the government has tried to do everything for him, he, for his part, is only too ready to call on the government for all his needs: he does not pride himself on his own efforts, has little taste for independence, and must almost be forced to be free.

The world's example has proven nonetheless that if individual energy and the art of governing oneself are useful in all societies, this is especially so in those that are born and develop as colonies, in forced isolation.

The history of the past centuries presents, it must be admitted, a singular spectacle.

We see France undertaking a vast system of colonies in the New World. The plans are ably conceived, the places it designates are well chosen: it sought to unite the Saint Laurence to the Mississippi by an uninterrupted chain of settlements, and to found a new French empire in the center of North America, with two outlets — Canada and Louisiana. France made great sacrifices of men and enormous sacrifices of money and trouble to attain this goal. The government is constantly preoccupied with its new settlements and never for a single instant does it abandon the duty of governing them. And yet, despite such efforts, the colonies languish; the land stretches out beyond the step of the French in vain, they fail to advance into the fertile wilderness that surrounds them, the population hardly increases, ignorance seems to spread, the new society remains stationary, gaining neither force nor wealth, and eventually it succumbs, after having fought with heroic courage against foreign aggression.

Nearby, on the ocean coast, the English come to settle. Some are sent by the mother country; others are rather fleeing from her. Once they have set foot on American soil, they become foreigners to England, so to speak, just as England appears little preoccupied with governing them. From the start, they have their political assemblies and tribunals, they appoint most of their magistrates, organize their militia, provide for their needs, and make their own municipal regulations [*règlements de police*] and laws. The metropole gets involved in almost none of their internal affairs; it acts only to protect their commerce and to secure them against attack by foreigners.

And yet these settlements, left to themselves in this way, costing the mother country neither money, nor concern, nor effort, double their population every twenty-two years and become centers of wealth and enlightenment [*lumières*].

We must recognize, because experience demonstrates, that for France to found a colony is for her to give herself up to an enterprise full of perils and of uncertain success.

To found a penal colony is even more dangerous . . .

FIRST LETTER ON ALGERIA
(23 JUNE 1837)

Great events have just occurred in Algeria.[1] One might believe, too, that others are about to happen, and so my time is not ill chosen, sir, to try to fulfill your request and tell you what I know of Algiers.[2] I do so all the more willingly because it seems to me that although this country has been much discussed, it is hardly known.

M. Desjobert, in a recently published book on our colony that in other respects was quite good, argues that in order to discuss a foreign country properly, it is well never to have been there.[3] This is an advantage I share with him, but I hardly pride myself on it. On the contrary, I take the popular view that in order to inform others about something, it is useful to know it oneself, and that to know something well, it is not useless to have seen it. So I do not pride myself on not having been to Africa, but I shall attempt to profit from the accounts of several of my friends who have spent a long time there, and to make it as little apparent as possible that I have never myself witnessed the things I am trying to depict.

I think that before speaking of the inhabitants, it would be well to say a word about the country itself. These two things are closely linked and explain one another.

You are surely aware, sir, that Algeria stretches practically in a straight line from west to east, over a space of . . . leagues.[4] Parallel to the sea rises a chain of high mountains called the Atlas. Sometimes the Atlas recedes abruptly to the south and opens up long, broad plains; elsewhere it suddenly reaches the shore and bathes its last slopes in the tide. From time to time, it folds back upon itself and encloses deep valleys within its contours.

A thousand small streams flow from all directions along the mountain-sides. But no part of the Atlas admits of a drop even briefly to the level of the plains and allows the formation of a great river that could easily carry the arms and arts of Europe deep into the deserts.

The Kabyles live in the Atlas, the Arabs in the valleys. Whenever you see a mountain, you can be sure that it hides a Kabyle tribe in its contours, and whenever you see a plain, you can expect that an Arab's camp will soon appear on the horizon. In this way the two races are always intermingled, but they never become one.

You undoubtedly will ask me, sir, what the origin is of these Kabyles, who are so remarkably mixed with the Arabs and yet always distinct from them. The Institut is still not sure.[5] I shall leave you to judge whether I might permit myself a conjecture. Some argue that they are Iberian and believe they recognize similarities between their language and Gascon.[6] Others think they are Arabs who arrived long ago from the frontiers of Judea. There are also those who believe they have discovered in them the descendants of the Vandals. You may be sure, sir, that no one knows anything at all about their origins. But in truth this hardly matters. It is the Kabyles of our day that we need to know, not their ancestors.

The Kabyles speak a language entirely different from the Arabs', and their mores are not at all alike. The only point of contact between these races is religion.

The Kabyles are always sedentary; they cultivate the soil, build houses, and have preserved or acquired several of the most necessary arts. They have developed iron mines, they make gunpowder, they produce all kinds of weapons, and they weave coarse fabrics. You mustn't imagine, sir, that all these Kabyles form one great people subject to a single government. They are still divided into small tribes, as in the first age of the world. These tribes have no power over one another or even any ties among them. They live separately and are often at war; each among them has its own little independent government that it establishes itself, and its own uncomplicated legislation. If Rousseau had known the Kabyles, sir, he would not have uttered such nonsense about the Caribs and other Indians of America: he would have sought his models in the Atlas; there he would have found men subject to a sort of social police and nonetheless almost as free as the isolated individual who enjoys his savage independence in the heart of the woods; men who are neither rich nor poor, neither servants nor masters; who name their own leaders, and hardly notice that they have leaders, who are content with their state and preserve it.

But Rousseau might not have approved so much of several of the Kabyles' political axioms. These people have as their fundamental maxim that no foreigner should set foot on their territory. They do not listen to reason on this point. They come to sell their wares at our markets, they climb down to the plains to hire out their services, they willingly enroll in our armies, but if it pleased you, sir, to decide, for the sake of reciprocity, to visit them in their mountains, even if you came with the best intentions in the world, even if you had no aim but to speak about morality, civilization, fine arts, political economy, or philosophy, they would assuredly cut off your head. It is a principle of government they obstinately resolve never to breach.

I have been assured that the Kabyles are quite indifferent to religion; that they are a prosaic and interested race who worry far more about this world than the other, and that it would be much easier to conquer them with our luxuries than with our cannon.

I could tell you much more about the Arabs, but I shall restrain myself. The limits of my journal require that I do so.

Europeans in general believe that all Arabs are herdsmen, and we like to picture them spending their lives driving large herds through immense pastures that are no one's property or that, at least, belong to no one but the tribe as a whole. This is indeed how they were 3,000 years ago, and you still encounter such people today in the deserts of Yemen. But they are not to be seen throughout the length of the Atlas. Can you believe, sir, that there is not an inch of land in the area around Algiers that does not have a known owner, and that there is no more vacant land in the plain of Mitidja than in that of Argenteuil [just northwest of Paris]. Each owner is provided with a title drafted in good form before a public officer. These, you will agree, are singular savages. What do they lack, if you please, to resemble civilized men entirely, but constantly to dispute the boundaries indicated by their contracts? But this is precisely what they never do, for the reason I am about to give you: if the Arabs have not remained completely herdsmen and nomads, they have not entirely become sedentary and agricultural. They are alternately one and the other. A small number among them have houses; the great majority have maintained the custom of living under a tent. Every year, they sow some of their fields and turn others into pastures for large herds. Every tribe thus has a very vast territory, of which the largest part always remains uncultivated and the rest is cultivated with little art. If a field is left fallow, each member of the tribe may lead his livestock to graze there; but from the moment the owner appears and sows the field, the harvest belongs to him alone.

You can see, sir, that the Arabs on the coast of Africa are at once cultivators and herdsmen. Most of them move about constantly, but they never pass beyond a certain radius. They have reached that period of transition when, placed between nomadic life and sedentary life, not yet strongly attached to the one, no longer solidly tied to the other, they can be fixed definitively into one or the other by fortuitous circumstances. I shall explain to you later the part that we can play in this state of affairs.

As you press toward the south, you see fewer cultivated fields and more herds; tents multiply, houses disappear; the customs of the population become less and less sedentary; nomadic life recovers the upper hand. And so you reach the great desert on the other side of the Atlas. There, it is said, you find the Arabs of the Bible and of the Patriarchs. There you find no more borders, no more boundaries to the fields, no more titles of land-ownership, but an immense solitude, where the tribes wander endlessly in the complete and full liberty of the desert, leading along a prodigious number of camels, horses, and sheep.

During the period when the successors of Muhammad invaded Egypt and Numidia, the Arabs followed them in tribes. These Arabs conquered everything they met up to the foot of the Pyrenees, and, in all the countries where they established themselves, they kept the same form of society. The Arabs of the African coast today are still divided into small peoples that are more or less independent of one another, as they were 1,200 years ago, when their great religious passion pushed them all at once toward the West.

Each of these small societies elects its leaders, who are called sheikhs, and discusses its own affairs in common. All these tribes, however, actually form but a single people. They all have the same origin, the same memories, the same opinions, and the same mores; they once formed a single nation, and not long ago, they were still, if not governed, at least ruled on certain points by a single government.

You do not see an equality among the Arabs as complete as that among the Kabyle peoples; you find, on the contrary, quite large inequalities. Each tribe includes a certain number of families, mostly old, which have vast domains, large herds, and many servants. The leaders of these families have fine horses, which they are always riding, and good, handsome weapons, which are always to be seen in their hands; they form a sort of military aristocracy, which more or less runs everything, by the tacit consent of the rest of the population.

But the main Arab aristocracy draws its origin from religion. I beg you to listen closely, sir, for this thing is at once important and remarkable. There are men who once acquired, through their piety and their wisdom, a reputation of extraordinary holiness. These men, called marabouts, were once surrounded by public respect throughout their lives and in general had a great influence on the thinking of the surrounding populations; and what is unusual is that they transmitted all this to their descendants. In each family of marabouts, there never fails to be born in each new generation a saintly and erudite man, who maintains the good name and the power of his predecessors. There is hardly a tribe in which one does not meet one or several marabouts, who generally live near the tomb of their most celebrated ancestor and who quite generously offer hospitality to those who come to make pilgrimages, as they are generally wealthy. These marabouts are men of religion and of science who feel or affect a great detachment from the tumultuous and deceitful occupations of this world. While the military aristocracy is always on horseback, yatagan or rifle in hand, the marabout rides a donkey and, without arms and meanly dressed, passes through the crowd of men of war, who eagerly open their ranks to let him pass and kiss his hand. Despite this poor appearance, the marabouts should no less be considered the most influential members of Arab society. They are the mind of this great body, of which the military aristocracy forms the heart and the limbs. It is generally the marabouts who reestablish peace among the tribes and who secretly direct the mainsprings of their politics.

You should note, sir, that Abd-el-Kader, whom you have heard mentioned, belongs to one of the foremost families of marabouts in the regency and that he himself is a marabout. This explains a great deal.[7]

As for the general traits of the Arab character, they have been known for many centuries, and you find them in Algeria just as you do everywhere else. Among the Arabs of the coast of Africa, you discover the brilliant and sensual imagination, the subtle, shrewd wit, the courage, and the inconstancy that their fathers displayed. Like them, they belong to a mobile and indomitable race that adores physical delights but places liberty above all the pleasures and would sooner flee into the desert sands than vegetate under a master.

The Arabs of the African coast also have a multitude of vices and virtues that are not peculiar to them but belong to the stage of civilization at which they find themselves. Like all half-savage peoples, they honor power and force above all else. Putting little stock in the life of men, and scorning trade and the arts, like those others, they love war, pomp, and tumult [*bruit*] above all; defiant and credulous, subject sometimes to an unreflective enthusiasm and sometimes to an *exaggerated* despondency, they fall and pick themselves up again without trouble, often excessive in their actions and always more willing to feel than to think.

After having told you about the two principal races that populate Algeria, it is well, sir, to finish by saying a word about a third that no longer exists, but whose power was preponderant for three centuries: I mean the Turks.

When the Spaniards had chased the Arabs from the Iberian peninsula, they soon followed them to the coasts of Algeria. The latter sought the aid of the Turks, who at that time were at the apogee of their power and their glory and who, after having beaten the Christians and seized Algiers, declared themselves masters of those they had come to defend.[8]

You mustn't suppose, sir, that the Turks, conquerors of Algiers and of part of the regency, wanted to found an empire there for their descendants. Not at all. These Turks were so proud of their country that they despised their own children born of Arab women. Preferring their race to their family, they had no desire whatsoever to recruit among their sons. But every year they sent to Turkey for new soldiers. Things, so established, continued. It was still the same in 1830. Every year the dominant race went to find recruits on the coast of Asia, leaving their own children to fall into obscurity and impotence.

I must tell you, sir, what were the Turks' principles and methods of government. This is necessary in order to understand everything that has happened since we took their place.

The Turks, the greatest number of whom lived in Algiers, formed a militia there that, although not numerous, was very brave, quite turbulent, and had the right to choose the head of government. Most of the civil and all the military functionaries were taken from this group.

These Turks thus formed an aristocratic corps and they possessed the faults and virtues of all aristocracies. Filled with immense pride, they also displayed a certain respect for themselves that made them speak and almost always act with nobility. They hardly worried about anything but the interests of their group, strongly despising all that was foreign to them.

As to what they called their government, here is what it comprised:

The Turks attempted to subjugate [*réduire*] the Kabyle tribes. But they never managed to make their sovereignty recognized by any but a very small number. All the others retrenched in their mountains and remained inaccessible.

I presume that it was the continual proximity of these Turks that caused the Kabyles to adopt the fundamental maxim I discussed above, according to which one cuts off the heads of all foreigners who come wandering over the slopes of the Atlas.

The Turkish domination was established more easily over the Arabs, who, as I told you, live on open plains. This is how they did it: 5,000 to 6,000 Turks confined to Algiers could not alone have subjugated these mobile tribes, who flee at the approach of the hand that would seize them. But tyrannies never would have been established if the oppressors had not found their instruments among the oppressed. The Turks distinguished certain tribes, granting them privileges and great independence in exchange for their help conquering the others. In addition, within those very tribes on which their yoke weighed heavily, they used similar means, especially tax exemption, to draw in most of the members of the military aristocracy I described to you above. In this way, they could use Arabs to dominate the Arabs. But these auxiliary Arabs were always commanded by Turks. Thus, each year a Turkish officer left Algiers followed by some soldiers of his nation, joined by those known as the cavalry of Marzem.[9] These were the Arab horsemen of whom I have spoken. Traversing the country with these troops, they collected taxes peacefully or levied them violently from the tribes who refused to pay. That was the basis of the Turkish government. You shouldn't believe, sir, that money levied in this manner served, as it does or at least as it seems to among all civilized nations, to assure the tranquillity and prosperity of those who paid it. Almost the entire amount went into the coffers of the dey or was turned over to his soldiers.

The Turks nonetheless had made several quite incomplete attempts to establish among the Arabs something that resembled a public administration.

They had divided the country, especially in the areas around the cities, into districts called *outans,* where several tribes lived. At the head of this population they placed a Turkish officer called a caid and several soldiers of the same nation, who were joined, as necessary, by the cavalry of Marzem. This officer's duty was to enforce criminal justice, and secure public peace and the safety of the roads — a duty he hardly fulfilled at all.[10] This was because the tribes, despite his efforts, were endlessly at war with one another and often

placed the caid himself at their head, who, to preserve some authority over
them, was obliged to share their passions and embrace their quarrels.

The Turks used another method to secure the towns. They supported a
garrison, which they took care to renew frequently. The soldiers, thus de-
tached, married Arab women and had children by them. The children born
in Algeria of unions between Turks and Arabs had a particular name; they
were called *coulouglis,* and they formed a race distinct from the other two. The
Turks, without granting the coulouglis either a part in the government or a
place in their militia, nonetheless assured them, through privileges, a preponderant position, which attached them to the government and separated their
interests from that of the rest of the governed. These coulouglis thus formed a
friendly population in the towns where they were born, who could be counted
upon, and who readily defended themselves as long as they were not entirely
abandoned.

This is how it was, then: in the mountains were the Kabyles, more or less
independent; in the plains the Arabs, quite incompletely subordinated; in the
towns, the Turks and the coulouglis and a mixed population without any fixed
character, about which I shall say just a word in finishing.

You already know enough to see, sir, that this supposed Turkish government was not truly speaking a government but a continuation of conquest, a
violent exploitation of the conquered by the conquerors. The Turks had not
merely established themselves on the coasts of Africa as foreigners but had
resolved the difficult problem of inhabiting,* for three centuries, a country
where they were always foreigners and where they always seemed to be new-
comers who were there to manage their own affairs and not at all to govern the
conquered people.

I have told you how things happened in the district of Algiers. They
proceeded in a similar manner in the three beyliks that recognized the authority of the dey. The Turks had divided Algeria into three governments: one
in the east, whose capital was Constantine; another in the south, called the
beylik of Tittery;[11] and the third to the west, which formed the province of
Oran. These three beys were named by the dey. Like the dey, who governed
from Algiers, each settled in the principal town of his province and governed
by the same means. But in general their power was more limited and more
contested than the dey's.

---

* [Variant: *de gouverner* (of governing).]

I have promised not to end, sir, without telling you a little about that part of the population of the towns that was neither Turkish nor coulougli. It included Jews, about whom you know as much as I, since they are the same there as elsewhere, and Moors.[12] These Moors belong to various races, but most of them are Arabs whose sedentary tastes and desire to enjoy their wealth in peace or acquire it in trade have kept them in the towns. They are a shrewd race, gentle, intelligent, and quite fond of order. The Arabs of the plains, who sleep under the stars, their sabers in their fists, and who are necessarily subject to the pains and joys of an adventurous existence, profess the most superb disdain for this peaceable and industrious portion of their compatriots. In their disdain they give these Moors a name that in Arab signifies pepper vendors, which could only be translated into French as *épiciers* [grocers]. I'm sure, sir, that you thought this epithet, so often repeated in our own day, was born among our own disturbances. You can see that it comes from far away and I believe it to be venerable in its antiquity. The Orientals change their sayings hardly more than their beliefs, and I would not be astonished if this one did not trace back to the first age of the world. I would add that it does not seem to me better for being old.

I have shown you in brief, sir, what Algeria was before our conquest. In the next letter I shall attempt to acquaint you quickly with what we have done and try to indicate to the best of my ability what remains to be done.

SECOND LETTER ON ALGERIA
(22 AUGUST 1837)

Let us suppose for a moment, sir, that the emperor of China, disembarking in France at the head of an armed force, were to make himself master of our largest cities and our capital. And that after having destroyed all the public records without even bothering to read them, after having destroyed or disbanded every administrative office without inquiring into their various purposes, he finally seized all the officials, from the head of government to the rural police, the peers, the deputies, and, in general, the entire governing class, and deported them at once to some distant country. Do you not think that this great prince, despite his powerful army, his fortresses, and his treasures, would soon find himself at a loss as to how to govern the defeated country; that his new subjects, deprived of all those who led or could lead affairs, would be found incapable of governing themselves, while he, coming from the antipodes and knowing neither the religion, nor the language, nor the laws, nor the customs, nor the administrative practices, and having taken care to remove all those who might have instructed him, would be incapable of directing them? You will have no trouble predicting, sir, that even if the parts of France physically occupied by the conqueror were to obey him, the rest of the country would soon be in a state of total anarchy.[1]

You will soon see, sir, that we have done in Algeria precisely what I have supposed the emperor of China to have done in France.

Although the coast of Africa is separated from Provence by only about 160 leagues of sea;[2] although the accounts of several thousand voyages to all parts of the world are published every year in Europe; although people here assiduously study all the ancient languages that are no longer spoken and many living languages one never has occasion to speak; even so, you can hardly imagine the profound ignorance in France just seven years ago about everything concerning Algeria. We had no clear idea either of the different races that inhabited it or of their customs; we did not know a word of the languages these people speak; the country itself, its resources, its rivers, its towns, its climate were unknown; it was as if the entire expanse of the globe lay between Algeria and us. So little was known even about matters relating to waging war, though it was the great business of the moment, that our generals imagined they would be attacked by a cavalry like that of the Egyptian mamelukes, when our principal adversaries, the Algerian Turks, fought only with infantry. It was in this ignorance of everything that we set sail, which did not prevent us from winning; for on a battlefield victory goes to the bravest and strongest and not to the most learned.

But after combat it did not take us long to see that to have conquered a nation is not enough to be capable of governing it.

You will recall, sir, what I told you earlier, that the entire civil and military government of the regency was in Turkish hands. Hardly were we masters of Algiers than we hastened to gather up every single Turk, from the dey to the last soldier of his militia, and transported the lot of them to the coast of Asia. In order to make the vestiges of the enemy domination disappear, we first took care to tear up or burn all written documents, administrative records, and papers, authentic or otherwise, that could have perpetuated any trace of what had been done before us.[3] The conquest was a new era, and from fear of mixing the past with the present in an irrational way, we even destroyed a large number of streets in Algiers so as to rebuild them according to our own method, and we gave French names to all those we consented to leave alone. In truth, I think, sir, that the Chinese I spoke about earlier couldn't have done better.

What resulted from all this? You can easily imagine.

The Turkish government had owned a large number of houses in Algiers and many estates on the plain; but its property titles had disappeared in the universal wreckage of the former order. Knowing neither what had belonged to it nor what remained in the legitimate possession of the defeated, the French administration thus either possessed nothing or believed itself reduced to seizing at random whatever it needed, with no regard for law [*droit*] and rights.

The Turkish government had peacefully collected taxes that we, in our ignorance, could not levy in its place, and we had to draw the money we needed from France or to extort it from our unhappy subjects by means far more Turkish than those the Turks ever used.

If our ignorance was such that the French government became irregular and oppressive in Algiers, it was altogether impossible elsewhere.

The French had sent the caids back to Asia. They knew absolutely nothing of the name, the composition, and the ways of this Arab militia that had served as auxiliary police and collected taxes under the Turks, and which was called, as I have said, the cavalry of Marzem. They had no idea of the division of tribes, and of the division of ranks within the tribes. They were unaware of what the military aristocracy of the spahis was,[4] and as for the marabouts, it took them quite a long time to figure out, when someone spoke of them, whether they were referring to a tomb or to a man.*

The French knew nothing of these things, and, to tell the truth, they hardly bothered to learn them.

In place of an administration they had destroyed root and branch, they imagined they would substitute French administration in the districts that we occupied militarily.

I beg you, sir, to try to envision these agile and indomitable children of the desert locked into the thousand formalities of our bureaucracy and forced to submit to the sluggishness, to the regularity, to the documents and minutiae of our centralization. We preserved nothing of the former government of the country but the employment of the yatagan and the baton as police equipment. Everything else became French.

This applied to the towns and the nearby tribes. As for the rest of the regency's inhabitants, we didn't even undertake to administer them. After having destroyed their government, we did not give them another.

I would be going outside the framework I set for myself if I undertook to tell the history of what has occurred in Africa in the past seven years. I merely want to place the reader in the position to understand it.

In the 300 years that the Arabs who inhabit Algeria were subject to the Turks, they had entirely lost the habit of governing themselves. The dominators' jealousy had removed their leading men from general affairs; the mar-

---

* The marabouts receive guests beside the tomb of their principal ancestor, and this place bears the name of the person buried there. This is the source of the error.[5]

about had descended from his steed to mount an ass. The Turkish government was a detestable government, but in the end it did maintain a certain order; although it tacitly authorized the tribes' wars among themselves, it kept down robbery and secured the roads. It was, in addition, the only link that existed among the various peoples, the center where so many divergent rays met.

Once the Turkish government was destroyed, with no substitute to replace it, the country, which could no longer run itself, fell into appalling anarchy. All the tribes fell one on top of another into an immense confusion; brigandage emerged everywhere. Even the shadow of justice disappeared, and everyone resorted to force.

This applies to the Arabs.

As for the Kabyles, because they had been fairly independent from the Turks, the fall of the Turks produced but little effect on them. Their habitual stance vis-à-vis the new masters remained fairly similar to what it had been vis-à-vis the old ones. They merely became even more unapproachable, inasmuch as their natural hatred for strangers combined with the religious horror they felt for Christians, whose language, laws, and customs were unknown to them.

People sometimes submit to humiliation, to tyranny, to conquest, but they never endure anarchy for long. There is no people so barbarous that it escapes this general law of humanity.

When the Arabs, whom we often sought to conquer and subdue, but never to govern, had surrendered for some time to the savage environment to which individual independence gives birth, they began to seek instinctively to rebuild what the French had destroyed. Enterprising and ambitious men began to appear among them. Great talents were revealed in several of their leaders, and the multitude began to cling to certain names as if to symbols of order.

The Turks had prohibited the Arab religious aristocracy from the use of arms and the direction of public affairs, but once the Turks had been eliminated, they almost immediately became warriors and governors again. The most rapid and certain effect of our conquest was to give back to the marabouts the political existence they had lost. They once again took up the scimitar of Muhammad to battle the infidels and lost no time in using it to govern their fellow citizens: this is a great fact and one that must capture the attention of all those who are involved in Algeria.

We have allowed the national aristocracy of the Arabs to be reborn; it now remains to make use of them.

A family of celebrated marabouts had long been settled to the west of the province of Algiers, near the frontier of the Moroccan empire. The family was descended from Muhammad himself, and its name was venerated throughout the regency. At the moment when the French took possession of the country, the leader of this family was an old man named Mahiddin. To the illustrious-ness of his birth, Mahiddin joined the advantages of having been to Mecca and having been for a long time energetically opposed to the exactions of the Turks. His saintliness was greatly honored and his ability well known. When the tribes of the area began to feel that unendurable malaise that the absence of power causes in men, they went to see Mahiddin and proposed that he be-come their leader. The old man gathered them all on a great plain; there, he told them that at his age one must be concerned with heaven and not earth, that he refused their offer, but that he begged them to transfer their support to one of his younger sons, whom he showed them. He enumerated at length the claims of this son to govern his countrymen: his precocious piety, his pil-grimage to Holy Places, his descent from the Prophet. He made known sev-eral striking indications that heaven had used to distinguish him among his brothers, and he proved that all the ancient prophecies that announced a liberator of the Arabs manifestly applied to him. With one voice the tribes proclaimed Mahiddin's son *emir-el-mouminin,* that is to say, leader of the believers.

This puny young man, who was at the time but twenty-five years old, was called Abd-el-Kader.[6]

Such is the origin of this remarkable leader: anarchy gave birth to his power, anarchy constantly developed him and, with God's grace and our own,[7] after having delivered to him the provinces of Oran and Tittery, it will place the city of Constantine in his hands and make him more powerful than the Turkish government that he replaces had ever been.

While these things were happening in the west of the regency, the east offered another spectacle.

When the French took Algiers, the province of Constantine was governed by a bey named Achmet [Ahmad]. This bey, contrary to all custom, was coulougli, that is to say, the son of a Turk and an Arab. It was a remarkably lucky chance that allowed him, after Algiers was taken, to support himself first in Constantine with the help of his father's countrymen and later to base his power on the surrounding tribes with the help of his mother's relatives and friends.

Thus, while all the rest of the regency that the Turks had abandoned and the French had not occupied fell into the greatest disorder, a certain form of government was maintained in the province of Constantine, and Achmet, by his courage, his cruelty, and his energy, founded an empire there that is so solid we are still trying to restrain or destroy it today.[8]

At this moment, then, there are three powers on Algerian soil.

In Algiers and at various points on the coast are the French; to the west and south, an Arab population that after 300 years is reawakening and acting under a national leader; to the east, a vestige of the Turkish government, represented by Achmet, is a brook that is still flowing after the source has dried up and that will not take long to dry up itself or to blend into the great river of Arab nationality. Between these three powers, as if enveloped on all sides, is a multitude of small Kabyle peoples, who escape from all these influences equally and pay no attention to any of the governments.

It would be superfluous to rehearse at length what the French should have done at the time of the conquest.

It can be said in just a few words that to the extent that our civilization permitted it, we simply should have put ourselves in the place of the defeated; that far from trying to substitute our administrative practices for theirs from the start, we should for a time have bent to their ways, preserved the political delimitations, taken on the fallen government's officials, accepted its traditions and guarded its practices. Instead of transporting the Turks to the coast of Asia, we clearly should have taken care to keep most of them on; deprived of their leaders, incapable of governing by themselves and fearing the resentment of their former subjects, they would quickly have become our most useful intermediaries and most zealous friends. This is what has happened with the coulouglis, who, although they were much closer to the Arabs than the Turks were, have nonetheless almost always preferred to throw themselves at us rather than at them. By the time we had learned the Arabs' language, prejudices, and ways, after having inherited the respect that men always feel toward an established government, we would have been free to return bit by bit to our own practices and to make French the country around us.

But now that the mistakes have been made, what remains to be done? And what hopes can we reasonably conceive?

Let us first carefully distinguish the two large races discussed above, the Kabyles and the Arabs.

As for the Kabyles, it is clear that there could be no question of conquering or colonizing their country: their mountains are impenetrable to our armies at present, and the inhospitable humor of the inhabitants leaves no security for the isolated European who might want to go there peacefully to find shelter.

The country of the Kabyles is closed to us, but the soul of the Kabyles is open to us, and it is not impossible for us to penetrate it.

I said earlier that the Kabyle was more positive, less devout, infinitely less mystical [*enthousiaste*] than the Arab. For the Kabyles the individual is almost everything, society almost nothing, and they are as far from yielding uniformly to the laws of a single government conceived among themselves as they are from adopting our own.

The great passion of the Kabyle is love of material pleasures, and it is by this route that we can and must grasp him.

Although the Kabyles have allowed us to penetrate their society far less than the Arabs have, they also show themselves to be far less inclined to make war on us. And while some of them take up arms against us, others do not stop visiting our markets and coming to hire out their services. The cause of this is that they have already discovered the material profit that they can draw from our proximity. They find it quite advantageous to come to sell us their produce and to buy those products of ours that are compatible with the sort of civilization they possess. And, while they are not yet at the point of achieving our level of well-being, it is already easy to see that they admire it and that they would find it quite sweet to possess it.

It is obvious that we should go about subduing such men by our arts and not by our arms.

If we continue to establish frequent and peaceful relations with the Kabyles, if the leaders have nothing to fear from our ambition and see that we have simple, clear laws that will protect them, it is certain that they will soon fear war more than we ourselves, and that we shall perceive the almost invincible attraction that draws savages toward civilized man at the moment they no longer fear for their liberty. We shall then see the customs and ideas of the Kabyles alter without their perceiving it, and the barriers that now shut us out of their country will fall by themselves.

The role that we have to play toward the Arabs is more complicated and more difficult.

The Arabs are not solidly attached to the land, and their soul is even more mobile than their dwellings. Although they love their liberty, they prize strong government and like forming a great nation. And although they appear quite sensual, they greatly value immaterial pleasures, and imagination continually lifts them toward some ideal it reveals to them.

With the Kabyles we must focus above all on questions of civil and commercial equity; with the Arabs, on political and religious questions.

A certain number of Arab tribes can and henceforth must be directly governed by us, but there are even more over whom we must not hope, for the present, to obtain anything but an indirect influence.

After 300 years, the Turks' power was established only very incompletely over the tribes that lived far from the towns. The Turks, however, being Muhammadans like the Arabs, had similar practices and had succeeded in keeping the religious aristocracy out of government. It is easy to see that for our part, having none of these advantages and being exposed to far greater dangers, we cannot hope to obtain the power the Turks had acquired over these tribes—nor even to approach it. On this point our immense military superiority is almost useless. It allows us to conquer, but not to retain under our laws, the nomadic populations, who bury themselves when they need to in deserts where we cannot follow, leaving us in the middle of a desert where we cannot survive.

The sole object of our present concern should be to live in peace with those Arabs whom we cannot hope to govern at present, and to organize them in the manner least dangerous for our future progress.

The Arabs' anarchy, so fatal to these peoples, is quite harmful to us as well, for having neither the will nor the power to subdue them all at once by force of arms, we cannot hope to have any effect on them except in the long term through the contact of our ideas and our arts, something that cannot happen except insofar as peace and a certain order reign among them. Besides, the anarchy that pits the tribes against one another throws them constantly onto us and leaves our borders completely insecure.

We thus have a great interest in recreating a government among these people, and it is perhaps not impossible to succeed in making this government depend in part on us.

Now that the scepter has slipped from the hands that held it for three centuries, no one has an incontestable right to govern, nor any probable chance of founding an uncontested power for a long time to come. All the powers that establish themselves in Africa will therefore be unstable, and if our support is given with firmness, justice, and durability, the new sovereigns will constantly tend to have recourse to it. They will thus depend partly on us.

We must aim first of all at getting the independent Arabs used to seeing us involved in their internal affairs and at familiarizing them with us. For we must realize that by the mere fact of the superiority of its knowledge, a powerful and civilized people such as ours exercises an almost invincible influence on small and fairly barbarous peoples. To force these peoples to incorporate themselves into us, it is enough to establish durable ties with them.

[margin note: amalgamation]

But if it is to our advantage to create a government among the regency Arabs, we have a much clearer interest in not letting them establish a single ruler. For the danger in this would be far greater than the advantage. It is indeed very important to us not to let the Arabs yield to anarchy, but it is even more important not to expose ourselves to seeing them united against us all at once.

From this point of view, the last treaty with Abd-el-Kader and the projected expedition to Constantine are of a nature to excite certain fears.

Nothing is more desirable than to establish and regularize the power of the new emir in the province of Oran, where his power had already been founded. But the treaty also grants him the government of the beylik of Tittery, and I cannot help believing that the expedition now being prepared will result finally in yielding the greatest part of the province of Constantine to him.

We can rest assured that with the degree of power Abd-el-Kader has attained, all the Arab populations that find themselves without a leader will come to him on their own. It is thus imprudent to destroy or even to disturb the Arab powers independent of Abd-el-Kader; we should much rather think of creating others that do not yet exist. Now, if our expedition to Constantine succeeds, as there is every reason to believe it will, it could hardly result in anything but destroying Achmet without putting anything in his place. We shall overturn the coulougli, and we shall be able neither to succeed him nor to give him an Arab successor. Our victory will thus grant the tribes under Achmet an independence that they will not wait long to surrender into the hands of the neighboring emir. We shall create anarchy, and anarchy will create Abd-el-Kader's power.

[margin note: divide and conquer]

This at least is what can be perceived from a distance and in ignorance of the details.

What we can affirm with certainty at the moment is that we can never allow all the tribes of the regency to recognize the same leader. Two is already far too few. Our present security, and concern for our future, demand that there be at least three or four.

Independent of the tribes over whom it is in our interest to attempt to exercise no more than an indirect influence at present, there is a considerable enough part of the country that our security as much as our honor oblige us to keep under our immediate power and to govern without intermediaries.

In that part of the country, a French population and an Arab population should be brought to live peacefully in the same places. The difficulty is great, but I am far from believing it to be insurmountable.

I do not intend, sir, to go into detail with you about the means that can be used to attain this end. It is enough to indicate roughly what seems to me the principal condition for success.

It is clear to me that we shall never succeed if we undertake to place our new Algerian subjects under French administration.

Nothing new can be done with impunity when it comes to political customs. We are more enlightened and stronger than the Arabs, and it is up to us to yield at first, up to a certain point, to their habits and prejudices. In Algeria as elsewhere, the great task of a new government is not to create what does not exist at all, but to use what does exist. The Arabs lived in tribes 2,000 years ago in Yemen; they traversed all Africa and invaded Spain in tribes; they still live in the same manner to this day. Tribal organization, the most tenacious of all human institutions, cannot, therefore, be taken from them for a long time hence without overturning all their sentiments and ideas. The Arabs name their own leaders; we must preserve this privilege. They have a military and religious aristocracy; we must by no means seek to destroy this, but rather to get hold of it and take part of it into our pay, as the Turks did. It is not only useful to draw upon the Arabs' political customs, but necessary to modify the rules of their civil law only gradually. For you know, sir, that most of these rules are traced to the Koran in such a way that for Muslims, civil and religious law are always mixed together.

Above all, in Algeria we must take care to give up this taste for uniformity that torments us, and to realize that it would be as dangerous as it is absurd to apply the same laws to different beings. At the time of the Western empire's fall, two laws ruled at once: the barbarian was subjected to barbarian laws, and the Romans followed Roman laws. This is a good example to imitate, because it is the only way we can hope safely to negotiate the transitional period that elapses before two peoples of different civilizations can manage to refound themselves as a single whole.

Where French and Arabs live in the same district, we must resolve to apply to each the legislation that they can understand and that they have learned to respect. If the political leadership is common to both races, but everything else is different for a long time, fusion will come later, of its own accord.

It would also be necessary for the legislation that governs the French in Africa not to be exactly the same as that in force in France. A newborn people cannot tolerate the same administrative hassles that an old people can, and the same slow and multiplied formalities that sometimes guarantee the security of the old prevent the new from developing and almost from being born at all.

We need in Africa, just as in France, and even more than in France, essential guarantees to the individual living in society; nowhere is it more necessary to establish individual liberty, respect for property, and guarantees of all rights than in a colony. But, on the other hand, a colony needs a simpler administration, one more expeditious and independent of the central power than those that direct the continental provinces of the empire.

We must therefore carefully preserve the substance of our political state in Algeria, but not hold too superstitiously to its form; and show more respect for the spirit than for the letter. Those who have visited Algeria claim to note the opposite: they say scrupulous care for the most trivial administrative methods of the mother country is observed there, and that the great principles that serve as the basis for our laws are often forgotten. By acting this way we might hope to multiply public officials, but not colonists.

I imagine, sir, as I approach the end of this too long letter, that you are tempted to ask me what, after all, my hopes for the future of our new colony are.

That future seems to me to be in our hands, and I shall tell you sincerely that with time, perseverance, ability, and justice, I have no doubt that we shall be able to raise a great monument to our country's glory on the African coast.

I told you at the beginning, sir, that the Arabs were at once shepherds and farmers, and that, although they held the entire extent of the land, they never cultivated more than a very small part. So the Arab population is quite sparse; it occupies much more terrain than it can possibly cultivate every year. The consequence is that the Arabs sell land readily and cheaply, and that a foreign population can easily establish itself next to them without causing them to suffer.

You understand, sir, how easy it is for the French, who are richer and more industrious than the Arabs, to occupy a large part of the soil without violence and to establish themselves peacefully and in large numbers in the very midst of the surrounding tribes. It is easy to predict a time in the near future when the two races will be intermixed in this way throughout much of the regency.

Pacification and colonization by settlement

But it is not at all enough for the French to place themselves next to the Arabs if they do not manage to establish durable ties with them and finally to form a single people from the two races.

Everything that I have learned about Algeria leads me to believe that this possibility is not as chimerical as many people suppose.

The majority of the Arabs preserve a lively faith in the religion of Muhammad; however, it is easy to see that in this portion of Muslim territory, as in all the others, religious beliefs are continually losing their vigor and becoming more and more powerless to battle the interests of this world. Although religion has played a large role in the wars that have been waged against us in Africa until now, and although it has served as a pretext for the marabouts to take up arms again, it can be said that religion was nothing but the secondary cause to which these wars must be attributed. We were attacked much more as strangers and as conquerors than as Christians, and it is the ambition of the leaders more than the faith of the people that has led them to take up arms against us.[9] Experience has shown that religion does not prevent the Arabs from becoming our most zealous auxiliaries whenever patriotism or ambition does not turn them against us, and they fight their coreligionists just as violently under our flag as those others fight us.

We may thus believe that if we prove more and more that Islam is in no danger under our domination or in our vicinity, religious passions will come to be extinguished, and we shall have only political enemies in Africa.

It would be equally wrong to think that the Arabs' civil customs make them incapable of yielding to a communal life with us.

In Spain, the Arabs were sedentary and agricultural; in the areas around the Algerian towns, a great number of them are building houses and devoting themselves seriously to agriculture. The Arabs are thus not naturally and necessarily shepherds. It is true that as you advance toward the desert, you see the houses disappear and the tent emerge. But this is because the security of property and persons diminishes as you leave the coasts, and because nothing is more expedient than a nomadic life for a people that fears for its existence and its liberty. I can well see that the Arabs prefer to wander in the open air than to remain exposed to the tyranny of a master, but everything indicates to me that if they could be free, respected, and sedentary, they would be quick to settle down. I have no doubt that they would adopt our style of life if we gave them a lasting interest in doing so.

Nothing, finally, in the known facts indicates to me that there should be any incompatibility of temper between the Arabs and us. I see, on the contrary, that in times of peace the two races intermix without trouble, and that they are growing ever closer as they come to know each other better.

Each day the French are developing clearer and better notions about the inhabitants of Algeria. They are learning their languages, familiarizing themselves with their customs, and even displaying a sort of unreflective enthusiasm for them. Moreover, the whole younger generation of Arabs speaks our language, and they have already partly adopted our mores.

Recently, when we had to defend ourselves in the area around Algiers against brigandage by several enemy tribes, we saw the formation of a national guard composed of Arabs and French, living in the same guardhouse and sharing the same hardships and dangers.[10]

There is, then, no reason to believe that time will not succeed in amalgamating the two races. God is not stopping it; only human deficiencies can stand in its way.

Let us not lose hope for the future, sir; let us not be stopped by temporary sacrifices just when an immense goal is revealing itself that can be achieved by persistent effort.

NOTES ON THE KORAN
(MARCH 1838)

Things that recur constantly. General spirit.[1]

CHAPTER I

Encouragement, commandments for holy war.

Necessity of obeying the Prophet, of obeying him as one does God.

Magnificent recompense for those who die with arms in hand.

Grandeur, horror of future afflictions.

Abomination of apostasy.

Entirely physical portrayal of paradise.

The violence of Muhammad's language principally directed against idolaters and Jews.

Faith constantly above good works.

Magnificent images of God appear continually.

He constantly assails the Jews and spares the Christians.

Like Christianity, the Koran is always connected to all the ideas of the Old Testament, to which it always presents itself as a continuation. It thus dates Islam back to the beginning of the world, which is the first requirement of all religions.

The Koran contains more or less all the general moral principles contained in all religions.

CHAPTER II

Unity of God, ubiquity, omnipotence, mercy.

Immortality of the soul.

Eternal rewards and punishments.

Immortality particularly promised to those who die for faith with arms in hand.

Muhammad complements the Jewish and Christian prophets. Roots of Islam in Judaism.

One turns toward Mecca and no longer toward Jerusalem to pray.

Prohibition against eating dead animals, pork, blood.

Almsgiving, good works, patience elevated to the rank of commandments.

The faith necessary to be saved.

Talionic punishment[2] for murder.

Fast of Ramadan.

Sanctity of holy war, encouraged with both energy and violence.

Pilgrimage to Mecca commanded.

Prohibition of wine.

Prohibition of mixed marriages.

Prohibition to approach women at certain times.

Rules about divorce.

Rules about the nursing of children, about the position and the rights of women in the house of their husband, about their dowry, etc. . . .

Necessity of prayer.

Utility of supporting holy war with one's property.

Usury proscribed.

Form of contracts.

CHAPTER III

He predicts schisms.

Last Judgment indicated.

Portrayal of paradise: gardens watered with rivers, and houris.

Jesus Christ recognized as a prophet; his miracles admitted; his birth recounted more or less as in the Gospel. His divinity alone is denied.

Influence of repentance.

He skillfully connects Islam to Abraham, father of the Arabs, who, he says, built the temple of Mecca as his first temple.

Love, pardon, good works recommended.

The end of human days is written (p. 70).

Happiness of those who die while fighting for the faith is exalted in a thousand ways.

CHAPTER IV

Commandment not to marry more than four women.

General rules of guardianship.

Laws of succession, advantage of males (81). Muhammad points out that these prescriptions emanate from God and promises paradise to those who obey them.

Punishment of death to be carried out against the adulterer.

Punishment against fornication.

Repentance useless on the last day; useless for infidels.

Rules about women's dowries in case of repudiation.

Rules about the stages [*les degrés*] when one can marry.

One cannot marry a married woman except when she is surrendered to you by war.

Permission to marry slaves in certain cases.

Prohibition against suicide.

Duties of women. Woman inferior to man (82).

Permission and commandment to kill infidels. Prohibition against killing believers.

CHAPTER V

Prohibition against eating pork, blood, animals that have been suffocated, beaten to death, killed by a fall (106).

Oblations before prayer (107).

Cut off the feet and hands of those who fight God and the Prophet (111).

Cut off the hands of robbers, that is God's commandment.

Christians shall be judged according to the Gospel (114).

The faithful, Jews and Christians who believe in God on the last day and practice virtue are exempt from fear and torments (117). The following verses suggest this to mean those who abandon their own beliefs to believe these things.[3]

Wine, games of chance, and statues are abominations invented by Satan; abstain from these (120).

The minister of the Prophet is limited to preaching (122).

Form of testaments (123).

CHAPTER VI

Never eat an animal over which the name of God has not been invoked (141).

Dead animals, blood, and pork are impure (145). We have prohibited Jews from eating all animals that do not have cloven hooves and the fat of beef and mutton except that of the back, the entrails, and that which is mixed with the bones. This prohibition is the punishment for their crimes (id.).

Never kill any one of your children for fear of poverty. We will provide nourishment for you and them. Avoid crime in public and in secret (146).

CHAPTER VII

The term of life is fixed. Nothing can forestall nor defer it for an instant (153).

My mission is divine, it encompasses the entire human race (172).

This very long chapter contains almost no commandments; it is the stories of the Old Testament slightly altered and apostrophes to Jews and pagans.

He speaks here of genies as beings almost identical to men. It is the second time this occurs. But it is obscure.

CHAPTER VIII

Spoils taken from the enemy belong to God and to his envoy. Fear the Lord (180). Whoever turns his back on the day of combat shall remain in hell (181). All infidels shall be reunited in hell (184). Fight infidels until the point when there is no more schism and when holy religion is universally triumphant (184). O believers! when you march on the enemy, be resolute, obey God and the Prophet, fear the discord that extinguishes the fire of courage. Be firm (185). The incredulous who refuses to believe in Islam is more abject than a brute in the eyes of the Eternal (187). If the fortune of battle causes those who violate the pact they have made with you to fall into your hands, use torture to terrify their followers (187). God will ease your task: 20 brave believers will crush 200 infidels, 100 will put 1,000 to flight. No prophet has taken prisoners without having spilled the blood of a great number of enemies (188). Feed on what you have taken from the enemy. You shall have no society with believers who have remained at home, until they have marched into combat. Believers who have left their country to fight under the standard of faith and those who have given aid to the Prophet are the truly faithful ones. Paradise is their portion.

CHAPTER IX

Loyally keep alliances contracted with idolaters if they observe them themselves (191). The sacred months having passed,* put idolaters to death wherever you encounter them. If they convert, perform their prayers, pay the sacred tribute, leave them in peace. The Lord is merciful (191). Fire shall be the eternal dwelling of idolaters (192). Believers who tear themselves from the bosom of their family to follow [God's] standard, sacrificing their property and their lives, shall have the first places in the realm of the heavens. They shall be the object of God's kindness[;] they shall live in gardens of delights and taste eternal pleasures (193). Cease loving your fathers, your brothers, if they prefer incredulity to faith. Those who hoard gold in their coffer and refuse to use it for the faith shall endure painful torments. This gold reddened by the fire of hell shall be pressed to their brows, their ribs, and their loins, and they shall be told: "Now enjoy your treasure" (195).

The All-Powerful made the year of twelve months:† four of these months are sacred. Shun iniquity during these days, but fight idolaters at all times (195). Young and old, enter combat, sacrifice your wealth and your lives for the defense of the faith, [for] there is no more glorious advantage for you (196). Some believers have let the Prophet go, they have said, "Let us not fight during the heat!" The fire of hell shall be much more terrible than that

---

* It seems that, during four months, war was not permitted among Arab tribes. It was a sort of holy peace similar to that of feudal times.
† The Arab calendar is lunar.

heat (202). The wealthy who demand exemptions are guilty (203). Those who do penance[,] serve the Lord, adore him, fast, carry out justice, respect and guard the divine commandments, shall be happy (206).* One must not intercede on behalf of idolaters, even if they are your kin, because they are buried in hell (id.). Fear the Lord and practice justice (207). O Believers! Fight your unfaithful neighbors. May they find implacable enemies (208).

CHAPTER X

The Koran confirms the truth of the Scriptures that precede it. It is the explanation of them (214).

Noah was treated as an impostor. Those who did not believe him were drowned in the waters. See what is the end of the incredulous! (218).

CHAPTER XI

Everything is written in the resplendent book (224).

He who suffers with patience and practices virtue shall receive a glorious reward.

If people demand that you do miracles, do not be distressed. Your ministry is limited to preaching.

Should they say: the Koran is his work? You shall respond: Produce ten chapters like those it contains.†

Most men shall persist in incredulity (226).

God shall give to each one according to his works; nothing escapes his knowledge (237). Pray at the beginning of each day, at sunset, and at night (id.).

The principal object of the eleventh chapter is to make known to the Arabs all the prophets that the peoples refused to believe and to hear, and to terrify them by the portrayal of the horrible punishments God has inflicted on their incredulity. As in practically all of the Alkoran, Muhammad concerns himself far more with making himself believed than with giving rules of morality. And

---

* Everything that relates to war is precise; everything that relates to morals, except almsgiving, is general and confused, as in the verse just cited.

† [In the margin:] Here Muhammad very skillfully makes use of the great writer to support the prophet.

he employs terror much more than any other motive. Muhammad evidently took a great deal from the New and Old Testaments, but much more from the Old than the New. You recognize Moses everywhere. He hardly strays from the Decalogue. He adds to it nothing but greater prescriptions for almsgiving.

CHAPTER XII

This chapter is nothing but the story of Joseph, son of Jacob, with some variations of little importance.

CHAPTER XIII

Those who are made constant in adversity by the hope of seeing God, who pray, who secretly or publicly give a portion of the property we have bestowed on them, and who erase their errors by good works, shall dwell in Paradise. They shall be introduced into the gardens of Eden: their fathers, their spouses, and their children who have been just shall enjoy the same benefit (258).

Should the Koran move mountains, divide the earth in two, make the dead speak, they would not believe you (259).*

The gardens of delights watered by rivers where shall be found eternal nourishment and perpetually green shade, shall be the prize for piety. The incredulous shall have flames as their reward (260).

CHAPTER XIV

Nothing new; always the same depictions of punishments that await those who refuse to believe the prophets.

CHAPTER XV

Depiction of the greatness of God. Threats against those who do not believe the prophets. Nothing exceptional or practical.

---

* The infidels asked Muhammad to perform miracles to prove his mission. Here is how he ordinarily gets out of this situation: "God could make me do it, but even so you would not believe."

CHAPTER XVI

Greatness. Goodness of God toward man. Violent attack on polytheism.

We have sent you the Koran in order to enlighten contested dogmas and to guide the faithful (II, 16).*

God commands justice, beneficence, liberality toward kin. He prohibits crime, injustice, and calumny (II, 19).

Avoid perjury. Whoever has practiced beneficence and professed faith shall enjoy a life strewn with pleasures.

Abraham is the leader of the believers. He worships the unity of God and refuses to worship idols. We have inspired you to embrace the religion of Abraham, who recognized the unity of God.

If you avenge yourselves, the vengeance must not exceed the offense. Those who have suffered with patience have performed a more meritorious action (id.).

CHAPTER XVII

Man carries his fate around his neck (II, 27).

God commands beneficence toward your parents. Always speak to them with respect. Be tender and submissive toward them. Give back to your neighbors what you owe them. Give alms to the poor and to travelers (II, 28).

Fear of indigence must not cause you to kill your children. That is a horrible crime. We shall provide for their needs and yours.

Avoid debauchery; it is a crime and the road to hell.

Never spill human blood. The murderer shall be under the power of the heirs of the deceased, but they must not exceed their limits by demanding his death.

Do not lay your hand on the orphan's property.

Fulfill your obligations.

Do not seek to penetrate that which you cannot know (II, 29).

---

* We see that Muhammad always makes connections with the Jewish and Christian religions and, through them, to the beginning of the world.

CHAPTER XVIII

Truth comes from God. Man is free to believe or to persist in error. We have lit furnaces for the wicked. Possessor of the garden of Eden where the rivers flow, adorned with gold bracelets, dressed in green garments woven in silk and gold, radiating glory, the believer shall repose on the nuptial bed during the season of delights (II, 42).

One day the earth shall be made plain; we shall assemble all men; not one shall be forgotten; they shall appear each in his turn before the tribunal of God (II, 44).

The works of those who have denied Islam and the resurrection are in vain. Falsehood presided over these works. They shall be without weight on the day of judgment (II, 51).

CHAPTER XIX[4]

NOTES ON THE VOYAGE
TO ALGERIA IN 1841

GENERAL APPEARANCE OF THE COUNTRY

7 May 1841

Arrived in Algiers from the direction of Oran, having gone too far west.[1] Cape
Caxine, a very green and furrowed mountain that plunges right into the sea.
The sky is hazy. The whole scene is like the one that the Hague's coastline
presents from the sea. As we approach, we perceive a multitude of small white
houses garnishing the mountain's furrows. As we round Cape Caxine, Algiers
appears: an immense quarry of white rock sparkling in the sun.[2]

First appearance of the town: I have never seen anything like it. Prodigious mix of races and costumes, Arab, Kabyle, Moor, Negro, Mahonais
[Balearic islanders, from Port Mahon on Minorca], French. Each of these
races, tossed together in a space much too tight to contain them, speaks its
language, wears its attire, displays different mores. This whole world moves
about with an activity that seems feverish. The entire lower town seems in a
state of destruction and reconstruction. On all sides, one sees nothing but
recent ruins, buildings going up; one hears nothing but the noise of the
hammer. It is Cincinnati transported onto the soil of Africa.

The French are substituting broad arcaded streets for the Moors' tortuous
little alleys. This is a necessity of our civilization. But they are also substituting
their architecture for that of the Moors, and this is wrong; for the latter is very
appropriate to the needs of the country, and besides, it is charming. The most
beautiful Moorish house shows, on the outside, only a wall with no opening

other than an arched door. This door leads into a vestibule supported by columns. From this vestibule a staircase leads to a square courtyard surrounded
by galleries, which are supported by arcades and columns. It is the same
on each floor. All the rooms open onto this courtyard, whose appearance is
fresher and more elegant than I can say. In all the better houses, the columns
are of curiously sculpted white marble, as are the edges of the arcades, and
festooned as if with lace. The whole very much presents the appearance of life
turned inward. Architecture depicts needs and mores: the architecture here
does not merely result from the heat of the climate, it also marvelously depicts
the social and political state of the Muslim and oriental populations: polygamy, the sequestration of women, the absence of any public life, a tyrannical
and suspicious government that forces one to conceal one's life and keep all
affections within the family.

Saturday 8

Visit to the environs of Algiers, at Couba.[3] Superb road that seems as
though it must lead to the provinces of a vast empire, and that one cannot
follow more than three leagues without being beheaded. Delicious country,
Sicily with the industry of France. Prodigious vegetation, the land dense with
vegetation. A promised land, if one didn't have to farm with gun in hand.
From the height of Couba we see the Metidja [usually Mitidja]: magnificent
plain, five leagues wide and thirty long, an entire province. Looks like Alsace.
Green, but not a house, not a tree, not a man. Astonishing contrast: the Sahel
the image of nature cultivated by industry and the most advanced civilization;
the plain: *wilderness.*[4]

Visit at the bishop's. An intelligent man, very intelligent. But a tint of
charlatanism.[5]

Evening, a trip to the Casaubah [Casbah or Qasba]. Old Algiers seemed
an immense fox burrow: narrow, dark, smoky. The population, at this hour,
seems idle and dissolute. Indigenous cabaret where Moorish public girls sing
and people drink wine. Mix of the vices of both civilizations. Such is the
external appearance.

ORAN — MERS-EL-KEBIR

We found about thirty cannons.[6] Sixty cannons would be necessary. . . .[7]
They plan to defend the fort with three batteries. Slight expense. Certain result.

Captain of the steam boat.

The port can hold fifteen to twenty warships.

Port Captain d'Assigny.[8]

The important task is to defend it from the sea. Almost impossible to attack by land. One could land only at Cap Falcon.[9]

SECURITY [*TENUE*] OF THE PORT AT MERS-EL-KEBIR

Commandant d'Assigny, who has commanded the station for eighteen months, gave us the following information:

The winds from the east and northeast are not felt in any way in the port. But they churn up the sea and produce a fairly strong surf.

The only winds that could present any danger are the west winds, which sweep into the harbor through a gorge and are tremendously violent. But they do not churn up the sea, and Commandant d'Assigny thinks it almost impossible for them to dislodge a warship well attached on a good mooring. Besides, since the sea is never churned up by this wind, the traction on the cable is always even.

If the cable happened to break, the accident could be quite serious, as it is not always very easy to reach the high seas when those squalls stir up the wind on the coast and tend to push ships trying to get out to sea onto the lighthouse rocks.

The most urgent expenses include everything necessary for the *defense* and the *securing* of the port of Mers-el-Kebir. The port of Mers-el-Kebir is thus far, as far as our overseas power is concerned, the most definite result obtained in Algeria.

The only drawback of Mers-el-Kebir is the lack of water. This lack of water is not absolute, however; the facilities we have already built and those that are to be built should be able to bring in 12,500 liters in twenty-four hours,* which might be enough for 6,000 men.

There are also the cisterns, which provide enough for the garrison.

Besides, communication between Mers-el-Kebir and Oran can never be interrupted by sea during the summer or by land during the winter. The road is superb and very easy to defend.

The Spanish left us a superb establishment at Mers-el-Kebir. At the moment, it is even superfluous, as it forms a very strong defense on the land

---

* We do not know yet if it would be significantly less during the summer.

side, where it would be quite difficult for Europeans and impossible for Arabs to ever attack us.

TRENCH DUG AROUND ORAN

This trench has been dug in three months by the army. It cost almost nothing, and people think it serves to break in the troops and prepare them for war. It is . . . feet deep and 9 wide at the opening. It is secured by occasional blockhouses. People believe that all the land within this trench is entirely sheltered from the Arabs. The total length of the trench is . . . meters. Lamoricière[10] has had this trench dug without authorization in 1841.

Nothing has been given to the soldier *diggers* who have dug it. As for the soldier *laborers,* they have had ten sous per day. Civilian laborers of the same type would have cost 4 to 5 francs per day. The troops, it is said, have done this job very willingly, regarding it as a *work of military defense.*

The plan of Colonel de Montpezat[11] to occupy a large part of the plain of Oran in the same manner. This should be examined.

It is often asked that Oran be made a transshipment port. The results would obviously be very great. A large part of the contraband commerce now passing through Gibraltar would go through Oran. But such a measure would be extremely hostile to Spain, and the question remains whether the interest is great enough to risk this drawback. We need Spain's friendship in the matter of Algeria. First, because of the foothold that Spain is letting us have in Mahon [Minorca], because of the security that we must grant her until we take possession of that island, and, finally, because she is neither giving the English the island nor allowing them to take it, which would be the loss of the colony. *Mahon must be French:* it is a question of life or death for Algiers.

PROVINCE OF ORAN

Lamoricière claims that his information leads him to believe that the population of the province could rise to 200 souls at least per square league.

He estimates at 80,000 the total number of horses found there, which would allow us to commission about 28,000.

Abd-el-Kader's government, far more powerful and centralized than that of the Turks, raises, Lamoricière believes, three million in taxes on the province of Oran alone.

CONFIGURATION OF THE COUNTRY

It is 35 to 45 leagues from the coast to the first desert, that is, to the country that produces neither grain nor large livestock, but only dates and grass suited to feeding sheep and camels.

This space is occupied by two transverse valleys, the first between Oran and Mascara, the second between Mascara and the desert.

For now, we can only harass the Arabs of the first valley, and we have harassed them so well since Lamoricière arrived that not a single one is left within 15 to 20 leagues of Oran. They have all taken refuge either in the mountains on the Mascara side, or on the other side of these mountains. Hence the need to have an army corps at Mascara that can, through razzias like Lamoricière's, harass them on the other side of the mountains and force them to go even farther. Thus, finding themselves pushed too far, they would come to terms with us. *(Information provided by Lamoricière on 17 May 1841.)*

Today I asked Colonel de Montpezat—who demonstrated quite well how four or five thousand men placed at Mascara could, in taking the population from the rear, bring about the submission of the tribes—how these four or five thousand men would live. He responded: "First, in making an enclosure that would allow cultivation around the town, where there is admirable land; second, in emptying the Hachems' silos, which allegedly could feed the army for eighteen months; third, in forcing the Hachem tribe—a tribe that could mount five thousand cavalrymen and that possesses admirable country to which it is quite attached—to submit. If an army of four or five thousand could live in Mascara, I would consider the province subjugated and Abd-el-Kader destroyed."[12]

CIVIL LABORS OF ORAN

Wharves to build: 200,000 francs, I think.
Jetties to build: 600,000 francs, I think.

ARZEU

On 21 May 1841, at 8 A.M., we were in the bay of Arzeu and went onshore.

A crenellated enclosure built by the French and occupied by 200 men. A few fathoms away, blockhouses beyond which one could not walk without risking one's head. Two or three wells of brackish and insufficient water. Such is the settlement. Arzeu harbor, which is very broad, gives excellent shelter to the commercial vessels. It would also shelter warships, but less safely, because it is shallow near the shore. The bay is not always easy to leave, and it would be difficult to establish good defensive structures. It is thus immensely inferior to Mers-el-Kebir. If we had commerce with the interior, the place would still be of some importance; indeed it will be from now on, because it is really the port for nearby Mostaganem.

CHERCHEL

The wind did not allow us to land at Cherchel. According to the maritime charts of the shore and the captain's report, Cherchel could shelter only three small ships, and it would be impossible to do anything better with it. The occupation of this town, where we are blocked, and which requires a fairly numerous garrison, is a great mistake.

DOUERS AND SEMALAS

The country occupied by tribes was to the south of the large lake. Not only did we allow this to be taken, but we gave it away in the treaty of Tafna. Enormous mistake. Country of admirable fertility. This same treaty ceded the territory of Ben-Zetoun in Algiers province to Abd-el-Kader, who soon took possession of it. The Ben-Zetouns, who were coulouglis, covered us admirably to the east. Another enormous mistake.[13]

In general, in Africa, as everywhere else, all our alliances have led to the destruction or the reduction of those who trusted us.[14]

23 May 1841

Today M. Hurtis,[15] a *very well-informed* colonist, led us a league and a half from Algiers into the hills of the massif on the Couba side to show us a property where he does excellent business. We first crossed the hills, covered with brushwood and brambles. He told us that three years ago, the land we were going to see had been just the same. Once we had passed this thicket, we found ourselves at the edge of a vast property planted with mulberry and olive trees, and under many of these grew vegetables such as potatoes and onions. . . .[16]

This field was 30 hectares large. It contained 3,500 cultivated and 2,000 wild mulberry trees, plus about 4,000 grafted olive trees. It was a very beautiful sight of its kind. All the mulberry trees had been planted three years ago. Not one had died, and *all* of them displayed uncommon vigor and growth. They were generally as big as an arm. Several were much larger. This, M. Hurtis told us, was because they had dug 16 inches deep. This land is of very ordinary quality in the massif (the average). This whole admirable plantation was profitable for the owner, including the purchase of land, which the administration sold at a very high price — 48,000 francs. The state had contributed nothing.

"We have heard it said that the soil of the massif wasn't worth anything."

— That is a lie: the soil is very good; only it is much worse than that of the Metidja, which is excellent. But since in the Metidja one is much farther from town, security is worse, even in peacetime, and one's health is at greater risk, for now, all things considered, it is still better to farm the massif.

— What kind of farming is preferable?

— Everything grows here. But for the owner who is not farming himself, wheat is bad, for the costs exceed the income. He can only succeed with orchards, mulberry, olives, chestnuts, almonds. There is only one planting, and the harvest is certain in this beautiful climate. Some day we'll be able to plant wheat, but only if it is farmed by small landowners who work the land themselves. The same is true of cotton: I am sure that this country will produce cotton very well, but on condition that the cotton is grown on small plots that the farmer and his family can oversee. To farm cotton in large quantities is inevitably to ruin oneself. Next year I plan to try something they say is done in Syria: to raise silkworms on the tree. If I succeed, the results will be tremendous, since it would eliminate almost all the labor costs. You can see that in the next field we've planted vineyards; they are growing with tremendous vigor, like everything else; but we don't yet know what the wine will be like. Besides, we must take care not to create troublesome competition with the vineyards of southern France.

— But couldn't this observation apply to everything else?

— No; as for olives, France is far from supplying its consumption, and besides, it is a kind of farming that is disappearing: the cold has forced us to cut our olive trees at the base three times. As for the mulberry, its production is also far from meeting consumption, and the artificial methods they are inventing these days will always be very expensive.

— What is most responsible for stopping the development of industry in the massif, where security is very good?

— The lack of small proprietors and workers. Almost all the land belongs to large landowners who do not farm and who cannot find farmers. As for workers, they hardly ever come on their own, and we are discouraged from bringing them, because as soon as you have brought a good worker, he is taken from you by another landowner. The remedy for this last problem would be, in my view, to require workers to carry a booklet in which they would register contracts of this kind; then an action for damages could be brought against a landowner who hired any worker carrying a booklet that proved that he was missing his prior engagement. That would undoubtedly be a departure from our law. But there have been useless and far more dangerous ones.

23 May, in the evening

We have just spent the evening with the bishop, who told us himself about the circumstances of the prisoner exchange. It was a scene out of the Crusades. Abd-el-Kader's Khalifa [lieutenant] got into the bishop's carriage and remained there chatting with him for three hours.[17] He revealed his exhaustion with the war, his terror of the way the French carried it out, his deep sense of the miseries that it led the Arabs to suffer. He finished with a very skillfully veiled overture of peace. The French can never ask us for peace, he said; nor can Abd-el-Kader; but you who are a minister of peace, can't you serve as intermediary between the two parties and bring them to an accord that, this time, will be stable?

This whole business of the exchange has put the bishop in a fine and important position. But, if I am not mistaken, he will soon abuse it. There is something of the saint and of the Gascon[18] in this man. He would submit himself heroically to martyrdom, and at the same time, he wants to act and to be seen. What I have seen of his clergy is admirable.

24 May 1841

We have just met with M. Lepécheux.[19] M. Lepécheux is the director of public instruction in Algiers. He has been living there for eight years. He is an intelligent and, it seemed to us, sensible man. Marshal Valée had very particularly recommended that we see him and talk with him.

Here is the substance of what he told us: "We could correct a thousand

details here without fixing the real problem. The problem is in the foundations. There is no *government* here, at least such as we mean by that word in the
civilized countries of Europe. On one side there is a military power that
conducts military affairs more or less as it likes and that can do anything it likes
in an instant by using violence. And as for the civil administration, it is entirely
in Paris, not Algiers. There is no permanent center for the civil administration
in Algiers. Everything is centralized in Paris in M. Laurence's hands.[20] The
tiniest affairs are decided according to his whim. We cannot grant an inch of
land to emigrants without endless formalities that last months and result in M.
Laurence's visa. When things are regulated in this way, we miss our chance and
the colonist leaves, or rather the prospect of such a state prevents him from
coming. The central administration in Paris continually takes the initiative on
a slew of measures without consulting the department heads. It sends men out
to the Algerian administration without ever requesting anyone to define their
mission [*une liste de présentation*]. So we are continually getting decrees, and
we learn from the newspaper about measures no one ever requested. For
example, the scientific commission,[21] whose salaries were put into the colonial
budget and that has already cost us 150,000 francs, was established without
asking advice from anyone about whether such a commission would have
anything to do and how the colony might usefully employ it. I would also
mention the foundation of the Arab college, also paid for with colonial funds,
which has not yet had and will never have any pupils, whose establishment
caused great harm by making the Arabs fear that we wanted to seize their
children (curious details on this point, altogether like those given by M.
Guyot and the bishop). Finally, I would mention the continual shipment of
very expensive objects, most of them worthless, which are sent, they say, to
make presents to the Arabs, which we must pay for, which we never requested
and on whose shipment we were never consulted. In sum, here we have the
most extreme abuses of French centralization, applied to a colony — that is, to
the kind of country that can least bear such a system. It is a thousand times
worse and more arbitrary than in France, and we have not had a single one of
those counterweights that, in France, help make it bearable, since we have
neither settled property, nor independent justice, nor press, nor local assemblies, small or large. What's more, all these vices, which, if not created by
M. Laurence, were at least exacerbated by him, were furiously described and
attacked by him in a speech he gave in Algiers in 1834, which I shall show you.

"You understand that the civil officials — caught between the coups d'état of the military power and the thousand times more crushing arbitrariness of the central authority — are conscious of nothing, have no common ties, think of nothing but returning to France as quickly as possible. Each goes his way without confidence, without direction and, I would add, without insight. This leads me to another set of thoughts.

"There is already 25 million in French capital invested here. These large interests are not represented in any way, directly or indirectly. All the local revenues are centralized in the hands of the central authority in Paris. As for the population, they have no way to express *their wishes:* the government council is made up of active public officials who are indifferent to the common project and uninterested in anything but their specialty. There is no colonial council. There is not even a municipal council. The latter was allowed to expire by not renewing its members. I am not very liberal — I wouldn't ask that any council, whatever name you want to give it, be elected. Choose it yourselves from among the notables. I don't ask that it be able to do anything but state its views. But create something that can at least make known, whether to the local or to the central power, the needs and wishes of the country. If you wish to have only public officials, at least have public officials who aren't busybodies, who would be required to prepare general decrees locally, and who have a sense of the whole. As long as we have none of these things, it is fair to say that there is no government and that an honest and reasonable population cannot consent to come and join such a country, despite the incomparable richness of the soil and the ease with which you can make your fortune. The place lacks the most necessary guarantees for man in society. What I fear is that we'll soon see the country's most respectable houses leave and return to France, because the place is so unbearable."

Q. I seem to have noticed that the population, which was first troubled by Marshal Valée, now misses him?

A. Yes. For a long time General Valée had no desire to stay. In the end, he embraced the country. What's more, he soon gave up the false idea that one had to fight first and colonize later. He finally understood that these two things must happen together. And this was where he directed his very vigorous and penetrating mind. He was going to establish colonial representation. He got actively involved in colonizing Blida. It is a great shame that he was removed.

M. Lepécheux added: "You may be sure that there is no man here, either official or citizen, who can stay on if either the governor-general or M. Laurence dislikes him. There is no need to make use of the decree that allows the governor to expel him without any form of trial. Nothing is easier than to make his life so unbearable that he is absolutely forced to pack up."

Q. What do you think of the latest decree on expropriation?[22]

A. It completes the picture. I understand that it forces landowners to use the land or sell it. But to grant the general ability to expropriate and to issue as a final decree the intention to expropriate cultivated lands in order to place new colonists on them: that seems to me barbarous and insane.

Q. What do you think of the new judicial ordinance?[23]

A. I find it dangerous. It removes rotation, but, what is far worse, it allows the attorney general to send the magistrate he complains of back to France, for reasons that he need give only to the minister. What's more, it prevents appeals in civil trials. Now that is a very necessary guarantee in a country where justice is still so unenlightened and so insecure.

24 May

M. Guyot,[24] director of the interior. He seemed to me a fairly mediocre man. He exaggerates the importance of the civil power just as others do the military power. I believe he is as opposed to any local representation as his predecessor was in favor of it, but it is curious to see with what passion he falls into line with him on other points. Thus, Laurence's ultra-centralization; the way each mailboat brings him decrees he didn't request and on which he had not been consulted; the deputies imposed on him without warning, mostly incapable or new to the job; the multitude and slowness of the formalities to which he is compelled so that centralization can function — on all these points, he is at least as passionate and as bitter as M. Lepécheux. He is even more passionate when he speaks of relations with the military authority. You can see his concentrated rage about the subordinate and truly humiliating position that the civil power holds here. He told us several very curious anecdotes on this subject: now it's a military leader to whom it suddenly occurs to ban carriages in a street and who begins by telling the director who objects to go to hell; another time, it's General Bugeaud giving him an immense job assignment at three o'clock in the afternoon and demanding that he bring it in at the crack of dawn the next day; then a military leader who suddenly prohibits Arabs from bringing certain goods to market. The director objects. He is told to get lost. He appeals to the general in charge, who finally decides against the officer. By this time a month has passed, a month during which quite a few baton blows have been showered on the Arabs. These anecdotes amused us but we learned nothing, since what could become of the poor civil official in the face of French insolence, with a knife at his throat? There was nothing strange about it but the deep, but submissive, rage of the poor director finishing all his sentences by saying, "You must admit, gentlemen, that this requires great patience!" To which we would respond in chorus, "Admirable, director."

24 May 1841

Today we also saw M. Henriot,[25] the attorney general. He seemed to us a very mediocre man, very discouraged and homesick. He has been here fourteen months. He left his wife and child in France and is burning to return. In his view nothing will come of Algiers; it is a country we should leave as quickly as possible. It is not the lack of judicial guarantees that troubles him; on the contrary, I think that in his eyes that is the good side of Algeria. But he can't cope with Laurence's arbitrariness. He is consulted on nothing. They want to run everything from Paris. They keep sending him magistrates he would like to send packing, and they impose all sorts of men on him without warning.

Some people argue for abandoning Algeria

It is with good reason that he is against having judges work alone [*l'unité du juge*]. He claims that the number of civil trials is so burdensome that a lot of judgments are drafted by the attorneys themselves. He says that the costs of trials are almost as great as in France. Regarding the judge working alone, he told us something of what is called justice in this wretched country: "Responsibility crushes a single judge," he said. "Recently there was a very grave affair in which eminent men were badly compromised. I put off the trial, because a single judge would never have been able to hold his own in such a matter." This is the attorney general casually saying such a thing.

General remark: everything I hear in this country proves to me that Laurence's shamefulness, his roguery, and in a word, his rubbish [*ordure*], is a commonplace. As long as that man stands at the head of this immense affair, there will be no hope. That seems axiomatic to me.

It seems to be notorious here, as much among the administrators as among the administered, that most of what is given out in the Chambers [i.e., parliament] about Algiers is full of lies and deserves not to be credited at all.

Doctor Trollier[26] made an apt remark to us this evening (24 May): he said that if it was vexing to have a country governed by officials without any kind of control on the part of the governed, it was all the more so in a colony where the officials, who are never more than passing through, are always foreigners, and especially in a colony such as Algiers where the law, in preventing them from becoming property owners, takes away even the chance that any of them might happen to identify with the country.

The fact is that *none of our colonies* has ever at *any* time been treated like Algiers. All, in one form or another, have allowed the local population some say or at the very least have allowed local authorities to administer local revenues. Algiers is singularly bad, even within our detestable system of colonization. Find out more exactly what Canada and Saint-Domingue [Haiti] used to be like and how the Antilles were ten years ago.

Nota. From now on, as long as I remain in Algiers, I shall continue on separate sheets that must be referred to *in order to follow the chain* of impressions.

25 May 1841. Visit to the school [collège]

It is quite a fine establishment, the old janissary barracks. There are 150 students, 30 of whom are boarders, who pay 600 francs. The day students pay nothing. The Arabic course is required for everyone. There are two systems of instruction in this school: Greek and Latin classes as in our *collèges royaux;* and nonclassical instruction, which lasts for four years and is more appropriate to the needs of the country.[27]

Q. Why is the basis of instruction classical?

A. There is tremendous mobility among our students. Most spend only a few months in the school. They are the sons of officers, who come from Europe and return there. The students would miss the education they had begun, or start one they could not finish, if the French educational system were not followed.

The school's director complains quite bitterly that no one prevents the bishop from having several students in a small seminary. "The bishop educates young Arabs for 300 francs a year; how could we compete?" It is indeed frustrating that instruction can be cheap. In any case, the college doesn't have *a single* Arab student. They say they would if there were scholarships. I doubt it.

I saw the library on the same day. There are some fine Arabic manuscripts, mostly taken from Constantine. Many others, also taken from that town, were mishandled and lost. Greek and Latin manuscripts are no longer found anywhere, nor Arabic manuscripts that could teach us anything new. I met a young Arabic teacher there, a student of M. de Sacy's, a man who seemed distinguished and very intelligent.[28]

Q. What difference is there between vernacular Arabic and written Arabic?

A. At least as much as between Latin and Italian. What is remarkable is that all Arabs who write use written Arabic, which is that of the Koran. A merchant writes his memoirs in the language of Muhammad and speaks modern vernacular, which has no grammar and thus cannot really be called a language. So the two languages exist side by side and are used by the same people.

Q. What is the best translation of the Koran?

A. ["] . . .[29] in Latin. Savary's is elegant and unfaithful.[30] Besides, there really is no good translation, because one would also have to translate the five or six principal commentaries that help explain the text. The Koran is, in fact, a collection of daily rules and proclamations about which we understand nothing, if the events that motivated them are not explained." (The Koran is the source of the laws, ideas, mores of this entire Muslim population with whom we are dealing; the government's first scientific task clearly should be to have the best possible translation made of both text and commentary. This would be much more worthwhile than spending 500,000 francs for a scientific commission that has no practical utility as far as I am concerned.)

Q. How long do you think a person of ordinary intelligence, with serious study, would take to learn written Arabic?

A. At least four to five years. As for the vernacular, you can get by after a few months, if you want to go to the cafés and spend time with the Moors.

After I left, I met Berbrugger[31] (he is not a man of great intellect, but he is the one who has lived most with the Arabs). He said: "During my last stay in the Chélif valley, I saw three or four thousand inhabitants of Algiers who had left us to go to Abd-el-Kader and whom Abd-el-Kader had put there. These people are extremely unhappy. Their women have to go about with their faces uncovered and to work. They weep when speaking of Algiers, bitterly regret having left it, and dearly wish to be able to return (Abd-el-Kader doesn't have any more towns and cannot hope to get any unless we want him to. The Arabs' lack of towns is an element that will have great consequences and should be examined). On this visit, as on the one I had made the week before to the Hadjoutes[32] for the exchange of prisoners, this is how the Arabs spoke to us:

— You admire our herds, but what use are these herds to us now? We can no longer sell them, and if we could sell them, what would we do with the money? we no longer have a town nearby where we could buy what we need. We are always on horseback and uneasy. War has made us miserable, but it will never make us abandon Abd-el-Kader. In the end, the French will only bring us to despair, and then, having lost all hope of peace, we shall do them far more harm than we have done so far. We could leave not a single house standing in the areas around Algiers. They think they are starving us by burning our harvests. Abd-el-Kader has cultivated a great deal of wheat behind the mountains and in places where the French will never go." (These speeches, which accord with everything the prisoners say, are quite remarkable. They indicate an exhaustion among the Arabs.)

When we tell the Arabs they started the war, they deny it passionately and claim that we were the ones to start it by passing the Biban.[33] They formally deny that Abd-el-Kader ever recognized French sovereignty and in this at least they are right; for on this point the wording of the treaty is very clear and permits only one interpretation. It says literally: "Abd-el-Kader knows that the sultan of the French has a force [*puissance*] in Africa."

VISIT TO M. FILLON

M. Fillon has been president of the superior court since 1834.[34] He will return to France with a permanent post. He is a man of intelligence. In all these capacities, he deserves to be trusted. In addition, it is clear that the man has grown bitter against the attorney general and the administration. Our goal in going to see him was to make sure that we had not been mistaken about the judiciary system of the colony, whose monstrosities astonished us.

Q. Nothing replaces the Council chamber and the court of indictments?

A. No.

Q. Then how are trials concluded and who is responsible?

A. The attorney general, who can prolong the trial or shorten it; suspend or cancel it; place the accused in prison or set him free; rearrest him or leave him at liberty, as he chooses.

Q. Does the latest judicial ordinance (February 1841) improve or worsen the state of things?

A. It worsens it immensely: first, in the former state, provisional liberty was given by the judge. Now it is given by the attorney general. Second, appeals of the Bône and Oran courts' decisions were strictly limited before. The new ordinance does extend these limits, but it also introduces two odious exceptions: political crimes, and crimes designated by the particular laws of the colony. Third, finally, and in my view this should be enough to make the country uninhabitable, it destroys appeal to the highest court of appeals in civil trials. This is to prevent the appeals court from hearing of . . .[35] . . . [to seize] the colonists' property, especially in bringing trials before administrative court.

Q. Don't you think that, in a country such as this, where all titles have a more or less administrative origin, that administrative justice might not end up by dragging everything into its own sphere?

A. Yes, without a doubt. In general, you should take for granted that there is no property, no justice here. So what astonishes me is, not that no one is coming, but that anyone is staying. Things are going more and more in this direction, and I know of several households in the process of liquidating.

The president of the commercial court, who was there, tells the following anecdote:

"In 1835, with the agreement of the authorities, the principal merchants taxed themselves voluntarily in order to establish a chamber of commerce, found an agricultural prize, and make other expenditures in the common interest. Then the authorities made this kind of tax mandatory, seized the proceeds, and did as they pleased with it." That's Algeria for you.

ANECDOTE TOLD AT THE SCHOOL

The scientific commission had expressed the desire to hire a young painter from the college, who had been here a long time and had shown a special talent for depicting the appearance and landscape of the country. M. Laurence agreed in principle, arranged for a large salary, and sent one of his relatives from Paris.

27 May 1841

Steamboat.[36] M. de Saint-Sauveur, captain. For one year the tribe's caid. Land of the beylik: the entire province. Tribes have territory; between these territories, vacant land. Each year the caid divides the territory into three parts, one of which is not to be cultivated; he distributes the other two among the various sections of the tribe. The sheikh of each section divides it among individuals. Only the harvest and not the land belongs to individuals. A sort of hereditary nobility. Magma,[37] in which the caid must be chosen. Tribe, complete society, priest, judge . . . The Arabs move easily from one tribe into another. It is in the caid's interest to keep them, because of the taxes he is paid. One plow represents a revenue of 3,000 francs. Often Arabs have three or four plows. The Arabs get used to houses. It would be possible to make this a habit with them if they were given individual property and if their farming system were changed, which is more difficult. The Arabs make no provisions for their herds, so they have to move about constantly. This country easily could be brought to resemble Egypt. Arabs of this province, farmers, fellahs. Complaints of the Arabs against their caids, cadis. . . .[38] French caids would be better. But we must not impose them, but rather get them to ask for them. Only through justice can we bring them to forgive us for our religion. To imitate the Turks is to be inferior to the Turks, since we are not Muslims. We shall probably have war as soon as we seriously try to colonize with Europeans. It would be better to make use of the land in the Egyptian manner, that is, have the natives farm it, but to the government's profit. The Arabs live a very idle life. Farming takes them no more than a month. The rest is spent in conversations that sharpen their wit and give them that subtlety and that ability to understand that makes them so superior to our peasants in France. There is nothing to be done with the Kabyles, except trade. If we stop threatening them on their land, they will come supply us with everything. The Kabyle tribes often fight among themselves; still, they form a sort of confederation. M. de Saint-Sauveur believes we could easily have a good effect on the Arabs' minds by distributing books; they are a curious and intelligent people.

29 May 1841

At six in the morning, we arrive at Bougie. Very picturesque town. Vast enclosure now filled with ruins. Lovely nature. To the left of the town the stream of . . .[39] flows down from the mountain and toward the sea through magnificent valleys. We are enclosed there as if in a sentry box, from which we can't stray even a rifle shot away without risking our heads.[40] Still, in the past several months, two shipwrecked crews were not assassinated. They were returned for ransom, but after having been circumcised and raped. We are told that the Bougie harbor is secure. The mountains drop right into the sea on all sides.

Leaving Bougie, we skirt the coast. Always the same sight: a chain of mountains runs parallel to the sea; behind the first we can see others always aligned in the same direction. Few or no valleys open onto the sea. No large rivers; only streams flow from the gorges. The mountain slopes on our side appear highly cultivated. Wooded summits. Enclosed and cultivated fields, planted with fruit trees. You can't see villages, they are undoubtedly hidden in the gorges. But the whole presents the picture of a very rich country, beautiful and well inhabited. It is true that we are skirting the large block of mountains that is essentially the Kabyles' country, which even the Turks were never able to penetrate.

It seems quite clear to me that as soon as we try to make use of our domination in the province of Constantine to colonize, peace will end and the domination will be challenged. But on the other hand, where will a domination that does not result in colonization lead us?

SECOND CONVERSATION WITH M. DE SAINT-SAUVEUR

He was caid of three tribes who had freely chosen him, in the area of Constantine. He is the only Frenchman to whom this happened. When he speaks of the farewells the Arabs gave him when he had to leave them, he has tears in his eyes. In the three tribes, he had 100 plows and about 2,000 men. He believes that the best system with the Arabs would be French caids (but would we find good ones, would we leave them, wouldn't the faults of the bad ones be blamed on the French in general? Talk about this in Constantine). I speak to him again about colonization. He persists in saying that it will lead to war. What's more, he says, the areas around Bône where it could be done are precisely those occupied by the tribes who are friendliest to us and who provide us with our spahis.[41] We couldn't take away these people's lands by compensating them. So they must be dispossessed. Now, two great drawbacks to this measure. Material effect: the spahis we have trained will take precise information to the enemy. Moral effect: injustice, and injustice that would fall, as always, on our allies and friends.

Q. You told me that the entire territory with minor exceptions belongs to the beylik. So where is the injustice?

A. The property itself belongs to the beylik, but when it has granted the use of a territory to a tribe, to take the land away when the tribe has committed no crime is outrageous in the Arabs' eyes.

Q. Then what would you have us do?

A. Use the Arabs to make the province productive. I think the taxes could rise and our trade could increase. We could bring down the cost of the army, if we gave some of the beylik's unoccupied territories to regiments that would farm it as collective property, as a sort of fiefdom.

Q. Why is it that all the produce, including wheat and barley, has grown so much more expensive?

A. The bad harvests partly explain it, but I think the biggest reason is that the Turkish administration used those vast territories that we leave vacant to farm for its own benefit, to raise herds. . . .[42] So the land produced far more in the Turks' time, and the number of consumers was smaller. We are immense consumers and we produce nothing.

Q. How are the conditions for women?

A. Easy enough, when they are pretty. The ugly ones work almost like beasts of burden.

Q. Does polygamy actually exist on a large scale?

A. Yes. Many men have the four wives they are allowed. Naturally, as a result, many men have no wife. So the vice against nature is very common.

General Galbois's system was to govern the Arabs according to Arab laws, but by Frenchmen as much as possible. General Négrier's[43] system is to govern Arabs through Arabs. Much to say for or against these two systems. This should be examined.

29 May, in the evening

At three o'clock we arrive in Gigelli,[44] a small village consisting of Moors' hovels and a superb hospital, the only truly French monuments there are in Africa. Surrounding the town, you can see a line of blockhouses, a cannon shot away. Charming and magnificent country, such as we've seen since the morning. From the point of Gigelli runs a line of reefs on which it would be easy and not costly to build a jetty. Duquesne's idea. In this way, the sea would never come into the port. But from what the sailors say, it will never be a very desirable port. Its position is bad, and it lies behind a deep and dangerous bay where ships are always hesitant to seek shelter. They would rather go to Bougie, a far more secure harbor, where you can enter and exit easily and that can be seen from far off. About 800 Moors who have returned live in the town. But they are very poor. The wealthy ones stayed in the mountains where they had property.

Visit to the commander;[45] he told us the following: "There are three

Kabyle tribes in the areas around Gigelli. I am in a fair way to establishing peace with them. And I would have done it already, if I could have gotten it out of their heads that sooner or later we mean to seize their territory. For they very much like trading with us and it would be easy to establish considerable communications with them. The tribes near us would ask no more than to be left in peace, but the more distant tribes, who have little to hope for and nothing to fear from us, make war on them if they don't make war on us. Still, I hope to have made a solid enough peace with the Beni-Caids, one of the three tribes I'm talking about. This tribe could put three hundred men under arms. The negotiation was difficult because this tribe is broken into ten sections, each of which [obeys] its own sheikh, without a common superior power. So I had to deal with ten men. I succeeded, especially by refusing to allow them to come to market. Since then, they have even returned a deserter and have stopped firing their guns at us. But this will last no more than a month and, despite this arrangement, I'll admit that I wouldn't go for a walk on their territory a hundred feet from the blockhouse. I couldn't settle anything else with the other tribes. Still, I am hopeful. But there is no way to do anything stable with a group of tribes who don't obey any common authority and who are constantly at war with one another, and when each tribe has a slew of little independent leaders whose consent you have to get. I can't imagine anything that seems less like a government than the Kabyle authorities. In a sense, the sheikhs are made by chance or force, and anarchy is perpetual.

"The example of the Beni-Caids proves that you can make a temporary treaty but not a true alliance with these peoples, and that they always take care not to get tied too closely to us. The Beni-Caids are about to go to war with their neighbors. I had us propose to help them. They were careful not to accept. They would have been forever compromised with their compatriots, and no momentary interests are worth this drawback to them."

According to the commander, the first task in Gigelli would be to bring into the town a fine spring that rises out of the ground a hundred paces from the last blockhouse and at which one cannot draw water without exposing oneself to the Kabyles' murderous fire. It would be necessary, as much to secure this aqueduct as to guarantee the small territory in front of the blockhouse, to build a wall [whose cost is] estimated by the commander at 30,000 francs. Otherwise the town is uninhabitable, since during the summer the springs more or less dry up, and water becomes insufficient and very unhealthy.

The commander believes in a great commercial future for Gigelli; the fact is that if we act wisely, Gigelli will, like Bougie, become the distribution point for a large trade with the Kabyles. These two towns border a large territory filled with this singular population. Little by little, communications of this type would certainly be established, if we had the wisdom not to do anything that could make the Kabyles fear we want to attack them on their land. But will we ever be able to *keep up* this wisdom? I doubt it.

The preceding explains the Kabyles better than a large book would. Here one sees: (1) their mistrust of the French; (2) their resolution not to deal with us at all; (3) their industrious character; (4) their need for outlets; (5) their division into small tribes; (6) their lack of any centralization and regular powers; and (7) their permanent state of anarchy and civil wars.

One wonders why peoples who have reached the first stage of civilization like the Kabyles never went further. This can hardly be explained except by their situation as mountain people, the proximity of the Arabs, their religion, and *especially* their division into small tribes, the organization that is best suited for a rough civilization and is the most resistant to high civilization. This same division in tribes is itself facilitated by the physical state of the country.

30 May

Philippeville appeared in view at four o'clock in the morning. We disembarked at six o'clock. The town looks American. Two years ago, a single shack. Now 5,000 souls. Houses thrown pell-mell on the hills amid Roman ruins. Disorder, confusion, life.[46] Lunch with the commander, a colonel [Colonel Jean Baptiste Simon Arsène d'Alphonse (1792–1875)]; "Nothing but force and terror, Gentlemen, succeeds with these people. The other day, I carried out a razzia. I'm sorry you weren't there. It was a tribe that allowed men to cross its territory on their way to rob and kill us. Still, I didn't want to push things too far: after having killed five or six men, I spared the animals. There was even a man from this tribe of our friends who had had two mules taken from him; I ordered another troublesome Arab to give him two cattle. Nothing but terror works with these men, Gentlemen. The other day a murder was committed on the road. An Arab who was suspected of it was brought to me. I interrogated him and then I had his head cut off. You can see his head on the Constantine gates. As for your so-called colonists in Philippeville, they are a bunch of scoundrels; men who think the army is there just so they can make their fortunes, thieves who would be nothing without us, and whom despite

all that I go to great trouble to protect. Yesterday, I requisitioned their wagons
and horses for making hay, and I announced that the first to refuse would be
sent until further notice to the Monkeys' blockhouse (it's an isolated blockhouse on a scorched and arid mountain)."

All this was said by a man who seemed to be the nicest fellow in the world.
A sailor who was there, and who owns some land, responded heatedly that it
was wrong to treat the colonists this way; that without a colony, there was
nothing stable or profitable in Africa; that there was no colony without land,
and that it would be better to dispossess the nearest tribes and put Europeans
in their place.

And I, listening sadly to all these things, wondered what could be the
future of a country subjected to such men, and where this flood of violence
and injustices would end, if not in the revolt of the natives and the ruin of the
Europeans?

What is apparent in all Africa, but especially here where it is master, is not
only the coarseness and the violence natural to military power, but the ardent
and unintelligent hatred of the soldier for the civilian. Even though the civilian
populations actually nourish the army, there is a sort of furious jealousy of
them in the army. The soldiers cannot own land. The idea that they spill their
blood to make the fortunes of those who come here only to enrich themselves
drives them mad. We have encountered this imbecile sentiment at all levels,
and General Bugeaud personifies it.

What happens between or went on his assessment of Bugeaud in 1847?

MISCELLANEOUS

The wool affair. General Négrier, because he wants to force the Arabs to sell
him cheap wool, prohibits them from selling it to anyone but him. Right away
the Arabs stop selling wool. They take it to Tunis. Stupid measure. Here is its
odious side: the Arabs generally sell their wool crop in advance. They had sold
theirs to French merchants in Philippeville. Most [of these] had paid in advance, so that the measure hurt only them. One of them who wrote to General
Négrier heatedly to complain was removed from Philippeville, forcibly put on
a ship and expelled from the colony. Intolerable.

When the civil commissioner at the head of the principal tradesmen presented himself to salute General Bugeaud, the latter, in front of the entire

general staff, told him, "I don't know why you were sent here. The civilian population has nothing to recommend it. It must remain under military rule. I mean everything here to remain under military power."

Note that the population of Philippeville has already increased by 5,000 in two years, that its most recent customs period has already produced 50,000 francs (check this), that it is becoming a very important commercial center, not only with the French, but with the Arabs. At a business I visited this morning, I was told that last month it had done 80,000 francs in business with the Arabs alone. This was in linens, cotton, wool . . . Already more than four million have been invested here, they say. Despite oppression and tyranny, there is great prosperity and very great hope. Material causes more powerful than the governors make this country prosper. Every moment, however, we learn something new. Houses are built on a certain *preordained* alignment and demolished because plans were changed. The military authority prevents the civilians (who lack water) from using a well, more than sufficient for the garrison . . . The idea that they must take care that the civilians don't profit too much, this idea so antipathetic to all colonization, is to be heard more or less explicitly in all the officers' conversation.

The markets. Prohibition on buying barley in Africa. Refusal to buy hay from the colonists. It is harvested by the army, which costs more (check all this).

ESSAY ON ALGERIA
(OCTOBER 1841)

I do not think France can think seriously of leaving Algeria.[1] In the eyes of the world, such an abandonment would be the clear indication of our decline [*décadence*]. It would be far less disturbing to see our conquest taken from us forcefully by a rival nation. A people in all its vigor and in the course of expanding its power can still be unlucky in war and so lose provinces. This is what happened to the English, who, after having been made to sign a treaty in 1783 that took away their finest colonies, managed, less than thirty years later, to dominate the seas and occupy the most useful commercial positions on every continent. But if France shrank from an enterprise in which she faced nothing but the natural difficulties of the terrain and the opposition of little barbarous tribes, she would seem in the eyes of the world to be yielding to her own impotence and succumbing to her own lack of courage. Any people that easily gives up what it has taken and chooses to retire peacefully to its original borders proclaims that its age of greatness is over. It visibly enters the period of its decline [*déclin*].

If France ever abandons Algeria, it is clear that she could do it only at a moment when she is seen to be undertaking great things in Europe, and not at a time such as our own, when she appears to be falling to the second rank and seems resigned to let the control of European affairs pass into other hands.[2]

Independent of this reason, the foremost in my view, I see several others that should bind us to our conquest.

People who say that we are buying the advantages Algeria has to offer with too great a sacrifice are right.* But they are wrong when they reduce these advantages to almost nothing. The truth is that if we can manage to hold the coast of Africa firmly and peacefully, our influence in the world's general affairs would be strongly enhanced. Algeria offers two positions that are or can become preponderant in the Mediterranean:

The first is the port of Mers-el-Kebir. This port, opposite Carthage at a distance of fifty leagues, stands at the head of the strait formed by the coasts of Africa and Spain, which continues to narrow all the way to Gibraltar. Such a position clearly dominates the entrance and exit of the Mediterranean. We discussed the surrounding areas with the sailors and especially with Captain d'Assigny,[3] a worthy man who has occupied the station for almost two years. These inquiries prove that in its current condition, without further work, the port of Mers-el-Kebir† could accommodate a fleet of at least fifteen vessels, almost impossible to attack by a landing or from the sea.

The second site is Algiers itself. The construction already completed in Algiers forms quite a considerable commercial port. The projected construction, whose success is almost certain at this point, could make Algiers a great military port with a complete maritime establishment.[5]

These two points supporting each other, opposite the French coast, on the *political* sea of our times, would certainly add a great deal to France's strength.

All this is incontestable. What is no less so in my view is that if these positions do not remain in our hands, they will pass into those of another European people. If they are not for us, they will be against us, whether they fall directly under the power of our enemies or enter the circle of their influence. What we saw in Egypt has occurred in Algeria: it happens every time there is contact, even the contact of war, between two races of which one is enlightened and the other ignorant, one progressing and the other declining. The great things we have already done in Algeria, the examples set by our arts, our ideas, our power, have had a powerful effect on the spirit of the very populations that fight us with the greatest ardor and reject our yoke with the greatest energy. If we abandoned Algiers, the country would probably pass directly under the rule [*empire*] of a Christian nation. But even if Algiers were

---

* Above all, it would be too much to let ourselves say that our conquest in Africa should be our part of the division of the Orient.

† Put the material from the diary in a note here.[4]

to fall back into the hands of the Muslims, which is possible, we can be sure that the Muslim power that would take our place would be very different from the one we have destroyed. It would aim higher, it would have other means of action, it would enter into regular contact with the Christian nations and would be regularly controlled by one of them. In a word, it is clear to me that whatever happens, Africa has henceforth entered into the movement of the civilized world and will never leave it.

Algiers must therefore be preserved. But what must we do to succeed? The first consideration that strikes me is that time is pressing. We must make haste for two clear reasons:

1. The first is that if war catches us by surprise during the early work of settlement, it will take the country from us easily and make us lose the fruits of all the sacrifices we have already made.
2. The second is that as long as this work lasts, our action in the world will be suspended, and it is as though the arms of France were paralyzed—a state of affairs that we must quickly bring to an end, for our security as much as for our honor.

We must therefore hasten and do everything necessary to attain the proposed aim as soon as possible. For me the question will always be whether what we do is effective, and not how much it costs. In this affair all useful expenditure is an economy.

But what are the effective means of success?

We absolutely must not separate domination and colonization and vice versa. There are two ways to conquer a country: the first is to subordinate the inhabitants and govern them directly or indirectly. That is the English system in India. The second is to replace the former inhabitants with the conquering race. This is what Europeans have almost always done. The Romans, in general, did both. They seized the country's government, and in several parts of it they founded colonies that were nothing other than far-flung little Roman societies.

It has often been said that the French should limit themselves to dominating Algeria without trying to colonize it, and some people still think so. Studying the question has given me an entirely contrary opinion.

It must be recognized that if we did not want to colonize it, domination

would be easier; for above all what makes the Arabs take up arms is the idea
that we want to dispossess them and sooner or later settle on the land they
have inherited from their ancestors. If, from the beginning, we had said con-
vincingly that we aimed only at government and not at land, it might have
been easy to get them to recognize our authority. But that moment has passed.
Now, the prejudices that we have brought about are so powerful that we
would have trouble making them believe in a change of the system, however
real and sincere it were on our part. Still, I have come to believe that if France
renounced colonization even now, we would have less trouble making our
domination accepted. But such domination would always be *unproductive* and
precarious.

In time, I think, we shall manage to govern the Arabs in a more regular
manner than we do today, with fewer soldiers and less money,* and that we
shall be able to impose more considerable taxes on them than at present. But it
can be said nonetheless that for quite a long time — we cannot know how
long — domination of the Arabs will be onerous. This is because of the social
organization of this people, their tribal organization and nomadic life, something we can do nothing about for a very long time, perhaps ever.† Very small,
nomadic societies require great effort and expense to be held in an order that
will always be imperfect. And this great governmental effort produces very
little, because the same causes that make them so difficult to govern also make
them poor, needing little and producing little.

In addition, as I shall set out later in detail in reference to Abd-el-Kader
himself, such rule [*empire*] is always precarious. A government over tribes and
especially nomadic tribes is never sure to remain standing. This is true of
indigenous leaders, and that much more true of foreigners and infidels. At the
first crisis such a domination undoubtedly would be in danger of dissolving.

Domination without colonization would be, therefore, easier to establish, but it would not be worth the time, the money, or the men that it would
cost us.

Total domination and partial colonization. This is what has suggested to
some sensible observers [*bons esprits*] that France should immediately and

---

* Say how somewhere.
† Perhaps put here, either as a note or in the text, that I have a lot to say about the
nomads and the *tribal organization*.

completely abandon the idea of dominating the interior and limit ourselves to occupying the *political* points of the coast and to colonizing around them.

In the end, we might have to return to this point and take up the question from this end. But my firm opinion is that that would be a great misfortune and that we must make the most energetic efforts to unite the two systems before we resort to supporting just one of the two.

Colonization without domination will always be an incomplete and precarious work, in my view.

If we abandon the Arabs to themselves and allow them to build up a proper power at our backs, our establishment in Africa has no future. Either it will dissolve bit by bit through the permanent hostility of the natives or it will fall suddenly at the hands of those natives aided by a Christian power.

To flatter ourselves that we could ever establish a solid peace with an Arab prince of the interior would, in my view, be a manifest error. The permanent state of such a sovereign would be war with us, whatever his personal inclinations might otherwise be, and whether he were as pacific by nature or as fanatical in his religion as one could imagine. The following reasons should convince us of this:

Unlike the kings of Europe, an emir does not rule over individuals who can be kept down by the social force at the prince's disposal. Rather, he governs tribes that are completely organized little nations,* which cannot normally be guided except in the direction their passions lead. But the Arab tribes' passions of religion and depredation always lead them to wage war on us. Peace with Christians from time to time, and habitual war, such is the natural taste of the populations that surround us. They grant power only to those who permit them to act on this taste.†

Although the tribes that compose the Arab population of the Regency have a single language and fairly similar ideas and customs, their interests differ prodigiously, and they are deeply divided by old hatreds. This is easily seen in the ease we have often had in arming them in our favor, some of them against others. The great difficulty in governing these people is to create and exploit a common sentiment in them, or an idea common to all of them, that we could use to keep them all together and push them from the same side. The

---

* Here the information I have on the organization of tribes.
† [In the margin of this paragraph:] Maybe omit this.

only idea that could serve as a link among all the tribes that surround us is religion; the only common sentiment that could be used to make them submit to the same yoke is hatred of the stranger and infidel who has come to invade their country. The prince who governs these tribes will always be the more powerful and tranquil in his power as he further exalts and more violently enflames these common sentiments and these common ideas. That is, his government will be the more assured and stronger according to the degree of fanaticism and hate he excites against us. This is especially true of a new government, which is supported neither by old habits of obedience nor by the superstitious respect that eventually attaches to everything that lasts.

Indeed, history shows us that no one has ever been able to achieve great things among all the Arabs as a whole except by this process. This is what Muhammad did, and the first caliphs, as well as the different princes who rose in succession on the coast of Africa during the Middle Ages. In order to turn these people to advantage, one must either destroy the tribal divisions in their hearts or excite in all the tribes at once a common passion that will hold them together artificially and violently, despite the vices of their social organization that are constantly dividing them.

Abd-el-Kader — clearly a character of the rarest and most dangerous sort, a mix of sincere and feigned enthusiasm, a sort of Muslim Cromwell — has understood this marvelously.* In all his external actions, he exhibits the prince far less than the saint: he constantly hides behind the interest of the religion for which he says he acts. It is as interpreter of the Koran, with the Koran in hand, that he orders and condemns; he preaches reform as much as obedience; his humility increases with his power. The religious hatred that we inspire created him, it raised him, it sustains him. To quell it would be to renounce his power. Therefore, he won't quell it but will constantly revive it, and he will always fight us, secretly or explicitly, because peace would leave the tribes to their natural instincts and soon dissolve the support on which he relies.

Moreover, neither Abd-el-Kader nor any other prince who might rule the Algerian tribes could possibly be satisfied and live in peace under the conditions we have created for him. Concern for our security obliges us to retain all the coastal ports in our power and to keep the entire coast under our control. To leave any important spot in the hands of the Arabs is to give the first Chris-

---

* Say what I know about this.

tian power that comes into conflict with us a place of security and refuge. It would mean providing all our enemies with a natural means of communicating with the natives and battling us. A large Arab population stuck between us and the desert can live only with extreme difficulty. Although the Arabs have fewer needs than the civilized nations of Europe, it would be wrong to think that they have no more than savages. Before the conquest of Algeria, there was considerable commerce at various points along the coast. The Arabs sold wheat, livestock, hides, wool, wax; in exchange, they bought European goods, although in small quantity. The impossibility of conducting these necessary exchanges except at our pleasure would make the position of an Arab nation of the interior very difficult; that fact is now clear. The greatest harm we can cause the indigenous people results from the interdiction of commerce. Their government would suffer as much as the people would from this state of things. For the government gets most of the things necessary for the establishment of its power from Europe. Only with the arts and even the ideas of Europe can it hope to rule the Arabs and battle the French victoriously.

We cannot concede a position on the coast to Abd-el-Kader's government, and he cannot do without it. So it will be impossible to establish a solid and durable peace between us.

It is vital for the future of colonization, therefore, that we absolutely do not allow a great Arab power to establish itself at our backs in the interior.* In my view, I repeat, it is only at this price that we can hope to found a prosperous and durable establishment in Africa.

I am under no illusions about the nature and the value of the sort of domination that France can found over the Arabs. I know that even if we handle it in the best possible way, we shall never create anything but an often troubled and generally onerous government there. I am aware that such subjects will never add anything to our force. Therefore France must not seek domination as our goal; rather, domination is the necessary means we must use for achieving tranquil possession of the coast and the colonization of a part of the territory, the real and serious goal of our efforts. We shall never have either security or any future on the coast if we do not somehow manage to make our authority respected in the interior, or, at the very least, prevent the

---

* Even if we cannot make the tribes accept our domination, it would be a great deal to prevent them from recognizing a single leader.

different tribes there from uniting under a single leader. In a word, partial colonization and total domination: such is the result that I am convinced we must seek, until the impossibility of achieving it should be demonstrated.

DOMINATION AND THE MEANS TO ESTABLISH IT

There is no time to lose if we want to destroy Abd-el-Kader's power. I do not need to argue that the newer a power, the easier it is to destroy. That is obvious. My point is that Abd-el-Kader's actions should make us fear that, if we leave him time to establish himself, he may soon become so powerful and durable that it will be very difficult for us to overthrow him.

Abd-el-Kader's government is already more centralized, more agile, and stronger than the Turks' government ever was. It more easily brings together a greater number of men and more money. In part, this results precisely from what I have described as the necessary consequences of European contact with other peoples. From Arab ways, Abd-el-Kader preserved everything necessary to exalt his countrymen; from us, he took everything necessary to subjugate them.

The greatest difficulty encountered by a prince who wants to govern a confederation of Arab tribes is this: at any moment he may find himself facing an organized force that resists him, while he is never sure of having at hand the means of making his power respected. The first condition of power, and even of existence, for such a prince is thus to possess an army that belongs to him, in addition to those that the tribes may provide: an army that, if not capable of putting down a general revolt, can destroy at least the partial resistances that are encountered every day.

Abd-el-Kader has managed to create such an army. He has done more: having learned from the Turks' example that he needed not only a cavalry but an infantry to manage the Arabs' disobedience,* he undertook to form such regiments. Here the difficulty was great, as the Arabs have the same scorn for infantry that Christians had in the Middle Ages. Abd-el-Kader, however, managed to gather a certain number of men, whom he formed into battalions, and,

---

* The Arab populations, being nomadic and living near the mountains, can always withdraw into places into which the cavalry could never follow them and subjugate them. The cavalry is necessary to surprise them, and foot soldiers to achieve victory and to seize men and herds.

using what he had learned from us just as he had used what he had learned from the Turks, he gave these battalions a European organization, an organization powerless against our own, but that made him master of his countrymen.[6] It was very difficult for him to achieve this, but once he did, the rest became easy.

With his army, he has levied regular taxes, which in turn have enabled him to maintain his army and keep it standing. With this permanent force, he has built up stockpiles, marshaled resources, and developed long-term plans that he can carry out smoothly. Thanks to this army, he is always ready to anticipate or destroy any resistance, while malcontents have to gather together and come to an understanding in advance in order to attack him successfully. In this way, he rules the majority through enthusiasm and the minority through fear. Such is the secret of his power; it is not difficult to understand, for what Abd-el-Kader is attempting is not new in the world. These half-savage African countries are now undergoing a social development very much like that which took place in Europe at the end of the Middle Ages. Abd-el-Kader, who has probably never heard of what happened in fifteenth-century France, is acting toward the tribes precisely as our kings, and in particular Charles VII, acted toward feudalism. He is creating a standing army. And with the aid of this independent force he is destroying bit by bit the small powers that, united, would control him easily. The French kings took advantage of each small rebellion to strip the great vassals of power and to bring new territories under their direct administration. Abd-el-Kader is seizing similar opportunities to do away with the most considerable men in each tribe who resist him. It is the same process applied in a slightly different manner. Without knowing the history of these princes, but obeying a similar instinct, he is constantly dispersing or destroying ancient and powerful families, and raising up new ones who owe him their authority and whose authority is not old enough and well-established enough to threaten his own. He is making war not only on the French but also on the hereditary aristocracy of his country.[7]

All this is quite new among the Arabs. The ambition shown by Abd-el-Kader has been shown with more or less success by many others. But he is the first who took from his contact with Europe the ideas that would make his own enterprise similarly durable. We must therefore not trust in the past and believe that this power, after having shone for a moment, will fade like so many others. On the contrary, it is much to be feared that Abd-el-Kader is founding among the Arabs who surround us a power that is more centralized,

more agile, stronger, better tested, and more regular than all those that have
succeeded one another in this part of the world for centuries. We must therefore strive not to allow him to achieve this formidable accomplishment.

We must not yet despair of destroying Abd-el-Kader. There is not a soldier or
even a simple traveler who, having been in Algeria, believes that Abd-el-Kader
can be destroyed all at once by force of arms. Abd-el-Kader knows that he does
not have the slightest chance of beating us in a pitched battle. He will never
wage such a battle of his own will, therefore, and there is no way to force him
to it. What compels a European prince to wage battle, even at a disadvantage,
is the need to secure a population that would fall to the enemy if he were to
retreat; it is the need to save warehouses, artillery, towns, the capital. In a
word, there are many greater misfortunes for civilized European powers than
to lose a battle. This is not the case in Algeria. The populations flee easily
before the enemy; the armies carry everything with them; there are no important towns or positions to be seized and occupied; there is nothing, therefore,
that obliges the Arabs to fight if they do not want to, and it would be insane of
them to want to fight. With them, then, war cannot be won at one great blow.

If Abd-el-Kader is destroyed, it will only be with the help of some of the
tribes that are now subjected to him; his alliance must be dissolved rather than
shattered.

Although Abd-el-Kader has destroyed many powerful men among his
countrymen, a great number remain who are irritated and outraged by his
power and whose position might cause them to raise the standard of revolt
against him if the populations would follow them. Although he has created a
force independent of the tribes, he has not destroyed the individual and collective force of these tribes. Several of them are actual nations, who in detaching
themselves from him would cause his downfall immediately.* The longer
Abd-el-Kader's power lasts, the more improbable this event will become. It is
not yet so today.

There are two ways to bring about the schism among the Arabs that
would be to our profit: We can win over some of the principals by promises or
largesse. We can dishearten and exhaust the tribes through war. I do not
hesitate to say that these two means can and should be used simultaneously
and that the time to renounce them has not yet come.

Experience has already shown a thousand times that, whatever the fanati-

---

* Details on the tribes of the Oran province.

cism and the national spirit among the Arabs, personal ambition and greed have always animated them even more powerfully and caused them accidentally to make those resolutions that are most opposed to their usual tendencies. The same phenomenon has always occurred among half-civilized men. The heart of the savage is like a perpetually agitated sea, where the wind does not always blow from the same direction.

The facts, not only of our time but also of earlier periods, have proven that the same Arabs who displayed the most furious hatred for Christians could suddenly take up arms for them and turn against their compatriots. We must therefore not despair of winning them over by either flattering their ambition or giving them money.

It is still worth attempting this, as the Arabs form quite an aristocratic society; the influence that birth, wealth, and holiness have among them is very great. Men there hold tightly together and in bringing one of them over to us, we can almost always get several others to follow.[8]

As to the rules of this necessary diplomacy, they clearly cannot be stated in advance. Everything depends on the prompt and subtle appreciation of the facts, in the honesty and the confidence of the hand that acts. Considerable secret funds are clearly necessary in Africa, but success depends entirely on the choice of the man who is to use them. Such funds have often been wasted by scoundrels. In any case, in the current state of things, diplomacy would be useless without war.

I am convinced that before Abd-el-Kader's power developed, it was possible, without exactly waging war but only stirring up the Arabs' passions and setting them against one another, to keep them dependent on us and prevent any of them from becoming the master. That moment passed long ago. Now that Abd-el-Kader stands at the head of a united army that can fall on those who would betray him, at any moment and upon the least suspicion, we cannot hope for defection except under two conditions. The first is to occupy military positions that allow us effectively to defend those who have declared themselves for us against unforeseen attacks by Abd-el-Kader. The second is to give the leaders who want to unite with us the support of tribes whose patience is wearing thin in the kind of life to which they have been condemned by Abd-el-Kader's domination. Only war can *fulfill* these two conditions.

What type of war we can and must wage on the Arabs. As to the manner of waging this war, I have seen two contrary opinions expressed, both of which I reject equally.

1)

According to the first, to subjugate the Arabs, we should fight them with the utmost violence and in the Turkish manner, that is to say, by killing everything we meet. I have heard this view supported by officers who took it to the point of bitterly regretting that we have started to take prisoners in some places, and many assured me that they encouraged their soldiers to spare no one. For my part, I returned from Africa with the distressing notion that we are now fighting far more barbarously than the Arabs themselves. For the present, it is on their side that one meets with civilization. This manner of conducting war seems to me as unintelligent as it is cruel. It could occur only to the coarse and brutal mind of a soldier. It was certainly not worth taking the Turks' place in order to recreate that aspect of their rule that deserved the world's abhorrence. It is far more destructive than useful, even from the point of view of interest. As another officer told me, if we aspire to equal the Turks we shall be inferior to them in that very fact: even if we act like barbarians, the Turks will always have the advantage over us of being Muslim barbarians. Thus we must appeal to a principle superior to theirs.

2)

On the other hand, I have often heard men in France whom I respect, but with whom I do not agree, find it wrong that we burn harvests, that we empty silos, and finally that we seize unarmed men, women, and children.

These, in my view, are unfortunate necessities, but ones to which any people that wants to wage war on the Arabs is obliged to submit. And, if I must speak my mind, these acts do not revolt me more than, or even as much as, many others that the law of war clearly authorizes and that have occurred in all the wars of Europe. How is it more odious to burn harvests and take women and children prisoner than to bombard the inoffensive population of a besieged village or to seize the merchant vessels belonging to the subjects of an enemy power? The one is, in my view, much more harsh and less justifiable than the other.[9]

If we do not burn harvests in Europe, it is because in general we wage war on governments and not on peoples;* if we take only soldiers as prisoners, it is because armies hold firm and the civilian populations do not escape upon conquest. In a word, it is because we can always find the means of seizing political power without attacking the governed or even making them supply the resources necessary for war.

We shall never destroy Abd-el-Kader's power unless we make the position

---

* [Variant: "populations."]

of the tribes who support him so intolerable that they abandon him. This is an obvious truth. We must conform to it or give up the game. For myself, I think that all means of desolating these tribes must be employed. I make an exception only of those condemned by humanity and by the law of nations.

The most effective means we can use to subjugate the tribes is the interdiction of commerce. I said earlier that the Arabs have greater need to buy and sell than we had supposed. They suffer a great deal when we trap them between our bayonets and the desert. I had long conversations in the province of Algiers with some intelligent men who recently found themselves among neighboring tribes, notably the Hadjoutes, on the occasion of the treaty relative to the exchange of prisoners. They all assured me that these Arabs, though they remain loyal to Abd-el-Kader, bitterly complained of their suffering under the cessation of commerce. They displayed their herds, saying: "What is the point of raising all these animals if there is no town in which we can sell them to buy the things we need that we cannot make?"[10]

This state of things is perhaps felt less in the province of Oran than in that of Algiers because of the proximity of Morocco; still, I do not doubt that the misery is just as great there.

The means second in importance, after the interdiction of commerce, is to ravage the country. I believe that the right of war authorizes us to ravage the country and that we must do it, either by destroying harvests during the harvest season, or year-round by making those rapid incursions called razzias, whose purpose is to seize men or herds.

There is great protest in France against those great military promenades that the African army dignifies with the name of campaigns. And rightly so, in the sense that very often these murderous voyages are undertaken only to satisfy the ambition of the leaders. But they seem to me to be indispensable sometimes, and in these cases it would be quite wrong to prohibit them.

In the long run, what an Arab tribe find unbearable are not the occasional marches of a large army across their territory, but the proximity of a mobile force that may descend on them unpredictably and at any moment. Likewise, we must recognize that what will protect our allies effectively is not a large army that occasionally joins them to fight the common enemy, but the possibility of calling us immediately to their rescue if Abd-el-Kader approaches.

One could say, then, as a general thesis, that it would be worth more to have several small mobile corps constantly moving around fixed points than to have large armies periodically crossing an immense space. Wherever you can place a corps in such a way that it can pick up and cross the country when necessary, you should do it. That, in my view, is the rule. But considerable expeditions are necessary now and then to set up or provision these small corps.

I would say as well that occasionally large expeditions seem necessary to me:

performance of strength

1. To keep showing the Arabs and our soldiers that there are no obstacles in the country that can stop us.

prevention of towns

2. To destroy everything that resembles a permanent aggregation of population or, in other words, a town. I think it is of the greatest importance not to let any town remain or rise in Abd-el-Kader's domain.

I have often heard two objections made in this regard, which do not hold up in the presence of the facts:

It is said: But why prevent the Arabs from founding towns? Once they are fixed in the towns, they will no longer escape you. And also: let towns be established, and these towns will become so many important military points that you can then occupy. I have asserted that these claims do not hold up in the presence of the facts.

If Abd-el-Kader tried to destroy the tribes' nomadic life and fix them in towns and villages, he should not be interrupted in such an effort. But he has neither the possibility nor the desire to undertake any such labor. Far from it: since he became a political man, Abd-el-Kader has not slept in a house. He has them built, but he never lives in them. His tent is set up outside, and he affects to sleep there every night. Indeed, he knows well that the nomadic life of his tribes is his surest defense against us. His subjects will become ours the day they attach themselves to the soil. Abd-el-Kader, moreover, while borrowing some of our ideas and many of our customs, presents himself to his compatriots as the representative and the restorer of their old mores and their ancient glory, and he is careful not to unsettle the prejudices, until now intractable, that attach the Arabs to their tents and keep them away from towns. All semi-barbarous peoples have great disdain for town-dwellers. This disdain is greater still among nomadic barbarians. The Arabs push these sentiments to the extreme. Their only contact with town-dwellers is for the sake of commerce; they hardly ever ally with them, they never take them into consideration at all. They even refuse to acknowledge that they have a common origin and do not give them the generic name Arabs; they disdainfully call them *agads,*[11] or townspeople. This explains why, when we seize a town, we soon discover that we hold nothing but stones. The population of the towns is not tied to that of the countryside; it exercises no influence over the other; it is just as incapable of serving us as of causing us damage.

The Arabs, however, are in greater need of the towns than they themselves imagine. No society, even if only half-civilized, can subsist without towns. Nomadic peoples do not escape from this necessity more than any others; indeed, they are even more subject to it than others, because the wandering life they lead prevents them from cultivating even coarsely the sciences and arts that are indispensable even to the least advanced civilization. Consequently, all the nomads of the world, unless they are purely savages,* have always had, either in their own country or near it, towns where they went from time to time to sell and buy, towns with workshops, temples, books, schools, and idlers, and that formed sources of well-being and enlightenment from which, often unawares, they went to drink. The Arabs of the Regency thus could not do without towns; despite the passionate taste they show for the wandering life, they need some fixed settlements. It is of the greatest importance not to let a single one emerge among them, and all the expeditions whose aim is to occupy or to destroy the old towns and the nascent ones seem to me useful.

Ways in which to wage war more economically and with fewer casualties. I think it is desirable for us to continue pressing on vigorously with the war. I fear that this will last some time. Finally, even if it is carried on in this manner, I believe the country will continue to be in an agitated and unstable state afterwards that will oblige us to leave a certain number of troops there, who will lead an active and exhausting life. We must try to find a way to make our soldiers' stay in Africa less deadly and less costly. I have joined together the idea of health and that of economy, because as will be seen, almost everything that serves to diminish mortality serves at the same time to diminish expense.

As to the means of diminishing mortality in the army, several are instantly clear.

---

* Besides, from the moment when savages enter into contact with towns, they can no longer do without them. The most barbarous Indian tribes that neighbor the United States come at least once a year to camp near a fixed settlement where the Europeans trade with them. The most powerful means that the United States has for making their citizens respected even in the deepest wilderness is to prevent the tribe among whom a theft or murder was committed from coming to this market.

Experience proves that what is unhealthy in Africa is less the climate than the conditions in which we live there. This was clear in Philippeville. During the year 1840, the garrison, which had . . . men, lost . . . ; while of . . . inhabitants, only 152 died in the same period.[12] These numbers are all the more grievous because the population of Philippeville includes old men, women, and children, while the army is composed of men in their prime. The sad outcome needs only one explanation: the inhabitants slept in houses and the soldiers in wooden shacks, where they were suffocated by the heat, drenched by the rain, and devoured by vermin.

It is clear that everywhere that we have to occupy with a fixed position, we must quickly build barracks.* Except in the neighborhood of Algiers, there are almost none. Philippeville and Constantine are almost completely devoid of them. This expenditure is urgent, not only because it has to do with men's lives, but also because such an expenditure avoids other much more considerable ones. A soldier in the hospital costs 20 sous per day, and during his stay we often have to bring another from France at great expense. The enormous sums that would be spared in sparing the lives of men can hardly be conceived.

We have recently built vast hospitals at almost every important point along the coast. I commend the government for this; but I cannot keep myself from noting that this expense is not the only important one; I am not sure we should even consider it the most important. A good hospital cures the soldier, but would it not be even more economical and more humane to keep him from falling ill?

There is one sanitary measure that seemed to be demanded by very reasonable men. Among these, I would cite General Lamoricière, who will certainly not be accused of excessive philanthropy.[13] The soldiers are not well nourished enough for the job they are made to do. The general made the same point I have just made. He told me: "Increase nutrition by 2 sous and you will still save; for the soldier will be sick less often, and each sick soldier costs you 20. I know well that the increase of 2 sous applies to all the soldiers, while the figure 20 now applies to just a portion of them. Still, I am convinced that this would represent a considerable gain." When these things are said by a man like the general, who wants to wage war cheaply because he wants to fight for a

---

* [In the margin:] Information on the medical corps. See the letter from the chief doctor of the army.

long time, and who holds the lives of his fellow men in such small regard, my view is that he should be believed.

But the question that I am about to address has much greater importance.* In it I see the entire future of our conquest.

To maintain 70,000 men in Africa, a portion of whom die in the hospitals every year and who cost France 100 million [francs]:† this is an intolerable state of things that, if it continues, will nullify our actions in the world and will soon force us to abandon Africa. We must therefore find a way to make the same effort with fewer men, fewer illnesses, and less money. The best means to achieve this is the creation of a special African army.‡

---

* [Variant: "But what follows."]

† [Variant written in the margin: "and who use more kermes powder (a dye, producing the color scarlet, and also an emetic — J.P.) than gunpowder."]

‡ The most obvious idea is to create a corps of natives in France's service. This idea is excellent if modified as follows:

It will always be impossible to raise an indigenous infantry, unless it is among the coulouglis, who still remain in the regency in very small numbers (this is how we formed a battalion in the province of Constantine, which does not trail a single of the battalions of our army in discipline and courage. The soldiers and a part of the subofficers of this battalion are sons of Turks or coulouglis. The officers are French). The Arabs, as I have said, have a practically invincible repugnance for service in the infantry. Those we managed to engage would always be scoundrels who, at the first opportunity, would desert with arms and baggage and retreat into the interior where we could not go to bring them back. The Arabs can and should one day provide us with excellent cavalry, but on condition, I think, that we leave them their national organization. We have tried to regiment the natives and make them into a European cavalry. If I am not mistaken, experience has shown our generals that this method was defective. We were well able to collect men for this type of service, and several of them belonged to distinguished families, but even they did not take long to leave us; the minute, insipid details of our discipline soon gave them an insurmountable distaste for the service. We shall thus never form a regular cavalry among the Arabs without great trouble and expense; but if we want to hire tribes who recognize our authority for an expedition that allows them to wage war in their manner with their leaders, we shall have an excellent light and irregular cavalry that would be at least as useful to us as the Cossacks are to the Russians. This is how the Douairs and the Smelas have fought with us for a long time.[14] But such auxiliaries are not always ready to march and they can vanish at the moment we have the greatest need of their help.

So we do need a French army in Africa; it should be numerous and include both cavalry and infantry. But I believe that there are ways to greatly shrink this army

I shall explain. There is not a single officer in Africa, I think, who denies that to wage war as it is done in this country, a regiment like that of the Zouaves,[15] for example, would be worth two regiments from France, not so much to fight in battle but to endure the fatigues and privations that make up the everyday life of a soldier. I think it can be said that 4,000 infantrymen supported by a cavalry proportionate to their number could easily do everything that is now done by an army of 8,000 foot soldiers, which is to say cross the country in every direction without having anything serious to fear. I, personally, do not doubt that 30,000 men of this kind could do more than the 60,000 now in Algeria.

As you can easily imagine, no country in the world resembles Europe less than Algeria. Everything is different in war and in peace; ways of living, of fighting, of being healthy are unique to the place. Nothing in a European education prepares one for this type of war nor is developed with a view to it. Thus the first thing the soldier must do on disembarking is change his clothes and his arms and learn new rules. Every war demands an apprenticeship, but this one does so more than all the others. They must learn to fight not merely to win, but to survive. It has been remarked a hundred times that where the French novice died of cold or hunger, the African soldier still found things to eat and ways to keep warm. Add to this a climate completely different from ours and that from the beginning shocks the body and changes all its habits. A regiment that is in Africa only to leave it never gets completely used to that war and that country. The soldiers and the officers who know that they will soon return to France apply their minds only halfway to understanding the job they must do. They never throw their hearts into their lives there, and they always remain inept at it; finally, almost all of them wish to leave, which is a bad disposition if we want them to serve well.*

---

without diminishing its force and to make it less costly while getting more from it than we do today.

* Nothing struck me more in Algeria than to see the difference in bearing and language between the officers living in Algeria permanently and those belonging to regiments that were merely passing through. It is said that both are equally brave on the battlefield. I would like to believe it. But, for all the rest, they differ so much that one would think they formed two distinct races. The first are ardent, ambitious, full of energy; they love the country and are passionate about its conquest. The others are sad, mournful, sickly, and disheartened; they think and speak only of France. In truth, the first wage war, the second endure it.

There must be regiments, therefore, that have Africa as their unique and special destiny, that are composed of soldiers selected for this task and led by officers who chose it. France will provide both in great numbers. In other words, it is not only that we need the French army force we send to Africa to stay there a long time; Africa must also have its own army. In any case, in this matter we need only expand what already exists. I am convinced that if we followed this route, we would manage to use half the money and three times fewer men to do something more considerable than we are doing now.

I have said that we would lose far fewer men this way. It has been re-marked that the troops settled in Africa are almost never ill compared to the others. This is not only because having been there longer they are more used to the life they must lead there, but also, and I would say especially, because they lead their life there with a different spirit. Having adopted it, no longer thinking of leaving, they finally live it resolutely; for them mental agitation, boredom, and nostalgia do not arise to complicate or aggravate the effects of the climate. The soul supports the body. Whereas the soldier who arrives from France expecting to return soon makes no attempt to reconcile himself to his condition. The foreign and barbaric aspect of this war strikes him as painfully on the last day as on the first.

However partisan I may be about the creation of special African regi-ments, I am still far from believing that only this kind of troops should be stationed in Africa.

That would give rise to several grave objections.

The result would be that only a few regiments would fight and learn to fight, while all the others would be kept far from the battlefield. The small army that served in Africa would thus become very different and much supe-rior to the French army in general; we can even say that it would enervate it. For little by little it would attract everyone in the army with an active spirit and warlike temperament. We would see certain officers constantly advancing in Algeria, while the mass that remained in France rose quite slowly. This would be intolerable.*

There is another danger people never think of, but that I admit worries me a great deal: we cannot deny to ourselves that the officer, having once

---

* Why not, if we think about it? Each would advance according to his accomplish-ments. Besides, wouldn't it be better to have an excellent core group than a vast mediocre army?

adopted Africa as his theater, will soon contract habits, ways of thinking and acting, that are very dangerous everywhere, but especially in a free country. He will pick up the practices and the tastes of a hard, violent, arbitrary, and coarse government. That is an education I don't care to generalize and spread. From the military point of view, I admire these men; but I confess that I fear them and I wonder what we would do with a large number of such men, if they returned home. It is with a secret fear that I notice several such men now emerging. Africa is the only place one hears the clash of arms today. All eyes are drawn to it. Reputations are made there, often very cheaply, that don't offend anyone. Men emerge who take on distorted proportions in the public imagination, because they alone are acting in the midst of universal sloth; they alone acquire the reputation of warriors among a people who love war and are not fighting. I fear that one day they will appear on the stage of domestic affairs with the force of opinion they acquired abroad, often undeservedly. God save France from ever being led by officers from the African army![16]

I think it necessary, therefore, to send a certain number of regiments to Africa that are to return to France after a few years. Still, I think the way this is done today is contrary to our financial interests as much as to humanitarian concerns.

War in Africa is nothing like large European wars, where a country attacked by immense armies is obliged to send all its available soldiers to the battlefield, at the risk of losing a great number in hospitals. There, if attention were too closely paid to men's wishes, countries would never succeed in raising large enough armies. But it is not like this in Africa.

What is needed in Africa is a small number of select men, and the French army will always supply the necessary number. These days we send entire regiments to Africa. Weak soldiers as well as strong soldiers, new recruits as well as men of many years' service. What is the invariable result? In the first year all those who aren't used to service, all those who were feeble or sickly, fall ill and die. Only energetic and vigorous men remain under arms. Isn't it expensive and inhumane to let death make the selection, rather than handling it ourselves?

Good sense and philanthropy properly understood clearly indicate that before sending a regiment to Africa we must subject it to rigorous inspection. All the weak or feeble soldiers must be left at the depot.

We must also remove all soldiers with fewer than two years of service. Not only do the regiments that go to Africa take recruits, but while they are in Africa, I think, they take on more through the annual recruitment. To do so is, I repeat, willingly and unnecessarily to send many of our countrymen to their death; it condemns us to supporting at great expense in Africa more men than we need. It is almost always young soldiers who succumb, not only because they often are not completely developed and haven't had a chance to get used to the physical trials of service, but especially because their spirit hasn't had time to strengthen. Coming straight from their villages, their undisciplined imaginations are struck by the foreign and terrible nature of this war, and they become prey to nostalgia and to illnesses that the climate threatens to inflict. They are the ones, in general, who succumb to delirium during the long summer marches and kill themselves for fear of not keeping up with the columns.*

I know that in proscribing all the men I've just described from the regiments we send to Algeria, we might be able to create only one war battalion. But what is wrong with that? If all the French regiments fought in Africa successively, so that the entire army was disciplined and inured to war, that is what would be useful. This goal is attained as easily when each regiment is represented by a set of men who form the elite, as when the entire regiment goes, only to be miserably decimated.

A further necessary precaution before sending a regiment to Africa, it seems to me, would be to garrison it for a year or two in the South of France. The transition would be less difficult. I repeat that it would be impossible to take such precautions for a large European war, but for war in Africa, it would be inexcusable for the administration not to take them.

Which officers should be entrusted with command? What I have said of the soldiers, I would say of the officers as well, especially of those who lead the large maneuvers. This war, as everyone knows, is unlike any other; recollections of European tactics are good for nothing and are often harmful. Officers

---

* Everyone knows that in Africa the artillery and engineering soldiers from France are little more affected by fatigue and the climate than the Zouaves are. Why is this? These men certainly have the same lungs and stomachs as the infantry soldiers. The only possible reason is that in general they are physically stronger, that they normally have been in the service longer, and especially that their minds are sharper and more energetic. All the regiments sent to Africa, should, as much as possible, be made up of men like these.

who are used to it and who were raised on it should thus be chosen to lead it. But there is another reason that seems to me even more pressing.

Unfortunately, there is little hope at the moment of finding a general in the French army who has not shown himself, in his actions in Africa, to be more concerned with his personal glory than with the desire to do the things most useful for the country. Officers in Africa are certainly no more exempt than others from coarse personal ambition, and we must expect that all of them will choose to achieve things through war that could have been done without it or to throw themselves uselessly into murderous enterprises in order to have the chance to shine. Still, it can be said that the ambition of officers who are stationed permanently in Africa is more enlightened and more contained than that of the generals who arrive from France for only a certain period. First, they are better acquainted with the difficulties, which makes them slower to act; second, since they are permanently stationed in Algeria, they are less likely to get caught up in brilliant expeditions that are troublesome in the long term. In a word, since their fortune is joined to that of the conquest, they act better without being any more honorable.*

To summarize, I shall say that in my view we must increase by a considerable proportion the number of regiments in Algeria that are destined to live there permanently. As for troops coming from France, they must not be composed of regiments transported to the African coast as a whole, but of detachments carefully chosen from among the strongest, oldest, and most resolute soldiers. I would dare to claim that if we follow this plan, we shall soon achieve things far superior to those we have achieved so far, and with a smaller army and smaller budget.

---

* Of these officers, the most eminent and, all things considered, our best choice, is General Lamoricière. He is a man of great faults and even greater vices, the worst of which I would say are an ambition without limits or brakes, an extreme disdain for human life, and an implacable and exclusive personality. But he knows the country marvelously well, [and] he possesses a will of iron and an indestructible activity. His intellect, although bizarre and incomplete, is in some senses vast. He loves Africa; he considers it his domain, and he identifies with it. He is the only officer I have met who was really favorable to colonization and to the colonists, and who understands that a civil society cannot be governed by the sword alone. This is not to say that there is an atom of liberalism in his person, but in this sense his intellect leads him in a direction that his tastes never would. I believe we should try placing Lamoricière in command. But he is a man to keep a close eye on at present and especially in the *future.*[17]

COLONIZATION

I have just shown the ways I believe we could fight and achieve domination. But domination, I have also said, is only a means to achieve colonization. I now take up the subject of colonization.[18]

Should we begin colonizing before domination is established and the war ends? We must address a preliminary question: Should we begin colonizing before domination is established and the war ends? I do not hesitate an instant to answer: yes.[19] There is no way to know when the war will end. If we wait for it to end before we colonize, we put off the main task indefinitely. I have already said, and I repeat, that until we have a European population in Algeria, we shall never establish ourselves there but shall remain camped on the African coast. Colonization and war, therefore, must proceed together.

A state of war, moreover, doesn't increase the difficulties of the enterprise as much as one might think. Domination over semi-barbarous nomadic tribes, such as those around us, can never be so complete that a civilized, sedentary population could settle nearby without any fear or precaution. Armed marauding will long outlast war itself. Even if the war were over, it would be necessary before colonizing to adopt certain means of security and self-protection. The type of war we have to fear requires us only to take precautions that aren't much greater than what would be dictated by prudence if this war were to end.

Finally, even if a European population is more difficult to settle in Africa during a war, this population, once settled, will make the war easier, less costly, and more decisive, by providing a solid base for the operations of our armies.*

Which part of the Regency should we colonize first? The French public has a childish taste for those enterprises whose general effect forms a complete and regular whole that satisfies the eye. In politics as in architecture, it would willingly install fake windows rather than sacrifice the regularity of the view.

It must be admitted that the administration serves the public taste. Whether undertaking canals or railroads . . . the administration presents the public from the first with plans that will satisfy at once all the present and future needs of every part of the territory. To begin with the easiest and most pressing thing would seem an indignity to both. The same spirit is displayed in the conduct of affairs in Africa. Algeria is composed of three large provinces: thus, each must have its own colonization effort, for how could the admin-

---

* [In the margin:] "Elaborate on this."

istration present the country with an incomplete* project. It would be better to do nothing. Consequently, last year, M. Laurence[20] came before the Chambers to say that colonization must be undertaken in three places at once: in the western province at Mostaganem, in the central province in the area around Algiers, and around Bône in the east.

After having seen these places, I can assert that in my view, nothing would be more absurd than to try at present to colonize Mostaganem.[21] Several reasons can be given to prove this point; they are, I think, unanswerable.

Nothing irritates and alarms the natives more than the introduction of European farmers; good sense indicates that we must not start in the province in which the most violent and hostile sentiments against us already exist, and that we have the greatest trouble subjugating. It is there that it is of the utmost importance not to confuse the question of war with the question of colonization. It is there, moreover, that colonization would be most difficult, not only because of the power and the hostility of the tribes that surround our establishment, but also because of the difficulties natural to the country. The country around Mostaganem is, in truth, very fertile. But it is a five days' walk from our principal settlement at Oran, and you can cross the intervening space only alongside an army. From the seacoast, the approach to Mostaganem is so dangerous that even during the summer months, men and merchandise can only rarely be unloaded safely. It is true that there is a fairly good port, Arzeu, a short distance from Mostaganem. But Arzeu has no water, and the hostility of the neighboring tribes is so great that we can say quite literally that the French occupy only the ground they stand on. In any case, despite the proximity, it is often impossible to reach Mostaganem from Arzeu for weeks on end. So even granting that the colony of Mostaganem could defend itself from Arab attacks, it would have no communication with the civilized world for part of the year. All this is absurd. The truth is that we really should not colonize the western province for the present, except perhaps around Oran; the land is undoubtedly mediocre, but there at least the rural population is directly attached to a town and a port. In all the rest of the province, we can only hope to fight and conquer. That is already difficult enough. Later, we can see whether colonization might follow.

It remains to consider the two other provinces.

It is a large and difficult question whether we should, at present, colonize

---

* [Variant: *boiteux* (crippled).]

in the eastern province, or that of Bône. My inclination is not to do so: around Bône and Philippeville, it is true, there is admirably fertile land ranged around considerable towns and along a coast whose approach, although not easy, is more or less practicable year-round. In addition, there is peace in this province and in particular along the coast, and the nature of the people in this part of the country is gentler and less uncivilized than everywhere else. These are great advantages. We must make use of them sooner or later. Has the time arrived to do so? I doubt it.

I have already said that what most worried and irritated the natives, reasonably, was to see us take and cultivate their lands. This irritates not only those we dispossess but the entire country. For three centuries the Arabs have been accustomed to being governed by foreigners. As long as we take over only the government, they are well enough disposed to let us do so. But the moment the laborer appears behind the soldier, they will conclude that we mean not only to conquer but to dispossess them. The quarrel is no longer between governments, but between races. It is probable, then, that the province of Bône, now so tranquil, will become agitated the day a European plow touches the soil. This is all the more likely since, in order for us to colonize to any extent, we must necessarily use not only violent measures but visibly iniquitous ones. We would have to dispossess several tribes and transport them elsewhere, where they very likely would be less well off. On this subject, the documents provided to the Chambers present facts that demonstrate either great ignorance or an impudent plan to fool us. It is said there that since the land belongs almost entirely to the prince, he can always remove a tribe from their territory without violating their rights. This is not at all the case. It is true that, according to Muslim law and the ancient custom of the country,* the land throughout the country belongs to the prince.[22] But if the prince invokes this abstract right to take a tribe's territory when that tribe has given him no cause to do so through rebellion, he commits a violent and unjust act at which the public conscience revolts. It is as if, in the Middle Ages, the king had deprived a lord of his fief although the latter had done nothing to incur the forfeiture. Now, not only have the tribes we would have to dispossess not been at war with us, but they have always proven to be our best *friends*. It would be all the more impolitic given that this would not be an isolated event, but would be added to many others as a final demonstration to the Arabs that they

---

* Something similar can be found throughout the Orient. I have since verified this.

have less to fear in being against us than in being for us. In Africa we have done in miniature what we've done throughout the world on a large or small scale for the past ten years: we have behaved in such a way that our friendship is always fatal. Almost all the tribes and almost all the men who have declared themselves on our side have been either abandoned or harmed by us. The treaty of Tafna transferred the admirable territory occupied by the Douairs and the Smelas to Abd-el-Kader.[23] The same treaty returned to him the unfortunate little Coulougli tribe of Ben Zetoun, the only one in the Mitidja that ardently embraced our cause. He slaughtered the entire tribe before our eyes.[24] A similar example in the province of Bône would not fail to destroy our reputation and undermine our power. Isn't it finally time to show, even if only in a tiny corner of the desert, that people can be France's allies without losing their fortunes or their lives?

Thus we must conclude that however we attempted it, an effort to colonize in the province of Bône would only cause a war. Such an event would be a great misfortune at any time, but especially now.

It is self-evident that as long as the province of Oran is not pacified and Abd-el-Kader destroyed, it will always be extremely dangerous to provoke the province of Bône against us.

But regardless of this reason, there is another that should make us avoid any revolt and even any agitation in the province of Bône. This province is the first place in Africa where Arab tribes have truly recognized our domination and have submitted to paying us taxes and obeying us almost as they did in the Turks' time. It has been so for only three years. It is a decisive experience for the future of our conquest. Prudence requires, it seems to me, that we do nothing to trouble these habits of obedience before they are consolidated. Let us allow our power to settle and to base itself on mores — the only solid basis for government in Africa as well as in Europe — before using it to attempt things that are too difficult and too dangerous.

These reflections lead me to believe that we should put off colonizing the areas around Bône, and that France should direct all its resources and efforts into the province of Algiers and the area around the capital.

Algiers is the center of our power in Africa. It is there that we have the greatest need to rely on a large agricultural population. It is Algiers that offers the greatest outlets for agricultural products, and that as a result will most quickly attract, and best retain, colonists. Besides, it is toward Algiers that all eyes are turned. It is there that the plow was first put to the soil and the work of colonization begun; it is there that we must prove we can colonize Africa. In Algiers, all the damage that colonization can do to us in the minds of the natives is done. Efforts at colonization have gone on there for ten years. To remain where we are is not to calm the irritation that we have produced, it is only to add to it the disdain that our impotence must provoke. In Algiers, as elsewhere, we cannot settle without taking territory from the tribes, but in Algiers, at least, we shall only be dispossessing tribes that have always been at war with us. The measure is violent, but in the mores of the country, it is not unjust. I would add a final consideration: what most threatens the future of our settlements in Africa are the vices and faults of those charged with administering them — soldiers as much as civilians. These men are kept infinitely more reined in in Algiers and its surroundings than elsewhere. The proximity of France and the presence of a large European population, whose complaints reach the metropolitan newspapers in a matter of days, all these things tend to keep a certain brake on authority and make it more moderate and reasonable than it is in any other part of the Regency. In Algiers the government is bad. But almost everywhere else, we found it absurd or detestable. *[margin: checks on power]*

It is therefore in Algiers that we must make the great effort on behalf of colonization.

The conditions essential for success. Good sense tells us that the first condition essential for success is to create a territory around Algiers where security reigns. The best way to achieve this seems to me to erect a continuous barrier around the territory. Many excellent officers seemed to me to prefer this method. What I myself saw in Africa leads me to believe that it is indeed the only means of defense that could succeed against the Arabs, and that it would be more effective and less costly than one might suppose. One of the first truths that strikes you upon arrival in Algeria is the difficulty or rather the absolute impossibility for the Arabs of seizing any sort of fortification. You find wretched houses everywhere that have withstood actual sieges without being taken. Something that wouldn't stop a European army for an instant is impregnable for an Arab army. What's more, the natives would always hesitate to penetrate such an enclosure, as they would never be sure whether they could leave again — themselves, their horses, and their plunder. *[margin: sequestration] [margin: fortification]*

We should thus state as the first point that a continuous barrier would have to be erected around the territory destined to receive the colonists. What shape should it take? This is a question I am not in a position to resolve. General Berthois, it seems, would build his trench along a line that would rise from the sea through Coléa to Blida, then descend to Boufarik and finally abut the Harrach, not far from the mouth of that river.[25]

The advantages of this plan are to cover the entire Massif and the fertile part of the Mitidja, that which extends from the Massif toward Blida.

Its disadvantages are: (1) that it does not encompass the most fertile lands of the Mitidja; (2) that, on the contrary, it encloses the entire swampy or infertile part of this plain; and (3) that it forces work to be carried out across a territory that is pestilential for the workers and would be so for those who had to guard it as well.

The colonists apparently support a different plan, one that would consist of following the base of the Atlas from Blida to the Hamiz, which would then serve as a natural rampart. This plan would lengthen the barrier by four leagues, but it would cover the most fertile part of the Mitidja, and, raising it above the swamps and the desert wind, would present no dangers to those building or defending it. This plan, in itself, would be worth far more than the other. That is certain. But is it wise to enclose such a large area from the beginning? Shouldn't we first limit ourselves, as the government plan does, to securing the Massif and an area to the west? This is the view of General Lamoricière, who is a very good judge of these matters. I myself am not in a position to judge. One would need information I do not have, and one would need to be on the spot to get it.

The sanitation of the plain. There is another preparatory task almost as necessary as that of the enclosure, if we want to move beyond the Massif and colonize the Mitidja: this is sanitation. All the swamps that make the plain unhealthy are located at the foot of the Massif, because the Massif stops the waters that pour from the Atlas to the sea and forces them to wind left and right on fairly flat land, where they spread and flow slowly and with difficulty.[26] I know of nothing that has been done to change this state of things. If we really mean to populate the Mitidja, however, we must lose no time in taking care of this problem, not so much, perhaps, to cultivate the fairly mediocre lands covered by the swamps, but rather to make the more fertile lands around them healthy and habitable. *

---

* We must realize that no kind of colonization is perfectly healthy at the beginning. People get fevers in even the healthiest countries when they first arrive to cultivate them. This has happened in every part of the world where Europeans have settled. We must therefore distinguish carefully between the troublesome but temporary situa-

Good sense tells us that of all operations necessary for colonization, the foremost is to procure territory to colonize. At the moment, as we have said many times, this does not exist.

Consolidation of property. In general I am quite hostile to violent measures, which usually seem to me as ineffective as they are unjust.* But we must recognize that we shall never manage to possess the land around Algiers without the aid of a series of such measures. As a result, we must resolve to make use of them.

The largest part of the Mitidja plain belongs to Arab tribes that, whether by choice or by force, have gone over to Abd-el-Kader's side. Once the administration has taken control of this territory, it must not be given back, even in peacetime. The tribes that occupy it have been at war with us; their land can be confiscated according to Muslim law. It is a rigorous law whose rigor, in this case, we must use.

As for the lands in the Mitidja and the Massif that belong not to Arab tribes but to Moors, it would be useful for the government to acquire them either by mutual agreement or by force, paying liberally for them. The Moorish population deserves our consideration because of its peaceful character. But in the countryside they create problems without being at all useful to us. They cannot serve as a link between the Arabs and us, as I have already explained, and they form a refractory element in the midst of our rural population that will never assimilate with the rest.

This dispossession of the natives is not the most difficult part of our task. The Arabs are already far away, and there are very few Moors. It is the European landowners who complicate the question.

---

tion of all colonial beginnings, and the permanent situation born of certain physical causes that never change and that would be the same in Europe. The one disappears on its own, and there is no need to be alarmed by it; the other persists and often worsens, if no remedy is applied. When Europeans began to cultivate the hills and valleys of the Algerian Massif to the east of the coast of Couba, Hussein Dey . . . they were taken by fevers, which led us to believe that the country was unhealthy, even if the cause was invisible. After several years, when the land had been cultivated and the population had grown, people no longer fell sick. But on the southern slopes where the swamps are, it seems likely that the sanitary conditions will not improve with time, because there the fever comes from a deep and permanent cause that will always make itself felt and that would lead to illness in whatever country one encountered it.

* [In the margin:] Begin differently by connecting to the preceding sentences.

On this same Mitidja plain, large stretches are unoccupied, but owned by Europeans who bought them from the natives. This is the case in almost all the uncultivated parts of the Massif. These men don't cultivate the land, and they don't sell it to those who would, for two reasons. Most of them are land speculators who don't sell because they think the time will come when they can do better than they can now. For many it is truly impossible to sell, because the property they own is uncertain, either because it has no recognized boundaries or because the right of the seller is in doubt. Much of the land was sold to several people at the same time, most of it has no boundaries, and the boundaries there are so badly designated that they are unrecognizable.[27] No serious colonist would acquire this type of property for settlement and cultivation. Thus as I said above, almost all the land, even at the gates of Algiers in the Massif, is owned but not occupied by us. This is absolutely intolerable, and I cannot imagine how an administration that so constantly and lightly violates so many rights has tolerated such abuses for so long.

In general, nothing is more dangerous in a new country than the frequent use of forced expropriation. I shall develop this idea further below. I cannot complain too much of this abuse, which is committed in Algeria every day. But in the present case, and in the prodigious disorder of property, such a remedy, administered once and for all in a single dose, is necessary. It is absolutely necessary that we manage to fix property and its boundaries using a summary procedure and an expeditious court established for that sole purpose. Having thus created a certain landowner and an alienable property, we should declare that if, after a term we indicate, the recognized owner does not cultivate his land,* this land will fall to the state, which will secure it by paying the purchase price. These are undoubtedly violent and irregular procedures, but I defy anyone to come up with another way to extricate ourselves from this problem.

An operation that must precede all these, and that alone will permit them to be done, is the survey. It is incomprehensible and inexcusable that the survey of the Massif, a district that hardly covers the area of an arrondissement in France, has not yet been done.[28] This alone would suffice to illustrate the unproductive or injurious activity that *characterizes* the civil administration of Algiers.

---

* By cultivating, I mean planting trees as well as harvesting crops. It seems that, especially in the Massif, planting trees is the best and most useful agricultural occupation.

Establishment of villages. The government finally controls a large part of the land by right of conquest, either through voluntary sale or forced expropriation. What should be done with it and how should it be populated? *population settlement*

Several systems have been proposed, but all agree and must agree on one point: the necessity of not allowing the population to scatter into the countryside, but rather of forcing them to live in villages that the state fortifies at its own cost, and whose defense it entrusts to a designated officer. All of them, as I've said, agree and must agree on this point. But they differ on all others. On this subject I have heard many theories advanced.

Nothing proves better than these theories the kind of irresistible attraction in our time and our country that little by little is leading the human spirit to destroy individual life in order to make every society into a single being. In France, this tendency has produced Fourierism and Saint-Simonianism. It has even attracted, unbeknown to themselves, Abbé Landmann,[29] General Bugeaud,[30] and many others who have written or spoken on colonization. All of them tend to cover Algeria with veritable phalansteries, theocratic, military, or economic; in other words, they all want to found little communities where *socialism → Tocqueville is opposed* property and individual life are hardly found, if at all, and in which each citizen works like a bee, following a single plan and a single goal, not for his own interests, but for those of the hive.

There is, however, this difference between M. Landmann's plan and that of M. Bugeaud: the former makes the property arrangements and the common life the permanent state, while the latter, if I am not mistaken, makes them only a temporary one. The members of his military colony, who are former soldiers, begin by cultivating in common and following a common leadership, but after a certain number of years, I think, they become free landowners.

All these plans can succeed to a point, in a particular case and for a certain time; we have seen such things in America. Abbé Landmann may persuade a certain number of German families to group themselves around him, and he may keep them united by his zeal. General Bugeaud may find enough former soldiers in his army who would consent to form one or two colonies, and officers able enough to lead them. All this is possible. But what is a pure dream is to imagine that we could populate the country with either of these exceptional methods.

All these fine plans for societies lack the first condition for success: men to test them.

Regarding the military colonies, let me say, first, that they would contain only unmarried men, at least at the beginning. This is an immense drawback. Colonization is achieved with families and not with individuals.[31] Let me say, next, that if one considers the state of our mores, the comfort that reigns among the French rural classes from which the soldiers are drawn, the love these people almost always preserve for their native villages, the hatred they generally feel for Africa and especially the horror of war, orders, and military discipline that more and more lies at the heart of their character, it seems quite unreasonable to think that we shall be able to find many soldiers who, after their service, would remain in Algeria to farm the land in military unison for the sake of distant and precarious advantages. You will find almost no such men, especially among good subjects, and if they come for awhile, they will eventually leave. That is the feeling of many well-informed men in Africa. I completely agree. Military colonies do not work except by bringing and keeping new residents there by force, which is to say that such colonies work only when they can be populated by serfs.

As for the religious or economic colonies that simply have communal property and life as their means and their end, I would say there is even more reason to believe it unreasonable to think that a large number of men would leave their homeland and expose themselves to the miseries and dangers of colonization in Algeria, and to what end? So that they can be masters neither of their own persons nor of their property and find limits placed on all their hopes. That, I repeat, has never happened, and never will, because to act this way is directly contrary to the natural movements of the human heart.[32]

All these artificial and complicated means of populating Africa could appeal only to those theoretical men who have never seen the landscape of colonial society for themselves. Those who have studied the matter practically know, to the contrary, that what is required to fight against the innumerable difficulties of an original settlement is nothing less than all the energy of the passions to which individual property gives rise; that, at the harsh early stages it is necessary to keep the colonist's movements as free as possible, and to give his hopes as broad a horizon as possible. We must never forget, as I said earlier, that the colonists are not serfs but independent and mobile men who can choose not to come or not to stay as they please. The point, therefore, is not to discover *a priori*, with pen in hand, the most suitable system for making the little society prosper, but rather to find the most effective means to attract and retain each man who will compose it, through his passions and tastes.

The colonies of all European peoples present the same spectacle. The part of the individual is always greater than that in the mother country, rather than smaller. His freedom to act is less restrained. We should learn from this fact.

I know that in this matter as in all others, much depends on the circumstances. It is clear that social power should be involved in more things, should guide and direct individuals more often in a colony like Algeria than in any other colony I know. I do not contest the claim that it should play a large part. I only want us not to forget that it should not play a larger part than necessary, and that we must count principally on the free, passionate, and energetic action of individuals for success.

When I try to discover what part the particular circumstances of our colony oblige the administration to play, this is what I find: the administration must carefully survey the country to be colonized, and as much as possible, acquire land in order to sell it to the colonists unencumbered and at a low price.* It should fix the location of the villages, lay them out, fortify and arm them, build each a fountain, a church, a school, and a town hall, and provide for the needs of the priest and the schoolmaster. It should force each inhabitant to lodge himself and his herd within the fortifications and to enclose his fields. It should subject them all to the rules of watch and defense that security requires;† and at the head of their militia, it should place an officer who will keep up certain military habits in the population and who can command them outside the village. In addition, the administration should, either on its own or through colonizing companies as intermediaries, provide either animals, instruments, or provisions, in order to facilitate and guarantee the foundation of the settlement. Above all, and this is crucial, it should ensure that the obligations it imposes are well defined and well known in advance. What most disheartens the inhabitant of a new country is not to know precisely what he can count on. Impose strict obligations if you will, but do not allow them to vary according to your whims. That is the administration's task.

That done, the colonist must be allowed to settle where he likes and farm as he chooses. To the greatest extent possible, he should be freed of the irritations and obligations imposed on him in France, and his village should call to mind the community in which he lived here at home.

---

* It would be best to give them the land on condition of military service in certain cases.
† [Variant: *à certaines règles de garde et de défense* (to certain rules of watch and defense.)]

Those who go to Africa must be given real financial incentive [un pont d'or].*
We have been tormenting ourselves trying to discover ways to attract farmers
to Algeria and settle them. There is one way these grand utopians never think
about that would be worth more than all the military and ecclesiastical colonies in the world, which is to make farming profitable. In order to make
money farming, one must be able to live cheaply and sell one's produce easily
and at a high price. Lower the tariffs so that they can buy everything useful and
agreeable for life, even foreign goods, at low prices. Allow all Algerian products to enter France freely, especially those produced not by indigenous industry but by colonial industry.[33] For instance, instead of buying the tobacco you
need from America, buy it in Algiers, where it grows marvelously and is
excellent. The allure of gain and comfort will soon attract as many colonists as
you could desire to the Massif and the Mitidja.†

I know that metropolitan commerce and industry will protest that we are
sacrificing them; that the principal advantage of a colony is to provide an
advantageous market for the mother country and not to compete with it. All
this may be true in itself, but I am not moved by it. In the current state of
things, Algeria should not be considered from the commercial, industrial, or
colonial point of view: we must take an even higher perspective to consider
this great question. There is in effect a great political interest that dominates all
the others. Our current situation in Africa is intolerable: ruinous for the treasury, destructive for our influence in the world, and above all precarious. Our
most pressing interest, and I would say our most national interest, is to resolve
it. It can be resolved only by the arrival of a European population that will
protect and guarantee the territory we have conquered. We must, therefore,
get them there at all costs, even if that means we must temporarily injure our
various producers. I say temporarily, since it is easy to see that this will be
merely a passing problem. Once Algeria contained a large French population,
we could reestablish, to great advantage, the protective tariffs that at this point
are almost useless to our producers, since the country is uninhabited and has
no needs.

---

* [Another title in the margin:] Other conditions essential for success; changes in the
customs laws.
† [In the margin:] Find out exactly the state of the customs laws . . .
     All this is just an idea that will become interesting only if I can add the details of
facts I don't know.

Let me repeat here what I have said and shall say many times: try to ensure that the money Algeria costs you is spent usefully, but don't be stingy, for nothing is more costly and at the same time more dangerous than the current status quo. I think that if France, in building, as they say, a bridge of gold [*un pont d'or*] for those who would populate Africa, managed to attract a large population in a few years, it would have done excellently, even if we consider the money alone.

Of social and political institutions and of the type of government best suited to *producing and ensuring colonization* It is not only by our cutting ditches, clearing rivers, building walls, granting lands, and laying out villages that a European population will be attracted to Algeria. The task is more difficult and more lofty. I do not hesitate to say that, whatever concrete efforts we make to create a populous and flourishing colony in Algeria, we shall fail unless we profoundly modify the institutions that now govern the country. To demonstrate this truth is the most important part of my task.

The government of Algeria displays several contradictory flaws that are rarely found in the same power. It is violent, arbitrary, tyrannical, and, at the same time, it is weak and impotent. It is easy to see the cause of this phenomenon.

The government is arbitrary and tyrannical because it does not protect citizens against the different agents of authority; and it is weak and impotent because no central power exists in the colony to force all these different agents to work together for the execution of the same plans and produce a vigorous and continuous social action.

It is essential to make the administration at once stronger and more limited, if we want Europeans, who are used to facing one or another of these characteristics in the authorities that govern their metropoles, to come and settle in Algeria.

I have already indicated what makes the Algerian government weak and impotent. I now return to this idea in detail.

This weakness and this impotence stem from two causes: the first is the lack of centralization in Algiers. You cannot imagine anything more miserably anarchic than the civil government in Algiers. The head of each department is independent in his sphere and, as the execution of almost all the projects demands the simultaneous cooperation of all of them, and since this cooperation is out of reach, nothing is begun on time or completed. It is true that over all the departmental heads is the governor, who has the right to force them all to obey. But this governor is a general who has no clear or practical notions of civil administration; who, besides, is quite preoccupied with war matters; and who is usually away at the head of his army. Such a man, whatever he may be, is hardly the right person to conceive plans of administration and, even when an idea occurs to him, his ignorance of details, his military preoccupations, and his being away almost always leave him incapable of putting his ideas into practice and getting the various departmental heads to work assiduously and in concert to realize them.

The civil administration in Algiers, therefore, needs a single head; there should be a man in charge of coordinating all the various officials in the administration to execute either his own projects or those of the governor-general.

I know that the difficulties of execution are very great. It would seem difficult to many people, in the current state of things, not to grant supreme power over African affairs to a general. Military affairs, they say, at this point represent such a large part of colonial government that to put the government in the hands of a civilian official is either to make a mess of military affairs if he tries to run them, or to ensure that the person who runs military affairs in his name is the real governor, or, finally, to guarantee constant conflict.* The destruction of Abd-el-Kader would not change this situation much, they add, for the means of governing Arab tribes even in peacetime closely resemble the procedures of war. They require knowledge and practice. People conclude that we shall need a military governor for a long time to come. But where, on the other hand, is the good man who will consent to lead the civil administration under a military chief and in a colony where all the effective power and all responsibility is in the hands of the army? We are likely to find for this important position only very mediocre men, who would offer no real guarantee of ability or even morality; or, if we managed to get a capable man with any weight in the country to take the position, he would soon rebel against the insignificant role the army left him, and anarchy would reemerge

---

* [In the margin, a crossed-out note suggests Tocqueville's uncertainties on this point:] "This, however, is almost always how the English have acted in India. The great things that we ourselves achieved in that country were done by men who were not soldiers, such as [Joseph-François] Dupleix [1697–1763].

"It can even be said that the government of India is essentially civilian, even though it was founded with arms in hand and remains so."[34]

in another form. That, I believe, is the greatest difficulty presented by the entire Algerian question.*

Later I shall examine in greater detail the great question whether the government-general of Algeria should be granted to a civilian or a military official. All I want to note now is that it is important really and effectively to centralize the real administration of the colony in the hands of one official, whether the governor himself or someone immediately under him.

The first cause òf the weakness and impotence of our colonial government was the lack of centralization in Algiers. The second is the absurd centralization that exists for the same affairs in Paris.

It would be futile to establish a central power on which all of the agents of the civil administration depended if, for each detail, the representative of this authority were obliged to take orders from a sovereign authority residing in Paris. The rights and duties [*attributions*] of central power and those of colonial authority diverge with good reason: all the measures of a legislative or political character, general regulations, especially those resulting in penal resolutions, in a word, everything with a general and permanent influence on the state of property and persons must be decided only with the approval and permission of the government. Because these measures are of great importance, because their necessity or appropriateness can be appreciated in Paris as well as and often better than in Algiers; because they are almost never so urgent that a delay of several weeks would be damaging, and finally because it is very necessary in this matter not to innovate lightly or often, even to improve things, instability being the most natural and the most dangerous malady to which new societies succumb.

On the other hand, whatever is only the application of general regulations, details of administration, and selection of subordinate agents should be left to the power governing the colony. Centralization in these matters is, in my view, bad, even in France and the areas around Paris, but it becomes much more dangerous as you move away from the center, and in the end it halts and disrupts everything by wanting to control it all, when this is attempted in a

---

* [In the margin of this paragraph:] *Note for Beaumont:* Everything that follows will show Beaumont the doubts in my mind on the important question treated here. He will see further on that I settle on the idea that all things considered the government should be civilian.

country far from France, whose administrative needs are almost always pressing and are known only to those who feel them.

This is certainly how things should be. Let us see how they are:

Every day the governor of Algeria, of his own accord, makes decrees concerning the European population of the Regency that could be considered actual general laws given that they profoundly modify the existing state of things and at the same time affect the position of everyone living in the country.*

The ministerial decree of . . .[35] which placed limits on the governor's power, allowed him to exceed them *in cases of emergency,* as long as he later consulted the minister. In time, this emergency declaration became what is known in legal terms as a formal clause. It appears at the top of all the governors' decrees, thus investing them with *de facto* legislative power — legislative power without guarantees or counterweights, since no precautions have been taken to keep them from exercising it dangerously. Governors have no advisers who could inform them and restrain them in this work, so foreign to their habits, nothing that does what the Conseil d'Etat [state council] does for the king. They intend to control the governor from Paris; failing this guarantee, there is nothing but the arbitrary will of a soldier improvising civil institutions.

In the administration strictly speaking, on the contrary, the governors can do almost nothing. All the colonial funds are centralized in Paris, and endless formalities are required before the smallest sum can be spent; similarly for lands, and for the most minute details of the various departments. All the documents must pass again and again through the minister's office. Correspondence takes up all the employees' time. When I asked the finance director why the survey of the Massif has not yet been done, he responded that he and his clerks hardly had enough time for their everyday work. In the year 1839 alone, he himself had written 9,000 letters to the minister. It has often happened, and still happens continually, that colonists return to France or starve to death a few months after arriving in Algeria because the formalities necessary to grant them a small plot of land have not been completed. You have to be French to understand and put up with absurdities of this kind.

Thus, there is at once too little and too much centralization. The governor is free where he should be restrained. He is chained where he should be

---

* Some examples.

free. It can be said more reasonably of him than of the king that he governs but does not administer, which certainly goes against common sense.

This state of things cannot last, I say with the most complete conviction, without making colonization almost impossible. We must have an administrative leader who can oversee and create this new society, and this leader must have reasonable independence from the Paris bureaus. In all administrative details, he must be given part of the powers that the minister now keeps for himself.

That is what should be done for the government. Let us see what the citizens need.

Guarantees to give the citizens. In the matter of colonization, we must not lose sight of a very clear and simple idea. In our time and in our part of Europe, it is not possible to seize a population and transport it at will from one place to another. They must be given the desire to go.* It is not an easy thing to suggest to Europeans the desire to leave their homeland [*patrie*], because in general they are happy there and they enjoy certain rights and certain goods that are precious to them. For even more reason, it is difficult to attract people to a country where from the beginning they encounter a scorching and unhealthy climate and a formidable enemy that constantly circles around you to take your property or your life. To bring inhabitants to such a country, they must, first, be given good chances of making their fortune there; second, they must encounter a state of society that agrees with their habits and their tastes. Because if the evils and irritations of a bad government join the inseparable evils born of the country, no one will either come or stay.

Now, let us see whether the colonist who lands in Algeria finds a single one of the guarantees of security and liberty that can be found more or less in all European countries, and that those who live in them are accustomed to consider the best thing in their lives and their prime necessity.

In his own country, the Frenchman takes part in the government of affairs

---

* This is not about conquering a natural obstacle for which a government needs only money and good engineers, or even about guiding a certain number of men who are strongly unified to each other and to their leader through military discipline. The task is far more delicate. This is what we constantly seem to forget. If you listen to those who are always talking about organization in Algeria, it seems that we own men as property and that there is nothing more to do than arrange them one beside the other in the most appealing order. All these great colonial founders would really make an American or an Englishman laugh.

either directly through elections or indirectly through freedom of the press. The laws are made by powers that he either elected or oversees. The general rules and the principal acts of the executive power emanate from the Conseil d'Etat, a great body that, placed outside the active administration, directs it and checks it. As for local affairs, the most important are conducted by assemblies, and the citizens compete to be nominated for these. The Frenchman in his own country can be arrested only by a mandate issued by an independent magistrate. He is detained by an equally independent court, charged by another, and finally judged by his fellow citizens gathered together on a jury. His property is perfectly guaranteed. The state can seize it only by paying in advance and using formalities that it cannot dispense with. In his disputes with the government, he is judged either by permanent magistrates or at least by a large assembly whose position makes it independent.

This is what he leaves in France. Let us consider what he finds in Algeria: The tribune, liberty of the press, the jury, electoral right, do not exist in Africa. These things, it must be recognized, could not exist there at the moment. But one does not even see the trace of an institution found even in the most absolute monarchies of Europe, of which I don't know that any colony of any nation has ever been completely deprived. I mean those bodies either elected or appointed whose function is to direct the purely local affairs or at least to give their opinion to those who direct them. There is nothing like a colonial assembly in Africa. At the beginning a municipal council was created in Algiers; the members were chosen by the authority. This shadow of municipality still seemed to bother the power that directs African affairs. It was made to disappear. What was worse, the centralization of the local revenues — as well as the use of these funds — in a common fund in Paris, destroyed the very principle of municipal life itself. At this time, there is not a colonist in Algeria who knows whether the community he lives in has revenues, what these revenues are, and how they are spent. There is not one who participates in the most distant and indirect way in the policing of his village, in the establishment or repair of his church, his school, his presbytery, his fountain; all these great affairs are settled in Paris. This is prodigiously absurd. All the colonizing peoples from the Greeks and the Romans to the English have endeavored to make municipal life in the countries they peopled very independent and very active, either because of the impossibility they perceived of directing the small societies, placed far from the metropole in quite different situations, down to the last detail, or because of the need they experienced to create a new homeland for their colonists and to tie them to one another by confiding in them common control over their common interests.

As for the high administration and the general rules that concern the fortune, and often the liberty and the life of each of them, the colonists possess not one guarantee, neither those we have in France nor any other, as I have already shown. Among these rules, some come directly from the Ministry of War, without having been submitted to the Conseil d'Etat. Others are improvised in Algiers by the governor-general, and what is called the governor's council in Algiers is composed only of departmental heads, each absorbed in his particular tasks, who have as little a vision of the whole as they have independence. What results is not only bad measures, but the perpetual alteration of measures, which is worse.

In the detail of its actions, the administration of Algiers is no more irreproachable.

One sees first of all the abuses that can spring from the military control this administration was given. This drawback is more striking at a distance than up close. The military power from time to time undoubtedly uses quite a brutal measure of violence. But this does not happen all the time. I am convinced that taken as a whole the most oppressive and injurious power in Algiers is the civil power. It is not that it permits itself great acts of tyranny. But it shows itself everywhere and always, ruling, directing, modifying, touching and retouching everything. You can easily understand the inconvenience and the social malaise to which this behavior gives birth if you imagine our French administration with all the dominating, inquisitive, *meddlesome* instincts it got from the Empire and the bureaucratic habits it got from the Restoration, acting in a country where neither public opinion, nor the civil courts, nor the criminal courts, nor even the administrative courts can be mustered against it.*

---

* In fact, not one of these barriers that are erected around the administrative power in France exists in Algeria. In France, when an administrator makes a mistake in the application of laws or regulations, his decision is appealed to the Conseil d'Etat to be redressed. When he commits a crime or a misdemeanor one can denounce him before this same Conseil d'Etat to obtain permission to indict the delinquent before the tribunals. In Africa, it is the government council that fills these different functions of the Conseil d'Etat; now, do you know who makes up the government council? All the chiefs of active service. That is to say, when you have a complaint about an official's mistakes, you must appeal to the man himself or to his superior; when an official commits a crime or a misdemeanor, you must request permission from his immediate

These institutional vices are compounded by human vices. In general, the civil administration in Algeria is poorly composed. This comes from the fact that a horde of creatures were put there whom people would not dare to employ in the bright daylight of publicity in France. The administration is, moreover, too large for the size of the country and the number of inhabitants. Many public services that presuppose a complete and advanced society were created in Algeria, but only with difficulty do they find things to do in this small new society.

In general, you can count on this:

Whenever it's a matter of administration, Algiers, in the eyes of the government, is a country essentially similar to France, to which all our officials and all our administrative practices must be introduced. When it's a matter of citizens, on the other hand, the colony forms a completely exceptional society where none of the rights and freedoms that are enjoyed in the mother country can be granted without danger. Algiers thus abounds with officials, each of whom, unable to extend his power over many of the administered, likes to make every one of them feel it at each moment. This fury to act at every turn, down to the least details, to stick their hands everywhere and to always shift around people and things, was born from yet another cause: in Algiers, the civil administration is in a false and humiliating position. The military power on one side, the centralization from Paris on the other, oppress and eclipse the civil administration: by perpetually tinkering with small affairs, it seeks to retrieve some of the importance it should have in great ones.

Algiers is thus a country where one has none of the great guarantees and liberties that one enjoys in Europe, but where on the other hand one finds all the commercial, financial, and administrative difficulties that one left in the home country, augmented by many others one did not even know existed.

It can be said with justice that in Algeria, the first of all the civil liberties, individual liberty, is not assured. Not only does individual liberty not attain the guarantees it has in France; it does not even have those it is given in most of the absolute monarchies of the continent. Things there are arranged in such a manner that almost all the courts of criminal justice are in the hands of the

---

superiors or his colleagues to sue him. Am I right to say that in Africa the natural vices of our administrative system develop on their own and quite freely, and, what's more, that our administration is subject to particular vices there, born of the circumstances and the country?

public minister. It is the prosecutor and not the examining magistrate who has the accused arrested and detained. The proceedings take as long as he likes; he can suspend them indefinitely, if he likes, or speed their course. It is he alone and not the council chamber or the council of arraignment [*chambre des mises en accusation*] who decides whether there is sufficient indication to inflict the glare of a trial on the accused. He holds the judges' destiny in his hands and has an immense influence on their decision. You could say he even dominates the defense, inasmuch as in Algeria the profession of defense attorney does not exist. Defense attorneys are replaced by defenders, a type of civil servant who are few in number and whom the administration has in its palm. Thus not only does the Frenchman who goes to Africa lose the guarantee of a jury and of the impartiality of the judges, which were difficult to maintain, but also many other very important guarantees, which nothing required that he be denied. He is arrested without a mandate, detained without recourse, prosecuted without a preliminary investigation by the council chamber and the council of arraignment, judged by a few dependent men and defended by defense attorneys who are not free. Finally, if he surmounts all these obstacles, the governor-general can, at his whim, have him seized, taken by force, and expelled from the colony within twenty-four hours.

There is another right less precious in itself, but perhaps dearer to men who have left their homeland to make their fortune: the right of property, which is still less assured. It is endlessly threatened and reduced in many ways: first by the military authority, which, from time to time, seizes animals or harvests for the army's use. I saw several examples of this during my stay in Algiers. The army behave this way not only because of their unconcern and scorn for rights, but also, it must be said, because it pleases them. One of the things that most strikes the visitor arriving in Africa is to see the envious and hostile feelings of the soldier for the colonist. I have already noted this, and I can't repeat it too often. This point deserves the careful attention of the government. It is there that you find one of the principal obstacles to colonization. For these feelings of hatred and jealousy fill not only the officers' hearts but also the generals'. You notice that more or less all of them watch the colonists making money with secret irritation, and they willingly seize occasions to lessen their profits or ruin their enterprises.[36] A government of such masters is always dangerous for property; still, let me repeat here, as above, that all things considered, the civil authority seems to me even more to be feared than the military power.

In effect, what always threatens property is, on one hand, the civil administration's immoderate use of forced expropriation, and the means it uses; and, on the other, the few judicial guarantees surrounding the right of property.

Expropriation in Algeria is carried out with savage speed: the governor makes a declaration of eminent domain; and within twenty-four hours, the administration seizes the property without prior indemnity. During these twenty-four hours, the owner has to name an expert who, together with the administration's expert, estimates the value of the property. If the owner cannot or will not choose an expert, the court designates one for him. Thus a man who leaves Algiers to spend eight days in Toulon could find his house razed on his return. What is more, for certain properties, those seized in order to build roads, no indemnity is due at all. The decree of 1834, which serves as the law regarding forced expropriations,[37] makes a point of stating it formally. There is more still: if the administration one day consents to pay for the properties it seizes, it reserves at least the right not to reimburse the capital, but only to pay the interest. I saw several examples of this during the short time I was in Algiers, including the following: a Frenchman's house suited the director of the interior[38] as a place for his offices. He had eminent domain declared, but agreed only to pay interest. The owner was a poor man who had done badly in business in Algiers, whose wife had just died, and who wanted to leave Africa to return to France. Interest in Algiers was not at all what he wanted: he hoped to take his small capital with him to France. But the administration held firm, and the poor devil was probably obliged to do as they said. It is easy to understand why administrators in Africa prefer to pay interest instead of capital for expropriated property. The registration of a rent is hardly noticed in the colonial budget, and this way one can carry out many expropriations without seeming to take too much from the public budget.

It is not only the law of expropriation that is dangerous but especially the use the administration makes of it all the time. It is in this matter above all that the damage done by the administration of Africa is demonstrated. The culpable wantonness with which the government of Algiers continually uses its exorbitant power to dispossess citizens can hardly be imagined or described. Its plans change constantly, and each of these changes amounts to a forced expropriation, executed as soon as it is known, in such a way that there is no owner in the towns or their surroundings who can consider, I do not say as certain, but even as probable, the preservation of his garden or his home. With my own eyes, I saw large, fine, newly built houses in Philippeville pulled down, even though they had been built along lines assigned by the administration, because it had since pleased the administration to change its plans. I heard complaints about the same abuses of power in all the provinces. While I was in Algiers, it occurred to General B. to give the lands adjoining the camps to the soldiers for them to cultivate. The idea was not bad, but good sense would suggest that it should only apply to the lands, still uncultivated, that surrounded the camps at a short distance. Instead of this, they undertook to apply it as well to the fields that are at the gates of Algiers, that is, to a considerable mass of very valuable and already occupied properties. I saw the decree that ordered the expropriation of these fields.[39] Is it possible, I ask, to imagine a more brutal, more absurd and more dangerous measure than one that consists of expropriating the colonists who are already settled in order to attempt to implement a new system of colonization at their expense?

I have said that the right of property was not yet surrounded in Algiers by the judicial guarantees one is accustomed to seeing in Europe. Indeed, there is hardly more civil justice in Algiers than there is criminal justice.

Instead of simply importing into the colony the practices and judicial laws of France, they were modified in a thousand ways, so that in the midst of this confusion caused by the mixing* of French legislation and colonial decrees, jurisprudence wavers uncertainly, and the judges adjudicate more or less at random. This is what most of them confessed to me. This introduction of a new judicial system is a big mistake even if we were to admit that the innovations were good, for there is nothing Europeans care about more when they emigrate than to find in the new country the judicial practices they had grown used to in the metropole. Let me say, in addition, that in my view, many of these innovations are, in themselves, quite unfortunate. Take unitary judgment as an example. It is a great question among theorists whether, instead of having courts composed of a large number of magistrates, it would not be better to invest all responsibility in a single man. This is what the English have believed, and the system works well for them. But in England these men who act as sole judges of litigants' fates are very few in number, occupy one of the highest positions in the state, and are paid with enormous salaries, so that they can be chosen from among the greatest jurists and lawyers of the country, and they offer litigants every sort of guarantee. In addition, in most cases, they judge only the law, once the facts have been established by a jury. It is a

---

* [Variant: *la rencontre* (the encounter).]

distinctly clumsy imitation of the English to borrow [the principle of such] unitary justice when this lone judge is just an obscure little official drawn from the lowest ranks of the magistracy or from the bar and to arm him at once with the right of establishing the facts and judging the law. These single justices who replace our district courts in Africa seemed to me to inspire great defiance in the population. And I cannot help adding that this defiance seems to me quite well founded.

If, at least, this new and exceptional justice people imagined they were creating in the colony remained, like ours, subject to inspection and examination by the Appeals Court [*Cour de Cassation*], the errors or the vices of the judges would be contained within certain limits. But the royal ordinance of . . . 1841,[40] which the minister of war brazenly called progress, destroyed recourse in civil matters, thus depriving the colonists of France's foremost judicial guarantee with a single blow.

This act of violence was led in part by the desire to conceal the greatest abuse of all from the Court of Appeal. I mean the unlimited extension of administrative law.

In Algeria, it is the governor-general who has final judgment in case of conflict, just as the king does in France. It is easy to see that his tendency, unresisted by anyone, is constantly to draw all the trials into the administrative legal division. In Algeria, he finds a thousand ways of doing so that the king would not have in France. Almost all the properties in Africa come either from the Beylik, which the government represents, or from the government itself, which sold or ceded the lands. In addition, as the largest producer and the largest consumer in Africa, the state is party to almost all transactions. There are thus few trials that could not give rise to an administrative interpretation and that would not be easy to bring before the government council. Now, as I have said, this government council is not composed, like the legal department in the Conseil d'Etat, of administrators or active officials. It is made up of departmental heads, who can be considered in most cases at once judges and parties to the case. Here even the French fiction that portrays administrative law as a sort of disinterested third party between the citizens and the state has disappeared, leaving only the administration judging its own cause and bit by bit nullifying civil justice in order to substitute itself in its place.

I have just depicted quite a bad state of society, but I have not mentioned its greatest vice: that it can change and does indeed change every day. Not only do the colonists not find the protective institutions that exist in their homeland, but they absolutely do not know what institutions they will have tomorrow. No part of the French society of Algeria rests on the *law*. The royal ordinance itself rules only on some matters; several of the most important are governed by ministerial decrees that can be modified every day in the darkness of an office, according to the whim of some clerk. The act in virtue of which the governor-general possesses his powers, and that allows him to make general regulations, inflict punishments, impose taxes, improvise services, and expel whomever he pleases from the colony, the act that gives him such exorbitant powers, is a ministerial decree. Thus, the instability is not only in the administration but in the very legislation itself. The very foundations of society rest on nothing solid and are indeed constantly being overturned. This is a great evil, even in old societies, and even if mores, traditions, and practices take the place of laws; such a state of things is absolutely intolerable in a newborn society whose naturally unstable elements have a particular need to be held firm and stable.

The truth is that there does not yet exist in Africa what Europeans call a society. The men are there, but not the social body. For myself, I declare in all honesty and after thorough examination, that if I were condemned to live on the coast of Africa, I would much rather live in the Regency of Tunis than in that of Algiers. I am not surprised at the small number of colonists who come to Algeria; I am astonished that any of them can come and stay. That can be explained only by ignorance or misery.

NECESSARY REFORMS

Modifications to make in the legislation. I have already said what can be done to occupy the country with a less numerous, less expensive army and to lose fewer men.

I have also said what the essential conditions for success in colonizing the country are in my view.

I have shown that fulfilling these conditions would not be enough, because the country's legislation does not yet offer any of the guarantees for the preservation of concrete gains that the government could promise. These gains, however important they might be, would never be able to attract quickly or to retain a large European population on the coast of Africa.

It remains to indicate what changes would have to be made to this legislation.

Whatever the institutions established in Algeria, the primary requirement is to make sure that they are well known in advance and that their durability can be relied on, for the obscurity and instability of the law are the worst of all social misfortunes.

There is only one way to achieve this; that is to establish the foundation of colonial society on the law or, at the very least, on royal ordinance.

There will never be anything stable in Algeria until the legislature itself has generally sketched the shape and limit of the different powers that must govern the colony. The law itself is quite unstable in France, but experience has always shown that what rests on law is infinitely more solid than everything else. Why would the Chambers have set aside such a large question, and one of such vital importance? I do not see a single good reason to leave it so. French society in Africa must be kept in an exceptional condition, it is said. All right. But it is still necessary to indicate in advance and permanently what the exception should consist in and where the rules apply. Finally, why could we not establish through law what had been founded on *organic* ordinances (that is, those relative to the creation and the division of powers)? Isn't it insane to decide the powers of the governor-general by a simple decree?

This step would be useful not only because it would place the colonial government on a firm footing, but also because it would prove to foreigners and to colonists themselves that France is decidedly engaged in the question of the possession and colonization of Africa.*

In this constitution of colonial society, the law cannot intervene except in a small number of very general prescriptions.

These points established, there are others, very important though somewhat less so, which will be left to either royal ordinance or ministerial decree. I have already noted that today the governor-general, either in exercising his powers or in using the pretext of an emergency to extend them, makes actual administrative, fiscal, and even penal laws. These are clearly royal rights that must be left to the great national powers. I am not at all opposed to allowing the *case of emergency* to remain. This is necessary, but instead of saying that decrees made in cases of emergency must be ratified by the government, which means nothing, we must fix a time after which the decree is nullified, and not rightful law, if it is not ratified.

---

* It is partly for this reason that [the government] does not want to and will not do it.[41]

As to the details of administration, I would centralize almost all of them in Algiers.

This is how I would accomplish what I have already mentioned above: I would lessen the governmental powers of the governor-general, and I would increase his administrative powers. His administration would become stronger and more regular, less arbitrary and more effective. Citizens' rights would be better guaranteed and public power greater.

After the question of what part it is appropriate for the central government to play in the administration of the colony, the most important question is who will represent the central government. In this matter, the current state of things is absolutely intolerable. To hand over the civil government of Africa to the minister of war's offices is, on the one hand, to ask that things be run badly and, on the other, that no one be accountable for the problem.

It is clear that the least appropriate men to organize and even to imagine a colonial civil society are the clerks in the War Ministry. There is natural antipathy between these men's preconceived ideas and acquired habits, and the task imposed on them.

In addition, no one is accountable for their mistakes. However great the Algerian affair, it is only a detail in the minister of war's immense portfolio, and what is worse, it is a detail alien to the rest, so that a marshal can be an excellent minister of war and understand nothing at all about it. Not only is this possible, but the Chambers know it and the minister himself has almost admitted it, which rids his accountability of any reality.[42] It is desirable that Algeria, to which the colonies could be added, should form a separate ministry.[43] But if, during the current state of war, it is judged impossible to separate the affairs of Africa absolutely from the War Ministry, at least it is urgent that we create an undersecretary of state for Africa within this ministry, whose sole business would be to govern the colony and who would be truly accountable to the Chamber for the way it was governed. The administration of Algiers must be represented by a political man who can be called on at any time. But first and above all, M. Laurence,[44] a man of notorious unworthiness, must be dismissed.

I believe that the *government* of Algeria must be centralized in Paris in the hands of an accountable official. I believe as well that it is necessary to centralize the *administration* in Algiers in the hands of a single official in charge of giving a common direction to all the departmental heads.

Would this official be the governor? In other words, could the general direction of our affairs in Algeria be entrusted to a civilian official?[45]

For a long time I was of the contrary opinion. But reflection led me more and more every day to believe that the creation of a civilian governor is not only possible but desirable.

I am firmly convinced that if the general direction is confided to a military man, the work of colonization, which is our greatest task, will not be done or will be done badly, either because the governor will have neither the knowledge nor the proper taste to succeed in such an undertaking, or because he will not have time to devote to it. War will always be his major preoccupation, whatever is done. To try to give a civil administration its proper place under a military leader seems to me an almost impossible task.

A military governor will never run a civil government well. Now is it true that a civilian governor could not (especially after the destruction of Abd-el-Kader, if it were to happen) govern generally and oversee military affairs as well?

If you make your civilian governor an official of the second order, a sort of prefect whose habits and position dismiss the whole picture and large political considerations, I concede it. But if you make the government of Algeria one of the great state positions, and if you entrust this government to one of your foremost political men, is it to be believed that such a man would not be capable of judging when and how to make war, even if he did not know the details of the profession, and even if he could not stand at the center of the generals who command the troops? Dupleix, who nearly conquered India for France, was not a general. The governors of British India who, thanks to an uninterrupted series of fortunate wars, acquired an immense empire in that part of the world, were almost all strangers to a military career; to wage war one must be a general, but to know under what circumstances it is appropriate to fight, it is unnecessary and may even be damaging. A military governor may desire to wage war for himself; a civil governor wages war only for the colony.

In this matter, for the rest, we must allow ourselves to be guided by circumstances. If a general with a genius for civil government presented himself, we should certainly be quick to place him at the head of our affairs in Africa. But we must not count on such an accident.

I predict that this creation of a civil government will encounter great obstacles in the government and perhaps even in public opinion. In any case, if general control of these affairs is left in the hands of a military man, at least the civil administration should be concentrated in the hands of an official who, as the head of all the departments, would give them a common and continuous direction. This is urgent and must not be put off.

Another task is no less pressing. It is the creation of a government council composed differently from the existing council and with more extended powers.

The civil administration has two responsibilities: the power of decision in particular cases, and the drafting of the general rules that govern both the officials and the citizens. These rules are in truth quasi-laws, and it is on this side that legislative power and administrative power meet and often become confused. I have said that the most important of these rules regarding Algeria came not from the governor of the colony but from the central administration, sometimes from the crown, others from the Chambers. But the greatest number of them incontestably are the work of the colonial authority.

In all the countries of the world, alongside the executive power are placed bodies in charge of judging the utility of these rules and drafting them or overseeing their composition. This is one of the primary functions of the Conseil d'Etat in France. Something similar is particularly necessary in a country where the civil administration is entrusted to a military power. Thus, alongside the governor-general, we have placed a council whose advice he must take in certain cases. But this council is composed entirely of department heads. The result is that it provides no guarantee. None of these officials, each absorbed in his own affairs, have either the time or the frame of mind necessary to judge general measures soundly.

It is urgent that we place beside this military power, to whom we have entrusted the right to promulgate real civil laws, a council that can actually guide and contain it in this matter, that is to say, one composed of men who do not have active and independent functions. Undoubtedly, the governor must not become dependent on this council, but in matters where he must take the advice of this council, if he finds himself in disagreement with it, he must not be permitted simply to disregard it, but should submit the case to the central power.

If this type of council is necessary for preparing the public administration's regulations, it is even more necessary that it be composed this way, since it is destined to exercise the powers of administrative law. In France, at the first level of that law, those who are to judge are not part of the actual active administration. The prefecture councils, which lack many guarantees, have this one at least. Algiers does not have it, and I have shown how it is a thousand times more necessary there than in France, because the scope of administrative law there is naturally much more extended, and the abuse that one can make of this pretended law much easier.

Guarantees to grant citizens. That is how I believe power could most appropriately be constituted. As for guarantees of a different nature that citizens should be granted, here is what I think:

I find that people infinitely exaggerate the necessity of doing something very different in Africa from what exists in France. The officials who have been sent to Algeria have often said that they must be armed with very exceptional powers, because this was very convenient for them and they quite enjoy breathing easy outside our uncomfortable legality. The public in France, which deep down has a certain natural taste for violent and summary proceedings when it does not suffer itself, was quick to take them at their word. Thus it was concluded that the rule was to act differently in Africa than in France; the exception is to act the same. Or rather, as I said earlier, Algeria has fallen into the common law whenever the subject is the powers of the administration, and it remains there except for everything that has to do with the guarantees that our laws grant citizens.

I believe that these are very false notions and very unreasonable ways to act.

I have already said many times, and I would like to say again, that what matters most when one wants to create and develop a colony quickly is to ensure that those who arrive there feel exiled as little as possible, and that they encounter, if possible, a perfect image of their homeland. All the colonizing peoples have done this. The thousand colonies founded by the Greeks on the shores of the Mediterranean were all very exact copies of the cities from which they had sprung. The Romans founded municipalities on almost all the points of the known world of their time that were nothing other than Romes in miniature. Among the moderns, the English have always done the same.

What prevents us from imitating these examples in Algeria?

What persuades men of good faith that everything must be quite different in Algeria than in France are, if I am not mistaken, these two reasons:

1. The population of the colony being composed of Arabs and Europeans, of Muslims and Christians, we could not govern it in the same way that we can our homogeneous societies.

2. In the dangerous circumstances in which the colony finds itself, surrounded as it is by armed enemies, with whom it must always make war, it is necessary to arm the government with exceptional and extraordinary powers it can do without at home.

The first objection could be made only by men who have never been to Africa. Those who have been there know that unfortunately Muslim society and Christian society do not have a single tie, that they form two bodies that are juxtaposed but completely separate. They know that this state of things seems to become more so every day, and that nothing can be done against it. The Arab element is becoming more and more isolated, and little by little it is dissolving. The Muslim population always seems to be shrinking, while the Christian population is always growing. The fusion of these two populations is a chimera that people dream of only when they have not been to these places. There can, therefore, and there must, be two very distinct legislative systems in Africa, because there are two very separate societies there. When it comes to the Europeans, nothing *absolutely* prevents us from treating them as though they were alone, since the rules that we make for them never have to apply to anyone but them.

As for the other objection drawn from the internal dangers that could threaten the colony if the government were not armed with very exceptional and very arbitrary powers, I find it puerile. In Africa we have four times as many soldiers as colonists. The latter are placed between the yatagan of the Arabs and the sea in such a way that at every instant they feel the need to support the power that defends them, and to aid it. I cannot be persuaded that, to maintain order in a population of this type, we must add a violent, irregular, and arbitrary civil government to 80,000 combatants. This, I repeat, is puerile.

Thus it should not be said that social organization in Africa must be exceptional, except for a few similarities, but on the contrary, that things should be conducted in Africa as they are in France, but for a few exceptions. For I certainly admit that some are necessary. This single difference in the point of departure would soon lead to a prodigious difference in the facts.

What are the exceptions I believe are necessary? I have already said that I do not believe that for the present our great political institutions can be introduced into Africa: the electoral system, freedom of the press, the jury. These institutions are not necessary for the infancy of societies. On the other hand, there are liberties that are not granted in France that could be granted without inconvenience in Africa. Let me mention, for example, liberty of instruction.* Isn't it insane, while we speak of nothing but the necessity of doing exceptional things in Africa, to transport the privileges of the University of France there? Isn't that carrying the taste for assimilation to extremes, while at the same time, on other questions, we are immoderately surrendering to a taste for innovation? If there is a place on earth where it is necessary to leave education free, it is assuredly Algeria, where the needs in this matter are so varied, so mobile, and can be so different from those we feel in France.

In any case, we can say in a general way that all the political liberties must be suspended in Algeria. But, for almost all the rest, I maintain that there are only advantages and no inconveniences in faithfully reproducing in Africa what exists among us.

The colonists have long demanded the creation of some sort of body that can be their organ before the government. An ordinance was passed prohibiting all civil or military officials from acquiring property in Africa.[46] The result is that all the colony's officials are outsiders who, during the time they live there, contract none of the interests or ideas of the inhabitants, and who in general are merely passing through. The colonists say, with reason enough, that an administration constituted in this way can know their needs only very imperfectly. They wish us to create for them a sort of colonial council formed of a certain number of them—not elected, but chosen by the governor—which would be allowed under certain circumstances to make their wishes known; something like the manufacturing and commercial councils in France. It seems that Marshal Valée, at the time when he was recalled, was in the process of organizing this sort of indirect representation. It is very much to be desired that this plan be taken up again. The existence of this council would allay many exaggerated fears and would dissipate many of the prejudices that, from one side and the other, today create a veiled but continual antagonism between the administration and the population it must rule.

But what is far more urgent, what is essential and cannot be postponed, is the creation or rather the reconstruction of a municipal power. All colonies began as communes; in antiquity as in our own time, they have almost all owed their birth and their development to the communal spirit. We have seen that, in recent years, the government destroyed the representation of this

---

* [In the margin:] One could find many other examples.

power in Africa in destroying Algiers's municipal body, and made its very substance disappear by centralizing communal resources in Paris. This is a detestable state of things that must quickly be changed. For my part, I see little disadvantage in having the municipal council (not the mayor) elected by the population itself. But I admit that the elements of this population are still not homogeneous enough to make an election anything but a disadvantage. So do not have any elected municipal bodies. But at least have appointed ones and give back to these bodies, from whom you have nothing to fear, as they come from you and are dependent on you, the responsibility of making use of the municipality's resources. You must move quickly to attach the inhabitants to this new land by giving them collective interests and action. It is these interests and actions that are lacking, and no one has ever created societies without them. It is an error to believe that there must be fewer municipal functions in Algeria than in France. On the contrary, there must be more. An active municipal power is at the same time more necessary and less dangerous there than elsewhere: more necessary because a social life that does not yet exist must be created there; less dangerous because there is no need to fear that municipal liberty will degenerate into political license. The circumstances in which Algeria finds itself—the small number of colonists, their isolation, the force of the army, the inevitable predominance of the military spirit and military government—will always give an irresistible force to power there.

People always try to confuse two very distinct ideas: the military government of each locality and its civil administration. That the Algerian colonist must be compelled to certain military customs; compelled to live behind walls, to protect himself, to defend himself, or even to leave them in certain cases to join the army, all this is clear. It would be fine for there to be a delegate of the military power in every village, in charge of making sure that these obligations are fulfilled. But it does not follow that the administration of the communal property, the responsibility for the public works, and the internal policing of the city should be in his hands. These are things, distinct in their nature, that can and should remain separate.

Finally, if many of the greatest and most precious liberties enjoyed in France cannot be granted to the Algerian colonists, there at least will be, I maintain, no acceptable reason for depriving them of two great civil liberties that one finds even in the most absolute monarchies, and without which a country is not habitable in the eyes of a European. I mean the liberty to make use of one's own person and property.

Liberty of persons is not assured because the governor can with one word instantly tear a man from his interests and his family and expel him from the territory without any form of trial.

It does not exist because the judicial power is so constituted and the criminal procedure of such a nature that there is no one that cannot be arrested, detained, and judged at the whim of the authorities, who offer no guarantees.

Property is always jeopardized by abuse and the manner of forced appropriation on grounds of eminent domain, by requisitions, by the unlimited jurisdiction and nature of the administrative courts, by the absence of a true civil justice.

As these evils are well known, the remedies come to mind naturally.

The formidable power granted to the governor to expel whomever he likes from the colony must be, if not removed, at least limited. There are two ways to accomplish this:

1. Oblige him to state the reason for his expulsion decree and have it appear in the *Moniteur de France*.
2. Have the decree canceled if during an indicated period a ministerial decree has not legalized this measure.

Establish by a law, or at the very least by royal ordinance, forms of expropriation that are less rapid and less savage than those used in Algeria. Impose the obligation of paying a real price for the property. Surround the *declaration of eminent domain* with certain formalities that prevent it from being as lightly used as it is now.

Impose on the right of requisitioning men and animals for army service certain limits that would make the exercise very rare. On this subject I have heard very stupid arguments from officers of great intelligence. They said that the primary interest of the colonists being to defend their territory, it was quite extraordinary that they refused to aid the army in its defense. Who does not see that one moves to a colony to make money and not to make war, and that no one will come if they know in advance that at every moment they risk having their cows, horses, and harvests taken for army service. If the army wants to continue using these resources, it will soon have a deserted territory to defend. Others say that it is a great savings for the treasury to take resources that are already there instead of having them brought from a distance. Absurd reasoning: since the most costly thing France can do is to keep its colony empty and prevent it from being populated. These are like the arguments of savages who sacrifice the future to the present.

But what must be done first of all to give to men's liberty and property the guarantees that one has a right to demand of the government in all civilized countries, is to establish true justice instead of the simulacrum that exists in Africa at this moment.

I have examined this question very closely, and I declare that I do not perceive a single powerful reason that should prevent us from transporting to Africa, with very few exceptions, our entire judiciary system: for my part, I would not see a single difficulty to giving magistrates in Algeria life appointments provided they were chosen in some way other than most of them have been until now. I understand, however, that judges will not be given life appointments until we have been able to judge the effects produced by our judicial system. I also concede that we should not transport several obviously defective details of our civil procedure to Africa. But aside from that, it is urgent that we set up our courts in Africa just as they are constituted in France, purely and simply; that is to say, the district courts [*tribunaux de première instance*] and a crown court [*une cour royale*]. The good produced by the changes introduced in their constitution would not equal the problems that would result from giving justice a novel and extraordinary appearance. It is urgent that we take back from the attorney general the extraordinary powers he has been granted;* that we make the judges, if not permanent, then at least settled in one place, to permit appeals to the Appeals Court [*Cour de Cassation*] as is done in France, and finally and above all to introduce the protective formalities [*formes*] of our code of criminal investigation; no one in the world has ever claimed that these formalities were too favorable to the liberty of the accused. The contrary reproach has been made with justice, especially regarding arrest and custody. If they are not very liberal as it is, why make them savage?

I repeat that all these things can be done without inconvenience and without danger.[47]

Almost all the civil trials have been among Europeans. That is where the

---

* Among others, those of issuing mandates, of making proceedings last as long as he likes or canceling them, and making judges sputter from one end of the territory to the other according to his whim.

main action of justice occurs. As for trials among indigenous people or between indigenous people and Europeans, these are exceptional cases for which an exceptional procedure has already been established and can be kept without inconvenience.

Most of the criminal trials are also conducted against Europeans. In the case where there are indigenous people, if one thinks that our formalities are too slow (which I do not believe), we could establish councils of war for them. This is of secondary interest, for the Arabs who live with us are few in number and not very dangerous. But what is not secondary is to give the European we invite to Africa all the judicial guarantees, civil as well as criminal, that he is in the habit of regarding as necessary to civilized life. After having created civil justice, we must concern ourselves without delay to giving precise limits to administrative justice. Above all we must quickly create a constitution for the administrative court that gives guarantees on property. As I have shown, at the moment it has nothing of the kind. And not only the administration, but also the interested official, is always the one to judge his own case.

In sum, I believe that the rapid colonization of part of Algeria by France is not an impracticable task. The greatest obstacles are less in the country than in ourselves. Let us change our method, and we shall change our fortune. But in the manner we have acted and continue to act, I believe we wouldn't have managed to colonize the plain of Saint-Denis [just north of Paris], if it were still uninhabited.*

---

* [Note by Tocqueville at the end:] The essay needs a recapitulation to really grasp the sequence of ideas. [In the margin:] I believe it would be good to provoke a new inquiry by the Chambers. The first produced very good results.

INTERVENTION IN THE DEBATE OVER
THE APPROPRIATION OF SPECIAL FUNDING
(1846)

M. DE TOCQUEVILLE — Gentlemen, no doubt the Chamber does not expect me to follow the previous honorable speaker [Desmousseaux de Givré] into the very interesting but very extended details into which he believed it necessary to enter. I believe the Chamber wishes the discussion to be confined and directed to the subject's central points instead of being diluted and to some extent shrinking and getting lost in the details.[1]

If I am not mistaken, what, definitively, are the Chamber's wishes? They are to examine, in few words, these three questions:

What is the real state, I say the real state, of our affairs in Africa today?

Where does the trouble lie?

What is the remedy?

These are the three questions that I shall attempt to discuss. (*Listen! Listen!*) And so, first, what is the real state of our affairs? Not the state we have been shown, not the one the minister of war described at this podium,[2] but the true state, as all those who return from Africa represent it to us.

Gentlemen, those recent events that in some respects have been so disastrous,[3] have nonetheless had the advantage of shedding considerable and decisive light on a large number of questions that until now have seemed indecisive enough, to me at least, that despite the particular study I have made of African affairs, I have not felt able to speak about them before the Chamber.

If the Chamber were so disposed, or if I myself desired to go into details, I believe I could show you clearly, with a small number of certain facts, the truth

I advance here. But I limit myself to placing this fact before the Chamber, and I am sure that all those who know Africa, that especially all those who have fought in Africa, are of my view, and say as I do: the war, although contained within certain limits, was reduced to a certain type of expedition that Marshal Bugeaud himself described quite well with reference to our civil wars in calling it *chouannerie;*[4] the war, I repeat, is still troublesome, still a burden, but it is no longer a danger.

uprising

This is the first point. There is another that the previous speakers have also demonstrated completely: that the idea of possessing Africa, of keeping Africa with the aid and support of the indigenous population — that idea, the dream of noble and generous hearts, is a chimera, at least for the present. As the war exposed us to these various populations, their mores, their habits, their social state, their passions, their antipathies, their mobility — as all this knowledge was acquired, Gentlemen — it demonstrated, and I could prove this just as well with facts, it demonstrated, I say, that the idea of keeping Africa under our laws, with the aid of the indigenous populations, is a chimera.

Without doubt, I want no more than my honorable friend M. de Corcelle, who spoke yesterday on this podium,[5] and who so nobly expressed such noble ideas, I want no more than he does to expel the natives. Above all, I do not want to exterminate them, as has been, if not proposed, then at least suggested or insinuated several times, and as those African newspapers that were mentioned yesterday have demanded in the name of philanthropy.[6] But I think that to trust to the goodwill of the natives to keep us in Africa is a pure illusion, to which it would be insane to attach ourselves.

M. DE CORCELLE — I said nothing of the kind.[7]

M. DE TOCQUEVILLE — A third idea, to which recent events have given the character of a certitude, is that from now on, the future of our domination in Africa depends on a single event, a single one, you understand: the arrival on African territory of a European population. That idea, which has often been opposed, is universally admitted today. The latest events have caused it to penetrate all minds without exception, not only the minds of the colony's civil officials, but also those of all the military leaders. I would call on everyone today to acknowledge — and I am sure that everyone will respond — that in their eyes the main thing to do to preserve Africa is not to defeat the natives; they are defeated. It is not to keep them under a regular government; many years will pass before we shall be able to do that; it is to import into Africa a European population, and I would add an agricultural population. (*Various movements.*)

Such are the three simple and clear truths that emerge with the utmost clarity for those who have followed and studied recent events closely.

Now what is the real state of this European and agricultural population that we must—that we want to—attract to the land, the population whose greatness contains the entire future of our greatness in Africa? Yesterday, I was, I would say not only troubled, but strangely surprised, to see the remarkably gratifying image that the minister of war, at this podium, painted of the state of this particular and important side of the African question.

I do not want to play the role of opposition here; I have declared myself in favor of the project. I should like to do complete justice to the intentions of the minister of war. I should like to do justice to the talent and zeal of the general officer who is placed at the head of Algerian affairs in France;[8] but, whatever desire I may have to agree with the views of the government on this matter, I cannot allow anyone to keep the country and the Chamber under the illusions that were presented here yesterday.

You have been told that the agricultural population was numerous, that the villages were numerous, that a large number were flourishing. Well, I am not afraid to say it, this directly contradicts not only what I, only a single individual, know of Africa, but also what the Chamber's two large committees know and have said.

Here is the truth: in Africa, the agricultural population, which you desire as much as we do, does not, in truth, exist; agricultural products do not, in truth, exist.[9]

You have created villages, that is true, but who lives in these villages? Half of their inhabitants are dead, and the other half live in misery.

In truth, when I hear such a seductive picture painted in the Chamber, and before the country, of what is happening in Africa, I think I must be dreaming. Don't you know as I do, and as the minister does, what is happening in Africa? Don't you know that at this moment some of the colonists live in the most horrifying misery? Don't you know, as I do, that you will have to create workshops [*ateliers*] so that this supposed agricultural population can support itself? Don't your own newspapers, printed in Africa, affirm this? Do we need an inquiry to prove these deplorable facts, when we have here in the Chamber men who have just returned from Africa? I am sorry not to see them here; I would have begged them to take the podium and to paint you the lamentable pictures that they have painted for us.

It is assuredly not for my own pleasure that I place such a scene before you; if others had not spoken of Africa's prosperity, I would have said nothing myself; but I cannot conceive . . .

THE MINISTER OF WAR — I didn't say a word about the agricultural population!

M. DE TOCQUEVILLE — Then about whom were you speaking? You can be quite sure that wherever you transport 100,000 soldiers, with their needs and their passions, a good deal of trade will grow up around them. If it was this population you meant, it proves nothing. What would prove something would be the agricultural population, and that, to put it better, doesn't exist. (*Interruption.*)

THE PRESIDENT — It shows real intolerance to prevent the speaker from explaining his point of view. Others will have the opportunity to respond.

A VOICE — He is telling the truth!

THE PRESIDENT — It is no better to interrupt to say that the speaker is telling the truth than to say that he is in the wrong. Would the Chamber listen in silence.

M. DE TOCQUEVILLE — Perhaps, Gentlemen, I have spoken with too much eagerness, in a heated state that the Chamber will understand, since we are dealing with the lives of men and the lives of our fellow citizens? What reassures me is that the facts I have just proclaimed at the podium are known; that they are known, not only in France, but in Europe as well.

Recently, moreover, I felt a real sense of shame when I saw this, in the advice that colonization associations in Switzerland offer the men who ask them: You can go to North America, you can even settle in the almost savage parts of South America, under almost barbaric governments. But beware of going to Africa: the country is beautiful, the soil is good, the climate is healthy, but as long as Africa remains as it is today, without a real government, don't go to Africa, for there you will find only misery or death. (*On the left: Very good!*)

Gentlemen, I believe that if, without my knowledge, my words have colored the truth, it is nonetheless the truth that I have just revealed to the Chamber: that is my profound conviction.

Now, I ask myself, where is the remedy for this state of things, and where is the source of the trouble?

This is what I ask the Chamber's permission to reveal to you in very few words.

Gentlemen, there are a certain number of men, the pessimists of the question, who maintain that what happens in Africa is what necessarily must happen; that the state of the country, a multitude of circumstances I don't want to dwell on, means that the trouble I complain of is an inevitable one.[10]

I believe they are mistaken.

For me, and, if the Chamber will permit me to speak only of my own personal experience, for me, who have studied questions of this order closely, perhaps more closely than anything else, who have visited new countries, I am profoundly convinced of the opposite. I believe the problems that are arising in Africa have arisen and still arise today, more or less, in every new country.

This is my profound conviction, and each of you, Gentlemen, to be sure that I am right, may go to the Chamber's library to read the inquiries that have been conducted for the British Parliament for the past ten years. You will be astonished to see that all the questions and all the difficulties we have faced appear in these inquiries, to see them study all the solutions that we ourselves are studying at this moment.

All new countries have presented some similar conditions and obstacles similar to those we now face in Africa. There is, I confess, one very great difference: while England has often met energetic resistance from the populations she sought to govern and often to oppress, nowhere has she encountered a population as warlike as the Arabs. But in addition, never has anyone sent 100,000 soldiers marching ahead of European civilization; this circumstance has not been seen anywhere, and it compensates and even more than compensates for the greater difficulties we face on Algerian soil.

There are other people, and these are the optimists of the question, who say: the African question can be solved, but its solution depends on a certain administrative stroke of luck that has not yet been seen; on an intellectual curiosity that has never been found. There is probably some idea in the world, some system, some institution that is being sought and that some day will be found, they say; when it has been found, the question will be very simple, for things will run themselves. On this point, I am still of the opposite opinion: I think that, to discover the cause of the trouble we complain of, it is not necessary to be so learned.

I think that our affairs in Africa suffer precisely from the lack of something, for lack of which all the affairs of the world, large or small, have always failed. This necessary thing is neither more nor less than a government: a good government, or even any government whatsoever.

I maintain that the African question (I use this term and not simply the word *Africa*); the African question, that is to say the complex of facts and all the ideas encompassed by this term, has never until now been controlled by anyone, and this cannot but seem peculiar.

In this African affair, you have the greatest affair of this country. I ask who governs this affair: is it the Chambers? No, it is not the Chambers. The African affair is not the Chambers' affair, it is the government's affair.

The Chambers can influence the African affair only by weighing on the government: and until now, who has represented the government before the Chamber in this question? Bureaus, and not a truly and effectively responsible minister. Who has been in control over Africa and in Africa?

Is it the governor-general? I shall prove in a moment that he has remained a stranger to that portion of his task that has always been, in my eyes, and which is now, in the eyes of the world, the foremost. Is it the minister of war? I shall prove in a moment that he has most often failed to understand what he had to do, and that when he knew, he could not do it. And when I have proven these things, what will be left for me to say, if not that this great African affair has been controlled until now by whom? By chance, Gentlemen. (*Movement.*)

I come to the first question that I pondered a moment ago. Is it the governor-general who controls the African affair? The Chamber does not fear, I hope, that my language contains any violence toward Marshal Bugeaud; I have several reasons to maintain this reserve.

The first is that M. Bugeaud is not here to respond; the second, that I truly believe that he has rendered great services to his country. It is not that I think, as one of my honorable friends seemed to think yesterday, that the dominant merit of M. Bugeaud is precisely his being a philanthropist: no, I don't think that; but what I do think is that M. Bugeaud has rendered a great service to his country on the soil of Africa, and here is the service. He is the first to have applied, everywhere at once, the type of war that in my eyes, as in his, is the only type of war practicable in Africa. He has practiced this system of war with an unequaled energy and vigor (*Very good!*): I recognize this; I owe it principally to him that I can say here that war in Africa is now a burden, an inconvenience, but no longer a danger. If he has not produced this result, he at least ensured it.

Thus, I fully recognize Marshal Bugeaud's great military qualities; but that said, I will be permitted to add that Marshal Bugeaud has done nothing, nothing — he has damaged — he has done nothing, to bring about what everyone today realizes as the great end that France must set itself: the establishment of a European society in Africa. Not only did he not do it, but he prevented it from happening. He did not do it, and why? First for a very simple reason: because Marshal Bugeaud never believed it was useful, possible, good to introduce a civilian population, a civilian element, into Africa. He never believed in it; not believing, he naturally—and I am not reproaching him here—he naturally contributed with bad grace, incompletely, with only half a will, and often a contrary will, to pursuing a goal he felt to be impossible or dangerous. He thus did nothing, and often prevented things from being done.

There is another reason. An affair of this nature can be led, carried out, completed, only with a very concerted effort; a series of actions that require, if not the continual presence, at least the habitual thought of the person at the head of such an enterprise.

Now, during the five years that Marshal Bugeaud has been in Africa, do you know how much time he has spent in Algiers? Hardly two years. And, during his absence, do you know what was going on? In truth I am ashamed to say: this immense enterprise, in which the honor of France was engaged to the utmost, was surrendered to the miserable rivalries of subaltern officials who thought they had been given a respect they perhaps did not deserve in dealing with these matters. (*It's true!*)

It fell prey to a complication of petty and miserable contradictory measures that would have impeded the establishment of a colony—I won't say in Africa—but on the plain of Saint-Denis, if the plain of Saint-Denis were empty. This is the manner in which, for five years, France's greatest affair, that of Algeria, has been controlled in Africa. (*Approval from the left.*)

Now, how is it controlled in France? If it is not controlled in Algeria, is it controlled in France? I am sorry to say it is not, and I say it with that much more freedom because most of the events to which my words refer happened before the current minister's arrival on these benches.

I could cite a whole multitude of events to show that the minister of war knew ill or incompletely what was happening in Africa.

I don't want to go into these details; I shall limit myself, in order to make myself understood, to alluding to a document that is before the Chamber, to events that are attested to not by me, but by a large committee of the Chamber.

What is most important for the minister who is in charge of directing the great affair of colonization to know? You might think it would be to know the exact number of colonists. The budget committee addressed this question to the minister of war; the minister replied that he did not know.

This is written in the report. What is important besides? It is to know what
is the nature of products, for that comprises the entire economic question.

This question was put to the minister of war: he didn't know. Again, it is
the budget committee that tells us this.

I shall go further: the most important question in the matter of colonization, assuredly, is to know which lands can be given to the colonists, which
lands are free, what has been done to possess them, how many we possess.

These questions were asked, and the minister of war didn't know. (*De-
nial.*) All this can be found in the budget committee's report.

Am I wrong to say, Gentlemen, that in numerous circumstances, what it
was important to know in order to run affairs in Africa was unknown. And it is
not only things that are not known, but men. You have heard of the countless
malversations that have occurred in Africa. Word of them must have reached
you. It took on an official character with the pursuit against the disloyal agents
that was led by the minister of war himself. To be sure, I avidly and sincerely
praise the war administration for having made use of those energetic measures
whose goal was to denounce and strike at the culprits. I think it sets an
excellent example that should be imitated everywhere, perhaps in France itself.
But there would have been something better than to pursue the culprits, and
that would have been not to appoint them.

And why were they appointed? It is said that it was because the ministry's
hand was forced. And why was its hand forced? It is well enough to tell the
Chamber this: you must know, Gentlemen, that, for a certain time, there were
a certain number of rich and powerful families who considered Africa approximately in the same light that the great families of the ancien régime considered the Bastille. That is, when they were not pleased with a young man's
conduct, they managed to have him sent to Africa. The difference is that in
Africa these men were not in prison but in command of citizens, and that often
they returned with the cross of the Légion d'Honneur.

M. DE SIÈYES — There was nothing wrong with that.

M. DE TOCQUEVILLE — I am aware, Gentlemen, that regarding several of
the reproaches I have just addressed to the minister of war, or rather to the
government as a whole, not only men but also, in part, institutions are to
blame. I understand that the war minister, who is charged with such an immense task and for whom the African affair, however big, is only a detail, that
the war minister naturally can be unaware of many things.

I understand, as well, that a minister who, by his specialty, is as far as possible from all the thinking and all the various plans that might be of service for the creation of a civil society, is equally excusable for not knowing all that must be done to achieve such an end. On this point I am ready to recognize that a part of the reproaches I have just made falls on institutions at least as much as on men; but here is what depends directly on men.

When you knew what was to be done in Africa, when you saw it, you could not carry it out, or you dared not.

Need I recall the remarkable and deplorable dissensions that arose between the government and its foremost official in Africa, especially in the past year? Need I say that this expedition that can now, with everyone's agreement, I think, be called insane, that this expedition of Kabylia was nearly done in spite of the government, and would have been done in spite of the government if the Chamber had not prevented it?

The Chamber remembers, as well, that at the moment when the government in Paris and the Chambers declared themselves in agreement against military colonization, the representative of the government in Africa declared in the presence of his army that military colonization was the only sound and profitable thing to do. Everyone knows that, when the government in France believed and declared—rightly or wrongly, that is not the issue—that civil colonization was the only means of colonizing Algeria, the governor-general opposed this colonization in the most systematic and energetic manner, both directly and indirectly.

Who does not recall the letter he wrote, which he meant to generate attention, whose object was to inform France and the world that there was a profound disagreement between himself and his employers, in which he had triumphed through circumstances stronger than they were themselves? Everyone remembers the sensation provoked by the publication of this letter.[11]

In the presence of such remarkable public signals of this disobedience, what did the government do?

In my view, Gentlemen, the government took the least noble and the most dangerous course, the course of resignation and at the same time of ill humor.

Marshal Bugeaud was not disavowed, he was not recalled, but he was allowed to be attacked by his friends. (*Various movements.*)

Marshal Bugeaud, for his part, waged a similar war: he had the king's government attacked by the newspapers he controls or influences in Algeria; and we witnessed that new and pathetic spectacle of a civil war erupting from,

I won't say a subsidized press — they say there isn't one (*Hilarity*) — but at least from an official press.

That, Gentlemen, was the deplorable, humiliating spectacle that we presented to the world.

It is true, Gentlemen, that today all that noise has died down. Today, Marshal Bugeaud has his newspapers say that he is the most obedient of public officials; and yesterday you heard the minister of war assure you, in the government's name, that his was the most obeyed of governments.

What is all this, Gentlemen? I don't like to say the word, but this terribly resembles a parliamentary comedy. (*Various noises.*)

What is causing them now to calm down? It is not hard to say: at the approach of the Chambers, they discovered that it was as dangerous for one as for the other to seem to be at war, and that, consequently, it was a wise measure for both parties to seem to be at peace. Are they really, Gentlemen? Not at all. Do you know, Gentlemen, why no one in Africa disobeys any more? The reason is quite simple: because they are hardly commanded at all any more.

On the left. — That's it! That's it!

M. DE TOCQUEVILLE — There is at this moment a perfect balance between the governor-general and the government in France: one wants military colonization, and it must be recognized that this can't be done; the other wants civil colonization, and he can't achieve that either. In this manner, as I have just said, the two powers hold each other in check, and we peacefully achieve impotence. (*Approving laughs on the left.*)

Gentlemen, was I wrong to say, in beginning this speech, that what prevents us from succeeding in Africa is not a cause inherent in Africa? This is the cause: govern such an affair in the way I have just described, and you will achieve the same result.

Let us seek remedies, then. A great number have been indicated; and recently two committees of the Chamber have proposed a remedy for a situation that everyone, except the minister of war, recognizes as very bad. They conceived the idea of uniting the direction of all Algerian affairs in the same hands, to create what they called a special ministry.[12]

Gentlemen, I confess, even if my opinion on this point scandalizes a large number of this Chamber's members, that I am a partisan of the special ministry. I believe the plan to be very constitutional; I do not believe it to be a revolution, as one honorable speaker yesterday or this morning called it.[13] On the contrary, I believe it to be a return to methods followed by all peoples who have done great things for their colonies; and I can affirm to the Chamber that if in England, for example, it was proposed to Parliament to place Indian affairs or colonial affairs in another ministry than the ministry of the colonies, it would seem a far more extraordinary idea than a special ministry could seem in France. And indeed it would be.

For myself, I think that it is a good and useful plan to unite all these immense African affairs into the same hands: to personify the African affair, so to speak, in a politician, so that when the Chamber had something to complain of about the way things are handled in Africa, it could address this man directly. So that when the government needed to inquire about what is going on in Africa, it could address this man directly. And finally, so that this man could see his own future entirely engaged, personified, so to speak, in the success of this affair.

But, Gentlemen, I hope the Chamber will do me the justice to think that I do not attribute to any institution whatsoever such great, such preponderant efficacy that it could in some way do without men's daily efforts; no, I do not commit such a great error, such a ridiculous blunder. No, Gentlemen, there is something more necessary in the African affair than the creation of a special ministry, and that is this:

Until now we have witnessed this remarkable anomaly; we have seen an affair that, in everyone's mind, taken individually, one by one, on these benches, is the country's greatest task; an affair that affects it in the present, that threatens it in the future; an affair that in a word is, I repeat, in everyone's mind, at the forefront of all the interests France has in the world. And this affair, Gentlemen, ranks only second, third, perhaps fourth in the attention of those who govern it.

Yes, until now the government has always considered Africa a secondary object. Rather different things have preoccupied the government: schemes, sometimes of personal interest, sometimes of general interest, but inferior to this great general interest of which I speak. Africa has been given limited and incomplete attention; no statesman has tied his political fate to that of this great affair; no cabinet has deigned to compromise its existence for it. It is not surprising, then, that the affair, left to itself, so to speak, should become what you know it to be and what I have told you. As long as it is so, Gentlemen, do not hope for anything.

Will this always be the case, Gentlemen? Once (perhaps the opposition will find me credulous), once I thought that the government, or rather the men in the government who put their hearts above their politics (*Movement*), that those men, tired of our internal and external affairs, would want to go abroad to create a great theater for their glory. I believed it, and if this supposition was once founded, perhaps it still is. But if it was, without ceasing to fight men in their internal and external politics, I believed that the first of all my duties, and the foremost duty of every decent man in this Chamber, was to grant them, on the neutral terrain of Africa, the most energetic and sincere support.

But, Gentlemen, what I once believed, I now doubt. (*Listen! listen!*) I have doubts, I say no more, but I stand by the word.

Why do I have doubts? Because of signs that seem to herald them: when I see a measure that I thought had come from the very soul of the governors fought publicly in pages that generally represent the government, when I see things I thought people disapprove of, things I thought they disapproved of secretly, praised publicly; when I hear that a resignation offered by Marshal Bugeaud was not accepted,[14] I cannot help supposing that Marshal Bugeaud is left in Africa far less for the good one expects from him there than for the evil that might be feared of him here in Paris. (*Objections in the center.*)

M. VATOUT. — What trouble do you mean he would cause in Paris?

M. DE TOCQUEVILLE. — From the ministerial point of view, of course, it's clear!

When, finally, I heard the minister of war come here yesterday to tell us that everything is going well in Africa, to paint us that fantastic portrait of the prosperity there is in Africa, I admit that I had trouble recognizing in him the feelings I believed existed in the government. Suspicion slipped into my mind, and before regaining my confidence, I await the future.

If this doubt, Gentlemen, is not verified, if I have been mistaken in my judgment, if what I believed to be true is an error, I shall be the first to bring excuses to this podium. But if I am not wrong, if all this noise has in fact been nothing but an expedient, and the most miserable of expedients, to escape the question's difficulties in the Chamber; if, after you have stated your decree, this immense African question sinks as usual back into oblivion, if it becomes once again the secondary and forgotten portion of governmental action, I shall say then, and I say from today that this conduct will have deserved the reproval and scorn of all good citizens. (*Numerous signs of approval from the left. The speaker receives congratulations from several of his colleagues.*)

FIRST REPORT ON ALGERIA (1847)

REPORT BY M. DE TOCQUEVILLE ON THE BILL ON
SPECIAL FUNDING REQUESTED FOR ALGERIA

Object and outline of the report.[1] Contrary to custom, gentlemen, this year the Chamber has appointed eighteen members instead of nine to the committee on special funding for Africa.[2] In taking such an exceptional measure, it undoubtedly wanted to express a thought whose true meaning your committee has had to investigate carefully.

Never has our domination in Africa seemed threatened by fewer dangers than at this moment. Submission in the greatest part of the country, following a war conducted ably and gloriously;[3] friendly or peaceful relations with our neighbors the Muslim princes; Abd-el-Kader reduced to committing acts of barbarity, which attest to his impotence even more than to his cruelty;[4] Kabylia disposed to recognize our authority; the instigator of the last insurrection reduced to putting himself into our hands and appealing to our generosity, after vainly having tried to resist our force:[5] such is the state of our affairs today.

It is thus not with the intention of averting danger that the Chamber has sought a more solemn inquiry into the question of Africa this year. On the contrary, we can say that, in the Chamber's eyes, it is the recent success of our arms and the resulting peace that have created a new situation and call for new resolutions.[6]

The long war that carried our flags throughout the old regency and showed us indigenous people in all aspects and situations, led us not only to conquer territories, but also to acquire entirely new, or more accurate, notions about the country and its inhabitants. One can study barbarous people only with arms in hand. We conquered the Arabs before knowing them. It is victory that, establishing numerous and necessary connections between them and us, led us to penetrate their customs, their ideas, their beliefs, and finally yielded the secret of how to govern them. We have made surprising progress in this direction. Today, indeed, indigenous society has been unveiled to us. The army showed no less intelligence and perspicacity when it came to studying the conquered people than it showed brilliant courage and patient, tranquil energy in subjecting them to our arms. Not only did it enable us to learn about the reigning ideas among the Arabs, to come to know the general facts that influence their public spirit and bring about their great events, but we were also able to delve into the details of secondary matters. We have recognized and explained the various elements that make up the indigenous population; the history of the different tribes is practically as well known to us as to themselves; we have accurate biographies of all the powerful families; finally, we know where the real influences lie. For the first time, we can thus find and declare, with certainty and assurance, the true and natural limits of our domination in Africa, what must be the normal state of our forces there for a long time to come, the instruments we need and the appropriate form of administration for the peoples who live there, what we may hope of them, and what it is wise to fear.

As we get to know the country and the indigenous people better, the utility and even the necessity of establishing a European population on African soil seem clearer to us.

Moreover, in this matter the choice is no longer ours to make.

The European population has arrived; civilized and Christian society has been founded. Now our only task is to know under what laws it must live and what must be done to hasten its development.

The time has also come to study this great side of the African question more closely and in greater detail than we have yet been able to do. Everything is on our side: our experience of the flaws in the actual state of affairs, the greater knowledge we have of the country and of its needs, the peace that allows us to devote ourselves to such a study without fear, and that will make it easy and fruitful.

Our domination over the indigenous people, its limits, its means, its principles.

The administration of Europeans, its forms and rules.

Colonization, its location, its conditions, its procedures.

These are the three great problems raised by the two bills that have been submitted to you, and whose solution the Chamber has asked us to present.

In the present report, we shall treat all the questions directly connected to the domination of the conquered country, and to the administration of the Europeans who inhabit it.

We shall examine all the questions of colonization in the report on the law of the agricultural camps.

PART I

Ruling and Governing the Indigenous Peoples

Is the domination we exercise in the territory of the old regency of Algiers useful for France?

Several members of your committee vigorously argued in the negative.[8]

The majority, gentlemen, with utter and deserved respect for the long-standing and very sincere convictions expressed by the honorable members, and acknowledging their opinion, did not believe it necessary once again to raise before you questions so often debated and long since settled.

We thus submit, as a demonstrated truth, that our domination in Africa should be firmly maintained. We limit ourselves to studying what that domination is today, what are its true limits and what is required to strengthen it.

Distribution of the indigenous population on the land. Its general appearance from the point of view of our domination. From the point of view of our domination, the indigenous population of Algeria should be divided into three principal groups: the first lives in the vast country generally known by the name Petit-Désert,[9] which extends to the south through the end of the workable land at the edge of the Sahara.

Petit-Désert. The Chamber knows that the inhabitants of this country are at once more nomadic and more sedentary than most of the other indigenous people of Algeria. The majority travel across immense spaces every year without, so to speak, recognizing any territory. The others live at oases, where property is individual, delimited, cultivated, and built upon. Our troops have not inspected all of the Petit-Désert; they occupy none of it. We govern the population that lives there through the mediation of the indigenous leaders, whom we supervise only from a great distance; the population obeys us without knowing us; they are really our tributaries and not our subjects.[10]

Independent Kabylia. Opposite the Petit-Désert, in the mountains along the sea, live the independent Kabyles. Until now we have never crossed their territory, but now, surrounded on all sides by our settlements, constrained in their industries, blocked into narrow valleys, these peoples are beginning to submit to our influence and are said to be ready to recognize our power.

The Tell. The rest of the inhabitants of Algeria, Arabs and Berbers, spread across the plains or on the mountains of the Tell, from the frontiers of Morocco to those of Tunisia, form the third population group that remains to be mentioned.

This is the part of the country where the towns are located, where the largest tribes live, and where you find the most fertile, best irrigated, and most habitable land. This is where the principal military expeditions and the large battles have occurred. Finally, this is where we have our large settlements and where our domination is not merely recognized, but stable.

Today this vast territory is at peace — a most profound peace; our troops cross it in every direction without encountering the least resistance. Even the isolated European can cross most of it without fearing any danger.[11]

Here there is submission everywhere; but it is not everywhere of the same character.

Division of the Tell into two distinct regions. To the east, our domination is perhaps less complete than to the west, but infinitely more tranquil and secure. In general, we administer the indigenous people in the east less closely and less directly, but our supremacy is less contested there. Many indigenous leaders in the east are our feudatories rather than our agents: our power is at once less absolute and more secure. An army of 20,000 to 22,000 men is enough to guard this part of the country, which nonetheless forms half of all the old regency, and which includes more than half the inhabitants. War has been almost unknown there for several years.[12]

The populations of the west, those who occupy the provinces of Algiers and Oran, are more dominated, more governed, more subjected, and at the same time more agitated. Our power over them is greater and less stable. There, the war routed everyone able to resist, violently shattered all the resistance we had encountered, exhausted the country, diminished its inhabitants, partly destroyed or drove out its military or religious nobility, and for a time deprived the indigenous people of any power. There, submission is at once complete and precarious; it is where three-quarters of our army is amassed.

To the east as well as to the west, our domination is accepted only as the work of victory and is the daily product of force. But in the east this is tolerated, whereas we are still only subjugating the west. In the former, it is understood that our power can have certain useful results that make it less onerous; in the latter, the only reason for submitting is the profound terror our power inspires.

Such is the general appearance that Algeria presents from the point of view of our domination.

Maintenance of military strength. In the face of this scene, gentlemen, in view of this state of affairs, which is satisfying as a whole but precarious in several of its parts, should we maintain the strength of our army as it is?

Two members have requested that the force be diminished, because, in their view, our occupation must be restrained; others thought that, without exposing our domination and without restraining our occupation, it would be possible to decrease the current size of our army by several thousand men.

The committee, while expressing the wish to decrease the force, did not, however, believe that it would be wise to refuse the government the 94,000 men it requests, for the government alone knows the facts perfectly and bears responsibility for their consequences.[13]

As a result, the committee proposes to grant the funds appropriated by the bill.

Reasons that suggest that a force of 94,000 must suffice from now on. Your committee, gentlemen, did not decide to propose the maintenance of the force, without having examined the consequences and the import of this resolution with great care; it asked itself whether the proposed figure of 94,000 was still a provisional figure that, like so many others, would soon rise.

The committee has not forgotten, any more than you have, the gradual and incessant increases the African army has experienced in the past seventeen years. In 1831, the French forces had no more than 18,000 men of all types of service; in 1834 this rose to 30,000; in 1838 to 48,000; in 1841 to 70,000; in 1843 to 76,000; in 1845 to 83,000; and in 1846 to 101,000.

Must this progression continue? Does the figure asked of us represent, as it did in the past, a provisional evaluation? Does it indicate a final level? It is important to know that, not only in France's interest but also in Algeria's. What exhausts the country, what could in the long term cause it to be disgusted with its conquest, is less the burden of expenses the army imposes than the uncertainty about its probable or possible extent.

We believe the time has come to clarify these doubts, and we shall attempt to do so.

If the African army is to expand, it is necessary to accept one of two things: either that our occupation will extend further still or that, within its current limits, our forces are insufficient to assure the continuation of our domination. Let us examine these two hypotheses.

Why our domination must not extend any further. It is undoubtedly very difficult, we must recognize, to know where to stop in the occupation of a barbarous land. As you ordinarily encounter neither constituted governments nor stable populations, you hardly ever obtain a respected frontier. The war that pushes back the limits of your territory settles nothing; it merely lays the ground for a further and more difficult arena for a new war. For a long time, this is how the situation has appeared in Algeria itself. A conquest never failed to demonstrate the necessity of a new conquest; each occupation led to a new occupation. You can well imagine that the nation, seeing the gradual and continual extension of our domination and sacrifices, should sometimes be alarmed, and that even the friends of our conquest should have wondered worriedly when it would finally reach its extreme limits and where the number of troops would stop growing.

These feelings and ideas grew out of the profound ignorance in which we lived for so long regarding the nature of the country we had undertaken to dominate. We knew neither how far it was appropriate to go nor where it was not only useful but necessary to stop.

Today we can say that light has been shed on both these points.

Let us simply remind the Chamber that Algeria presents that bizarre phenomenon of a land divided into two countries that are completely different from one another, but nonetheless united by a close and indissoluble tie. One, the Petit-Désert, contains nomadic shepherds; the other, the Tell, is the home of relatively sedentary farmers. Everyone now knows that the Petit-Désert cannot survive if the Tell is closed off from it. Thus, from the beginning of the world, the master of the Tell has been the master of the Petit-Désert; he has always commanded it without occupying it, governed it without administering it. Today, we occupy, other than Kabylia, the entire Tell; why should we occupy the Petit-Désert? Why should we do more or other than the Turks, who ruled there in this way for three hundred years? The interest of colonization does not force us to establish ourselves there, because we cannot dream of settling European populations in these areas.

Thus we can say, without misleading anyone, that from now on, the natural limit of our occupation in the south is certain. It is set at the edge of the Tell itself.[14]

It is true that within the borders of the Tell, there is an area that we have not yet occupied, and whose occupation would not fail to augment considerably the strength of our army and the size of our budget. We mean independent Kabylia.

The Chamber will permit us not to expand at this moment on the question of Kabylia; we shall have occasion to speak of it later, when we describe an incident that happened in the committee itself. We shall limit ourselves to establishing here, as a certain fact, that there are particular and peremptory reasons not to occupy Kabylia.[15]

Thus, we are justified in saying that today the true and natural limits of our occupation are set.

How we came to know the best means by which to dominate the country. Let us now see whether it can also be said that within these limits, the forces we possess today will be sufficient from now on.

Experience has not only shown us where the natural setting of war was; it has taught us how to fight. It has shown us the strong and the weak among our adversaries. It has shown us the means of defeating them, and, after having defeated them, of remaining their masters. Today we can say that war in Africa is a science whose laws are known to everyone and that can be applied almost with certainty. One of the greatest services that Marshal Bugeaud has rendered his country is to have extended this new science, perfected it, and made it clear to all.

First, we came to understand that we faced not a real army, but the population itself. The perception of this first truth soon led us to another: given that this population would be as hostile to us as they are today, in order for us to remain in such a country, our troops would have to be almost as numerous in times of peace as in times of war, for it was less a matter of defeating a government than of subjugating a people.

Experience has also taught us the means we must use to subjugate the Arab people. Thus, we quickly discovered that the populations that rejected our rule were not nomads, as we had long thought, but only much more mobile than Europeans. Each had its well-defined territory, from which it did not easily stray, and to which it was obliged to return. If we could not occupy the inhabitants' houses, we could thus seize harvests, capture herds, and arrest people.

From there, the true conditions of war in Africa appeared.

It was no longer a matter, as in Europe, of assembling huge armies destined to operate en masse against similar armies, but to cover the country with small, light corps that could overtake populations on the run, or who, placed next to their territory, would force them to remain there and live in peace.

To make the troops as mobile as possible and always to keep them within range of suspect populations: these were the two aspects of the problem.

We first gave up almost everything that encumbers soldiers' marches in Europe. We almost entirely abolished the cannon; for carts, we substituted camels or mules. Storage outposts, placed at distant intervals, allowed the soldiers to carry very few or no provisions with them. Our officers learned Arabic, studied the country, and led columns there without hesitation and without going astray. As speed achieved far more than numbers, the columns themselves were composed only of selected soldiers already inured to fatigue. We thus attained an almost incredible speed of movement. Today our troops, as mobile as the armed Arab, move more quickly than a tribe on the march.

At the same time that we were making the troops so mobile, we were seeking and finding the most useful places to billet them. War allowed us to distinguish the most energetic, the best organized, the most hostile populations. We settled among or near these last in order to prevent or suppress their revolts.

The entire Tell is now covered by our outposts, as if by an immense net whose mesh, tightly woven in the west, will loosen to the degree that it extends to the east. In the Tell of the Oran province, the average distance between all the outposts is twenty leagues. As a result, there is hardly a tribe that could not be seized on the same day from four sides at once, at the first movement it chose to make.

Whether the outposts are all placed where they should be to provide the best service is still open to debate (we shall discuss this question with regard to special appropriations); it is worth investigating whether it would not be appropriate to increase the strength of some of them by decreasing that of others. But we are agreed that the strength of the African army largely suffices for the organization of all the necessary outposts, and we are sure always to remain masters of the country conquered today. This truth, gentlemen, is important, and it was worth taking the trouble to prove it.

We do not want to exaggerate our point. We do not pretend to say that with the aid of current forces, Algeria could fight against all the perils that might grow out of a foreign war, nor even that it is safe from the fatal effects that might be produced by the passions or faults of those who will govern from now on. If we undertook futile expeditions and settlements in the Petit-Désert, it is probable that our forces, however considerable they may be, would have difficulty sufficing. If, contrary to the wishes expressed repeatedly by the Chambers, and, we may say, contrary to the light of experience and reason, we undertook military occupation of independent Kabylia, instead of limiting ourselves to possession of its outlets, it is incontestable that we soon would have to increase the size of our army; finally, if through bad government, by violent or tyrannical behavior, we pushed the populations who live peacefully under our empire to despair and revolt, we assuredly would require . new soldiers. We have not attempted to prove otherwise. There is no physical force, however large, that could allow men to dispense with moderation and good sense. It is the government's task, not ours, to prevent such missteps. All we want to say is this: for a long time we have not known what were the true limits of our domination and our occupation in Africa. Today they are known. For a long time we had no accurate notions about the type and the number of obstacles that we might meet at these limits; today we do. For a long time we could wonder with the aid of what forces, by what means, according to what method, we could be sure to defeat the natural and permanent difficulties of our enterprise; today we see them clearly. Current forces, even if they could not, perhaps, satisfy the factitious and momentary needs created by ambition and violence, should respond largely to all the natural and habitual needs of our domination in Africa. A very attentive and detailed study of the question has profoundly convinced the majority of the committee.

By what means can we gradually diminish our forces? But we do not want to stop there; we desired to study what steps we could take gradually to decrease these forces and finally to reduce them to much smaller proportions, without putting our settlement in danger.

Several members thought that perhaps it would be possible to distribute the troops in such a manner as to produce the same effects with fewer numbers. Others have said that settlement and the perfection of the roads would facilitate our domination powerfully and would allow us to decrease the size of the army. We return, in another part of the report, to this crucial question of the roads. We do not deny, gentlemen, that these means would be very effective; we believe that their judicious use would allow us notably to diminish our army; but we do not believe that it would suffice.

In our view, it would be an illusion to believe that, by a new organization of the physical forces, or in making these forces more mobile, we could bring about a very great decrease in the size of our army. The art of the conqueror would be too simple and too easy if it consisted only of discovering such secrets and surmounting difficulties of this type. The real and permanent obstacle that stands in the way of the decrease of the forces, we must recognize, is the indigenous people's attitude toward us.

What are the means of modifying these attitudes? By what form of government, with the aid of which agents, by what principles, by what conduct, can we hope to achieve this? Here, gentlemen, are the real and serious questions that the subject of the reduction of troops raises.

Structure of indigenous government. In fact, the system that we follow to govern the country that has submitted to us, although somewhat varied in the details, is the same everywhere. Different indigenous officials, established or recognized by us, administer, under various names, the Muslim populations; they are intermediaries between them and us.[16] According to whether these indigenous leaders are near to or far from the center of our power, we submit them to a more or less detailed surveillance, and we become more or less closely involved in monitoring their activities; but almost no part of the tribes are administered by us directly. It is our generals who govern; their principal agents are the officers of the Arab bureaus. No institution has been more useful in our domination in Africa than the Arab bureaus.[17] Several of the Chamber's committees have already said this, and we are pleased to repeat it.

This system, which was partly founded, organized, and generalized by Marshal Bugeaud, rests entirely on a small number of principles we believe to be wise.

1) Everywhere, political power, that which gives the primary impulse to affairs, should be in the hands of the French. Such an initiative can in no part be securely relinquished to the indigenous leaders. This is the first principle.

2) Here is the second: most of the secondary powers of the government should, on the contrary, be exercised by the inhabitants of the country.

3) The third maxim of government is this: our power must seek to rely on already existing influences. We have often tried, and we still sometimes try, to remove the religious or military aristocracy of the country from affairs to substitute new families, and create influences that are our own doing. We have

almost always failed in such efforts, and it is easy to see, in fact, how premature such efforts are. A new government, and especially a conquering government, can easily give physical power to its friends, but it cannot transfer moral power and force of opinion that it does not have itself. All it can do is to interest those who have this force and power in serving it.[18]

We believe these three maxims of government to be just in their generality; but we think that they have true value only in the wise and able application made of them. We understand that they must be rejected or adhered to according to places, circumstances, and men. That is the natural field of the executive power; there would be neither dignity nor utility for the Chamber in trying to enter into it more deeply than we have just done.

But if the Chamber cannot undertake to indicate in advance and in a permanent and detailed way what should be the structure of our government in indigenous affairs and which agents it is appropriate to use, the Chamber has not only the right but the duty to study and say what the spirit should be, and what permanent goal should be proposed.

What the general spirit of our government with regard to the indigenous people should be. If in a single glance we envision our conduct toward the indigenous people up to now, we cannot fail to note that we meet with great inconsistencies. We see quite different appearances depending on time and place; we pass from the extreme of benevolence to that of rigor.

In certain places, instead of reserving the most fertile, best-irrigated, best-prepared lands of the territory for the Europeans, we have given these to the indigenous peoples.

Our respect for their beliefs was pushed so far that, in certain places we built them mosques before building churches for ourselves; each year, the French government (doing what even the Muslim prince who preceded us in Algiers did not do) provides free transport to Egypt for pilgrims who wish to visit the tomb of the Prophet.[19] We have bestowed on Arabs the honorific distinctions designed to recognize the merit of our citizens.[20] We often received the indigenous peoples, after betrayals and revolts, with a remarkable forbearance; we have seen those who, the day after they had abandoned us to go bathe their hands in our blood, get back their estates, their honors, and their power. What is more, in many places where the European civilian population is mixed with the indigenous population, it is complained, and not without some reason, that in general it is the indigenous person who is better protected, and the European who has more difficulty obtaining justice.[21]

[handwritten marginal note:] Tocqueville complains that natives are more respected and better protected than Europeans.

If these scattered traits are collected, one will be drawn to conclude that our government in Africa pushes gentleness toward the conquered to the point of forgetting its position as conqueror, and that in the interest of its foreign subjects, it does more than it would do in France for the well-being of its citizens.[22]

Let us return now to the portrait and look at the reverse side.

The indigenous towns were invaded, turned upside down, and sacked by our administration even more than by our arms. A great number of individual properties were, in time of total peace, ravaged, disfigured, destroyed. Numerous property titles that we had taken in order to verify them were never returned. In the vicinity of Algiers itself, the very fertile areas were torn from the hands of the Arabs and given to Europeans who, not being able or not wanting to cultivate them themselves, rented them to these same indigenous people, who thus became the mere farmers of the domains that had belonged to their fathers. Elsewhere, tribes or factions of tribes that were not hostile to us, or even more who had fought with us and sometimes without us, were pushed off their territory. We accepted conditions we did not fulfill, we promised indemnities we did not pay, thus allowing our honor to suffer even more than the interests of these indigenous peoples. Not only have we already taken a great deal of land from the former owners, but, what is worse, we left the idea hanging over the entire Muslim population that in our eyes possession of the soil and the situation of those who live on it are pending questions that will be settled as necessary and following a rule we still have not worked out.

Muslim society in Africa was not uncivilized; it was merely a backward and imperfect civilization. There existed within it a large number of pious foundations, whose object was to provide for the needs of charity or for public instruction. We laid our hands on these revenues everywhere, partly diverting them from their former uses; we reduced the charitable establishments and let the schools decay, we disbanded the seminaries.* Around us knowledge has

---

* In an excellent memoir, which the minister of war recommended to the committee, General Bedeau explains that in the town of Constantine at the time of the conquest, in 1837, there were secondary and superior schools where 600 to 700 students studied different commentaries on the Koran, learned all the traditions relating to the Prophet and, what is more, took courses whose purpose was to teach arithmetic, astronomy, rhetoric, and philosophy. In addition, in Constantine at about the same time, there were 90 primary schools, attended by 1,300 or 1,400 children. Today, the number of young people who pursue higher studies has been reduced to 60, the number of primary schools to 30, and the number of children who attend these to 350.[23]

been extinguished, and recruitment of men of religion and men of law has ceased; that is to say, we have made Muslim society much more miserable, more disordered, more ignorant, and more barbarous than it had been before knowing us.

It is undoubtedly good to use indigenous people as agents of the government, but on condition that we guide them according to the sentiments of civilized men and with French maxims. This has not happened always or everywhere, and we can be accused sometimes less of having civilized the indigenous administration than of having lent its barbarity the forms and intelligence of Europe.

Sometimes theories have joined actions. Various writings have professed this doctrine: that the indigenous population, having arrived at the utmost degree of depravity and vice, is forever incapable of any amendment and of all progress; that, far from enlightening them, we must rather end by depriving them of the knowledge they possess; that, far from settling them on the soil, we must push them little by little off the territory in order to settle in their place; that by waiting we have asked nothing of them but to remain in submission, and that there is only one means of obtaining their submission, which is to repress them by force.

We believe, gentlemen, that such doctrines merit the highest degree not merely of public reprobation but of the official censure of the government and the Chambers; for it is such ideas that the facts will eventually breed.

We must avoid the two excesses that have been mentioned. We have just described two excesses; the majority of your committee believe that our government must carefully avoid falling into one or the other.

There is neither utility in allowing, nor a duty to allow, our Muslim subjects exaggerated ideas of their own importance, nor to persuade them that we are obligated to treat them under all circumstances precisely as though they were our fellow citizens and our equals. They know that we have a dominant position in Africa; they expect to see us keep it. To abandon it today would be to astonish and confuse them, and to fill them with erroneous or dangerous notions.

Half-civilized peoples have difficulty understanding forbearance and indulgence; they understand nothing but justice. Exact, but rigorous, justice should be our sole rule of conduct toward the indigenous population when they act reprehensibly toward us.

What we owe them at all times is good government. By this, we mean a power that guides them, not only toward our interest, but in theirs; that shows itself to be truly attentive to their needs and sincerely seeks to provide for them; that is concerned for their well-being; that looks to their rights; that works ardently for the continual development of their imperfect societies; that does not believe itself to have completed its task when it has obtained submission and taxes; that governs them, finally, and does not restrict itself to exploiting them.

It would undoubtedly be as dangerous as it would useless to seek to suggest to them our mores, our ideas, our customs [*usages*]. It is not along the road of our European civilization that they must, for the present, be pushed, but in the direction proper to them; we must demand of them things that suit their ways, and not those contrary to them. Individual property, industry, and sedentary dwelling are in no way contrary to the religion of Muhammad. Arabs know or have known these things elsewhere; they are known and appreciated by some in Algeria itself. Why do we despair of making them familiar to a greater number? This has already been attempted in some places with success.* Islam is not absolutely impenetrable to enlightenment: it has often admitted certain sciences or certain arts into itself. Why do we not seek to make these flourish in our empire? Let us not force the indigenous peoples to come to our schools, but help them rebuild theirs, multiply the number of teachers, and create men of law and men of religion, which Muslim civilization cannot do without, any more than our own can.

Public instruction among the indigenous population. The religious passions that the Koran inspires are hostile, people say, and it is good to let them die out in superstition and ignorance, for want of jurists and priests. It would be committing a great imprudence to attempt this. When religious passions exist among a people, men are always found who take it upon themselves to make

* Already a great number of important men, desiring to please us, or profiting from the security that we have given the country, have built houses and live in them. In this way the greatest indigenous leader of the province of Oran, Sidi el-Aribi,[24] has already built a home. His coreligionists burned it during the last insurrection. He built it again. Several others have followed this example, among other the bachagha of Djendel, Bou Allem,[25] in the province of Algiers. In that of Constantine, great indigenous owners have already imitated in part our agricultural methods and adopted several of our tools. The caid of the Bône plains, Caresi, cultivates his land with the aid of European labor and intelligence. We cite these facts, not as proof of the great results already obtained, but as hopeful indices of what might with time be obtained.[26]

use of these and to lead them. Allow the natural and regular interpreters of religion to disappear, and you do not suppress religious passions, you merely cede control to fanatics or impostors. It is already known that there are fanatic mendicants, belonging to secret societies, a sort of irregular and ignorant clergy, who have enflamed the spirit of the populations in the last insurrection and who brought about the war.[27]

How we should proceed regarding land. But the vital question for our government is that of land. What, in this matter, is our right, our interest, and our duty? In conquering Algeria, we did not intend, like the barbarians who invaded the Roman Empire, to take possession of the territory of the conquered.[28] We had as our sole goal to take control of the government. The capitulation of Algiers in 1830 was drafted according to this principle. The town surrendered to us, and in return we assured all the inhabitants of the preservation of religion and property. We have since treated all the tribes who have submitted on the same footing. Does it follow that we cannot take possession of the lands necessary to European colonization? Undoubtedly not; but it strictly obliges us, for the sake of justice and good policy, to indemnify those who own them or enjoy their use.

Experience has shown that this could easily be done, either in concessions of rights, or in an exchange of lands, without costing anything, or for a little money. We shall explain this in much more detail elsewhere; all we want to say here is that it is important for our security, as well as for our honor, to show a real respect for indigenous property and truly to persuade our Muslim subjects that we do not mean to take away any part of their patrimony without indemnity, or, what would be even worse, to obtain it with the aid of deceitful and derisory transactions in which violence takes on the guise of purchase, and fear the appearance of sale.

We should strengthen the tribes' ties to their territory, rather than transport them elsewhere. In general such a measure is impolitic, as it has the effect of isolating the two races from each other and, in keeping them separate, leaving them enemies. It is, in addition, very harsh, however one chooses to execute it.*

---

* Starting with the notion that the Arab populations are, if not entirely nomadic, at least mobile, it was too easily concluded that one could at will, and without too much violence, move them about; this is a great error. The transplantation of a tribe from one area to another, when it has not chosen to move voluntarily in return for very

The indigenous population has the greatest need of tutelage at the moment when it manages to mix with our civilian population and finds itself, partly or completely, subjected to our officials and our laws. It is not just violent behavior that must be feared. Civilized peoples often oppress and dispirit barbarous peoples by their mere contact, without intending to and, so to speak, without knowing it: the same rules of administration and justice that seem to the European to be guarantees of liberty and property, seem an intolerable oppression to the barbarian; the delays that irritate us exasperate them; the forms that we call tutelary, they call tyrannical, and they would rather withdraw than submit to them. This is how, without recourse to the sword, the Europeans in North America ended by pushing the Indians off of their territory. We must take care that it is not the same for us.

The property transactions between Arabs and Europeans must not be free. It has been said as well that wherever uncontrolled property transactions are allowed between barbarian proprietors and civilized Europeans, land passes rapidly and cheaply from the former's hands into the latter's, and the indigenous population ceases to have any roots in the soil. If we don't want to produce such an effect, we must everywhere prevent transactions of this sort from being completely free. We shall see elsewhere that this is no less necessary for the European than for the Arab.

---

great political privileges (such as was the case with the Makhzen populations); such a measure has always seemed, even in the time of the Turks, extremely harsh, and was taken very rarely. Only a few examples can be cited during the last century of Ottoman domination, and these examples occurred only at the end of long wars and repeated insurrections, such as those of the great tribe of the Righas, who were transported from the vicinity of Miliana to that of Oran.

The story of this tribe of the Righas merits the attention of the Chamber in several respects. It shows at once how difficult it is to displace tribes, how powerful the feeling for individual property is, and how sacred individual property is.

The Turks, tired of the incessant revolts that they had put down among the Righas, one day surrounded the whole tribe, transported them to lands owned by the Beylik in the province of Oran, and allowed the neighboring tribes to occupy their territory. The tribe of the Righas, dispossessed in this way, continued for 50 years to entreat the Turkish government to grant them permission to return to their country. They were finally granted it. The Righas returned at the end of this half-century and retook possession of their territory; what is more, the families who had long ago owned particular bits of land brought with them their titles and reestablished themselves exactly on the properties that their fathers had cultivated.

We have cited some facts, made allusion to circumstances. The Chamber should not mistake our intention: in doing so, we have not attempted either to enter into a special examination of any measure or to judge any measure in particular. The summary nature of this report does not permit it. We merely wanted the Chamber to understand the permanent tendency and the general spirit of our government.

What effects we can hope to produce on the indigenous people through good government. What will be the probable effect of the conduct we advise toward the indigenous population? Where does permissible hope in this matter end? Where does the chimera begin?

There is no government so wise, so benevolent, and so just that it can suddenly bring together and intimately unite populations whose history, religion, laws, and practices are so profoundly divided. It would be dangerous and almost puerile to think that we could. We believe it would even be imprudent to think that we can manage easily and in so little time to destroy in the heart of the indigenous populations the blind hatred created and sustained by foreign domination. It is thus necessary, whatever our conduct, to remain strong. This should always be our first rule.

What can be hoped for is, not to suppress the hostile sentiments that our government inspires, but to weaken them; not to make our yoke liked, but to make it seem more and more tolerable; not to annihilate the repugnance that Muslims have always displayed for a foreign and Christian power, but to make them discover that this power, despite an origin they condemn, can be useful to them. It would be unwise to believe that we shall manage to tie ourselves to the indigenous population through the community of ideas and practices, but we may hope to do so through the community of interests.

We already see this type of connection forming in several places. If our arms have decimated certain tribes, there are others whom our commerce has enriched and strengthened considerably, and who feel and understand this. Everywhere the prices that the indigenous people can get for their wares and their labor have increased greatly by our presence. In addition, our agriculturalists gladly make use of indigenous manpower. The European needs the Arab to make his lands valuable; the Arab needs the European to obtain a high salary. In this way, two men so widely separated by education and origins are naturally brought together in the same field, and united in the same inevitable conclusion, by their interests.

It is in this direction, toward this goal, that we must move, gentlemen.

The committee is convinced that the future of our domination in Africa, the size of our army, and the fate of our finances depend above all on our manner of treating the indigenous population; for in this matter questions of humanity and budget are joined and mingled. The committee believes that, in the long run, a good government can lead to real pacification and a very notable diminution in our army.

If on the contrary we were to demonstrate by our behavior — without saying so, for these things are often done but never admitted — that in our eyes the old inhabitants of Algeria are merely an obstacle to be pushed aside or trampled underfoot, if we surrounded their populations, not to lift them in our arms toward well-being and enlightenment but to destroy and smother them, the question between the two races would be that of life or death. Sooner or later, Algeria would become a closed field, a walled arena, where the two peoples would have to fight without mercy, and where one of the two would have to die. May God save us, gentlemen, from such a destiny!

Let us not, in the middle of the nineteenth century, begin the history of the conquest of America over again. Let us not imitate the bloody examples that the opinion of the human race has stigmatized. Let us bear in mind that we would be a thousand times less excusable than those who once had the misfortune of setting such examples; for we are less fanatical, and we have the principles and the enlightenment the French Revolution spread throughout the world.

Slavery in Africa. France does not only have free men among its Muslim subjects. Algeria also contains a very small number of Negro slaves. Should we allow slavery to continue on soil we control? One of the neighboring Muslim princes, the bey of Tunis, has declared that servitude has been abolished in his empire. Can we, in this matter, do less than he?

Surely you know, gentlemen, that slavery among the Muhammadans is not the same as slavery in our colonies. Throughout the Orient, this odious institution has lost some of its rigor. But in becoming less harsh, it has not become less contrary to the natural rights of humanity.

It is therefore desirable that we eradicate it, and the committee has expressed this desire most explicitly. Doubtless the abolition of slavery must proceed with caution and measure. We have reason to believe that if this is done, abolition will face no sustained resistance and will create no new perils.

This opinion has been expressed by several of the men who know the country well. The minister of war himself is in agreement with it.

PART II

Civil Administration — Governing the Europeans

Algeria is administratively divided into three territories: one, populated mostly by Europeans, is called the civil territory [*le territoire civil*]; another, populated by Europeans and Arabs, is called the mixed territory; and the third, where only indigenous people live or are supposed to live, is known as the Arab territory. The mixed and Arab territories are solely or principally administered by the military, and according to military regulations. Only the civil territory approximates French common law. We shall concern ourselves above all with this last, although it is by far the smallest of the three. It is on the civil territory that we create and establish European society; permanent regulations can govern it there. The Europeans who settle in the mixed territories, by contrast, are in an exceptional and temporary position. As their numbers increase and their interests become more varied and more respectable, they will demand and obtain the institutions of the civil territory, which will soon expand toward them. What happens in the civil territory is what must happen everywhere, bit by bit. It holds the majority of the Europeans in Algeria, and, in some sense, it holds the future of all of them. Its administration thus deserves our particular attention.

We ask the Chamber's permission to state that at this moment the Algerian administration properly speaking, that which has as its principal mission to settle and govern the European population in the country, functions only very imperfectly, that its machinery is remarkably complicated, its procedures very slow. Despite many officials, it is unproductive; often, despite a great deal of work, effort, and money, it performs poorly. Later we shall have occasion to clarify these truths with examples. For the moment, we limit ourselves to stating them. We believe that the Algerian administration's vices are among the principal causes of the missteps that have afflicted us in this country, and that administrative reform is the most pressing of all our needs today.

This fact stated thus, let us now examine the causes.

Administrative personnel. How much should be attributed to the poor selection of men? The committee is under no obligation to examine this question. It is a question of personnel, into which the Chamber should not enter. Here all the power, but also, you must understand, all the responsibility, lies with the government.

On this subject, we can say that it would be wise, before sending officials to govern Algeria, to prepare them for this task, or at least ensure that they have prepared themselves. A special school, or at the very least special examinations, would seem necessary to us. This is what the English have done in India.* The officials we send to Africa, by contrast, know almost nothing of the language, the customs, the history of the country they go to govern. What is more, they act in the name of an administration whose particular structure they have never studied, and they apply an exceptional legislation whose rules they know nothing about. How can we be surprised that they often are not up to the task?

We shall say nothing more about the personnel. We wish to inform the Chamber about the structure of the services itself.

No society has a greater natural need for certainty, simplicity, and swift administrative action than those founded in new lands. Their needs are almost always badly foreseen and pressing, requiring immediate and easy satisfaction. Faced with every kind of obstacle, people should be less constrained there by their government than anywhere else. What they want above all is security for the fruits of their labor and freedom to do the work itself.

We should have created for Africa, then, a governmental machine with simpler workings and prompter movements than the one we have in France.† We have done precisely the opposite. A rapid survey will prove this to the Chamber.

---

* Young men who hope to join the civil service in India are required to spend two years at a special college in England (called Haileybury College). There, they undertake all the particular studies that relate to their career, and at the same time, they acquire general ideas in public administration and political economy. They are given the most famous men as professors. Malthus taught a course of political economy at Haileybury, and Sir James Mackintosh taught law there.[29] Eight Asian languages are taught there. Students must pass an examination to leave. And that is not all. Once they have arrived in India, these young men are required to learn to speak and write fluently in two of the country's languages. Fifteen months after their arrival, another examination ascertains that they possess this knowledge, and if they fail this examination, they are sent back to Europe. But as soon as they have taken their place in the administration of the country, after so many tests, their position there is assured, their rights certain; their advancement is not entirely arbitrary. They rise by degrees, and according to rules known in advance, up to the highest positions.

† The centralization of affairs in Paris, were it not even more complete for Africa than for our departments in France, would already be a great problem. The very principle

Centralization of affairs in Paris. What is most striking about the rules that govern the Algerian administration is the extreme centralization in the metropole. To say that the centralization of government in Paris is just the same for Africa as for a department in France is to understate the case dramatically. It is easy to see that it extends much further and much deeper. In France, secondary officials can solve a great number of administrative questions on the spot. Also, prefects and mayors are intermediaries who can interrupt the course of things and make final decisions, subject to appeal. In Africa, municipal and departmental life do not exist at all; everything is controlled by the central authority and must wind up, sooner or later, in the center. The final budgets of

---

that, in this matter, should be maintained as protective in the territory of the kingdom becomes destructive in the colony. A single example will make this clear.

What could be more natural or more necessary than the rules established in France for the alienation or renting of state lands? Nothing, in this matter, can be done except by virtue of a law, an ordinance, or a ministerial act; in other words, it is always the central power that acts in one form or another. Rigorously apply the principles of this legislation to Africa, and you will suspend social life itself. The creation of a colony is not, properly speaking, anything but the continual alienation of state land in favor of private individuals who come to settle in the new country. It is understandable that the state that wants to colonize reserves for itself the right to fix the conditions and rules according to which the public domain will be granted or rented: in this matter, it is the law itself that should set the rules. It is entirely appropriate that the central power alone reserves the right to alienate in one blow a vast expanse of territory, but we should be permitted to say that it is unreasonable that someone in a colony seeking to sell or rent any parcel of land, however small, should have to apply to an authority of the metropole. For the disposition of land in a colony in favor of emigrants, we repeat, is the reason for the whole operation. To make this slow and difficult is more than to interfere with the social body: it is to prevent it from being born.

The commission for which Mr. Charles Buller was the reporter,[30] and that was sent, in 1838, to Canada, under the presidency of Lord Durham, to research the causes that prevented the population from developing as quickly as that of the United States, attributes as one of the principal causes the necessity placed on all emigrants who wished to settle in the colony of going to Quebec, the chief town of the province, to obtain title to their property, instead of obtaining it on the spot, as in the United States.

In Africa, one cannot buy or rent a meter of soil belonging to the state without a long inquiry that ends only upon reaching the minister of war.

A single exception was made to this rule, on behalf of the province of Oran. There, the local government was authorized to grant territory without ratification by

most of our towns are set in the department; but in Algeria the minister of war must authorize the most minor local expenditure. To tell the truth, and with only rare exceptions, all the public authority's actions in Africa, however trifling they may be, all the details of social existence, however paltry, are settled by the offices in Paris. This explains how it is that in the year 1846, the Algerian administration alone received 24,000 dispatches and sent more than 28,000. However great the zeal and activity demonstrated by this administration, and we recognize it willingly, such a concentration of affairs in the same place cannot help but slow down the operation of all services significantly.

As such a state of things is profoundly contrary to the country's current needs, it happens that at every instant, fact rebels against law, so to speak. The local government claims in license what we deny them in liberty; their independence, theoretically nonexistent, is often very great in practice; but it is an irregular, intermittent, confused, and poorly limited independence, one that interferes with good administration rather than facilitating it.

All affairs of whatever sort that begin in Africa end up in the Ministry of War; but, once there, they are divided and scattered among many hands. The official who controls administration, strictly speaking, for example, is a complete stranger to the political side and the general government of the country. None of these things, however, can be done well in ignorance of the others. The central power in France that governs Algeria would exercise much clearer and greater power if, in restraining its competence, it centralized its action more effectively.

There would be far fewer problems if the African issues that go to the Ministry of War never left the country and were solved immediately and

___

the minister, under certain conditions, and up to a certain limit, indicated in advance. All those who know the province of Oran believe that the great movement of emigration and colonization that has occurred in this part of Algeria is mainly because colonists who arrive are certain to be placed right away.

We believe we should call to the Chamber's attention to the report of the Canadian commission we have just mentioned, a useful document to consult. This report throws light not only on the question of Canada but on that of Algeria. The factors that will make colonization fail or succeed in a new country are so similar, whatever the country, that when you read what Mr. Buller has said about Canada, you might think he is speaking of Africa. The same faults produce the same mistakes. We find there, as in Algeria, the same misery of emigrants upon arrival, the disorder of property, the unplowed wastes, the absence of capital, the ruin of the poor who prematurely seek to become landowners, the speculation that leaves the soil barren ...

definitively; if issues were studied less, they would at least be solved more quickly. But this is not the case: many of them, before being settled by the minister of war, are examined, discussed, and debated by several of his colleagues. The principal public works are submitted to the royal council on Ponts et Chaussées, religious and legal affairs are ordinarily sent to the minister of justice, those of public instruction to the minister of that department. As a result, we have the inconvenience of having all services centralized in a single administration without any of its advantages.

Centralization of affairs in Algiers. After the excessive centralization in Paris, the greatest vice of the African administrative structure is excessive centralization in Algiers. Just as we have forced every matter of any kind that has to do with Algiers to end up in Paris, we have forced all African affairs to go through Algiers.

The two centralizations are equally complete; but they have different consequences. All matters, small or large, that are sent to Paris are at least handled and resolved, whereas when they arrive in Algiers, it is simply to be looked at. Not only are they not decided in Algiers, but a great number of them could not possibly be settled properly there.

Politically, Algeria forms a single indivisible unit; the government of indigenous tribes, the management of the army, and even more that of war, must all derive from a single line of thought. But the administrative unity of the three provinces, at least as to details, is a result of convention, a purely arbitrary conception, that exists only by the will of the legislator. It is not justified by proximity, since it is usually quicker to get from provincial capitals to Paris than to Algiers. Nor is it explained by community of interests, since each of the three provinces has a separate existence, special interests, and particular needs. These are hardly better known in Algiers than in Paris. Each one of them has real relations with France, but they hardly have any contact among themselves. This point is illustrated by the financial and industrial crisis that has struck Algiers and its dependent towns but has not affected Philippeville and Oran. The rate of interest hasn't varied in Oran, while in Algiers it has risen to an almost incredible level.

Why go to such effort to transport the provinces' administrative affairs, from the smallest to the largest, a long distance, to a place with such industrial and commercial problems?

The provinces' military managers, the directors of fortifications and artillery, and the quartermasters [*intendants*] correspond directly with the minister of war. This significantly accelerates and facilitates the service without destroying its unity. The civilian administration has not imitated this example: everything it might have to deal with is sent to Algiers from every spot it occupies; there they accumulate. Let us now explain how they are dealt with.

Organization of services in Algiers. It will surprise you to see to what extent we have abandoned this same principle of centralization that was so excessively abundant in the previous discussion.

Let us take a department of France for comparison, in order to understand it better.

There are numerous government officials. Some are concerned with providing for the society's general and unforeseen needs: that is the administration properly speaking. Others fill more specific functions: some are in charge of collecting taxes, others of constructing public works. Each of these officials reports to a different minister in Paris; but in the department all are subjected to central oversight and, in many respects, to a common leader — the prefect. This prefectural concentration of power [*unité*] is one of the most fortunate creations, and assuredly one of the most novel in the matter of public administration, that we owe to the genius of Napoleon.

Let us see what exists in Algiers to compare to this simple and powerful structure.

Centralization of the directors of the interior, finance, and public works. Instead of the single centralization of the prefect, three centralizations were created, those of the directors of the interior, of finances, and of public works.[31]

Each of these department heads has under him all the subordinate officials of the different services I have just named. He retains power and preliminary inquiry over all the affairs these men handle.

These three directors behave toward one another with an independence that is all the more anxious and caviling because their high place in the hierarchy gives them such an exalted idea of their dignity and power. Still, their agreement is continually necessary for the proper and prompt handling of affairs.*

---

* Again, if the sphere of activity of these three powerful figures had been outlined by a steady hand, each of them at least could act effectively in the sector assigned him. But their various responsibilities were determined so confusedly that often two directors, dealing at the same time with the same matter, hinder, duplicate, or cancel out each other's efforts. In the matter of colonization, for instance, it is the director of the

Centralization of the director-general of civil affairs. Above these three large administrations into which everything is centralized, a fourth has been placed to serve as a link among them: the department of civil affairs. The mission of the director-general of civil affairs is to guide the action of the three specialized directors toward a common goal: but he is powerless to do this. There are two reasons for this: first, he has been given no real power; the initiative for everything is reserved for the governor. On his own, the director-general can't take a position on issues or move anything forward: he listens, he examines, he receives, he transmits, he doesn't control anything, he can't even communicate with the executors except through intermediaries. If he had any real power, he would have even more trouble exercising it over three officials placed almost as high as he is in the hierarchy and armed, as he is, with centralized authority. Thus, for the moment, all relations between them and him have led only to conflicts.[32]

Centralization of the governor-general. Above all these superimposed centralizations, there is, finally, the centralization of the governor-general; but this is by nature more political than administrative. The governor can give a general direction to the administration, but it is difficult for him to follow it up and to coordinate the processes. His principal mission is to rule [*dominer*] the country, govern its inhabitants, take care of peace and war, provide for the army's needs, and oversee the distribution of the European and indigenous populations on the land.

Thus we can affirm that our great and guiding principal of administrative unity does not exist in Africa today. Later we shall examine the consequences of this state of things. For the moment, we shall merely describe it.

Administrative councils. Alongside the administrative powers, there is a large government council, called an administrative council,[33] before which matters are brought and discussed. If this council had been limited to the resolution of only the gravest administrative questions, it could have injected a certain unity and harmony into the administration. As it was, the council was

---

interior who is in charge of settling colonists in villages; the finance director oversees the foundation of isolated farms. As if these two operations, although distinct, were not part of the same operation and did not need to be guided by a single conception! If the Mitidja is to be surveyed, each of them has the right to undertake it separately, so that many areas are surveyed twice, and even today many have not been surveyed at all.

made to go into the smallest details; its jurisdiction was extended over an ever greater space, which it could not possibly cover. In wanting to know everything, it brings everything to a halt.

Beside this council, which overflows with useless powers, they have placed another, the litigation council [*conseil du contentieux*], which has, so to speak, nothing to do. The ordinance that created it does put under its jurisdiction all the questions that come before our prefectural councils, but many of these questions cannot arise in Africa. In addition, the questions that arise from Algeria's special position, being naturally under the jurisdiction of administrative tribunals, have until now been retained by the administration itself.

Besides, for the administrative councils to perform any real service in Algeria, there would have to be one in every province.

Organization of services in the provinces. We have just shown the number, the extent, and the respective positions of each of the powers in Algiers. Let us now return to the provinces and see how things are done there.

The independence that each of the different administrative officials has from the others is even greater and more destructive of good administration than that of Algiers.

At least in Algiers, if the heads of departments, isolated from one another in their particular spheres, are not forced to act in common, they *could* do so if they chose. When the directors of the interior and of finances have a common project to execute, they can communicate their respective views directly and immediately and resolve difficult questions without losing time. Their subordinates in the provinces cannot do the same. Let us suppose that the deputy director of the interior and the director of the Bône area wanted to establish a village: a conflict follows; they have hardly any chance to come to agreement, since, for one thing, there is no one on the spot who could force them to come to agreement, and even if they wanted to do it themselves, they don't have the right to do so. Each must write to his respective department in Algiers; there, the department heads, having learned separately of the difficulty that has arisen, meet and come to agreement on a matter that is not immediately before them, and then each sends his subordinate the instructions they have worked out together.

In Algiers, at least, the governor-general's power dominates everything, and at a given moment, he can make all the department heads agree. This remedy, although intermittent,[34] can resolve the problem at least in part. It cannot be used in the provinces.

By an extraordinary arrangement, the officials that represent the governor's military and political power in the provinces have none of his civil or administrative power.*

Such a state of things is filled with inconveniences and even perils, as we shall prove with a single example, which the Chamber will find striking. Everyone knows the importance of the town of Constantine; it can be said that this town is the key to the province. Almost all the country's important men have property and many family members there. Nothing involves politics more than the administration of such a town. Well! the superior commander of the province can exercise no control, nor even any oversight, over the civil officials who govern the population of Constantine. It is only out of condescension that they ever follow his advice. If the superior commander of the province believes that the civil commissioner, who administers the town, is about to take a measure of a nature to compromise public tranquillity, he has only one legal means of opposing it, namely, to notify the governor-general in Algiers, who will first appeal to the general director of civil affairs, who himself must go to the director of the interior, who turns to the subdirector of Philippeville, who will, finally, present the civil commissioner of Constantine with an order to desist.

All this, we are not afraid to say, is just as contrary to good sense as it is to the interest of the service. It is never wise, but especially not in a conquered country, to keep the administrative authority and the governing political power completely independent of one another, whatever the nature of the representative of that power, and to whatever class of officials it belongs.

Problems that result from the current administrative structure. Such is the

---

* It would be hard to find an example that would better show the arbitrary and incoherent fashion in which the rules of our administration in France have been alternately invoked and brushed aside. Sometimes people take great risks to remain faithful to them; at other times they are needlessly rejected.

In France a lieutenant general who commands an army division is in charge of nothing but troops. He cannot exercise any control or powers of inspection over the civil administration. This has been imitated in Africa; but there, the imitation has been quite unfortunate. For the position of the lieutenant general commanding an Algerian province bears no resemblance to that of the commander of an army division in France. He not only commands the troops but also governs the European populations living on military territory. He rules not only the Europeans but also the Arabs. He represents not only the minister of war, but also, by delegation, the sovereign himself.

structure of civil services in Africa. Let us examine the many problems and abuses that result.

If you calculate the sum total of the salaries accorded to the officials or to the various European agents of the civil service in Algeria, you will discover that it is over 4 million [francs],* even though the population they govern has hardly reached 100,000 Europeans. This should not astonish us, when we consider the multitude of cogs that have been loaded onto the administrative machine, and especially the large number of central administrations that have been created. What always costs the most in administration is the leadership. By unnecessarily multiplying the number of high officials, we have accumulated innumerable high salaries.†This has led directly to far more troubling financial consequences: by creating a very elevated sphere of parallel or nearly equal authorities, we have sparked the most heated rivalries and jealousies. That was inevitable: and as there was no single superior power to keep each of these secondary powers in check, the following two things resulted, to the great detriment of the treasury:

Each of the central administrations sought to install itself in a vast building, which resulted in a great cost to the treasury; then each of them sought to surround itself with numerous bureaus. These bureaus were not always created only with a view to their tasks, but also with a view to the importance that the administration under which they were placed had or hoped to have. Algeria now contains far more than 2,000 European officials in the civil service.‡

---

* About 3.7 million francs were requested from the state budget for 1848 for this purpose. More than 600,000 francs were allocated for the same purpose by the local and municipal budget for that year. It is important to note that this covers only the European civil administration: the indigenous civil administration is excluded from this figure. We should also consider that we have counted only the officials' salaries, and not the indemnities for the houses that were granted to most of them, an expense that, if it were counted, would bring the total to nearly 5 million.

† By themselves the salaries of the four directors discussed above, and of their offices, represent nearly 600,000 francs in the 1848 budget.

‡ The number mentioned in the 1848 budget is 2,000; but there are still a large number of officials in Africa whom we know of without knowing their exact number. The mayors (although these officials have hardly any of the powers of mayors in France, they are at least well paid), the collectors of municipal revenues, the militia officers, the directors and doctors of the charitable establishments, the police personnel . . . the 600,000 francs in the budget, mentioned above, are distributed to these various officials in the form of salaries.

In Africa we already find almost all the officials found in France, as well as a great number of others that we don't have here. Still, people complain that there aren't enough officials, and rightly so. Indeed, we don't have officials to carry out policies in many services. What we have in abundance are clerks.*

There is an even greater lack of *good* officials to carry out policies. The best men in each service are not employed in the field; they are attracted to and kept in the directors' offices; instead of managing affairs, they summarize them.

Since, amid all these jealous and discordant powers, no unified plan for expenditures can be either conceived, developed, decided, or followed, and since each of them presses ahead in isolation on those tasks that will increase its importance, money is often spent without need or foresight. In administration, foresight must be the business of a single person: a complex and confused administration will demand large appropriations, and it will often spend more than it is allotted. This is what has happened, notably last year, as members of the Chamber could see on the occasion of the discussion that recently took place before them.

Administrative consequences of the current organization of services. If we stopped examining the costs of the administration in Africa and considered what it is doing, we would see an even more regrettable spectacle.

What is immediately striking when you watch it in action is that you do not perceive any powerful, central conception guiding it toward a common end and keeping each of the parts that compose it within their natural limits. On the contrary, each of these is a world of its own, with its own particular spirit that develops freely and reigns uncontrolled.

Absence of unity in the conduct of affairs. Let's take an example: people have often complained of the fiscal tendencies shown by the financial services in Africa. Indeed, the financial administration has worried far more about getting revenue from Algeria than about settling inhabitants there. It has sought to sell state lands regularly and at high prices, rather than making good use of some of them for settlement. This is true. But it is wrong to reproach the financial officials for succumbing to this tendency when it is natural and even legitimate for them. We should be sorry only that there is no power over them

---

* So it was that while the finance department included 55 employees in its offices, they could not, for lack of personnel, either study or verify the state lands; we still don't have that information.

to keep sight of the general interest, one that could direct them and when necessary compel them.

The abuse of the particular spirit in each service or, in other words, the absence of unity in the general conduct of affairs is the greatest problem created by the administrative structure we have just described. The others are impotence and slowness.

Impotence and slowness of administration. Since centralization in Algiers is boundless, since local and municipal life does not exist, the smallest matters are brought to the attention of the principal officials, mingled with the largest. *

When the high functionaries in Algiers have thus taken everything upon themselves, they collapse under the burden. Details of administration distract them from the society's principal interests. After they have exhausted themselves resolving questions of pavement and lighting, they neglect, for lack of time, the great tasks of European colonization. Studying the country, exploring the lands that the state controls, acquiring those it does not yet possess, surveying and distinguishing the one from the other, mapping the sites of new villages, overseeing the proper choice of colonists and wisely settling them on the land, all this they leave to some future moment of leisure.

In whatever they undertake, they act with an almost incredible slowness. It usually takes longer for a dispatch from the Ministry of War to go from the governor's cabinet to the hands of the implementing official, even if he is in Algiers itself, than for it to travel across France, cross the Mediterranean, and reach Africa. This makes sense if we realize that whereas in France, there might be only one intermediary between the ministry and the executing agent, one finds three and even four in Africa.

No business, however great and however general, is finished on time. Let us take, for example, the most important and the most general of all, the preparation of budgets. The ordinance of 2 January 1846 provided that the general schedule for the subdivision of funds that is made in the annual finan-

---

* The facts are even worse than the law on this point. The ordinance of 15 April [1845, art. 99 (Duvergier 1845, 91)], without creating municipal institutions, still charged the mayors with exercising, in the government's name, certain powers concerning the maintenance of order, public safety, health, sanitation, town lighting, the safety of the public roads, and local and municipal police. In fact, the mayor of Algiers exercises none of these powers, for the director of the interior has snatched them, even though the ordinance does not in any way authorize him to do so. Such abuses can be seen everywhere.

cial legislation for Algerian civil expenditures should be drawn up in Africa and sent to the minister of war before 1 October of the preceding fiscal year, so that this same schedule, after having been approved, can be sent back to Algeria before the beginning of the fiscal year, just as the proper ordering of finances and good sense would require. Now, this schedule has never been sent to the minister of war on time; from which it follows that it could not be sent back to Africa until the fiscal year has already begun. In 1846, it was only in November that the plan for division of funds was known by the department heads. In other words, it was only at the end of the year that they learned what they should have been spending from the beginning.

As for minor matters or those that only have to do with particulars, not only do these go slowly, but often they never come to any conclusion at all. After having moved painfully through the administrative maze we have just described, they often simply disappear. What becomes of them? No one has any idea; the interested parties don't know, and the administration doesn't know any better than they do, because among all the functionaries who passed them from hand to hand, not a single one was directly and uniquely responsible for them.

Wealthy French landowners who have gone to Africa several times to visit sites, with the minister of war's authorization, have waited for four or five years without being given a concession as they had been promised.

Many poor emigrants have died in the streets of Algiers before anyone told them where they had been assigned to settle.

Colonists established temporarily on a plot of land have had time to build a house, clear a field, and harvest several times before receiving the response informing them they could settle there permanently.

Some concessionaries, after largely having fulfilled the conditions imposed on them in order to receive the definitive title that the state had promised them, demanded it in vain without being able to obtain it. They had transformed their capital into houses or cultivated lands, and they could neither alienate these nor mortgage them to get the money they needed. Many were thus brought to complete ruin, not because they could not produce wealth, but because they were prevented from making use of the wealth they had produced.

Does it follow that the public officials in Algeria are idle? On the contrary, they are quite active. Everything that is regulated in France is regulated in Africa, and in addition the administration gets involved in many things that it has never done in France. The police decrees alone issued by the director of the interior in Algiers would fill a volume. But almost all this vigor is lost in sterile debates or unproductive activities. The civil administration of Africa resembles a machine constantly in action, all of whose parts operate separately or cancel each other out. With much movement, it goes nowhere.

The picture we present here is not exaggerated. If the Chamber could investigate in detail, it would be convinced that we have understated rather than overstated the truth.

Can such a state of affairs endure long, gentlemen? In France, an administration as complex, awkward, and powerless as that in Africa would slow the progress of affairs and damage public prosperity. But we mustn't forget that in Algeria it also leads to the ruin of families, to citizens' despair and death. We have attracted or led thousands of our compatriots onto the soil of our conquest; should we leave them there to fight miserably against obstacles that are not inherent to the country or to the enterprise, and that we have created ourselves?

Your committee, gentlemen, has reason to believe that the government, struck by the defects of the administration's current structure, intends to reform it. We ask you to strengthen us in this thought by associating yourselves with it. As a result, we propose to insert at the end of the bill submitted to you, an additional article as follows:

"The Chambers will be informed in the 1848 session of the structure of the civil administration in Algeria."

Nonetheless, it must be said that this resolution was not taken unanimously. The whole committee recognized that the current structure of the civil services in Africa was defective. But several members thought that it was enough to express the desire to see this structure modified, without indicating the precise date by which the changes had to be made.[35] To do more was at once dangerous and useless. The majority, which disagreed, persists in proposing the additional article that we have just stated for your adoption.

Changes to make in the administrative structure. What changes should be made? The committee, gentlemen, does not intend to explain these in detail here. We can only indicate in a general manner in what spirit we think it best to act, or rather we already indicated this when we demonstrated the defects of the current situation. A summary will suffice here.

Restrain centralization in Paris within narrower bounds, in such a way that even if the government of African affairs remains in France, part of the administration will be in Africa itself. In Algeria, deprive the central powers of some of their functions and restore these to the municipal authorities. In Algiers, simplify the machinery of the central administration and introduce subordination and unity. Create this same unity in the provinces: return responsibility for all secondary affairs to the local authorities, or permit them to deal directly with Paris. Place all the administrative authorities under the direction or at least under the surveillance and control of the political power.

This, gentlemen, is the general direction that would seem wise to give to the reforms.

Algerian legislation must be given a clearer and more stable form. The power that directs African affairs having thus become more unified and less dependent, more agile and stronger regarding particulars, the majority of the committee believes it necessary to place some new limits on that power and to give citizens greater guarantees than those they now possess.

The first need that one feels when one has just settled in a new country is to know precisely what laws are in force, and to be able to count on their stability. Now, we do not believe that there is anyone today who can say with complete accuracy and absolute certitude which French laws apply in Algeria and which do not. The officials do not know much more about it than the governed, the magistrates little more than those they judge. Everyone acts at random and from day to day. The committee believes that it is necessary finally to determine officially and exactly which part of Algerian law is exceptional, and which part is simply French common law.

Already, in some special matters, royal ordinances have declared precisely where the law diverges from French legislation. What was thus decided for part of the law should be done for all of it. We even believe that for matters of primary importance, we should do in Algeria as we have in the colonies: appeal to the law itself.[36]

To what extent, at this moment, can the legislation that governs Europeans in Africa resemble that of France? This depends very much on circumstances, subject matter, and location. We do not pretend to resolve such a complex question in detail. This is neither the time nor the place. Today, it is enough to demonstrate the final goal we ought to have in view. We should set out to create, not a colony properly speaking in Algeria, but rather the extension of France itself across the Mediterranean. It is not a matter of creating a new people, with its own laws, its customs, its interests, and, sooner or later, its separate nationality, but of implanting in Africa a population that resembles us in everything. If this goal cannot be attained immediately, it is at least the only one for which we should constantly and actively strive.

Individual liberty. We can already get closer to it on several points.

Today citizens' liberty is still threatened in two ways in Algeria: by the defects of the judicial system, and by the arbitrariness of political power.

The Chamber knows that justice is not set up in Africa as it is in France. Not only can the judge there be removed, but he remains deprived of most of the rights that in France are considered the best safeguard of the citizens' liberty, honor, and life. The public ministry, on the other hand, is given immense privileges that it has never possessed among us. It is [the minister] who, by his will alone, arrests, incarcerates, informs, releases, and detains suspects. He is the sole and omnipotent agent of justice. He alone proposes advancement of the magistrates, he alone has the right to impeach them to the minister of war, who can censure, reprimand, and suspend them.

If the time has not yet come to make judges in Africa permanent, at least we can say that from this moment on, there is no social need that justifies, by its particularity and urgency, the exceptional position and the exorbitant powers that have been granted to the public ministry. We believe that many eminent men who at different levels once represented or still represent the magistracy in Africa are themselves of the same opinion.

The majority of the committee also considers alarming and ineffective the privilege that has been granted the governor-general arbitrarily to expel from Algeria the men he judges dangerous to keep there. We must say, however, that on this point our views were divided. Some members thought that there were not sufficient reasons to withdraw from the governor-general a power that has not yet been abused and that, in the precarious state of a conquered country, it was very necessary for him to have. These same members observed that similar power has been exercised by the governors of all our colonies; they noted, finally, that its exercise in Algeria is not entirely arbitrary, as the governor-general cannot act thus without having received advice from the superior council — advice, to be sure, that he is not obliged to follow.

The majority of the committee, without suggesting that the governor-general's power of expulsion has been abused, persisted in thinking that such a power should not be left in his hands without providing much more serious guarantees against its abuse than those that exist today. It did not seem to the majority that the civilian population of Algeria — confined as it is between the indigenous people and the sea, defended but at the same time dominated by an army as numerous as itself — could pose a serious threat to the administration that governs it. The majority believed that to arm the government with such an exceptional and rigorous right was to exaggerate the importance that a citizen in our African settlement could have. The danger we face in Africa stems from the absence of a European population, not from its plots or turbulence. Let us first attend to attracting and retaining French colonists: we can worry about suppressing them later. Now, if we want them to come and stay, we must not lead each one of them to believe that his person, his fortune, and his family are constantly to be at the mercy of one man's will.

Property guarantees. Your committee also believes that more complete property guarantees must be given than those that exist at present.

The landed property of Europeans in Africa has two origins: some acquired land from the indigenous people, others bought or received it from the state. In barbarous or half-civilized countries, all titles that do not originate with the state provide only an unstable claim to property. The European nations that allowed property in their colonies to be assigned according to indigenous titles were soon thrown into inextricable difficulties. This is what recently happened to the English in New Zealand,[37] and it is what is happening to us in Africa. Everyone knows that the lands around Algiers and Bône were bought from indigenous people in the first years that followed the conquest, even before they could be visited. As a result, property there has remained confused and unproductive. Confused, because the same fields have been sold to several Europeans at once, by sellers whose right was either doubtful or nonexistent, and who in addition never indicated their boundaries. Unproductive, because it was confused and also because, since the lands had been acquired cheaply and unconditionally, their owners generally preferred to wait for an increase in value, leaving them uncultivated rather than turning them to account by cultivating them.

It is to remedy this problem — limited in extent but very profound — that various measures have been taken in the last three years.

The ordinance of 1 October 1844, that of 21 July 1846, and finally three ministerial regulations of the same year, were written with this goal.[38] It is not the committee's intention to analyze these different acts for the Chamber; we shall limit ourselves to a single remark. It could be useful and even necessary to reestablish property on a solid base, with one action and by an extraordinary procedure, and to give it certain limits. But it is regrettable that we have had to revise such exceptional and delicate legislation so many times.

People worried, and with good reason, when they saw, first, a royal ordinance submitted for consideration to the Conseil d'Etat according to which questions of property were sent to the courts; another ordinance granting judgment on these questions to an administrative body soon followed; then came several ministerial rules modifying the ordinances, under the guise of interpretation. Meddling with the existence of a particular type of property in this way has disrupted all the others and given the impression that no one owned anything in Algeria that was not subject to the arbitrariness of the king's ordinances or to the even more formidable fluidity of ministerial decrees.

The first operations that took place in virtue of these ordinances and regulations showed to an alarming extent, it must be said, the evil that must be cured.

According to the figures communicated to the committee by the minister of war, the lands laid claim to already exceed by a third the entire extent of existing land and, if we use the start of the procedure as a clue to what must follow, ten out of every eleven properties should already be claimed by two owners at once.

All this would not have happened if the state had begun by acquiring the lands, as it has done elsewhere, and had then given them or sold them to Europeans. Our committee believes that this is how things must happen from now on. The interests of both races demand it. Only then shall we be able to preserve old indigenous property and establish new European property.

Once property is well established by a title originally granted by the state, people must not have to fear that it will be taken away.

Today the concession is granted by royal ordinance, and it can be withdrawn by ministerial decree absent appeal to the king-in-council. The act that removes the concession ideally should be as solemn and surrounded by the same precautions as that which grants it.

The Chamber knows what deplorable abuse was made, in times past, of expropriation for the sake of public utility, and how the right of property itself became obscured and weakened. The ordinance of 1 October 1844 put an end to these disorders, but it governs only civil territories. In the rest of Algeria, the system prior to the 1844 ordinance is in force: expropriation is decided on by the governor-general; any reason suffices, and possession is taken immediately; the indemnity, which is fixed by the administrative council and paid as an annuity, comes only later. Now, every day a crowd of Europeans are summoned to become landowners outside civil territories [*territoires civils;* see p. 147 above]. It is neither just nor wise to refuse their properties the guarantees granted to others.

Municipal structure. We have said that it was very necessary, in the interest of the administration itself, and to facilitate its liberty of movement, to create municipal councils in Algeria. Doing so is no less important to the interest of the citizens than to good administrative order. A country where even the traces of a village council do not exist, where a town's inhabitants are deprived, not only of the right to administer their affairs, but of the benefit of seeing them managed in their sight, that, gentlemen, is entirely new in the world. Nothing like it has ever been seen, especially in the foundation of colonial societies. When a city has just been born, its needs are so numerous, so varied, so changeable, so particular, that only a local power can know them in time, understand their extent, and satisfy them. Municipal institutions are not only useful in such times, they are absolutely necessary; colonies have been established almost without laws, without political liberty, and literally without government, but in the whole history of the world, we cannot find a single one that was deprived of municipal life.

It would be impossible to calculate the loss of time and money, the social suffering and the individual miseries, that have been caused in Africa by the absence of municipal power. The village, unrepresented by anyone in particular, without a single director of its finances, often located far from the power that governs it, hardly ever obtains in time or in sufficient quantity the funds necessary for its needs.

The committee realizes that the government is at the moment working on instituting municipal power in Africa,[39] and we are pleased to see that. The task is pressing, and we can predict that it will be difficult. The current state of affairs, as flawed as it is, has already created habits and prejudices that will be difficult to overcome. Its overturn will, besides, necessarily shrink the jurisdictions of several existing powers, taking from them the care of part of the public funds and demeaning them in their own eyes. People will seek, therefore, either directly or indirectly, to block these reforms. We hope that the government will have the energy necessary to overcome such resistance.

Participation of citizens in local administration. Article 104 of the 15 April 1845 ordinance sought to involve a number of local Europeans in district consultative committees alongside the department heads; this introduced into the country's administration the principle of indirect participation by citizens.

It is desirable, gentlemen, that this germ develop, and that the interests and ideas of the European population find not only easy access to, but regular and official organs in, local authorities.

Regulating the press. Without giving the press unlimited liberty, it would be wise to grant it less narrow limits than those that restrict it today.[40] An ordinance regulating the press should be put in place of the censors who now suppress it. It is possible and perhaps necessary to prohibit the press from treating certain subjects that are dangerous for our domination in Africa. Even French legislation contains similar restrictions; but free discussion of the rest should be granted.

Several members argued that it was impossible to find an intermediate state for the press, between total independence and complete enslavement; that any preventive measure would radically destroy liberty and would leave the writer no guarantees; that we would find nothing between a purely repressive legislation and censorship.[41] The majority of your committee were not of this view. They did not believe the problem to be as insoluble as the others claimed; they thought a solution should be sought, and that it was very important to find one. It is important to both the government and the citizens. As long as the African press is under a censorship regime, the local administration in Algeria will be responsible for everything that is printed in the newspapers it authorizes, even if it hasn't seen everything; and we shall be forced to witness the scandal of an official press blaming and sometimes insulting high government officials.

Undoubtedly the administration that controls matters in Africa should be armed with great powers; it must be able to move with agility and vigor; but at the same time, the country must be in a position to know what it is doing. Officials granted such great prerogatives, so far from the public view, acting on rules so unusual and so little known, should be daily scrutinized and kept in check. Don't the disorders that have erupted many times in the African civil administration indicate how necessary it is to surround everything that happens in the administration with the greatest and most constant publicity?

State of foreigners. After having examined the condition of the French in Algeria, we should say a word about that of foreigners.

The foreigners living in the territory of the former regency today bear certain responsibilities from which they are released in France, such as service in the militia, for example; but legally they do not possess any more rights.

This state of things is at once a nuisance for them and awkward and even dangerous for us. Most foreigners who come to Algeria do not do so, as in France, for a short stay. They want to settle there. On this point, their wishes and our interests coincide.

To keep them for a long time in the difficult and unusual situation in which our laws place them is to deprive them, if they have not obtained the king's permission to establish their residence there, of the enjoyment of civil rights. It is to submit them to the rigor of the procedural code's measures; it is, until they have been naturalized as specified in the constitution of the year VIII [whose adoption, under Napoleon, was announced in February 1800], to close off all careers to them, and to prevent them from performing any public functions whatsoever. It is to impose an intolerable condition on them, to make them restless and anxious, and to work against our stated goals.

Nor could we leave things as they are without throwing the judicial administration into profound agitation. In Algeria as in France, litigation between foreigners on most of the most important questions, especially on those of state, falls under the consuls' jurisdiction. They do not come before our courts, or at least they are brought to their attention only by the free choice of the litigants. There is no drawback to this in France, because the foreigners are few in number compared to the rest of the population, and consequently litigation between foreigners is rare. But in Africa, where the number of foreigners is equal to or greater than that of Frenchmen,[42] such cases are so common that the jurisdiction of our own courts loses its character and becomes so to speak the exceptional jurisdiction.

We know that the Government is looking into this question. We emphasize that it should be resolved soon.

What is the foremost condition of success for our enterprise? Throughout the preceding remarks, we have indicated succinctly and generally the manner in which we think it would be best to govern and administer Algeria. We have not yet said anything about the foremost condition of success, the one that contains and sums up all the others: this one is to be found not in Africa, but in France itself. Until now, the African affair has not received the degree of attention in the Chambers, and especially in government councils, that its importance merits. We believe this may be affirmed without giving anyone in particular the right to complain. The peaceful domination and rapid colonization of Algeria are assuredly the two greatest interests that France has in the world today; they are great in themselves, and in the direct and necessary relation that they have with all the others. Our preponderance in Europe, the order of our finances, the lives of part of our citizenry, and our national honor are engaged here in the most compelling manner. Yet we have not thus far seen high state officials focus consistently on the study of this immense question, and nor do any of them seem clearly and directly responsible for it to the country. Nothing in the conduct of African matters has appeared to demonstrate that ardent, provident, and sustained solicitude that a government usually devotes to the principal interests of the country or to concern for its own existence. Nothing up to now has revealed a single powerful conception, a plan decided upon and followed. The enlightened and energetic will that invariably directs and sometimes constrains subordinate powers is not to be found here.

The committee, gentlemen, would have believed ourselves to have failed in our primary duty to you and to ourselves if we had hidden our thoughts from you on this point. We express them at this time in moderation, but we do not hesitate to express them.

We believe that what we have just said had to be said, and we say it without concern for persons or parties, for the pure and simple love of the public good. As long as things continue in this way, you must understand, improvement of details, administrative reforms, replacements of men, will all remain ineffective. The most salutary views will be lost, the best intentions will grow sterile. Everything will be possible and almost easy, on the other hand, the day that the government and Chambers, finally taking in hand control of this great affair, conduct it with the resolution, the attention, and the single-mindedness that it demands.

Incident relating to the Kabylia expedition. Before moving on to the discussion of different funds that you have requested, the committee believe we must inform you of a serious incident that happened in our midst.

The committee had not been assembled long when we were informed that an expedition with the goal of entering Kabylia was being prepared in Africa. This development could not but surprise and acutely concern us, being likely to cause profound changes in the situation of things in Africa; it might powerfully affect the forces, and, through the forces, the funds that you had given us to examine.

Every member heard these rumors with regret, and we all appeared to share the desire that the expedition not take place.

In order to dispel our doubts, the committee asked that the minister of war meet with us. We requested him to tell us whether the news we had heard was well-founded. The minister of war acknowledged that in fact an expedition was being prepared; that it was to march on Bougie from Algiers and Sétif in early May; but he added that it would be of an entirely peaceful nature. He read the committee, in support of his words, a letter from Marshal Bugeaud, who, while giving the same assurances, seemed to regret that he could not fight, because the submission of the indigenous people was never certain until, in their words, *the gunpowder had spoken.*

The measure, thus having been announced officially, became the object of debate within the committee. Several members appeared satisfied with the explanations given by the minister of war;[43] the large majority persisted in thinking that the expedition was regrettable, and that it was much to be desired that the government agree to prevent it. It even seemed appropriate to draft the committee's opinion, in order to be reproduced later in the report. It was declared that the majority of the members found the expedition impolitic, dangerous, and of a nature to necessitate an increase in troops. This resolution, contested as too absolute in its ideas and too strong in its wording even by some of those who had denounced the enterprise, was recorded in the transcript of the committee's proceedings.

Would it be made known to the government? The majority of the committee's members believed this to be urgent and indispensable.

But how?

Some thought that the minister of war should be asked to come before the committee again, and that we should communicate to him in person the impressions that his first interview had left. Others said that it would be more fitting and more in line with the respect the committee owed to the king's ministers that the chairman himself should call on the minister, express to him the committee's opinion, and explain the motives on which this opinion was founded.

This method was attacked by several members of the minority, who declared that such a form would turn the view of the majority into an injunction, and might lead to the accusation that the majority was trying to undermine the crown's prerogative.

The majority responded that its move could not seriously provoke any such suspicions; that it wanted merely to express to the government an opinion that the government itself would want to hear; that in requesting its chairman to leave a certified copy of its transcripts in the hands of the minister of war, the committee was merely seeking to give a precise and certain character to its thought, which would permit the government properly to grasp its meaning.

In virtue of these deliberations, the committee's chairman called on the minister of war, acquainted him with the committee's opinions, and left him with a copy of the transcript that stated them.

On 11 April, the committee received from the minister of war a letter in which the king's government, *after expressing its surprise at seeing the committee deliberate on a question falling exclusively within the jurisdiction of the royal prerogative, refused to receive the communication made to it.*

Here are the facts, gentlemen; the Chamber will understand that they are very serious.

Was the majority of the committee wrong or right to think that the Kabylia expedition was dangerous and impolitic?

Was the majority, as the government clearly charged, exceeding its powers and those of the Chamber in expressing its opinion in this regard to the minister of war? This is what we shall examine.

The Kabylia question is not new, gentlemen; hardly anything has been examined more often by the government and the Chambers. Not only has it often been the subject of examination, but until now high state officials have always resolved it in the same way. All the committees that have been concerned with African affairs for several years, those of 1844, 1845, and 1846, have expressed with increasing energy, the idea that an expedition should not be made into the Kabylia.[44] The government has been no less explicit.

Marshal Soult has expressed the same opinion to the Chambers on several occasions. This opinion was professed, not long ago, by the minister of war. He himself provided proof of this to the committee, by showing us several pieces of his correspondence with the governor-general.

Now, is the same expedition to Kabylia at issue today that was in question until now, or is the expedition of another character? They have spoken of a military outing [*promenade*], a peaceful exploration. Gentlemen, we must take serious things seriously. They can say, if they like, that today the Kabylia expedition confronts circumstances more favorable than those that existed previously; that may be. But they should not attempt to give it a new character, one that even those who are conceiving and executing it do not envision.

The *Moniteur algérien* of 10 May states that people in France are strangely wrong if they believe that all of Kabylia has submitted. *There are still thirty to forty leagues in Kabylia, along a length of twenty-five leagues, that, except for the three tribes near Bougie, contain nothing but unsubdued populations.*

The same day, the governor-general announced to these people, in a proclamation, that the army would enter their territory in order to hunt down those adventurers who preach war against France. He declared to them that he had no desire to fight and devastate property, but that if there were men among them who wanted war, they would find him ready to accept it.[45]

Let us not mince words, gentlemen. To subjugate Kabylia through arms the way we have already subjugated the rest of the country: today as before, this is the goal they propose.

Ten thousand excellent troops, divided into two army corps, are at this moment marching against the Kabyles. However energetic the latter may be, however entrenched in hard-to-reach mountains, they will crumble before our arms: that is quite certain. Today we know the indigenous people of Algeria and their manner of fighting too well to doubt this. It is possible and even probable that the preponderance of our forces will make resistance short-lived, or even prevent it. That is not where the drawbacks and perils of the enterprise lie.

What are we going to do in Kabylia? Is it a matter of acquiring a country where European agriculture and industry can be established? But the population there is as dense as in some of our departments. Property is divided and owned as in Europe. There is therefore no room for colonization there.

If we cannot usefully go to the Kabyles' territory, should we at least worry that they will disturb us on ours? Marshal Bugeaud himself said it to the Chamber: *The populations of Kabylia are neither invasive nor hostile; they defend themselves vigorously when you enter their territory, but they do not attack.*

It is true that their submission completes the conquest of the former regency. But who was pushing to complete it? Few conquerors have had such an easy time of it as we, by good fortune, have met with in Algeria, in a country divided into two entirely distinct zones and shared between two races so completely different that we could take each of them separately, conquer them at our leisure, and subjugate them in isolation. Is it wise to neglect such a stroke of luck?

We shall conquer the Kabyles; but how are we going to govern them after we have conquered them?

The Chamber knows that a Kabyle tribe is nothing like an Arab tribe; among the Arabs, the constitution of society is as aristocratic as you can imagine; when you dominate the aristocracy, you hold all the rest. Among the Kabyles, the form of property and the organization of government are as democratic as you can imagine; in Kabylia, the tribes are small, restless, less fanatical than the Arab tribes, but much fonder of their independence, which they will never surrender to anyone. Among the Kabyles, every man is involved in public affairs; the authority that governs them is weak, elections are always moving power from one to another. If you wanted to find a point of comparison in Europe, you might say that the inhabitants of Kabylia are like the Swiss of the small cantons of the Middle Ages. Can you believe that such a population will remain tranquilly under our rule for a long time, that they will obey us without being watched over and repressed by military establishments based in their midst? That they will docilely accept the leaders we undertake to give them, and that if they drive them back, we shall not be forced to return several times, arms at hand, to reestablish or defend them? Forced to administer peoples divided by age-old animosities, could we adopt the interests of some without attracting the hostility of the others? If our friends and the dissidents, as the marshal's proclamation states, make war among themselves, shall we not be forced to intervene once again? The measure taken today is thus only the beginning of a long series of measures that must be taken; it is clearly the first step on a long road that will then by necessity have to be taken, and at the end of which, gentlemen, we shall find, not a failure of our arms, but an inevitable growth of our entanglements in Africa, of our army, and of our expenses.[46]

The committee on special funding said it last year: *We believe that peaceful relations are the best, and perhaps the fastest, means of assuring the Kabyles' submission.* Never has a prediction by the Chambers been better or more quickly realized: a large number of Kabyle tribes, attracted by our industry, have already entered of their own accord into relations with us and offered to recognize our supremacy. This peaceful movement disturbed those who had not yet granted anything. Were we not permitted to believe, gentlemen, that at the moment when peace was succeeding so well we should not have taken up arms?

You will not find it strange, then, that on learning of the expedition being launched, your committee was as nervous as you yourselves are.

Now, was it wrong of the majority of the committee to display to the government the impressions created by this unexpected piece of news? Did they deserve refusal even to be heard, to be told that they were overreaching the Chamber's powers and interfering with the rights of the crown?

The Chamber will understand why such reproaches were greatly resented and could not stand without response.

What! gentlemen, the government submitted all African questions to the Chamber in presenting us with legislation enabling the funds necessary for the different services; in its turn, the Chamber charged us with examining the situation of affairs in Algeria and with proposing how the Chamber vote on the funds that we believed useful. Then there transpires, no mere detail of military operations, but a great event, an entirely new and unexpected event, which must soon put a new face on things; the force that we are asked to determine might change as a result; the funds we have been asked to review will undoubtedly become insufficient; but in letting the government know what it regards as the inevitable consequences of the step it was about to take, the committee has overreached its powers! In truth, such a thing could well be said, but it would be incomprehensible. What the committee has done here, two of the Chamber's committees have done before. If they acted unconstitutionally, why did the cabinet listen to them?[47] If they remained within the limits of the constitution, why does this same cabinet refuse to listen to us and send us a reproach that it never sent them? As for the reason given of the form the committee's majority gave to their communication,[48] the Chamber will permit us not to take this reason seriously. What was done in this circumstance was done in a thousand others. Committees, and especially finance committees, daily put observations and views that they believe they should submit to the government in writing, sending a draft that makes their thinking clear.

They say the charter grants the king the free disposition of land and sea forces. Who is denying that? Have we claimed to dispute the king's use of this prerogative, or to hamper any exercise of it whatsoever? Were we preventing the government from authorizing the expedition in asserting that it seemed to us, as it still seems, impolitic and dangerous? The government remained absolutely free to undertake it. We wanted only one thing: to discharge our responsibilities and yours, gentlemen, and to perform our duty.

The majority of the committee persist in believing that it would have failed in its clearest and most pressing obligations if it had acted otherwise than it did. We continue to think we gave powerful reasons to enlighten the government in time on the political and financial results of the expedition that was to take place, and that it was easier for them to refuse to listen than it was to respond to us in a convincing manner.[49]

SECOND REPORT ON ALGERIA (1847)

REPORT BY M. DE TOCQUEVILLE ON THE BILL REQUESTING A CREDIT OF THREE MILLION FRANCS FOR ALGERIAN AGRICULTURAL CAMPS

Algeria must be colonized.[1] Gentlemen, we do not undertake to demonstrate to the Chamber that the peaceable establishment of a European population on the soil of Africa would be the most effective means of placing ourselves there and guaranteeing our domination.[2] This truth has been made clear many times, and we have nothing to say about it here, except that your committee has admitted it as demonstrated.

Only two members, without denying the utility of the result to be attained, have contested the humanity and wisdom of attempting such an enterprise.[3]

The country to be colonized, they said, is not empty or populated only by hunters, like certain parts of the New World; it is already occupied, possessed, and cultivated by a population that is agricultural and often sedentary. To introduce a new population into such a country is to lengthen the war and to pave the way for the inevitable destruction of the indigenous races.

They add that in addition the climate repulses us. That numerous experiences have proven that the European never acclimatizes, and that his children cannot live there.

These objections, gentlemen, however grave they might seem in themselves, and whatever force they might derive from the talent of those who present them, have not held up the committee.

Factors that facilitate the introduction of a European population. The country is occupied, it is true, but it is not full, nor even actually owned. The indigenous population there is very sparse and thinly scattered. Thus the conquering population can be introduced onto the land without disturbing the conquered population.

Study the history of the country, consider the practices and the laws that govern it, and you will see that greater and more remarkable means for leading such an enterprise peacefully and to good result are nowhere to be found. We shall merely recall them very summarily to the Chamber.

It has been remarked that wherever society has long been unstable and power tyrannical, the properties owned by the state are numerous and vast. This is the case in Algeria. The public domain is of immense proportions, and the lands owned by the state are the best in the country. We can distribute these lands to European farmers without injuring anyone's rights.

We can do the same with part of the tribes' lands.

This is neither the time nor the place to explain and discuss before the Chamber the rules on which the right of property rests in Africa. These questions are obscure in themselves, and they were further obscured and muddled by the attempt to impose a single, common solution, which the diversity of facts resisted. We shall limit ourselves to establishing as general and incontestable truths that, in many places, individual and patrimonial property does not exist; that in many others, the tribes' communal property does not rest on any title, and that it is held by reason of the government's tolerance rather than of any law.

These, gentlemen, are the rare and particular circumstances that assuredly make our work easier than that of most conquerors.

First, the Chamber will readily understand that it is easier to introduce a new population to a territory that is owned only communally than onto land where every inch of soil is protected by a right and by a particular interest. You will also understand that in a country where property is rare enough that most individuals and even some of the tribes have none — a country in which nonetheless enough property exists for all to sense its charms and to desire it ardently — that in such a country there will almost always be people offering transactions of their own accord. It is easy to bring a tribe with a territory too large for it, but that it does not own, to give up part of it on condition that it gets secure title to the rest. The title we give is the price of the land we keep.[4]

It is thus not correct to say that the introduction of European farmers onto African soil is an impracticable measure. Undoubtedly, it presents difficulties and would even present great dangers if it were done haphazardly, if it were not done delicately, humanely, and competently: that we do not deny. We are only saying here that success is possible and, on certain points, easy to achieve.

But what does it matter, people say, that you have gotten the land ready, if the European cannot live there!

Your committee, gentlemen, cannot admit that the facts justify such fears.

The effects of the climate on Europeans. First, a word on the health of European adults. It cannot be denied that when our troops in Africa were exposed, without shelter, to the intemperance of the seasons or to excessive fatigue, many of them fell ill. It is beyond doubt as well that when civilian populations were placed in unhealthy places or were reduced to the horrors of need and misery, they were cruelly ravaged by death.[5] But were these fatal events owing to circumstances or to the country itself? That is the whole question. We can cite plenty of facts to prove that mortality is due far less to the climate itself than to the particular and temporary circumstances in which Europeans found themselves; but to do so we believe a single remark will suffice.

Everyone knows that what most afflicts Europeans' health in hot countries is manual labor — outdoors and during the summer. In the tropics, the same men who are healthy when their work allows them to avoid the heat of the day are exposed to great dangers when they must brave it. Work in the sun is the ultimate hardship and the most certain sign by which to judge the real influence of the climate of a hot country on the European's different organs.

Now, this hardship was suffered a hundred times by the troops, and the results were confirmed officially. The army performed immense tasks in Africa: they built roads, hospitals, barracks; they cleared the soil, farmed, harvested. Whenever the troops performed these tasks in healthy places, the health of the soldiers was unaltered. It has even been noted repeatedly that fewer soldiers fell ill or died among troops occupied in this way than among those in the garrisons. On this point we may rely on the testimony of our military officers and doctors.

It is more difficult, at present, to determine the effect of the Algerian climate on children's health.

 There is no doubt that in several places the mortality of young children was very great and entirely out of proportion to European averages. But there is no reason to be astonished, when we call to mind the particular circumstances in which these facts occurred. Most of these children who were taken by death had recently been brought from Europe by poor parents, who, even in Europe, were among the rabble of the population. It can easily be imagined that such children, born in misery, sometimes amid moral collapse, and exposed, upon entering the world, to all the risks of disease faced by a new settlement in an unknown climate, succumbed in great numbers.[6] What happened to them happens, even among us, to so many unfortunates who are born to bad parents, or who are deprived of the care that is indispensable to their age. We know that these children rarely survive the first years of life. In France, it has been ascertained that three-fifths of foundlings die before the age of one, and two-thirds before reaching their twelfth year. Should we conclude that the French climate is hostile to the reproduction of the human race?

Is the child who is born in Africa to healthy and well-off parents, raised in a city or in a village that has already been founded, treated with all the precautions that the particular hygiene of the country requires — is this child subject to more illnesses and exposed to a greater chance of dying than the child born, for example, on the coasts of Provence and placed in similar circumstances? This comparison was made, and its results do not justify the fears that are being expressed.

We ask the Chamber to permit us to reject all the reasons that may lead people to believe that we should not colonize Africa, and to focus on the question of which method of colonization we should follow.

The most effective way to understand what must be done is to know what has already been done. What exists today in the matter of colonization is the necessary point of departure for all the resolutions that must be taken. Let us speak first of the maritime zone, which is the real zone of colonization, and examine the province of Algiers.

Province of Algiers. Around three indigenous towns — Algiers, Coléa, and Blida — that were partly rebuilt and are now mainly populated by Frenchmen, many European farms and a fairly large number of villages had already been undertaken or founded. The countryside around Algiers and Blida was populated fairly slowly, and agricultural populations languished there, but, as we shall discuss in a moment, Algiers and Blida exhibited extraordinary prosperity. The number of inhabitants grew rapidly, new neighborhoods were constantly being built, and great fortunes were made overnight thanks to the sale of lands for construction or the rent of newly built houses.

Current state of colonization. For nearly a year, a violent financial and industrial crisis has overtaken these towns, halting development, and slowing and almost halting the movement of affairs.

This crisis stems from several causes that we shall not examine here,* for this report is concerned above all with agricultural colonization. As long as we

---

* This crisis has been attributed to many diverse causes, to financial troubles in France, which slowed the movement of capital toward Africa, to worries caused by the latest indigenous insurrection, to the slowing down of public works in the colony, to late or incomplete payments made by the state to its contractors or even to its workers, and finally to delays in the establishment of a bank branch.

It cannot be denied that all these facts have had considerable influence over the event; but its principal cause is simpler and more general. We need look no further than the excessive speculation and the creation of an enormous mass of fictive or very exaggerated values, which time finally shrank to their true proportions.

It would be difficult to describe the degree to which the speculators of Algiers and Blida allowed themselves to get carried away on the issue of houses. What happened in France in 1825 can scarcely give an idea of it. Lands that until that point could not find buyers were suddenly being sold for prices almost as high as those in the richest and most populous neighborhoods in Paris. Magnificent houses were built on this bare soil. These lands were bought not with capital but with securities [*rentes*]; the houses were built not with acquired wealth but with credit. On the ground floor, one borrowed the money to build the next floor, and so on. The houses passed through several hands before they had been completed, and the price doubled or tripled overnight; they were rented before they had a roof. When people couldn't give any security, they submitted to prodigiously usurious interest. Since the population in these two towns was constantly growing, people believed that their prosperity was unlimited; they did not perceive that most of the new immigrants were attracted by the large industrial activity itself. The population occupied in building the new houses installed itself in houses that had already been built, and continually raised the price of rents. The time came when this illusory prosperity vanished, when people had to recognize the exact proportion between the capital invested and the revenue it produced. From that moment the crisis began, and we can believe that it will last until the price of houses comes to represent exactly, not the fictive and temporary value that speculation gave to real estate, but their real and constant value.

These problems are great, no doubt, but they carry a useful lesson. Instead of looking to the cultivation of land, most of the colonists in Algiers, or those who arrived in that center of our settlements in Africa with some capital, thought of nothing but speculating in the towns. The current crisis will teach those who would imitate their example that in a new country, there is only one way to get rich, which is to produce; it is on the surrounding agriculture that the true prosperity of urban populations rests, and large, wealthy towns can exist only in the midst of a cultivated and civilized territory.

have a large army in Africa, it will be easy to create towns. To attract agricultural populations to the soil and to keep them there: that is the real problem that needs to be solved.[7]

Around Algiers, within eight or ten kilometers, there are gardens where the land, carefully cultivated, is immensely productive, supports a fairly dense population, and generates large revenues for its owners; it is beyond this area of gardens, on the hills of the Sahel and in the plains of the Mitidja, that agriculture properly speaking begins.

The Chamber has no need for us to recall the circumstances under which the lands of the Sahel and the Mitidja passed from indigenous into European hands. It knows what strange disorder in landed property resulted from these haphazard purchases made with no knowledge about the true owners and the true boundaries, and with a view to speculation rather than agriculture. What is important to know at this point is what the land has become in the hands of those who own it.

Most of the large European properties, in the Mitidja plain and even in the Sahel, are still uninhabited and uncultivated. The uncertainty of property itself and of its boundaries is one of the principal causes of this state of things, but it is not the only one. The country's insecurity in the beginning, then the lack of roads, the distance of markets for many landowners, and for others the proximity of a large capital that seemed to raise the value of their lands without their taking the trouble to clear them and to offer the imminent and happy prospect of speculation, were some of the secondary reasons that explain, without justifying, the abandonment of so many fertile lands.[8]

We must not exaggerate the problem, however. It is quite inaccurate to say that the large European landowners have done nothing around Algiers. In the Sahel, several considerable properties have been cleared, built upon, and planted, and have yielded a good profit. At this moment, in the Mitidja plain, large agricultural settlements have been founded or are being founded; the capital already engaged in these enterprises is estimated at no less than 1,800,000 francs.

A certain number of lands still owned and cultivated by Arab owners, and territory where small indigenous tribes stagnate, fill the space around the European farms and villages. We shall now discuss these villages.

The villages around Algiers were not all created in the same way.

The system according to which the villages were built. In some, the government merely provided the colonists, in addition to the land, with help in building their houses and clearing their land.[9] In others, the state went further: it built houses and cleared part of the land itself;[10] some villages were founded by contractors, that is to say, the state granted certain privileges, or gave certain assistance, to an individual who was in charge of settling inhabitants there. Finally, in the three villages of Fouka, Mahelma, and Beni-Mered, the majority of the population was composed of colonists who had left the army, or soldiers still subject to military law.[11] We shall return to this last fact, to examine it separately.

Behind these diverse exteriors, we find the same ideas everywhere.

Nowhere did the state limit itself merely to spending for the public utility, building fortifications, founding churches and schools, laying roads. It went further: it took it upon itself to make individuals' affairs prosper, and it gave them, wholly or partly, the means of settling on the land. Almost all the families placed in the villages belonged to Europe's poorest classes. Rarely did they arrive with any capital at all. The portion of land that the administration distributed was always very minimal. These lots rarely reached and almost never exceeded 10 hectares. The governing idea seems to have been to settle a purely laboring population on the land of Africa at the public expense.

The Chamber does not expect us to discuss in detail the history of each of these villages. We shall merely give the general impressions suggested by their appearance.

Population of the villages. In speaking of the villages, people have greatly exaggerated both the good and the bad. It has been said that the men who live in them came from the dregs of European society, that their vices equaled their misery. This is not accurate. If we look at the agricultural population as a whole, it will appear at once beneath and above most populations of the same type in Europe. It will seem less regular in its mores, less stable in its habits; but also more industrious, more active, and far more energetic. Nowhere has the European farmer better and more easily become familiar with abandonment, illness, destitution, and death, and nowhere has he carried a more virile and, so to speak, warlike soul into the adversities and dangers of civilian life.

Above all, it has been said that all the expenditures the state made for these villages were lost, that the results obtained were nothing: this again was to distort the truth.

To remain within the exact limits of the truth, we can only say that the result obtained by the state is entirely disproportionate to the efforts made to achieve it.

Economic situation of the villages.[12] The villages founded in this way have up to now generally led a very weak and precarious existence. Many of them have been decimated and are still devastated by illness, nearly all by misery. Even today, the government, after having created them, is forced to help them survive. Still, most of them will not disappear. You can already see in them the lively seeds of an agricultural population. Even in those where things are worst, it is rare not to find, in the midst of a very miserable or unprosperous crowd, several families who are making good in their position and appear not to be discontented with their fate.

For the rest, it would be unjust to blame the system itself for all the individual misfortunes and public miseries that have emerged. Errors of all sorts committed in its actual practice make up many of the causes of its reverses.

On this point, the metropolitan government and the colonial administration equally deserve severe criticism.

If we imagine that the colonists sent at the state's expense to cultivate Africa were assembled with so little care that many of them were complete strangers to agriculture or made up the poorest part of our agricultural population, that after having awaited the promised concession for months and sometimes years in the streets of Algiers, subjected to all the physical and moral evils bred by idleness, misery and despair, these men, so ill prepared, were often placed in ill-chosen spots, on foul soil, or on soil so covered with undergrowth it would cost more to clear a hectare than it would cost to buy one in France; finally, if we add to all these causes of ruin the daily influence of an incoherent administration, and thus one without foresight, at once inert and meddlesome, we may be permitted to doubt whether under such conditions it could have been possible to create prosperous villages, not only in Algeria, but in the most fertile parts of France.

These accidental causes undoubtedly contributed to the ruin of a large number of colonists. What, now, are the particular circumstances that led to the prosperity of others?

We begin with one striking point. Nowhere was the success of the colonists proportionate to the sacrifices the state underwent for them, but because of circumstances independent of the state, or that it caused only indirectly, such as the particular fertility of a place, the rare virtues of the colonists, the proximity of a market or a road . . . Of these circumstances, the most ordinary one and the one most worth pointing out was the availability of sufficient capital, either in the colonist's own hands or in those of his neighbors.

In some villages, such as that of Saint-Ferdinand, for example, the state pushed its solicitude so far that it built the colonists homes quite superior to the houses of nearly all the well-off farmers in France; around these dwellings it cleared four hectares of fertile land. On these farms, it placed families whom it obliged to pay only 1,500 francs, and it did not enforce even that payment; it gave them seeds, it lent them farm implements.[13] What has happened there, gentlemen? Today the majority of these families have had to vacate these places. They did not have time to wait for prosperity to come.

Since in giving them houses and fields the state had not given them the means to live — for they had no resources of their own and found around them no means of getting any — they languished and in the end would have died out, their hands still full of all the tools of prosperity they had been given free.

Nearly all the colonists who succeeded elsewhere, on the other hand, had arrived with some capital, or if they had not brought any themselves, they managed to earn it by working for those who already had capital.

When four or five rich landowners had already settled in the area around a village that was entirely made up of poor people, such as Cheragas,[14] for instance, the village provided these landowners with the laborers they needed and they, in turn, supported the families of the village with wages. This is how they have all lived, and soon enough all of them will lead comfortable lives.

This is what we have to say to the Chamber about the agricultural population of the Mitidja and the Sahel.

Colonization in the provinces of Constantine and Oran. The crisis that devastated the central province has not reached the other provinces; there they have not had to face the problems that caused it in Algiers. The towns have developed only in exact proportion to needs, and capital seems principally to have been directed at the cultivation of the land.

A certain number of villages, in the provinces of Constantine and Oran, were founded according to the system we have already discussed, that is, they were populated with poor families subsidized by the state.[15] Almost all these villages developed very slowly, and some are surviving only with difficulty.

Outside these villages, other European farmers settled on fairly large estates;* they are not subsidized by the state but on the contrary pay the state a rent. These have already done considerable work; they have built houses, dug

---

* Around Oran, 2,000 hectares have been distributed in this way, in plots of 4 to 100 hectares.

wells, cleared the land; they appear to be prospering, even though they are doing with their own resources what others have failed to do or have done incompletely with state funds.[16] Many new estates are requested near them.

In any case, it must be said that there are not yet very many of these settlements, and they are almost all recent; if they shed light on the subject at hand, they do not yet offer any certainty about which system to follow.

A number of European towns are already being built beyond the maritime zones, in mixed or Arab territories: they have been created and supported by the presence of our army, and a small number of farmers already live in the surrounding areas.

This is the general appearance of Algeria at present, from the point of view of European colonization.

The purpose of the bill that we now turn to discuss is to develop these sketchy accomplishments.

Analysis of the bill. The Chamber is already aware of the principal ideas behind this project. We shall merely mention them again briefly. An appeal is made to the army. Among the willing soldiers who still have three years left to serve, those most capable of carrying out an agricultural enterprise are chosen, and they are given a leave of six months to go to France to get married. During their absence, their fellow soldiers who have remained in Africa build the villages and clear and sow the fields. On his return, the soldier who has been chosen to become a colonist is placed on a property with his wife; the state gives him furniture, animals, farm implements, trees to plant, and seeds; for three years it continues to give him his pay and clothing, and provides him and his family with provisions. Until his term of service expires, that is, for three years, he remains subject to military discipline, and the time he spends in this situation counts as if he had spent it doing military service. After three years, the military colonists enter the civilian regime.

None of these details of execution can be found in the bill, as we might have expected. Only the bill's preamble explains them. The bill only says, very laconically, that agricultural camps will be created in Algeria, where land will be granted to military men of all ranks and services, who are serving or have served in Algeria.

This bill cannot be compared with any similar enterprise attempted elsewhere. Let us first dispense with any analogies that might be made between what has been done in other times and places, and what this project would attempt to do.

Austria, in the early eighteenth century, hoped to protect itself from the Turkish incursions that threatened its borders on the Croatian side by creating military colonies there; these still exist and are prospering.

Russia, at the end of Alexander's reign, similarly created settlements known as military colonies in the south of its empire.[17] Several fell into complete ruin soon after their founding; others survive today.

It would be a useless waste of the Chamber's time and our own to study the many ways in which the Austrian and Russian military camps differ from the agricultural camps the bill proposes. We shall note only the three main ones.

The first is that in those two countries there was no intention of founding a civil society with the help of the army; the intention was to create actual military societies, entirely subject to military discipline and preserving this character and this power forever.*

The second is that these societies were not formed by first placing the soldier in uncultivated areas and then attracting a wife and family to him; rather, they found populations already settled on the land and merely billeted regiments among them, or formed military organizations out of the populations themselves.

The third, finally, is that the populations who were subjected to this condition already lived under the yoke of servitude or in semi-barbarism, so that there was nothing new or very difficult to bear in the exceptional situation to which they were subjected. They took to it without trouble, and put up none of the resistance or obstacles that free or civilized peoples would not have failed to oppose to such transformations.

The plots of land promised by the law of 1 floréal year XI [21 April 1803] to soldiers mutilated or wounded in the war of liberty (these are the terms

---

* In Austria's military colonies, for instance, as described in a very curious memoir addressed to the emperor Napoleon in 1809, which the committee has learned of, landed property is inalienable and belongs not to individuals but to families. All the families eat together; everyone dresses in the same way, and the colonel is at once administrator and judge. The peasant cannot dispose of the produce of his land; he has to get permission to sell a calf or a sheep; he does not have the power to sow his fields or to leave them fallow; he cannot leave the limits of the colony without authorization.

This discipline is rigorously enforced with the cudgel.

used in the law) are also completely unlike the settlement we have suggested, in spite of what the bill's preamble says.*

The emperor's plan had nothing to do with settling soldiers on uncultivated land far from France, in a different climate and a barbarous country, but of distributing to them, as a supplement to their pensions, cultivated land located in rich and populated areas. These camps, although placed, in this way, in excellent economic conditions, fared badly, and they had even less success as military institutions. Although the veterans who lived there were kept under a sort of discipline and required to wear uniforms, it seems certain that at the time of the 1814 invasion they were of little use; this at least is what several eyewitnesses have attested. These former soldiers, turned laborers, acquired the habits, ideas, and tastes of civilian life so well and so quickly that they had become almost strangers to the labors of war and performed them ineffectively and with repugnance.

The only plan for military colonization that in some ways approaches the ideas contained in the bill is the one found in the papers of Vauban, who drafted it exactly 148 years ago (28 April 1699); it has since been published.†
In this work Vauban proposes to send several battalions to Canada, not to defend it but to colonize it. According to him, these battalions would begin by cultivating the land in common; after a certain period each soldier would become a landowner and the society would little by little lose its military character.

It is unnecessary to note that the soldiers Vauban intended to use were engaged in military service for an indefinite period; that the king could use them as he chose; that it was legal for him to force them to remain in the

---

* See the law of 1 floréal year XI [21 April 1803] and the decrees of 26 prairial year XI [15 June 1803] and 30 nivôse [21 January] and 15 floréal year XII [5 May 1804].[18]
† This account, written 28 April 1699, is entitled *Means of Establishing Our Colonies in America and Enlarging Them in a Short Time.* Nothing equals the meticulous pains with which Vauban, as was his custom, goes into the smallest details of execution that his plan discusses. He takes the soldier from his regiment, accompanies him to the port of embarkation, and indicates all the provisions he should be given; it is "a very essential operation," he says, "which must be presided over by a king's commissioner, one who is not a rogue." From there he follows the battalions to America and describes at length all the transformations through which the soldiers must go to get rid of their military character and become, as he says, bourgeois.[19]

colony and to keep them as long as he liked under military discipline, and after having freed them, to keep them under a very exceptional regime. Besides, Vauban's ideas were never carried out.

Let us not seek to clarify this question with examples that would be misleading, gentlemen. Let us examine it in itself, and judge it by the light of our reason alone.

Within the committee, the bill was attacked from several points of view.

Various objections made to the bill. Several members thought that the result of the proposed measure would be a profound transformation of the current system of recruitment law, changing its spirit and increasing its rigors.[20] The heavier the burden this law places on families and in particular on poor citizens, they say, the more inappropriate it would be to extend its application to other cases than those the law had foreseen. The goal of the recruitment law is to provide the state with soldiers, not colonists; it was created to give France an army, not to give Algeria an agricultural population. Let us not ask of it more than was desired by those who drafted it. Even if the proposed measure would not change the spirit of the recruitment law, it would probably increase the size of the French army, since it would be necessary to replace the soldiers who went to the agricultural camps.

This opinion, vigorously defended, was also vigorously fought. It was observed, regarding the first point, that since soldiers were not forced to become military colonists and remained in the agricultural camps only of their free will, the rigors of the recruitment law would not increase. As for the size of the army, it seemed doubtful to the honorable members that the result of the measure would be to increase it, since the agricultural camps could make part of the African army unnecessary.

Other members criticized the project in the army's own interest.

According to them, there were disadvantages in creating differences and inequalities in the condition of the soldiers, of sending some to France to get married and then turning them on their return into laborers and landowners, while alongside them their comrades remained stuck in military service. Such a state of things seemed to them contrary to the preservation of the army's order and strict discipline.

Several members restricted themselves to pointing out the difficulties, obscurities, and many lacunae in the plan.

To find a large number of soldiers who would agree to go to France for six months on condition that they get married, that, no doubt, would be simple;

but how can they be compelled to conform to such a condition? How, besides, are they to choose a wife in such a short space of time? What are we to expect of the morality and goodness of a union contracted in such haste, on orders, and in view of material advantage? What would happen to the military colonist's wife if he died? What would she do if the plot of land were taken away from her? If she kept it, how would the purpose of the law, which is to create a virile and warlike population, be achieved? The project says nothing of these problems.

Many other criticisms of detail were also made. These need not detain the Chamber; it seems above all to have been more general considerations that determined the majority of the committee.

It first studied what exactly the scope and character of the proposed measure were.

The proposed measure must be judged by economic rather than military considerations. What does the plan really intend, or rather do? Must it really place a military population ahead of the civilian one, a military population with the force of organization, the power of resistance, and the vigor of action that an army's hierarchy and discipline give? Such a goal would be useful and great; it would legitimate great sacrifices. It is the idea that the emperors of Germany [i.e., Austria] carried out in Croatia, and Czar Alexander in the Crimea. It is the idea that, in the beginning, Marshal Bugeaud himself seemed to favor.[21] Is this idea applicable to Frenchmen? Clearly not. No one today would dare say it is. Once the soldier has fulfilled his military engagement, nothing can force him to live under exceptional laws, whose burdens would be unbearable to him. No one has the right to force him to do so, and there is no hope of getting him to agree to it. Thus the bill proposes nothing of the kind. As soon as the soldier, placed in the new village, completes his service, he becomes a simple citizen again, subject to the home country's civilian laws and customs. This project thus concerns not military colonization, but civilian colonization with the aid of the army. The military side of the question immediately loses almost all its importance, and the economic side becomes the one to which we must turn.

In all the new countries where Europeans have settled, the work of colonization is naturally divided into two parts.

The Government takes on all projects of a public character and that concern collective interests. It has laid roads, dug canals, drained swamps, and built schools and churches.

Individuals have undertaken every project of an individual and private character alone. They have brought the capital and the labor, built houses, cleared fields, and planted orchards . . .

It is no accident that this division of colonial labor naturally developed everywhere; indeed, there was nothing arbitrary about it.

If the state abandoned the realm of public interests to take up the individual interests of the colonists and attempted to give them the capital they need, it would undertake a project at once onerous and fairly sterile.

Onerous, because there is no agricultural settlement in a new country that is not very expensive relative to its importance. No colony stands as an exception to this rule. If the individual spends a great deal when the money he uses comes from his own purse, how much more will he spend when he draws from the public treasury.

The project is, in addition, sterile, or at least not very productive. The state, whatever efforts it makes, cannot provide for all the costs entailed in settling and supporting a family. Its aid, which is enough to begin the enterprise, is almost never enough to carry it off; it has merely resulted in inducing imprudent men to attempt more than their own strength allowed.

Even if the state imposed unlimited sacrifices on itself, these sacrifices would still often be useless. We must not think that a colonist only needs the money necessary to cultivate the land to turn it to good account. The man who lacks the capital necessary for such an enterprise rarely has the experience and capacity necessary to succeed at it. Besides, when he is not exposing his own resources or counting on himself alone, he rarely displays that ardor, tenacity, and intelligence that make capital productive — that sometimes replace capital, but can never be replaced by it.

As to the question of colonization, whatever one does, one must always return to this alternative:

Either the economic conditions of the country to be populated are such that whoever comes to live there can easily prosper and settle, in which case it is clear that the men and the capital will come or stay of their own accord. Or there are no such conditions, and then it can be affirmed that nothing can ever replace them.

In stating these general principles again, gentlemen, we do not claim to be saying anything original or profound. We merely speak with the voice of simple good sense and repeat the ideas taught to us by experience.

If such truths needed to be proven by facts, what has happened until now in most of Algeria's villages would provide a slew of them.

Now, putting words aside and looking only at things, what is the purpose of creating agricultural camps, if not to reproduce these villages in another form?

The agricultural camps would have many similarities to the villages that have already been founded. What is an agricultural camp, gentlemen? What if not a village in which the state takes upon itself, not only to build projects of a public character, but on top of these to provide individuals with all the resources that are necessary for them to make their fortunes: houses, herds, and seeds, a village that it populates with people most of whom were day laborers in France, and whom it undertakes to transform instantly at its own expense into leaders of rural development?

The subsidized villages and the agricultural camps have only secondary and superficial differences; they are similar in their fundamental characters, and whoever rejects one rejects the other.

It is said that the original colonist will be better chosen in military villages than in the civilian villages. Very well. Let us grant that he will be vigorous, more intelligent, more moral; but, on the other hand, he will be in worse economic condition: he will not have his family with him, he will be placed farther from the large centers of colonization that already exist in Africa, from the large markets where his produce will sell at high prices, from the dense populations, where he could get inexpensive labor.

His settlement will impose a much greater cost on the state, and, what is more, a cost whose limits are unknown.

The costs will be greater because only assistance was given the civilian colonist, whereas here the state would provide for everything.

The costs will be less limited. When you have attracted a family to a new land through an appealing subsidy, it is quite hard to stop giving them assistance as long as their needs last. You have supported a man halfway through the job, why not carry him through to the end? What decisive reason is there to stop along this road on one day rather than another? The state still comes to the rescue of the villages first founded around Algiers. If it is so difficult to leave a civilian colonist to his own devices, someone who has never served the country, how much harder will it be to abandon a former soldier, whom the government prevented from returning home to settle him on African soil?

Will we ever be able to leave such a man to his fate and let him languish or die in misery?

It is said that this is just a trial. But, before we take the risk of carrying out such a trial, shouldn't we make sure that it might succeed? To attempt what one believes to be a good idea makes sense; but to attempt what one thinks is a bad idea is to show great disdain for money, for the state funds, and for the citizens one draws into the enterprise.

The attempt at agricultural camps has already been made. It is inaccurate, in any case, to say that no such efforts have been made.

For several years, there have been three villages in the area around Algiers that have, in part, a military origin: Fouka, Mahelma, and Beni-Mered.[22] The first was populated with discharged soldiers; the two others were founded exactly in the manner described in the bill's preamble. What must we conclude from this triple experiment?

We shall not go into a detailed examination of the condition of these villages. The elements of such a study would be unreliable and difficult to assemble. We shall only say that the three military villages just mentioned cost far more than the neighboring civilian villages and produced no different result. Those in mediocre or bad economic conditions languished and had trouble surviving. The third, Beni-Mered, which is located in one of the most fertile parts of the Mitidja, a league away from two towns that until recently were very prosperous, Boufarik and Blidah, presents a more satisfying appearance.[23] But you should note that the prosperity is not peculiar to the military population; there are a certain number of civilian families in this same village of Beni-Mered. The government did far less for them than for the neighboring military families; if one examines the state of each, one finds that their condition differs very little, and that, if there is any difference between them, one would have to declare it is to the advantage of the former.

Rejection of the bill. Seen as a whole, the considerations that have just been listed have convinced your committee, gentlemen, that the bill could not be adopted in the form in which the government has presented it. This resolution was made unanimously by the members that were present.

But the committee is divided on the question of whether to propose something to take its place. One member[24] suggested replacing the first article with an article conceived as follows:

Measure proposed to replace it. "A sum of 3 million francs will be used for the settlement in Algeria of discharged and married soldiers of all ranks and branches of the army and navy, with preference given to those who have served in Africa.

"These discharged soldiers will be divided among various agricultural centers that have been or will be created, and assimilated in every way to the civilian colonists.

"In addition to this sum, a fund of 1 million [francs] will be made available to the minister of war, to be appropriated under chapter XXXII of the war budget (colonization in Algeria).

"Funds that are not used by the expiration of the fiscal year title for which they are appropriated will be carried over, with full rights, to the subsequent year."

Reasons for and against the amendment. Here are the principal reasons that were given in support of this amendment. In adopting the proposed measure, it has been said, we avoid most of the drawbacks of the agricultural camps and keep most of the advantages they may produce.

Thus, on the one hand, the recruitment law remains unchanged; no inequality is created in the soldiers' conditions; we are not exposed to all the problems of execution the bill would face. The men chosen are already discharged from the military; they are married; they come of their own will, attracted by the subsidy offered. They are not gathered together to form separate agricultural societies; they are spread among the existing population and placed in good position for success.

On the other hand, we thus introduce into the civilian population more energetic and virile elements than those that now compose it. We give the army striking evidence of our support, and at the same time we do it an act of justice. What could be more just, indeed, than to put the land the soldier has conquered to use for his own benefit?

The soldiers we subsidize in this manner will have no capital, no doubt, but they will have what is no less necessary for success in such an enterprise — moral vigor, health, and youth.

The adversaries of the proposal responded: we must not exploit the army's name. What man, having been involved in Algerian affairs, and having traveled across Algeria, has not been struck by the rare and grand sight of the army? Who has not admired in particular, in the simple soldier we are discussing here, that modest and natural courage that achieves even a sort of unwitting heroism; that tranquil and serene resignation that keeps the heart calm and almost joyful in the middle of a foreign and barbarous country, where deprivation, illness, and death threaten every day, everywhere? On this question there is neither a majority nor a minority in the committee, any more than in the Chamber. Everyone is agreed that public interest and national justice require that we allow the army as well to take advantage of colonization. Only the means and the measure are in question.

What some want to do through a special law can be done quite naturally through the use of funds already included in the budget. There are considerable funds included in the budget whose object is to help settle colonists in Algeria; from now on, these funds should be employed principally to help the soldiers who want to settle in the conquered country; no one disputes that this fund can easily be increased as the need arises; but it is unnecessary to create a separate, completely similar, fund through a special law. It is unnecessary and difficult: for how are we to set the total amount today for the new funds that will be requested? We have always been assured of finding soldiers in numbers sufficient to fill the agricultural camps; but who can say now how many married former soldiers who want to settle in Algeria we shall find, and whether the funds that already exist in the budget are not enough to provide for their needs? The committee does not know; the government itself has no idea, as it has made no inquiries of this kind. This is easy to understand, for the proposed measure is not in fact a modification of the bill; actually, we should note, it is a completely new project the government had not thought of, and for which it could not provide any information. Why should the Chamber hurry, as early as this year, to create special funds when it is not even certain that we shall be able to use them?

The measure is thus useless in its effects, and in the form that some want to give it, it could be dangerous. Perhaps the government and the African administration will see in the proposed special bill a solemn recognition and a consecration of the general system that involves colonizing Africa through subsidies from the treasury. Now, this system, as a regular means of populating the new country, is condemned by reason and refuted by experience.

After long discussions, your committee being divided equally, the amendment was not adopted, and we have nothing to propose today but the pure and simple rejection of the bill.

A glance at the colonization plans proposed for the provinces of Constantine and Oran. Our work, gentlemen, could if need be stop here: but the committee believes it is acting as the Chamber would wish in pressing a bit further.

In the preamble to the bill, the government felt it should announce that there were two distinct colonization plans: one for Constantine province and the other for Oran province.[25] The government has distributed the documents best suited to introducing these systems and allowing you to evaluate them. The committee necessarily was asked to deal with them as well; it will do so very briefly.

However different on certain points, the two plans are founded on similar ideas.

Both recognize that colonization must be prevented from proceeding haphazardly, and that it cannot be the result of individual transactions between the colonists and the natives; this for them is a fundamental necessity. It belongs to the state alone to set the place where Europeans can settle. It alone can deal with the natives; the colonist must get his property title from the state. This is their first principle.

The second is that the state should not take on the task of providing individuals with the means of establishing their agricultural enterprises, nor give them the capital they might lack. In general, its costs should only be those of a public character, relating to a collective interest.

These, gentlemen, setting aside all details, are the principles that form the common base of the two projects discussed in the bill's preamble.

The committee agreed unanimously with the first of these two principles. A minority requested that we reject the other. According to the honorable members who made up this minority, the state should in general be responsible for choosing the colonists and helping them to settle on the land. Colonization using individuals' capital would not work at all or would go badly. It was not to be hoped, they felt, that small capital would willingly venture to Africa. As for large capital, it would go there for trade rather than for agriculture. If large capital were to seek territory, it would attract only an ill-chosen population, whose maintenance sooner or later would fall on the state. Such colonization would in the end be more expensive and less profitable than that undertaken from the start by the state itself.

The large majority of the committee was of the contrary view; it thought that the two principles stated above are equally true and it fully approves their adoption.

On what conditions and to which persons will the state grant the land it has acquired from the natives and designated for colonization? This must depend a great deal on circumstances and locations. Generally speaking, what is preferable is to give the landed property one is creating an individual character, and to grant it to an individual rather than to an association. Still, it might sometimes be useful and even indispensable, to return to the mode of colonization by company. But in this case, the state's primary duty is to devote the greatest care to seeing that the most serious moral and capital guarantees are provided. For here it is a matter of an industrial operation that can have the greatest influence on men's lives, and compromise an entire population associated with it.

What are the natural conditions for the success of colonization? In addition to the two colonization projects just discussed, many others have been produced at different times. We shall not discuss these with the Chamber. No problem has provoked more thought than that of the colonization of Algeria. It has given rise to almost innumerable writings.[26]

The authors of all these works, and the public itself, seem to have believed that the success of colonization in Africa depended on the discovery of a certain secret that had not yet been found. We have come to believe, gentlemen, that that is an error: there is no secret to discover in this matter, or at least the good sense of the human race long ago discovered and divulged what they are looking for.

It must not be imagined that the method to follow to create and develop new societies differs much from that which must be followed to keep old societies prospering. Do you want to attract Europeans to a new country and keep them there? Create institutions they recognize from home or those they hope to find: make sure that civil and religious liberty are the rule; that individual freedom is assured; that property is easily acquired and well guaranteed; that work is free, administration simple and prompt, justice impartial and rapid; that taxes are light and commerce free; that economic conditions are such that one can easily attain comfort and often wealth; in a word, ensure that people are as well off as in Europe — and if possible better — and the population will not lose time in coming and settling. That is the secret, gentlemen: there are no others.

Before abandoning ourselves to exceptional and singular theories, it would be good first to see whether the simple method we have just discussed might not by chance be enough; it certainly is not the one that has been most often followed in Africa.

Economic conditions. In Algeria, the state, which has made every sacrifice to make the colonists' fortunes itself, has hardly thought about putting them in a position to make their fortunes on their own.

The state has almost always acted in such a way as to make production difficult and expensive and to leave the products without any outlets.

Why production is difficult and expensive in Africa. Algeria still had only a few thousand inhabitants when France imposed a number of tariffs on it: registration fees, patents, stamp taxes, which the English colonies in America rejected after 200 years of existence; sales taxes, a tariff on our judicial costs, the customs system, the tonnage duty. Many of these taxes are lower than in France, it is true, but they weigh heavily on a society much less able to bear them. It is easy to see why we have been drawn down this path. As the government was demanding from the Chambers not only the millions necessary for war, but still more money to subsidize colonization and to populate the country at the state's expense, people wanted to make the revenues Africa produced comparable to the sacrifices it imposed. The public treasury thus undertook to take back in the form of taxes what it gave in the form of aid. It would have been better to dispense with both expenditure and collection.

But what has been far more harmful to production in Africa than taxes is the rarity and high price of capital.

Why is capital so rare and so expensive in Algeria? There are several factors on which legislation could exercise a large and direct influence, which it has not done. First, the absence of credit institutions. The Chamber knows what happened regarding the foundation of a branch of the Bank of France in Algiers. The bank agreed to create this branch only reluctantly; the committee has proof that it delayed the preliminary formalities as long as it could; and that when, finally, it was obliged to reach a verdict, it flatly refused to exercise its right. So the Bank of France, after having, through its presumed competition, prevented any other credit establishment from settling in Algeria, ended by not setting up there itself. This, gentlemen, was quite deplorable. The bank, by these calculated delays, and the government, by putting up with such delays, have certainly contributed to the crisis that is now destroying some of the principal places in Africa.

The absence of credit institutions is one of the reasons for the rarity and high price of capital; it may be said that it is not the main one.

Above all, what prevents people from being able to get abundant and inexpensive capital is the difficulty of giving a guarantee to the lender: as long as this first difficulty exists, the services the banks provide will be limited and the very existence of the banks difficult.

There are two reasons that the farmer in Africa cannot borrow, for want of guarantees. The first is that since most of the lands were granted by the government in return for the fulfillment of several conditions, as long as the conditions are not fulfilled, the land can neither be sold nor serve as the basis for a mortgage.

The second reason, and the main one, is that the mortgage system we imported to Africa, which is copied in part from our own, as well as the accompanying laws of procedure, prevent land from serving easily as security.

Without seeking to examine here all the flaws in our mortgage system, and without expressing any opinion on the changes that might or should be made to it, we shall only say here that this system, however good or in any case bearable it may be in France, will paralyze agriculture, the chief industry, in Africa. The farmers in a new country are unstable; their history, fortunes, and resources are not well known. They have only one way to obtain the capital they need, and that is to pledge the land they cultivate, which they can only do as long as the legislation allows the lender to take possession of it quickly and cheaply. Generally speaking, it can be said that the newer the society, the simpler and prompter the formalities of real estate sales should be. In Algeria, they are still very complicated and very slow, so the farmer there has far more trouble than farmers in France getting the necessary money and has to pay infinitely more for it.

Why there are not enough outlets for products in Africa. All the reasons that we have just indicated summarily contribute to making production difficult and expensive in Africa: still, these circumstances would not prevent production if there were accessible outlets for the products.

What generally makes the beginnings of all colonies so painful is the absence or the remoteness of markets. Products become abundant before the surrounding consumption can grow apace; once the goods are produced, no one can sell them. In this regard, the colonists of Algeria find themselves in far better economic conditions than those of most Europeans who have founded distant colonies. In settling them on the land, France also artificially brought into being a great center of consumption by putting part of its army there.

Instead of drawing from this the immense results that it might have produced for colonizing the country promptly, the government made it almost useless. Until now, the military administration has appeared to be preoccupied only with obtaining the colonists' goods at the lowest possible price. Thus, while the government was making great sacrifices to settle farmers in Algeria, it refused to make farming profitable. It may be said, gentlemen, that this showed little sense, and that money that might have been spent to assure the colonist in Africa of a regular and lucrative price for his products would have been far more useful to France and to the colonists themselves than that wasted on aid to the villages.

This outlet would be very precious, but it would soon become insufficient. European agriculture in Africa will have trouble developing if it is not given another — through the opening of the French market.

It would be easy to prove, if we went into details, that this measure could not have serious drawbacks in the long run, and that it would have great immediate advantages. It would be worth far more than budget subsidies. Your committee, gentlemen, will not develop this investigation. In everything we have said, we have wanted less to indicate this or that particular measure to take, than to call the attention of the government and the Chambers to this important and neglected side of the African question.

Until now, the solution to this immense question has principally and almost uniquely been sought in expedients of government or administration. It is much rather to be found in the economic condition of the new country. If the farmer in Africa can produce his goods cheaply and sell them at a good price, colonization will take care of itself. If capital is in danger or remains unproductive, on the other hand, all the governors' arts and all the treasury's resources will be exhausted without attracting and keeping the desired population on the land.

Bill (rejected by the committee).

1ST ARTICLE. Agricultural camps will be created in Algeria, where land will be granted to soldiers of all ranks and all divisions, who are serving or have served in Africa.

2D ARTICLE. The time spent in agricultural camps by the officers, non-commissioned officers, and soldiers, will count toward their pension as if they had spent it in military service, but only up to a maximum of five years.

3D ARTICLE. A sum of 3 million francs will be allocated for the anticipated expenses of the present law, during the fiscal years 1847, 1848, and 1849.

In addition to this sum, funds of 1,500,000 francs are available to the secretary of state's minister of war [*ministre secrétaire d'Etat de la guerre*] in fiscal year 1847, to be appropriated under chapter XXXII of the war budget (*Colonization in Algeria*).

The funds that have not been used by the expiration of the fiscal year title for which they are appropriated will be carried over, with full rights, to the subsequent year.

THE EMANCIPATION OF SLAVES (1843)

I

We are often unjust toward our times. Our fathers saw such extraordinary things that in comparison with their accomplishments, all those of our contemporaries seem commonplace. Still, the world today offers some great spectacles that would astonish us if we were not weary and distracted.[1]

Sixty years ago, if the foremost maritime and colonial nation of the globe had suddenly declared that slavery would disappear from its vast domains: what shouts of surprise and admiration would have broken out everywhere! With what concerned and passionate curiosity the eyes of civilized Europe would have followed the development of that immense enterprise! What fears and hopes would have filled every heart!

This bold and remarkable task has just been undertaken and completed before our own eyes. We have seen something unprecedented in history: slavery abolished, not by the desperate effort of the slave, but by the enlightened will of the master; not gradually, slowly, over the course of those successive transformations that have led insensibly from bondage to the soil toward freedom; not by the successive efforts of customs modified by beliefs, but completely. In an instant almost a million men together went from extreme servitude to total freedom, or better put, from death to life. Just a few years were enough to accomplish something that Christianity itself could only do over a great number of centuries. Open the annals of all peoples, and I doubt you will find anything finer or more extraordinary.

Must such a spectacle simply be an object of astonishment for us, or should we take the idea as an example to follow? Should we, like the English, seek to abolish slavery? Must we use the same means as they did? It is difficult to think of greater or more important questions today. These questions are great in themselves, and they seem even more so if we compare them with all those raised by the politics of the day.

France possesses 250,000 slaves. The colonists declare unanimously that the emancipation of these slaves would be the colonies' ruin, and they pursue all men who express a contrary opinion with their abusive clamor; they don't spare even their sincerest friends. Such anger should not surprise us: the colonists are in great distress, and their irritation toward everything they see as likely to aggravate their problems is assuredly quite excusable. Moreover, the colonists form one of the most exclusive aristocracies that has ever existed in the world. And what aristocracy has ever allowed itself to be stripped of its privileges peaceably? If, in 1789, the French nobility—who by then were distinguished from the other enlightened classes of the nation by hardly anything but imaginary signs—obstinately refused to open their ranks to these classes, and preferred to have all their prerogatives wrested from them at once, rather than voluntarily giving up the least part of them, how could the colonial nobility, who have skin color as a visible and indelible trait, prove to be more tolerant and moderate? The émigrés responded with outrage to those of their friends who demonstrated the futility and the peril of resistance.[2] So do the colonists. We should not be astonished by this, for human nature is the same everywhere.

The colonists have often said before what they are saying today. Thirteen years ago, when it was a question of abolishing the infamous slave trade,[3] the trade, to hear them, was indispensable to the existence of the colonies. Now, the trade, thank God, has been abolished in our overseas possessions, and work has not suffered. The number of blacks has even increased, and the same men who opposed the measure for so long are now happy it was taken. The emancipation of people of color was supposed to throw the colonial world into confusion and anarchy. The people of color have been emancipated and order has not suffered.[4] Were the colonists wrong, then? We may state that they are still wrong today. It is the status quo that will be the colonies' ruin; every impartial observer easily recognizes this. And if there is a way for France to keep [its colonies], it will come only from the abolition of slavery.

The colonists seem to believe that if they succeeded in silencing the men in France who pronounce the word *abolition*, or if they obtained from the government the positive assurance that the whole idea of abolition were abandoned, slavery would be saved, and with it the old colonial society. This is to cover one's eyes in order to see nothing. Can a sensible man believe that two or three tiny slave colonies, surrounded and so to speak enveloped by large emancipated colonies, could long survive in such an environment? And that, moreover, abolition in the English colonies could be considered an accident? Must we see in that event an isolated fact in the particular history of one people? Undoubtedly not. This great event was produced by the general movement of the century — a movement that, thank God, goes on. It is the product of the spirit of the times. The ideas, the passions, the ways of all European societies have pressed in this direction for fifty years. When, among free men, races mix and classes grow closer and merge throughout the Christian and civilized world, can the institution of slavery endure? We still do not know what accident will put an end to it in each slave country, but it is already certain that it will end in all of them. If slavery has trouble surviving in colonies that belong to those peoples of Europe among whom the new institutions and mores have not yet established their empire, how can the colonists who belong to the freest and most democratic nation of the European continent flatter themselves that they can preserve it?

The Chambers, the government, almost all political men of any merit have already solemnly acknowledged that colonial slavery must soon end. Is it up to them to retract? Can such words, spoken on such a question, be taken back? Isn't it clear that the idea of the abolition of slavery in a sense grew inevitably from all our other ideas, and that as long as abolition is not carried out, there will be numerous voices in France to demand it, a public opinion to applaud it, and soon a government to declare it? Every reasonable man who is beyond the prejudice of color perceives this with the utmost clarity and sees that colonial society is, every day, on the brink of inevitable revolution. Colonial society has no future. As a result, it lacks the first condition of order, of prosperity, and of progress. Already the slave cannot, without shuddering, carry the chain that must soon be shattered. What is slavery today, says one of our colonies' foremost magistrates,[5] if not a state of things in which the worker works as little he can for his master while the latter *dares not say anything to him*? For his part the master, with no certainty about the morrow, dares not change anything; he dreads innovation and improves nothing; he hardly has the courage to preserve [his estate]; colonial properties are worthless; no one buys things that will not last. The colonial landowners are without resources and without credit. Who could consent to share in a destiny one knows nothing about?

The troubles thus multiply daily, the uneasiness increases, distress and discouragement continually mount. Instead of making energetic efforts, the colonists resign themselves more and more to vain regrets, impotent rages, unproductive despair; and the metropole, turning its gaze from such a sad spectacle, ends by persuading itself that such settlements are not worth the trouble of saving them.

It is incontestable that the colonies will quickly consume themselves amid such a deplorable status quo; in addition it must be recognized that the least external action would precipitate their ruin.

In the English islands, not only is labor free, but it is enormously well paid; the laborer's wage is rising to four, five, even eight francs a day, apart from other advantages also granted to workers. Despite this immense premium granted to workers, there is still a lack of hands. All the British greed and British activity are devoted at the moment to procuring them. They are seeking them on every shore; the smuggling of men has become the most necessary and the most lucrative commerce. Already we know that on the English islands nearest ours, islands that were once French and are still populated by Frenchmen,[6] there are recruitment companies whose purpose is to facilitate our slaves' escape. If this method were put into effect on a large scale, it is likely that our planters would soon see the primary instruments of their industry escape. How could it be otherwise? Here the black man is a slave, there he is free; here he vegetates in misery and hereditary degradation, there he lives in an opulence unknown to the European laborer. The two shores on which such contrary things occur face each other across a narrow channel that can be crossed in just a few hours and that every day is crossed by rivals who want to provide the fugitive with the means to break free from his chains.[7] What, then, keeps the Negro among us still? The answer is easy: the hope of imminent emancipation. Deprive him of this hope and he will soon escape.

If, at this moment and in peacetime, the English can harm our colonies so immensely, what would it be like in wartime?

Since emancipation in the English colonies, the former slaves have conceived such an ardent, one could say almost fanatical, attachment to the metropole that, if a foreign attack were to occur, there is every reason to believe that they would rise en masse to resist it. Everyone in England agrees on this point; even those who deny the other benefits of the measure admit this one.

On the other hand, the observations of all the governors of our colonies, the views of the special councils, and the very language of the colonial assemblies suggest that in their current state, our slave islands would be very difficult to defend. The thing speaks for itself: how could we resist an external attack that would take as its point of departure the evident interests and the passions, so often excited, of the immense majority of the inhabitants? In Martinique and in Bourbon [Réunion], the slave population is double the free population; in Guyana it is triple, and almost quadruple in Guadeloupe. What would happen if the black regiments of the English islands disembarked in these colonies and called our slaves to freedom?[8]

We need not demonstrate the impossibility of withstanding such a battle successfully. It is quite obvious. At the first cannon shot on the seas, we would have to unleash a sudden emancipation, which necessarily would be a disaster because ill prepared, or resign ourselves to seeing our possessions conquered. Where do we go from here, then? If peace lasts, the status quo will bring about gradual but certain ruin; if war breaks out, it inevitably will lead to catastrophe. A convulsive and miserable existence, slow agony or sudden death, such is the only future in store for our colonies. No politician who has studied the facts even a bit fails to perceive this with the utmost clarity, nor are there any who suppose that when these things do happen we could save our overseas possessions without subjecting their social state to profound modification. But even among these men, a good number do not want to abolish slavery. Why? We must understand this properly. It is because they believe that the colonies are not worth the time, money, or effort such an enterprise would require. In this matter, as in many others, the colonists have created a remarkable illusion; they attribute the resistance that the abolition of slavery has encountered in the Chambers and in the crown councils to a sort of colonial ardor. Unfortunately, they are mistaken. People reject emancipation because they care little about the colonies and would rather let the patient die than pay for the remedy.

For my part, I am so convinced that the increasing indifference of the nation for its tropical possessions is now the greatest and so to speak the only obstacle that prevents emancipation from being seriously undertaken that I shall believe the cause of emancipation vindicated the day that the Government and the country are convinced that keeping the colonies is necessary for the strength and greatness of France. Thus we must commit ourselves first to establishing this foremost truth.

II

At first, the commercial importance of the colonies was greatly exaggerated. It is quite true that a considerable part of France's maritime commerce is conducted with them, and that the merchant marine, which handles commerce, employs a large number of vessels and several thousand of our sailors. But such facts are not conclusive, since if there were no colonies, we would go elsewhere to find the tropical goods that we have to get from our islands, and our commerce with the countries that provided these goods would certainly be equal and probably superior to that we have with our colonies. On the other hand, recently the commercial importance of our overseas possessions has been undervalued. The principal merit of these establishments is not the size of the market, but the stability they offer.

Here is what we see today in all the great nations of Europe: the working class is increasing everywhere; it is growing not only in numbers but in power; its needs and its passions so directly influence the well-being of states and the very existence of governments, that all the industrial crises threaten more and more to become political crises.

Yet what principally leads to these formidable perturbations is the instability of external outlets. When a great industrial nation depends for the export of its products solely on the interests or whims of foreign peoples, its industry is perpetually subject to the hazards of fate. This is not the case when a considerable part of its external commerce is carried on with its colonies, because there are rarely very considerable variations and especially very sudden variations in the markets of our colonies. Commerce there is established on bases that hardly ever change, and if at certain times this commerce is less considerable than it might be with foreign countries, at least it never stops abruptly. The profit is often smaller, but it is certain, and the metropole, if a bit less wealthy, is more tranquil. This, in my eyes, is the great benefit that colonial commerce offers, a benefit that undoubtedly must not be bought too dear, but that it would be very unjust to mistake, and very imprudent to neglect.

I recognize, however, that the principal merit of our colonies is not in their markets, but in the position they occupy on the globe. This position makes several of them the most precious possessions France could have.

This truth will become clear if we look for a moment at the map.

The Gulf of Mexico and the Caribbean Sea [Mer d'Antilles] together form an interior sea that is already, and, above all, must become, one of the principal sites of commerce.

I shall set aside everything that is merely probable: the piercing of the isthmus of Panama, which would make the Caribbean the regular route to reach the Pacific Ocean; the development of civilization in those vast, half-deserted, barbarous regions that line the Caribbean on the South American side; the pacification of Mexico, a vast empire that already has almost as many inhabitants as Spain; the commercial progress of the Caribbean islands [Antilles] themselves. If all these admirable countries, different in the customs of their inhabitants, in their tastes, and their needs, and yet so near to one another, were to be populated with civilized and industrial peoples, the sea that unites them all undoubtedly would be the most commercial of the globe. All this is problematic, you may say, and may never happen. It has already partly happened. But let us move on to what is certain. The Mississippi River, and the incomparable valley through which it flows, empties into these waters. No one can doubt that the Mississippi soon will be called the greatest commercial waterway in the world. The Mississippi valley is, in a way, all of North America. This valley is a thousand leagues long and almost as wide; it is irrigated by fifty-seven large navigable rivers, several of which themselves, like the river into which they flow, are a thousand leagues long. The soil of most of the valley is the richest of the New World. That is why this valley, which was deserted forty years ago, contains more than ten million men today. Every day, new hordes of immigrants arrive; every year they form new states.[9]

Now, to connect most of the points in this immense valley to the rest of the world requires going toward the Mississippi;[10] the river's mouth in the Gulf of Mexico is, so to speak, the only way out. Thus more and more of the wealth that is contained in the whole northern continent and exploited by the Anglo-American race with such prodigious success and such rare energy will come through the Mississippi. The sea that serves as the commercial road of the Antilles themselves, of Colombia, Mexico, and perhaps China, and which is in addition the outlet for almost all the products of North America, this sea certainly must be considered one of the most important points of the globe. To make myself clear, in a word, I would say that it is already and it will become more and more *the Mediterranean* of the New World. Like the latter, it will be the center of business and of maritime influence.

It is there that domination of the ocean will be fought for and won. The

United States already represent the third naval power in the world; in the near future they will challenge England's dominance. The Gulf of Mexico and the Caribbean will undoubtedly be the principal theaters of this battle, for maritime war always occurs where commerce is. Its principal object is to protect or damage that commerce.

Today, around the Gulf of Mexico, at the entrance to the Caribbean, and south of the isthmus of Panama, France possesses colonies where 200,000 inhabitants speak our language, share our mores, obey our laws. One of these islands, Guadeloupe, has an excellent commercial port,[11] and the other, Martinique, possesses the largest, the most secure, and the finest military port in the Caribbean.[12] These two islands form two citadels from which France can observe at a distance what happens in these waters, which are to have such a great destiny, and where France can be ready to play the role that her interest or greatness indicate. Could there be a question of abandoning or, what is the same thing, allowing ourselves to lose such positions? How long will they remain open to the first adversary? Surely there is no party in France that could support such an idea; the opposition, especially, could not accept it, as they are always loudly denouncing our apparent tendency to forget our strength and our dignity. What are they saying to calm the legitimate impatience that the country feels when it sees the reserved attitude, or, to use the official language, the *modest attitude* of their policies?[13]

They say that the current epoch, an epoch consecrated to the necessary acquisition of wealth, is not suited to remote enterprises; that it resists the execution of vast plans. That may be; but if in effect the nation's fatigue, or rather the interests and pusillanimity of those who govern it, condemn us to remain outside the great theater of human affairs, let us at least preserve the means of rising to it again, of taking up our role when circumstances become favorable. Let us not deploy our forces, I agree; but let us not lose them. If we do not acquire remote new positions that would allow us easily to take a principal part in the approaching events, let us at least try to preserve those that we have prudently acquired.

If it is proven, made obvious to all, that as long as slavery is not abolished in our colonies, our colonies will not, so to speak, belong to us; that up to that point we shall have nothing but costs, while the benefits will pass into other hands the day they can be used, let us have the courage to abolish slavery; the result will be well worth the effort.

In any case, nations cannot, with impunity, show indifference to the ideas and sentiments that have long characterized them, and that they have used to rouse the world. They cannot abandon them without quickly sinking in the public esteem and entering into decline.

These notions of freedom and equality that are weakening or destroying servitude everywhere: who spread them throughout the world? This sentiment, disinterested and yet impassioned with the love of men, which all at once made Europe hear the cries of slaves — who propagated it, directed it, illuminated it? We were the ones. Let us not deny it. It was not only our glory, but our strength. Christianity, after having fought long against the egoistic passions that reestablished slavery in the sixteenth century, was tired and resigned. Our philanthropy took up its work, reawakened it, and brought it into battle as an auxiliary. We were the ones to give a determined and practical meaning to this Christian idea that all men are born equal; we were the ones to apply it to the facts of this world. We were the ones, finally, who, seeing new duties for social power, imposed upon it as the first of its obligations the need to come to the aid of the unfortunate, to defend the oppressed, to support the weak, and to guarantee each man an equal right to liberty.

Thanks to us, these ideas have become the symbol of the new politics. Shall we desert them now, when they are triumphant? The English are doing nothing at the moment but applying *our* principles in their colonies. They are acting in accordance with what we still have the right to call the *French sentiment*. Are they to be more French than ourselves? England, despite its financial troubles, despite its institutions and its aristocratic prejudices, has dared to take the initiative and shatter the chains of 800,000 men with a single blow. Will France, the democratic country par excellence, remain the sole European nation to patronize [*patroniser*] slavery? When all inequalities disappear at her word, will she keep part of her subjects under the weight of the greatest and the most intolerable of all social inequalities?

If so, she must resign herself to letting that standard of modern civilization that our fathers first raised fifty years ago pass into other hands, and she must finally renounce the great role that she had the pride to take up, but that she does not have the courage to fulfill.

It does not necessarily follow that what I have said must lead blindly to an emancipation measure, nor that it would be appropriate to proceed without taking any of the necessary precautions to ensure the benefits and to restrict the costs and perils. Emancipation, I recognize, if not a very dangerous enterprise, is at least a very considerable one. We must be resolved to do it, but at the same time we must study with the greatest care the most certain and the most economical means of succeeding.

The English, as I have said, have taken the initiative. It makes sense, first, to examine their actions and learn from their example.

A commission of peers and deputies, formed in 1840 to study this question, has just proposed a new plan. It is the public's right and duty to judge it.[14]

This double task will be the object of the subsequent articles.

III

It is important to know how to be just even toward one's rivals and adversaries. It has been said that the English nation, in abolishing slavery, was moved only by self-interest; that its only aim was to cause the collapse of other peoples' colonies and thus to give its Indian establishments a monopoly in sugar production.[15] This claim does not withstand investigation. A reasonable man cannot suppose that England, in order to destroy other peoples' sugar colonies, began by ruining its own, several of which were in a state of extraordinary prosperity. That would have been Machiavellianism of the greatest conceivable insanity. At the time abolition was declared, the English colonies were producing 220 million kilos of sugar, that is to say, almost four times more than the French colonies did at the same time. Among the British colonies were Jamaica, the third in the Caribbean in beauty, fertility, and grandeur, and, on the continent, Demerara,[16] whose territory was so to speak unlimited and whose wealth and products had increased prodigiously in recent years. It was these admirable possessions that England supposedly sacrificed in order indirectly to destroy sugar production in all the countries where it is cultivated by the hands of slaves, and to concentrate it in India, where sugar could be procured at a low price without slavery. This would have been less difficult to imagine if, on the one hand, India had already been a large producer and, on the other, if sugar had not already been cultivated elsewhere and with greater success by free labor. But at the moment when abolition was declared, India still produced less than 4 million kilos of sugar annually, and the Dutch had already created the fine colony on Java that, from its inception, sent 60 million kilos to the markets of Europe.[17] Thus, after having destroyed the competition of slave labor in one hemisphere, the English immediately would have found themselves grappling in the other with a competition of free labor. To achieve such a result, this people, so enlightened in its interests, not only would have brought its finest possessions to ruin, but in addition would have imposed on itself, among other sacrifices, the obligation to pay 500 million in indemnity to its colonists! The absurdity of such a scheme is too obvious to require demonstration.

The truth is that emancipation of slaves was, like parliamentary reform, the work of the nation and not of its governors. It must be seen as the product of passion and not the result of calculation. The English government fought as hard as it could against the adoption of the measure. It resisted the abolition of the trade for fifteen years; it resisted the abolition of slavery for twenty-five. When it could not prevent it, it sought at least to delay it; and when it lost hope of delaying it, it sought to minimize the consequences, but always in vain; the popular tide always dominated it and swept it along.[18]

It is quite certain that once emancipation was resolved and accomplished, England's statesmen devoted all their skill to ensuring that other nations took as little advantage as possible from the revolution that they had just brought about in their colonies. Certainly it was not out of pure philanthropy that they worked so tirelessly to impede the slave trade on the world's waters and so to halt the development of countries that still kept slaves. The English, in abolishing slavery, gave up certain benefits whose enjoyment they did not want to leave to nations who did not imitate their example: that is clear. It is obvious that they employed every means to achieve this end, as was their way: sometimes violence, sometimes ruse, often hypocrisy and duplicity. But all these facts are subsequent to the abolition of slavery and do not prevent it from being the case that a philanthropic and above all a Christian sentiment produced this great event. This truth is incontestable as soon as one studies the question practically, yet it was obscured by all those who are bothered by England's example. It was necessary to make it entirely clear before explaining the details of even the English emancipation, which otherwise would have been ill understood.

It was on the 15th of May 1823 that the principle of the abolition of slavery, which had been debated for so long in the British Parliament, finally triumphed. That day, the House of Commons declared that Negroes should be made ready for freedom and given it as soon as they were in a condition to enjoy it. This resolution, apparently so wise, had only destructive consequences: the masters, who were thus alerted in advance that all the progress made by their slaves toward civilization would also be steps toward freedom, refused to share the Parliament's beneficent view. For their part, the slaves, who were shown freedom without being told when they would be given it, became impatient and unmanageable. There was an insurrection in Guyana and three in Jamaica. The last especially was one of the bloodiest ever seen.[19] Thus the solemn inquiry of 1832 demonstrated that hardly any progress had been made during the nine years that had just passed. The slaves remained as ignorant and depraved as before. Parliament, pushed by the incessant cries of the nation, finally resolved to cut the knot they had vainly tried to untie.

The act of 23 August 1833 thus declared that on 1 August 1834, slavery would cease to exist in all English colonies. There were nineteen slave colonies: eighteen in America and one in the Indian Ocean.[20] Still, the act of 23 August 1833 did not move slaves immediately from servitude to freedom; it created an intermediate state called apprenticeship. During this preparatory period, blacks continued to work unpaid for their former masters; only the unremunerated work that could be required of them was limited to a certain number of hours per week. The rest of their time was their own. It was actually still slavery by another name; but it was a temporary slavery. At the end of seven years, this last trace of servitude was to disappear.

The goal of the apprenticeship was to be in a sense a trial period that would show slaves independence and prepare them to handle it. It was above all, in the eyes of the English government, a way to reduce the indemnity that the metropole owed the colonists. In granting the latter the free labor of their former slaves for several more years, the government could pay them less.

This indemnity was set at 1,400 francs for each slave, whatever their age and sex. About half was paid in cash immediately; the rest was represented by the free labor of the Negroes for seven years. They made sure, in addition, to keep the tariffs that closed the English market to foreign sugar very high, so that during the expected crisis the colonists at least would be assured of selling their merchandise at a profit.

So, general and simultaneous abolition of slavery; an intermediate and preparatory state between the end of servitude and the beginning of freedom; preliminary indemnity; guarantee of a profitable price for sugar production, such, in its general aspect and leaving aside details, is the English system. We shall now see the results.

Perhaps never before in the world has there been an event that has created as much talk and writing as the English emancipation. The English, and foreigners as well, published a multitude of books, brochures, articles, sermons, official reports, and inquiries on the occasion; the subject has come up a

hundred times in ten years in the British Parliament's discussions; those documents alone would fill a large library.[21] One is at first surprised and then almost
frightened when reading them to see in what different and often opposing
ways men can evaluate the same event, not men who were born long after it
happened, but contemporaries before whose own eyes it unfolded. This truly
prodigious diversity can, however, be excused and explained if we look on the
one hand to the personal interests and party passions that animate most of the
witnesses and especially to the immensity of the revolution they were trying to
grasp. Such a social transformation occurring in nineteen different countries at
the same time must necessarily, according to the moment and the place one
studied it, have presented extremely different and often contrary aspects, and
those who spoke of it could have said things that were at once very contradictory and very true.

To oblige our readers to work through these opposing depositions would
be like leading them into a labyrinth: it is shorter and more effective to stick to
facts, to choose those that are incontestable and present these.

The colonists insisted that as soon as the Negroes were freed, they would
resort to the most condemnable excesses. They predicted scenes of disorder,
pillage, and massacres. This is the same language used by the planters in our
colonies.

Let us look at the facts: the abolition of slavery in the nineteen English
colonies has thus far not given rise to a *single* insurrection; it has not cost the
life of a single man, and yet in the English colonies there are twelve times as
many blacks as there are whites. As the report of the committee on colonial
affairs rightly remarks, summoning 800,000 slaves to freedom, on the same
day and at the same hour, has not caused in ten years a tenth part of the
troubles that ordinarily, in the most civilized nations of Europe, are caused by
the least political question that ever so slightly agitates people, that, for example, was caused in France by the simple question of the census.[22]

Not only have there not been crimes against society, but crimes against
individuals, ordinary crimes, have not increased or have increased only by
imperceptible proportions, and as a result it can be said that they have diminished, as a great number of offenses that have been punished by the magistrate
since the abolition of slavery would have been punished in the master's house
in the days of slavery without anyone knowing about them.

Another incontestable fact: since the Negroes felt the stimulus of freedom, they have rushed into the schools. This zeal for instruction seems truly incredible when one realizes that at the moment there is one school for every six hundred souls in the English colonies. One person in nine attends school; that is more than in France.[23] And just as the mind is being enlightened, habits are becoming more regular: we have equally unimpeachable evidence for this development.

We know what disorder of mores, approaching promiscuity, exists among the Negroes in our colonies. The institution of marriage is, as it were, unknown there, which is not at all surprising when on reflection we realize that this institution is incompatible with slavery. Marriages were also extremely rare among the Negroes of the English colonies: they multiplied quickly when freedom was granted. In 1835, 1,582 marriages were celebrated in Jamaica; 1,962 in 1836; 3,215 in 1837, and in 1838, the last year for which we have figures, 3,881.

With enlightenment and the regularity of mores must come the taste for well-being and the desire to improve one's condition. Just as the colonists predicted that the emancipated slaves would indulge in all sorts of violence, they insisted that they would revert to barbarity. The Negroes, on the contrary, once free, have lost no time in displaying all the tastes and acquiring all the needs of the most civilized peoples. Before emancipation, Great Britain's exports to its slave colonies never exceeded 75 million francs; this number has successively increased, and in 1840 it exceeded 100 million. It has thus grown by about a third in ten years. There can be no retort to such figures.

These are the incontestable results of emancipation among the blacks. It must be recognized that in other respects its effects are much less satisfying. But here again we should hasten to dispel the clouds of contradictory allegations in order to place established facts on solid ground.

Most of the adversaries of English emancipation themselves now recognize that this measure has led to the results just shown; but they still hold that if emancipation has not been as fatal to the tranquillity of the colonies, to the commerce of the metropole, and to the civilization of the blacks as one might have believed, it has been and will be no less disastrous for the colonists than they feared.

It is quite true that a fairly large number of Negroes, since they were freed, have stopped working in the sugar refineries that are the major industry in the English colonies, as in our own.

Among those who have remained in the factories, many have worked little or have demanded greatly exaggerated wages. This is a continual problem. But what is its precise extent? Is it as great as many predicted, or as it is imagined? Here too are figures that will provide an answer.

From 1830 to 1834, under slavery, the colonies produced 900,237,180 kilograms of sugar, which were sold for 578,536,395 francs.

From 1838 to 1841, a period of complete freedom, the colonies produced 666,375,077 kilos, which were sold for 650,579,649 francs.[24]

Thus, in the second period, real production diminished by a quarter.

As a result of the increase in sugar prices on the British market, the colonists in fact have received more money since slavery was abolished than before that time, as we have just seen. Still, their position has undeniably become far worse, as wages in the colonies were higher in comparison to the price of sugar in the metropole, and thus in selling at a higher price, the colonists actually did less well. Many of them were ruined, and almost all are suffering considerable difficulty.

In sum, no disorders; rapid progress of the black population toward good mores, enlightenment, and comfort; an increase by a third of exports from the metropole; decrease by a quarter of sugar production in the colonies; a notable rise in that product's price on the metropolitan market; an excessive increase in wages and, as a result, difficulties for the colonists and ruin for some: these are the good and bad results that emancipation has produced, as they emerge from proven facts and official figures.

When we consider the immensity of the revolution that has been effected, we must recognize that all in all, never has a greater change happened so peacefully or with so few costs.

This is what the Whig minister, author of the measure, proclaimed in 1841, and it is what the Tory minister who replaced him recognized in 1842.[25] In sum, as Lord Stanley said on 22 March 1842 in the House of Commons: "The result of the great experience of emancipation has surpassed the liveliest hopes of even the most ardent friends of colonial prosperity."

And it must not be said that these results apply uniquely to the particular character of the English colonies and to the education they had given their slaves. Among the nineteen colonies in which slavery was abolished, many once belonged to France and are still populated by Frenchmen: emancipation produced no more disorder there than elsewhere.

IV

It is true that in many respects the English emancipation had remarkable success, and, in Lord Stanley's words, it surpassed the hopes of the friends of colonial prosperity. It is easy to recognize, however, that in the execution of this great measure, the British government made many very considerable errors that led to most of the difficulties that the colonists and the metropole have endured and will continue to endure for a long time to come. So as not to exceed the limits of an article, I shall point out only the principal ones:

You will recall that after having abolished slavery nominally, the English in a sense reestablished it for a certain time under the name of apprenticeship. The apprenticeship was a preparation for freedom; when it was completed, complete freedom was granted, and colonial society entered into the same conditions of existence as European societies. Whites formed the wealthy class, Negroes the working class; no power was instituted to oversee and regulate the relations that developed between these two parts of the social body. The workers of the colonies had precisely the same rights those of the metropole enjoyed; like them, they could, at their pleasure, decide with sovereign power how to use their time, set their rates, and determine what to do with their wages.

This complete transformation of colonial society into free society was premature. The English had realized, during the semi-freedom of the apprenticeship, that most of the fears the colonists had conceived of the nature of the blacks were ill-founded. The Negro seemed to them perfectly like all other men. They saw him active when he worked for wages, avid for the goods offered by civilization when he could acquire them, loyal to the law when the law had become benevolent toward him, ready to learn as soon as he had perceived the utility of instruction, sedentary when he had a home, regular in his mores when he had been permitted to enjoy the joys of family. They concluded that these men were not different enough from us for it to be necessary to apply to them different laws from our own. The colonists, in constantly threatening the government with imaginary dangers, had turned their attention away from the real dangers.

The true peril they should have prepared to fight was actually born less of the particular character of blacks than of the special conditions in which colonial society was to find itself.

Before emancipation, there was in fact only a single industry in the English colonies: the sugar industry. Everything it did not produce was imported from elsewhere. Each colony was a vast sugar factory; this was clearly an artificial state that could be maintained only because the entire working population, being slaves, could be tied to the same work. From the moment that the workers were free to choose their industry, it was natural that a number of them, according to the diversity of faculties and tastes, would choose one other than sugar, and, without giving up on work altogether, would leave their former factories [*ateliers*] to seek their fortunes elsewhere. Above all, from the moment that the workers, instead of working for a master, could acquire land and earn more by working for themselves than by working for a wage, many of them left the sugar refineries or went there only from time to time, when the cultivation of their own fields left them leisure.

Since the number of sugar factories remained the same, and the number of workers who worked for the sugar industry was smaller, the former relationship between demand for and supply of labor suddenly changed, and wages rose at a frightening rate. If the cause remains, we must fear that the effect will continue, until the number of sugar factories declines or the mass of workers increases so that a balance is reestablished between profits and wages. But before this occurs, the emancipated colonies will suffer a long and profound malaise.

All this conforms perfectly to the general laws that govern production in free countries, and to explain the causes of such troubles it is useless to turn to alleged differences among the instincts of various human races. Place English or French workers in the same circumstances, and they will act in precisely the same manner.

The cause of the problem being well known, what were the remedies? Many presented themselves, but one in particular would have been very easy and very effective That a certain number of workers would leave the sugar refineries, preferring other industries, was the necessary consequence of freedom. But things could at least be arranged so that they would rarely have the desire to leave. To achieve that, it would be enough to prohibit them for a certain period from becoming landowners.

In all the English colonies, there exist vast expanses of very fertile terrain that have not yet been improved. There are colonies where the lands of this type infinitely exceed cultivated lands in extent. Almost all these lands can be acquired at a very low price. When the Negroes were freed, they naturally turned this way. Since they could easily become small landowners, they did not want to remain simple workers.[26] All the money they could save from their wages was used to buy these lands, and the possession of land allowed them to demand higher wages. One can well imagine what occurred in the English colonies by recalling what happened in France after the Revolution placed landed property within reach of the people. Everywhere the farm laborer has managed to become a landowner, he usually works at least half the year for his own benefit; he hires out his services only occasionally and consents to do so only for a high salary. The emancipated Negro acts likewise. The only difference is that because the price of land in France is high, workers can only become landowners gradually, whereas in the colonies, land being cheap, most blacks have been able to buy it at once.

In France, the change occurred slowly, and the national wealth has greatly increased; but in the colonies, where it has happened abruptly, it cannot but deliver a fatal blow to the sugar industry. Since the sugar industry is still the primary means of production — necessarily what big capital is used for, and almost the only source of trade — it cannot be ruined without bringing about a general crisis that, after first striking the whites, will necessarily extend to all the other classes.

The English government should thus have refused, at least for some time, to grant Negroes the right to acquire land; but it never had a very clear idea of the peril when there was still time to avert it. At the moment when slavery was abolished, such a restriction of freedom would have been accepted without murmur by the black population; later, it would have been imprudent to impose it. The English, however, did not give up; the same people to whom so much indifference to the fate of the sugar colonies is attributed made gigantic efforts to repair the unfortunate results of their error. They went to Africa, India, Europe, and the Azores to find the hands they needed. None of the slaves that British cruisers detained on the high seas in such great numbers were returned to the places from which they had come: they were transported as free workers to the emancipated colonies. Today, it is the English who take the greatest advantage of the slave trade, which they work to suppress, and perhaps it is to this consideration that we should attribute the extraordinary zeal with which they seize slave ships, and the remarkable apathy they display when effective means are proposed for suppressing the markets where the Negroes are actually sold.[27]

Soon, if Europe allows them, they will go to the coast of Guinea to buy blacks in order to make them free workers in Jamaica and Demerara, thus promoting the development of slavery in Africa just when they are abolishing it in the New World.

Despite these heroic remedies, we can predict that it will still take the English government a long time to cure the evil that its inexperience created.

The English, in abolishing slavery, simultaneously showed all other nations what should be done and what should be avoided. They have provided both great examples and great lessons.

We shall see in a later article what France can make of both.

V

In the preceding articles, we have seen where the question of the emancipation of slaves stands among the English. Let us now see in what state the same question finds itself in France.

One of the first acts of the July government was to stop the slave trade in our colonies. Since that time no new slaves have been introduced; from that moment, each slave already there became an instrument of labor that was more difficult to replace, and thus the recipient of greater care, and the black population, which fell by 3 percent annually during the days of the trade, stabilized and soon began to grow.[28]

Public opinion lost no time in asking for more. The mitigation of slavery and finally its abolition were demanded. Many of the most considerable men in Parliament took this great cause in hand. On a proposal made in 1838 by the honorable M. Passy, a committee was named. This committee was led by M. Guizot, and it gave rise to a very remarkable report, whose author was M. de Rémusat.[29] The committee did not ask for the immediate abolition of slavery, but nor did it hide that it considered that event imminent and necessary, and that all the measures it proposed had its preparation as their goal. Since the Chamber had been dissolved, the report was not discussed. In 1839, the question was taken up in a similar proposition by M. de Tracy. A new committee, which included M. Barrot, was named. The committee of 1839, for which M. de Tocqueville was the reporter, following the same course that the preceding committee had done at the outset, but, drawing more rigorous conclusions from the principles it had set out, decided in favor of the abolition of slavery and proposed a plan to bring it about.

This report of 1839 did not reach discussion, any more than the earlier one had, for M. Thiers, speaking for the ministry, had declared to the tribune that he shared the views of the committee and would undertake to prepare a plan for abolition himself. He gathered a number of peers, deputies, admirals, and former colonial governors to carry out this preliminary work. The duc de Broglie was their chairman and their reporter.[30]

After many years of research and labor, whose traces are borne by the voluminous minutes that were published recently, this committee published its report six months ago. By its extent, and more still by the manner in which the subject is treated, this report must be set apart from all other documents of this sort. It is a book — a fine book — that will endure and marks an epoch in the history of the great revolution that it recounts and prepares.

We have often had occasion to oppose the duc de Broglie. But the high esteem we have always professed for his talents and character allow us to seize with pleasure every opportunity to do him justice. We willingly recognize that better than anyone else, the duc de Broglie unites the necessary qualities to excel in the work the committee put him in charge of: a practical knowledge of the great affairs of government, and the habit of philosophical study as well as the taste for it; a true love of humanity, enlightened by political experience of men, and, finally, leisure.[31]

The committee of which the duc de Broglie was the organ recognized that the uncertainty in which the colonists, the slaves, and the metropole have been living for several years could not safely last much longer and believes that the moment has arrived to set a time for the abolition of slavery. But how should it be abolished? Here the committee is divided. Two plans are proposed. We shall limit ourselves to describing the one the majority adopted.[32]

A law would set the irrevocable termination of slavery ten years from today. These ten years would be used to prepare the Negroes and the colonists to uphold the new social state destined for them. While remaining subjected to forced and usually unpaid labor, the principal sign of slavery, the Negro would, however, acquire certain rights that until now he has never enjoyed, and without which there can be no progress in morals and in civilization: such as rights to marry, to acquire [property], to buy his freedom; schools would be open to him; religious education and instruction would be furnished abundantly.

You can see that between the end of slavery and independence properly speaking, the committee, like the British government, thought it appropriate to place an intermediate period principally dedicated to the education of Negroes; but the committee conceived this intermediate state differently from the English. The latter had begun by declaring slavery abolished, but each slave, transformed into an apprentice, nonetheless remained under his former master and worked for him without wages. This mixed condition, where freedom, after having been granted, seemed to have been retracted, was not well understood by anyone. It gave birth to interminable discussions between the races: the Negroes grew exasperated, and the whites were not the least bit satisfied. Enlightened by this experience, the committee judged that the name of slavery should not be suppressed until the moment that the principal traits that characterize it are truly erased; instead of announcing more than one is giving, as the English have done, the committee found it wiser to grant in reality more than seems to be promised.

At the end of this preparatory period, the forced relations between servant and master would end; work would become productive; servitude would cease in fact as in name.

But this does not mean that colonial society must all at once take on exactly the same appearance as greater French society, nor that the emancipated Negro is to enjoy on the spot all the rights that our worker possesses. The English example is there to prevent us from making such an error. The committee understood this perfectly; it judged that the greatest danger for the colonies at the time of the emancipation did not stem, as had been thought until then, from the bad inclinations of the blacks, and that, even though during the last years of slavery the slaves had achieved all the progress in morals and civilization of which experience had shown them capable, it would still be imprudent to accord them all at once the same independence that the French working classes enjoy. The committee understood that if, at the moment when forced labor no longer existed, artificial means were not used to attract and retain Negroes in the sugar refineries, and to prevent an excessive rise in wages, sugar production would receive a sudden and grave blow, and that the colonies, exposed to a sudden perturbation in their principal and almost only industry, would suffer greatly.

In the years immediately following the abolition of slavery, the committee therefore proposes to qualify the freedom of the emancipated Negroes in the following three main ways:

The former slaves will be required to reside in the colony.

Although free to choose their profession and the master under whose direction they want to work, they will neither be permitted to remain idle nor to work only for themselves.

Each year, the maximum and minimum wages will be fixed by the governor in council. Prices will be debated between these limits.

The motives behind these three transitional resolutions are easy to grasp.

With the first, the committee seeks to prevent English recruitment, which would quickly and significantly diminish the laboring population of our islands.

The goal of the second is to prevent the Negroes of our colonies from imitating those of the English colonies and abandoning large industries to settle on portions of fertile soil they would acquire at a very low price or usurp.

The principal object of the third, finally, is to prevent the masters, for their part, from abusing the blacks' obligation to hire out their services, and from abusing their ability, given their small number, to join forces and impose excessively low wages on their workers.

It is understood that these arrangements are transitional: they are intended only to facilitate the colonies' passage from one social state to another and to prevent a rapid decline of workers and, as a result, an industrial disturbance just as prejudicial, it cannot be said too often, to the black race as to the white race.

When the Negroes, after having adopted a fixed residence, have conclusively chosen a profession and learned its customs; when practice has imposed certain limits on wages, the last traces of servitude can disappear. The committee estimates that this transitional state could end after five years.

The Chambers will have to examine whether, instead of having recourse to this set of exceptional measures, they might not restrict themselves, on the one hand, to rigorously implementing the existing laws against vagabondage, and, on the other, to prohibiting Negroes from buying or occupying land for a few years. This would seem simpler, clearer, and perhaps just as effective.

It is principally the possession and cultivation of land that, in the English colonies, has caused blacks to leave the sugar refineries. The same causes infallibly would lead to the same effects in ours.

Of the 263,000 hectares in Martinique and Guadeloupe, 180,000 are not cultivated.

Guyana, which is 125 leagues by nearly 200 leagues, has only cultivated 12,000 hectares.[33] Thus there is not a Negro in the colonies who could not procure land, and who would not procure it if he were given liberty to do so. For as long as the trace of slavery is not erased, the blacks naturally will have little desire to work for the benefit of a master. They will prefer to live independently in their little domain, even if by doing so they live less comfortably. If on the contrary the emancipated Negroes were neither allowed to live as vagabonds nor to procure a little domain for themselves, and were reduced to hiring out their services for a living, it is very likely that most of them would remain in the sugar refineries, and that the cost of running these establishments would not increase immeasurably.

When one examines it closely, the temporary prohibition on landownership is not only the most effective but also in reality the least oppressive of all the exceptional measures to which we could have recourse.

It is not by any natural or necessary consequence of freedom that the Negroes of the colonies could pass all at once from the state of slaves to that of landowners: it is as a result of a very extraordinary circumstance, that is, the proximity of fertile lands that belong so to speak to the first occupant. Nothing like it has ever happened in our civilized societies.

Despite all the efforts we have made in France to put real property within reach of the working classes, land has remained so costly that it is only with great effort that the worker can acquire some. He manages to do so only in the long term and after having earned money by his industry. In all European nations, it is almost unheard of for a worker to become a landowner. For him, the land in a sense lies beyond reach.

In temporarily prohibiting Negroes from possessing land, what are we doing? We are placing them artificially in the position in which the European worker finds himself naturally.

Assuredly, that is no tyranny, and the man on whom only this obstacle is imposed as he leaves slavery would not seem to have any right to complain.

VI

However important the position of the blacks may be, however sanctified their misfortune must be in our eyes, for it is our doing, it would be unjust and imprudent to be concerned with them alone. France cannot forget those of her children who live in the colonies, nor lose sight of her greatness, which demands that these colonies progress.

If the Negroes have the right to become free, it is incontestable that the colonists have the right not be ruined by the freedom of the Negroes. It is true, the colonists have taken advantage of slavery; but it was not they who established it. For two hundred years, the metropole has favored the development of this detestable institution with all its power, and it was the metropole that inspired in our overseas compatriots the prejudices that now astonish and irritate us.

The insults and often the calumnies that the colonists level at so many honorable men every day should not prevent us from seeing that there is some justice in their demands and some foundation to their grievances.

Reviewing this aspect of the matter, the committee did not hesitate to recognize that if the metropole owed freedom to the colonies' slaves, it owed the colonists many guarantees, which it summarized in this manner:

First, [there should be] a delay long enough for colonial proprietors to prepare themselves to endure the anticipated revolution and to procure what they need to meet the new costs that the production of sugar by free labor will occasion.

One of our colonies has just suffered an immense disaster: we must give it time to recover.[34]

At this moment, moreover, colonial property everywhere is encumbered by debt; one could almost say that it does not exist, for as most colonists have more debts than assets, no one knows precisely who in reality owns the lands they cultivate. Only forced expropriation in the colonies could bring about an end to this disorder: liquidate properties and bring the true owners to light. Only then will the colonists with capital or credit be able to make the advances necessitated by the substitution of wage labor for free labor.

A bill proposing to introduce forced expropriation to the Antilles has now been submitted for the Chamber's consideration, and it is likely to be adopted next year. It is a good idea to let the new expropriation law function for a while before abolishing slavery for good.

The second guarantee that the colonists, according to the committee, have the right to demand of the mother country, is a profitable price for their sugar. Indeed, emancipation, however carefully it is brought about, will necessarily lead to a certain degree of disturbance in colonial labor, as the committee reporter points out. In the first moments, production will necessarily be reduced. If the price of sugar does not rise at the same time, and even more if it falls, the colonists, already strained, will suffer a loss of revenue that will make it very difficult and perhaps impossible for them to fulfill their new obligations.

A small sacrifice imposed on consumers would, by contrast, be enough to help them through this period and put the business to rights. Some figures will make this clear. The colonies today sell us 80 million kilos of sugar at a rate of 125 francs for 100 kilos; this earns them 100 million francs. Suppose that after the abolition of slavery, the importation of colonial sugar falls to 70 million kilos, and that, as a result of the introduction of foreign sugar or thanks to a particular favor granted to beet sugar, the sale price remains at 125 francs for 100 kilos, the colonists' revenue will fall by 12,500,000 francs — an overwhelming loss, which will be borne by a very small number of producers. If the price of sugar, by contrast, rises to 145 francs for 100 kilos, which would not be at all extraordinary and has happened several times in recent years, the colonists would lose nothing, and the consumer would pay no more than two sous extra for a pound of sugar.[35]

This is precisely what happened in England. The production of colonial sugar fell by a quarter after emancipation, as we have seen. But thanks to protective tariffs, the price of colonial sugar rose as a result of the very rarity of the product, and the colonists received no less money, which has allowed them until now to resist the disastrous consequences of the rise in wages.

Indeed, a quite remarkable circumstance occurred. In 1840, when the government wanted to lower the duty levied on foreign sugar by almost half, the House of Commons, that is to say, the legislative branch that most directly represented consumers, opposed this plan; rather than allow it, they preferred to turn out the ministry.[36]

These considerations led the committee for colonial affairs to declare that in its opinion it was necessary, before proceeding to emancipation, to establish equality between beet sugar and colonial sugar, and that as long as the crisis produced by this great event persisted, the import duty on foreign sugar should not be lowered.

The last guarantee it is fair to grant the colonists is an indemnity representing the monetary value of the freed slaves. During the ten years that would elapse, under the committee's system, between the moment the principle of abolition is adopted and the moment slavery is actually done away with, the slaves are prepared for freedom and colonial property is liquidated. During this period, the colonists would suffer no prejudice and consequently would have no right to indemnity. But the day servitude ends and Negro labor ceases to be unpaid, we shall have to deal with the question of indemnity. Is the slave truly property? What is the nature of this property? What is the state, who made it disappear, obligated to do by law and by equity? The duc de Broglie has treated this most difficult and delicate part of his report as an economist, a philosopher, and a statesman. This is the most striking part of this great work; we would like to be able to place it before our readers, but the limits we have imposed upon ourselves prevent this. We shall merely say that the committee manages to show that it would be contrary to all notions of equity, and to the evident interest of the metropole, to take their slaves from the colonists without indemnifying them for their loss.

After long and conscientious study, the committee decided to fix this indemnity at 1,200 francs per slave. The English settled the indemnity in two ways: upon abolition, they paid half the sum promised to the planters, and in addition they guaranteed them a part of the labor of the freed slaves for seven years. They calculated that at the end of the seven years the value of this work would be equivalent to the money that had not been paid. The committee adopted a measure that, if not identical, was at least similar.

As the capital owed for the colonies' 250,000 slaves, at 1,200 francs a head, comes to 300 million, half that, or 150 million, represented by interest at 4 percent of 6 million, would be granted the colonists and placed at their disposal at the deposit and consignment office. Through this arrangement, the metropole pays off half its debt and acquires as a result the right to withdraw from the colonists half the unpaid labor of their slaves; otherwise, it would continue to allow them to enjoy the full benefits of unpaid labor for ten years. Now, the price of the daily work of a Negro could be valued at 50 centimes. It is thus 25 centimes a day that the metropole gives the master, and this benefit, maintained for ten years, would be worth precisely the 150 million that was not paid.

As we can see, the costs of emancipation are distributed in a manner that seems equitable among all those who have an interest in the success of the measure: half the indemnity is furnished by the metropole, the other half by the labor of the blacks, and the rise in price of labor is borne by the colonists.

In sum, complete freedom is granted to the slaves after ten years; until then, a series of measures whose goal is to morally improve and civilize the Negroes and to liquidate the property of the whites. After this time, [there will be] special legislation whose object would be to help colonial society to resettle, with freedom given to slaves and a sufficient indemnity granted to masters.

Such, in its principal aspects, is the emancipation plan that the majority of the committee proposes. It would be difficult, it seems, to attain a greater goal at smaller cost, and to bring together any better the requirements of humanity and France's interest with the commands of prudence.

Will this plan, so laboriously prepared by the committee and presented with such great talent by the duc de Broglie, be sincerely adopted by the government and seriously presented for adoption by the Chambers? This is highly doubtful.

M. Guizot has too elevated a spirit to be insensible to the beauty and grandeur of the work proposed. We shall do him the justice to believe that he would carry it out if he were free to do so. But who does not know that M. Guizot is not the master, and that the role he settles for is merely to be the first among those who obey?[37] We might believe that many of the ministers favor emancipation, but all those who have a close view of affairs know well that the government does not favor it. This is not a time of generous enterprises, not even one of useful enterprises, when they are also large and difficult.

There are many ways to resist emancipation. One can preserve slavery resolutely, as Napoleon and the Restoration did. But this is not easy in these times of democratic liberty, when we represent a revolution that was undertaken entirely in the name of equality, and whose symbol and strength is this glorious principle.

Without upholding slavery, one can at least not undertake to destroy it. Inasmuch as it is impossible to emancipate Negroes if the government is not at the head of the enterprise, it has no need to resist the efforts of the abolitionists in order to negate them; it is enough to refrain from action. This has been our policy for six years.

A final expedient consists of preaching emancipation but exaggerating its perils, uncertainties, and costs to the Chambers, so that the obstacle comes from them. In this way, one preserves the honor of one's principles without placing one's power in jeopardy, and one remains at the same time liberal and a minister, a difficult thing to do. It is to be feared that the ministry will follow this method: several things said at the end of the last session seem to indicate this. Questioned on the intentions of the government, M. Guizot first protested his devotion to the cause of abolition; then he obligingly displayed the difficulties and costs of the measure, immensely exaggerated, before the Assembly. He did not hesitate, among other things, to announce officially that emancipation would cost the public treasury more than 250 million, which, as it was easy to predict, gave rise to disapproving exclamations from the Chamber.[38]

Now at that very moment, M. Guizot had in hand the duc de Broglie's report, a report that makes it clear that 6 million in interest on 150 million in capital represents the total cost very closely.[39] What do such words mean, then? Must we attribute them to ignorance? But how can we accept the ignorance of the government in such a large and well-known affair? Do they want to antagonize public opinion in advance and stir up a healthy resistance? This is what the next session will make clear.

If the ministry clearly takes the route of emancipation, showing that our suspicions were unjustified, the duty of the opposition is to support the ministry with all its power, for what is at stake are France's interest, greatness, and honor, the doctrines that her Revolution spread throughout the world and that the opposition in particular prides itself on professing. But the opposition must take care not to satisfy themselves with vain words; they should know that, when they are told of new delays for the purpose of new studies, they are being fooled.

Everything that statistics can make known has been learned; everything that experience can show has been seen. Never has a question better illuminated from all sides been placed before the Chambers. The measure is necessary, as all sensible men recognize. The time to enact it has arrived; no one can contest it seriously; the means for carrying it out have been found; it is enough to read the duc de Broglie's report to be convinced of this. There remains only one thing to decide: whether it is paying too much to add six or seven million francs more to our debts in order to preserve for the country positions that dominate a large part of the globe's commerce, in order to release 250,000 of our fellow beings from the slavery in which we keep them against all right, and, finally, in order to remain loyal to our role and not to desert the noble principles that we ourselves have made triumph among our neighbors. There is no other question than that.

NOTES

The notes are substantially drawn from Alexis de Tocqueville's *Œuvres complètes,*
edited by J.-P. Mayer (Paris: Gallimard, 1958–98) and have been modified where
necessary for purposes of this English edition. Aside from those to the Introduction, notes or parts of notes added by the translator appear in brackets. Tocqueville's own addenda are printed as footnotes to the text.

INTRODUCTION

1. Two important sources for this biographical sketch are Jardin 1988 and Mayer
1960. See also Pierson 1938 on Tocqueville's American journey, and Drescher 1964 on
Tocqueville's long-standing interest in England and his trip to England and Ireland in
1835.

2. Tocqueville's cousin and close friend Louis de Kergorlay ended his political
career at the time by refusing to swear loyalty to Louis-Philippe. In 1833, the young
soldier, who had participated in the June 1830 capture of Algiers, proposed to Tocqueville that they purchase land in Algeria and become settlers, and both entertained the
idea for some time.

3. Quoted by Jardin 1988, 90.

4. The Johns Hopkins University Press has recently republished a 1958 translation
by Barbara Chapman of Gustave de Beaumont's *Marie, or, Slavery in the United States: A
Novel of Jacksonian America* (Baltimore, 1999).

5. Jardin 1988, 224.

6. Tocqueville, "A MM. les électeurs de l'arrondissement de Valognes," quoted by
Drescher 1964, 11.

7. See Richter 1988.

8. Other prominent Englishmen with whom Tocqueville discussed colonial questions included Lord Edward Hatherton M.P. (1791–1863); Henry Reeve (1813–95),

who translated *Democracy in America* (see n. 15 below); and the economist Nassau William Senior (1790–1864).

9. His notes on India are published in *OC* 3, pt. 1.

10. As his French editors have noted in their informative introduction to the Gallimard edition of Tocqueville's writings on empire, Tocqueville's career is often imagined in three parts: the sociology of his early years, culminating in *Democracy in America;* the politics of his middle years, which "remain the most obscure," and during which empire was perhaps the subject of his greatest interest; and the history of his later years, which produced the *Old Regime and the French Revolution.* The writings collected here thus represent a crucial aspect of his work during an important and neglected period of Tocqueville's life. See André Jardin and Jean-Jacques Chevallier, *OC* 3, pt. 1: 7–8.

11. This volume also includes Tocqueville's striking series of articles on the emancipation of slaves in the French West Indies, written in 1843: these appeared in a translation by Seymour Drescher in 1968, now out of print: *Tocqueville and Beaumont on Social Reform* (New York: Harper & Row, 1968), 137–73. Their intrinsic interest, their connections with the themes of this volume, and the relative inaccessibility of the Drescher volume prompted their republication here, in a new translation.

12. Lawlor 1959, 175.

13. Richter 1963, 385. Richter's article offers a subtle and finely contextualized account of Tocqueville's writings on Algeria.

14. Richter 1963, 364. The other main commentator on Tocqueville's writings about Algeria, André Jardin, dismisses altogether the question of a clash of principles, saying that Tocqueville "did not question the legitimacy of such a conquest, having none of the bad conscience on this matter that people of the twentieth century have" (Jardin 1988, 318). It should be clear from the following discussion that criticism of empire on either moral or practical grounds is not a twentieth-century development, nor was it foreign to Tocqueville.

15. Tocqueville, *Democracy in America*, trans. Henry Reeve, ed. Phillips Bradley (1945; reprint, New York: Random House, Vintage Books, 1990), 1: 355. Henceforth cited as *Democracy*.

16. Pierson 1938, 596. G. W. Pierson collected and translated a great deal of unpublished material for *Tocqueville in America*, including Tocqueville's valuable essay "A Fortnight in the Wilderness," which records his horseback journey with Beaumont and some Amerindian guides to the fringes of European habitation in Michigan.

17. Berlin 1965, 204.

18. "Some Ideas about What Prevents the French from Having Good Colonies," which Tocqueville wrote in 1833 and originally intended to include, in some form, in *Democracy in America*.

19. Tocqueville presents conflicting opinions about the degree of choice the Amerindian tribes had either to accept European ways and survive or to decline them and be corrupted and ultimately exterminated. At times he suggests that their alleged pride or savagery played no part in their annihilation, but that it was inevitable given the rapacity

of the Europeans. In any case, he is clear that to the extent that he believed that if any choice existed, it was between total assimilation and extermination. In Tocqueville's view, while the Americans occasionally used the formal language of international politics with the Amerindian tribes (such as treaty-making), they never seriously considered allowing the tribes to remain as separate, neighboring nations.

20. *Democracy*, 1: 347.

21. Ibid., 331.

22. An ideal of French Algeria quickly entered the French imagination in the 1830s after the conquest of Algiers; the shifting view of the conservative historian and politician François Guizot offers some evidence for this change. In the 1820s, Guizot had criticized imperial conquest as the irresponsible acting out of personal fantasy; by the 1830s and 1840s, however, he had come to view the total domination of Algeria as necessary for France. Compare *L'Histoire de la Civilisation d'Europe* (Guizot 1828, 18) and *Memoirs to Illustrate the History of My Time* (Guizot 1865, 116–17). See also Louis Blanc's *History of Ten Years, 1830–1840* (Blanc 1844–45).

23. The *Recollections* are the best source both for Tocqueville's early anticipation of revolution (chapter 1) and his judgments about the mediocrity of French politics in his day (Tocqueville 1986 passim; see esp. p. 11).

24. In 1830, Tocqueville wrote to his brother Edouard, "In the midst of all this we are preparing for war with incredible activity (the expedition to Algiers). It is worth remarking that, since the war has been resolved on, the liberal papers have, in general, ceased to criticize both the end in view and the preparation. The unanimity of opinion on this point shows the spirit of the nation" (letter of 6 April 1830). Tocqueville was perhaps too quick to note unanimous support for conquest, for the left-center paper *Le Constitutionnel* announced several weeks later: "This war lacks two things: a cause, and an aim; moreover, it lacks a third, more important still — a vote: that is, the consent of the nation to the considerable expense that will be involved" (26 April 1830; see Lawlor 1959, 132).

25. See pp. xxxv–xxxviii for a brief history of French Algeria in the 1800s.

26. His biographer André Jardin notes the significance of Tocqueville's choice to write about Algeria as he formally entered elective politics. The "Letters" were published in *La Presse de Seine-et-Oise*, a newspaper he played a small part in running. No copies of the printed articles exist, and so our sources for these pieces are Tocqueville's manuscripts. The articles were anonymous by custom, but their authorship was widely known. See Jardin 1988, 320.

27. See Lorcin 1995, a thorough and compelling analysis of the "Kabyle Myth" in French thought, its role in nineteenth-century French racial theories, and its consequences for both the military and the civilian administration of Algeria. The crux of the myth lay in the binary contrast between Arabs (cast as fanatical, nervous, and weak) and Kabyles (seen as secular, vigorous, honorable, and appropriate allies for the French). Lorcin argues that what began as a rough Arab-Kabyle dichotomy hardened into the Kabyle Myth, with a pseudo-scientific apparatus and the active participation of ethnological and anthropological societies, in the 1850s, slightly later than the time of

Tocqueville's writings. Tocqueville's second parliamentary report of 1847 condemned the administration's effort to defeat the Kabyles militarily rather than co-opt them through trade.

28. *Le Moniteur universel* announced their arrival in Algiers in May 1841; see Lawlor 1959, 133, and *OC* 5, pt. 2: 199.

29. Letter of 12 May 1841, in *OC* 14 (*Correspondance familiale*, 1998): 216.

30. Letter of 30 May 1841, in *OC* 14: 221.

31. Tocqueville sent the manuscript to Beaumont as soon as it was drafted. He had apologized earlier for the poor quality of the prose. But in an effort to encourage Beaumont to write about Algeria as well, he wrote that "it is a very great question, about which we are already well enough informed to be able to throw into circulation many new and true ideas" (letter of 21 October 1841).

32. Melvin Richter has written that the essay, "never intended for publication, is altogether free from the edifying tone its author assumed on occasion in his more deliberate dialogues with his public and posterity" (Richter 1963, 365).

33. In this preference for property rights over political participation, Tocqueville came far closer to supporting the priorities of the July Monarchy he so disdained than he ever did in debates on domestic politics. For a discussion of the "bourgeois monarchy" of Louis-Philippe and its hostility to extension of suffrage, see Furet 1992, 340 ff.

34. In British debates over the government of India at this time, the utilitarians, James Mill in particular, were advancing similar arguments for improving imperial governance by placing responsibility on the shoulders of particular individuals. See Stokes 1959, 73-75.

35. *OC* 6, pt. 2: 514.

36. General Thomas-Robert Bugeaud de la Piconnerie (1784-1849) was a member of the Chamber of Deputies from 1831 to 1847. Sent to Algeria as a lieutenant general, Bugeaud was authorized to conduct negotiations with Abd-el-Kader (Toqueville's spelling of the name is used throughout in this volume for consistency, but it is often transliterated by modern writers as Abd al-Qadir), which led to the treaty of Tafna of 20 May 1837. Appointed governor-general in November 1840, General (and later Marshal) Bugeaud became notorious for his violent and uncompromising attacks on indigenous tribes and villages and for his hostility to civilian settlers. He was also known for organizing "drumhead marriages" between soldiers in Algeria and French orphan girls. Bugeaud proved unable to gain support for his plans for military colonies, as Tocqueville discusses in his Second Report on Algeria of 1847. For the most complete work in English on Bugeaud, see Sullivan 1983.

37. The Chamber of Deputies followed Beaumont's suggestion that a single committee of eighteen (instead of the usual nine) members be convened to consider both questions; Tocqueville was chosen (in preference to Beaumont) to draft both reports. The committee included Beaumont, Tocqueville's friend and frequent ally Claude (Francisque) Corcelle, and the anti-imperialist Amédée Desjobert, among others. *OC* 3, pt. 1: 308 n. 2. Richter notes that Tocqueville "was directly involved" in Bugeaud's

resignation, which came on the heels of the Chamber's rejection of his proposal for military colonies (1963, 392).

38. Because Tocqueville's wife joined him on the second trip and wrote on his behalf to his family, we do not have the rich documentation of his immediate impressions that we do for the first (when Tocqueville himself wrote extensively to his wife, as well as to his father and his brother Edouard). The most complete account of his tour with Bugeaud was written by the journalist A. Bussière, who accompanied them (Bussière 1853).

39. Quoted by Chevallier and Jardin 1963, 32; also included in *OC* 7: 127.

40. See, for instance, Tocqueville's *Correspondance anglaise*, in which he asks his friend Henry Reeve about the effects of warfare with the indigenous people on settlement and wonders whether the state should be involved directly in founding villages for settlers (*OC* 6, pt. 1: 93–94). Tocqueville had also learned about indirect governance during his extensive study of the British empire in India, where he believed the British had preserved the most effective elements of the former Mughal administrative structure (see *OC* 3, pt. 1: 456 ff.). However, see Stokes 1959, 310, for the argument that although indirect governance was widespread in the later British colonies in Africa, it was not much practiced in India.

41. Tocqueville noted that Algerian education prior to the French conquest was more extensive than that of rural France.

42. On Haileybury College, see First Report on Algeria, n. 29, below.

43. See Richter 1963, 379.

44. Tocqueville last wrote about Algeria in the parliamentary reports of 1847; after leaving government in 1852, following Louis-Napoléon Bonaparte's coup d'état, he turned his attention to French history. He continued to write occasionally to his British friends about imperialism, however, and we see a renewed burst of interest in empire in 1857–58 in particular, when the sepoy rebellion among Indian soldiers prompted a crisis in Britain that precipitated the abolition of the East India Company and the establishment of direct rule over India by the British state.

45. French slave colonies at this time included Guadeloupe and Martinique in the Caribbean, Guiana, and Réunion (the former Bourbon) in the Indian Ocean.

46. Other members of the society were Beaumont, Remusat, Guizot, Odilon Barrot, and the well-known abolitionist Victor Schoelcher; Victor Hugo, Louis Blanc, Lamartine, and General Cavaignac later joined; see Blackburn 1988, 485–92, and Drescher 1968, 161 ff. Blackburn 1988, ch. 12, provides a thorough account of the question of slavery in France from 1818 to 1848.

47. The report, published in *OC* 3, pt. 1, first appeared in English in 1840, in a translation by Mary Sparks, published in Boston; it reappeared in a modified translation by Drescher in *Tocqueville and Beaumont on Social Reform* (cited n. 11 above), 98–136; quotation at 136. For a discussion of the report's enthusiastic reception by American abolitionists, see 98–99, n. 1. Drescher's excellent editorial notes, as well as his chapter on the "Abolition of Slavery" in Drescher 1968, offer a good account of the historical and political background for both the report and the articles.

48. *OC* 3, pt. 1: 11.

49. Slavery was in fact abolished in French colonies in 1848, the second act of the provisional government, after its declaration of universal suffrage. Abolition was effected suddenly and completely, with the destructive results for colonial economies that Tocqueville had predicted. Cobban 1961, 137.

50. Some of these arguments can be found in the report; see Tocqueville 1968, 125, where he attributes (British) Antigua's smooth transition to a free economy to the absence of land available for purchase by freedmen, which forced them to labor for their former masters for relatively low wages.

51. This letter was published after Tocqueville's death in *Letters on American Slavery* by the American Anti-Slavery Society (Boston, 1860), 8.

52. Valet 1924, 145; cited by Lawlor 1959, 134.

53. Desjobert, a disciple of J. B. Say and the British economists, was a deputy in the Chamber from 1833 to 1848, and then a moderate member of the 1848 Constituent Assembly. For a decade, Desjobert kept up an impassioned and well informed, if somewhat monotonous, stream of anti-imperialist publications: *La Question d'Alger* (1837); *L'Algérie en 1838; L'Algérie en 1844; L'Algérie en 1846; Algérie* (1847).

54. After Louis-Napoléon's coup, 10,000 opponents of the new regime were exiled to Algeria. See Tocqueville 1985 and Furet 1992, 445.

55. Denis Diderot, *Political Writings,* ed. John Hope Mason and Robert Wokler (Cambridge: Cambridge University Press, 1992), 177. This passage appears in the *Histoire des Deux Indes*, 3d ed. (Neuchâtel and Geneva: Libraires associés, 1783), bk. 8, ch. 1.4.

56. John Stuart Mill, *On Liberty* (1859), in *On Liberty and Other Writings,* ed. Stefan Collini (Cambridge: Cambridge University Press, 1989), 13.

57. Mehta 1999, which restricts itself to the British case, attempts to identify elements in the liberal tradition of Locke, Bentham, and the Mills that explain their support for British imperialism. These include, Mehta argues, a disregard for the importance of territory and a sense of "place" to members of a political community; and a commitment to a narrow conception of progress. Although a subtle account, even this work tends to generalize about a tradition of liberal thinking that, in fact, has been much more heterogeneous in its views on empire than he implies.

58. Indeed, Jon Elster makes a good case that Tocqueville is the most self-contradictory of all great political thinkers. See Elster, *Political Psychology* (Cambridge: Cambridge University Press, 1993), 112.

59. For informative accounts in English, see Ruedy 1992, Ageron 1991, and Johnson 1976.

60. It is estimated that in 1830 the Berbers made up half the total population of three million (within the current borders of Algeria); see Johnson 1976 and Yacono 1955. For the term *qabā'il,* see Ageron 1991, 4 and 20.

61. For a discussion of the frequent arguments (French, British, and American) for European conquest of Algeria to eradicate piracy and slavery, see Ann Thomson,

"Arguments for the Conquest of Algiers in the Late Eighteenth and Early Nineteenth Centuries," *Maghreb Review* 14 (1989): 108–18.

62. A recent account of the conquest, which replaces reliance on the fly-swatter myth with attention to persistent French interest in North Africa and in particular to the pressure for conquest from commercial interests in Marseilles, can be found in Amar Hamdani, *La Vérité sur l'expédition d'Alger* (Paris: Balland, 1985). Also see Stora 1991 (who also dismisses the fly-swatter tale) and Bouche 1991 for accounts of the conquest.

63. Ordinance of 22 July 1834; reported in *Le Moniteur universel,* 3 August 1834. See Lawlor 1959, 142.

64. See pp. 66–69 in this volume, where Tocqueville describes Abd-el-Kader's rise to power and his successful combination of appeals to tradition to attract supporters and adoption of European organization and strategy. Abd-el-Kader "not only had an elaborate network of informants but also perused French newspapers to keep abreast of parliamentary debates in Paris" (Clancy-Smith 1994, 8).

65. See Johnson 1976, 110 ff.

66. See Clancy-Smith 1994, 88–89. As she notes at 71, the two leaders' efforts at state building differed significantly: Ahmad Bey attempted to "resurrect an Ottoman bureaucratic state," while Abd-el-Kader sought to build a "classical tribal-based theocracy."

67. See Ageron 1991, 28–30. Algeria was unusual, although not unique, in this regard; the only other overseas departments were Martinique, Guadeloupe, Réunion, and Guiana. Most French colonies were not granted departmental status and thus were not as thoroughly integrated into the metropolitan administrative and political structure.

68. See James S. Olson, ed., *Historical Dictionary of European Imperialism* (Westport, Conn.: Greenwood Press, 1991), 10.

69. See ibid. and Ageron 1991.

SOME IDEAS ABOUT WHAT PREVENTS THE FRENCH
FROM HAVING GOOD COLONIES (1833)

1. "Some Ideas about What Prevents the French from Having Good Colonies" comprises several pages of the manuscript that Tocqueville wrote in collaboration with Beaumont on the "Penitentiary System in the United States and Its Application in France" (1833). Marginal notes in pencil in Beaumont's hand tell Tocqueville that this passage — whose interest Beaumont acknowledged — went beyond the bounds of their study. By comparing these pages and the definitive manuscript, we can easily find the precise place where this passage would have been inserted: in the "Appendix on Penal Colonies" (1st ed., 257–58), where a brief summary appears instead.

Beaumont published a large part of the text, slightly edited (*OC* [B] 8: 267–72), but he arbitrarily inserted it in "Notes of the Voyage to the United States" under the heading "Québec, 4 September 1831." On that date, however, Tocqueville and Beaumont were far from Québec: they had taken a carriage from Whitehall and were to arrive in Albany the next day (see Pierson 1938, 345).

2. Cf. Tocqueville's description of the Canadian woodsman in the short essay "Quinze jours dans le désert" (*OC* 5, pt. 1: 378; see also Pierson 1938, 231–82, where the entire essay appears in translation as "A Fortnight in the Wilderness"):

> This man, however, has no less remained a Frenchman — enterprising, glorious, proud of his origins, a passionate lover of military glory, more vain than self-interested, a man of instinct obeying his first impulse rather than his reason, more interested in reputation than money. . . . Left alone, he would naturally feel a domestic temper: no one has a greater taste for the domestic hearth; no one enjoys more than he the sight of his native parish, but despite himself he has been torn from his tranquil habits, his imagination has been struck by new scenes, he has been transplanted under another sky; this same man has all of a sudden felt himself possessed by an insatiable need for violent emotions, vicissitudes and dangers. The most civilized European has become the adorer of savage life. He prefers savannahs to city streets, the hunt to farming. He delights in existence and lives without a care for the future.
>
> The whites of France, say the Canadian Indians, are as good hunters as we are. Like us, they despise the comforts of life and brave the terrors of death. God created them to make their home in the Indian's cabin and to live in the wilderness.

FIRST LETTER ON ALGERIA (23 JUNE 1837)

1. Tocqueville's two letters on Algeria appeared unsigned in the journal *La Presse de Seine-et-Oise*. The editors have been unable to find copies of the issues containing these articles, and, because they were not reprinted subsequently, we have based the text on Tocqueville's manuscript.

2. In June 1837, Algerian affairs had been the subject of important debates in the Chamber of Deputies, and the Molé government, while trying peacefully to resolve the problem of French penetration into Algeria, had obtained supplementary appropriations to reinforce the French army there. See Christian Schefer, "La Politique algérienne du ministère Molé," *Revue des études historiques* 79 (1913): 1–28. In Algeria, General Bugeaud, the commander at Oran, had just signed the treaty of Tafna with Emir Abd-el-Kader on 30 May [1837, in which the French recognized his territory as sovereign and conceded him the right to buy arms. For his part, Abd-el-Kader recognized "the sovereignty of France in Africa" (in the French, but not the Arabic, text of the treaty). For the text of the treaty and a thorough discussion of Abd-el-Kader's relations with the French from 1832 to 1839, see Danziger 1977. — J.P.]. In eastern Algeria, Governor-General Damrémont, who had replaced Marshal Bertrand Clauzel after the latter failed in the first expedition to Constantine, attempted to deal with the other notable Algerian leader, Ahmad Bey. But the French government had already decided, even if these

negotiations should fail, to launch a new expedition against Constantine; this took place on 13 October and resulted in the French conquest of the town.

3. Amédée Desjobert (1796–1853) was a deputy from 1833 to 1848, a "representative of the people" after the 1848 revolution, and a member of the legislative body under the [Second] Empire. A disciple of Jean-Baptiste Say and an economic and political liberal until the coup d'état of 2 December 1851, he was a prominent and prolific anticolonialist. He denounced the occupation of Algeria in books and parliamentary speeches, arguing for free trade and the right of the Algerian nation to self-government.

When Tocqueville's essay was written, Desjobert 1837 had just been published. Tocqueville seems to be referring to the following passage: "Aren't the accounts of witnesses, of interested parties, of specialists preferable to the notions of an isolated man who seeks to travel to the spot himself? . . . Convinced of the uselessness of such a pilgrimage, I have sought knowledge, even in the reports of those who, either out of error or out of interest, produce a conclusion contrary to my own" (ibid., vi–vii).

4. A blank in the text. It should say "just over 250 leagues."

5. [Tocqueville refers here to the Institut de France, the national literary and scientific body founded by the Convention in 1795. The Kabyles are a Berber group from the mountainous regions east of Algiers and west of Sétif, from the Mediterranean to the southern slopes of the Djudjura mountains. The name Kabylia applies to the mountainous region of the Tell (or Atlas) in eastern Algeria; its primary town is Tizi Ouzou. See Naylor and Heggoy 1994, 242–45. — J.P.]

6. Here Tocqueville clearly means Basque.

7. Tocqueville noted the following observations on a separate sheet, without indicating precisely where they should be placed:

> In all parts of the regency that they occupied, the Turks uniformly adopted a very profound political maxim I must tell you about.
>
> The Turks, who had common sense rather than shrewdness, understood that the marabouts, who already had the advantages of birth and religion, could easily become very dangerous adversaries if they were allowed to get involved in government.
>
> The Turks thus honored the marabouts greatly; they kissed the hems of their tunics and went devotedly to pray at the tombs of their ancestors. But they did not allow a single one openly to get mixed up in public affairs. They never employed them themselves, and they did not permit them to take up the arms they had abandoned after they stopped making war on the Christians.

8. In 1516, the Spanish, already in control of Oran, occupied a small island at the entrance to Algiers, on which they built the Peñon fortress: the Algerians appealed to the famous corsair Aruj, son of a potter from Mytilene (ancient Lesbos), who used Djerba as his base. Aruj defeated the sheikh of Algiers, Selim, but he was killed in 1518 in operations against the Spanish.

His brother Khayr al-Din (Barbarossa), surrounded by enemies, sought the support of the Porte, which sent him Turkish reinforcements. Obliged to take refuge in Djidjelli (1520–25), he soon reconquered the Mitidja, returned to Algiers, and took the Peñon (1529). By the time he was recalled in 1535 by the Porte, he had established the Turks' power base in Algeria.

9. *Sic.*

10. Julien 1931, 564, describes the administrative organization before the French conquest as follows:

> Each beylik was subdivided into many cantons (*outâns*), generally comprising several tribes and administered by commissioners (caids) who had civil, military, and judicial powers. These caids controlled the tribal chiefs (sheikhs), who were aided by the douar leaders in their administration. Their primary duties were to oversee the division and cultivation of land, on which the tax distribution was based; they undertook the collection of taxes with the assistance of the sheikhs. They were appointed by the beys and received a seal and a red burnous. They were always chosen from among the Turks, whereas the sheikhs generally belonged to the most important tribe of the *outân*. Sometimes the *outân* consisted of a single large tribe, whose sheikh became caid.

11. Tittery was the region between the Mitidja and the desert; it was bordered by the provinces of Oran (on the west), Algiers (on the north), and Constantine (on the east). Its capital was Médéa.

12. [The Moors were a Muslim population of mixed Spanish (Andalusian), Arab, and Berber origins who had fled the Spanish Reconquista and settled as refugees in North Africa between the eleventh and seventeenth centuries. — J.P.]

SECOND LETTER ON ALGERIA (22 AUGUST 1837)

1. [emended] Here Tocqueville seems to be paraphrasing Saint-Simon's parable that asks rhetorically whether France would be worse off if the country lost its nobility, its government ministers, and its 10,000 wealthiest property owners or if it lost 3,000 of its best artists, artisans, scientists, and industrialists. [See *Henri Saint-Simon (1760–1825): Selected Writings on Science, Industry and Social Organisation,* trans. and ed. Keith Taylor (New York: Holmes & Meier, 1975, 194–97. — J.P.]

2. [The shipping community at Marseilles were among the strongest advocates of the French conquest and occupation of Algeria. — J.P.]

3. See Esquer 1923, 428–31. The author points out that the occupation of Algiers by French troops was undertaken in great disorder, that the French failed to collect the administrative documents, and that many soldiers lit their pipes with government papers. To know the state of properties and public revenues, they had to trust the declarations of the people involved.

4. [emended] The term *spahi* (from the Persian *sipahi,* from which the term

sepoy — French, *cipaye* — in India is also derived) originally simply meant "soldier." But in the Ottoman Empire, the name was reserved for irregular cavalry corps, then for the elite cavalry. The Turks organized formations of these cavalrymen in North Africa.

5. The idea of a marabout is far more imprecise than Tocqueville suggests here: not only tombs but piles of stones, storks, etc., could be *marabouts*. See Edmond Doutté, *Notes sur l'Islâm maghribin, les marabouts* (Paris: E. Leroux, 1900).

6. Mahiddin, Abd-el-Kader's father, belonged to the Hachem tribe and was a venerated marabout of the powerful Kadria brotherhood. When the tribes of western Algeria decided to fight the French installed at Oran, they hoped to place him in command. But at the meeting at Essebieh near Mascara (22 November 1832), Mahiddin, enlightened by a dream, had them put in his place his son Abd-el-Kader, who had just turned twenty-four.

7. The Desmichels treaty of 26 February 1834, named for the general who commanded at Oran, affirmed Abd-el-Kader's power from the start by recognizing his title of emir and by fixing neither his territorial boundaries nor his precise obligations. The treaty of Tafna, signed by Bugeaud on 20 May 1837, reiterated this earlier recognition when it granted him Oran province and the Tittery.

8. On Achmet (Ahmad Bey), ruler of Constantine from 1826 to 1837, his tyranny and his greed, but also his virtues as a leader, see Ernest Mercier, *Histoire de Constantine* (Constantine: J. Marle & F. Biron, 1903), 371–436. On his relations with France in 1837, see First Letter on Algeria (23 June 1837), n. 2, above.

9. "Many French and Arab observers noted that the war did not, at the beginning of the French occupation, have the character of a holy war. It was rather an Arab resistance movement in response to soldiers from a foreign power to whom they had no reason to submit" (Emerit 1954a).

10. On 24 December 1830, Marshal Clauzel had created an urban guard in which French and indigenous residents of from twenty to sixty years of age possessing property or industrial establishments could take part. But on 17 August 1832, the duke of Rovigo decided to include only Frenchmen. On 26 October 1836, however, Clauzel, who had just become governor-general, reversed this decision by creating an African militia to which indigenous residents could be admitted on an individual basis.

NOTES ON THE KORAN (MARCH 1838)

1. Tocqueville took these notes from Savary 1793, and his quotations from that edition of the Koran are almost invariably word for word, with parenthetical citations of the correct pages. Three years later, in Algiers, he noted that this translation was "elegant and unfaithful" (see p. 49 below).

2. [According to the retributive principle of the lex talionis, a punishment should correspond in degree and kind to the crime or offense committed, as an eye for an eye, a tooth for a tooth. — J.P.]

3. These are the two passages to which Tocqueville refers: "The Faithful, Jews,

Sabeans, and Christians who believe in God on the final day, and who have practiced virtue, are exempt from fear and torments." But the following verses anathematize Jews and Christians who have refused to convert, and the text goes on: "Among Christians you will find humane men who are devoted to the believers, because they have priests and religious men dedicated to humility.

"When they hear the reading of the Koran, you will see them weep with joy to have heard truth. Lord, they cry, we believe. Number us among the witnesses."

4. Tocqueville stopped taking notes on p. 52 of Savary 1783, vol. 2, which has 464 pages.

NOTES ON THE VOYAGE TO ALGERIA IN 1841

1. [For the French original of Notes on the Voyage to Algeria in 1841, see the Gallimard *Œuvres complètes,* 5, pt. 2: 189–219. — J.P.] These notes were recorded for the most part in a bound notebook, labeled in Edouard de Tocqueville's writing:

Notes on Algeria by my brother Alexis de Tocqueville, in 1841.
Viscount de Tocqueville (Edouard), 1870.

Several other notes, written on separate sheets, which can without difficulty be integrated into the journal, have been added here. Beaumont published only these isolated notes in an abbreviated form (*OC* [B] 8: 475–84).

2. Tocqueville had left Toulon with his brother Hippolyte and Gustave de Beaumont on Monday, 4 May 1841, at 7 A.M. After a stop at Mahon [Minorca], they arrived in Algiers on 7 May. [See Tocqueville's letters to his wife, father, and brother Edouard (*OC* 14: 215–22, 417–34) for a complementary account of the journey. In his letter of May 9, Tocqueville wrote that the coast in the morning fog reminded him of Normandy; when the fog burned off, "then the real Africa appeared" (418). — J.P.]

3. Couba is about 8 km SE of Algiers.

4. In English. In the May 9 letter to his wife, Tocqueville wrote: "Beyond the last outposts war and desert begin. I say desert in the sense of *wilderness* and not desert" (*OC* 14: 419).

5. Monsignor Dupuch (1800–1856), first bishop of Algiers, named in August 1838, resigned because of his disputes with the lay authorities in December 1845. In Algiers, his charities were such that he was pursued by his creditors until 1852, when Louis-Napoléon Bonaparte paid his debts.

6. Tocqueville left Algiers by sea on 15 May with General Bugeaud, landing on 16 May at Mostaganem, where he met General de Lamoricière [see n. 10 below] (whom he had known since October 1828 through his friend Louis de Kergorlay). He left for Oran on the morning of 18 May and (after a short stop at Arzeu on 21 May) was back in Algiers on May 22. (See Tocqueville's letters to his wife of 14, 16, 17, and 22 May 1841, in *OC* 14: 421–27.)

7. There is an indecipherable word here.

8. Lieutenant Commander d'Assigny, who commanded the brig *le Dragon*. He had succeeded in saving the Swedish ship *Göteborg* on 15 February 1841, in Oran harbor.

9. Cap Falcon is 11 km west of Mers-el-Kebir.

10. General Christophe-Louis-Léon Juchault de Lamoricière (1806–65) had arrived in Algiers in 1830.

11. Marquis d'Aizeny de Montpezat (b. 1788), commander at Oran, March 1838–May 1842 (Vincennes military archives).

12. Lamoricière took Mascara on 30 May 1841 and left Lieutenant Colonel Géry in charge there, but although the latter retained control of the fertile Eghris plain, the Hachems submitted only very provisionally in the spring of 1842.

13. The Douairs and the Smelas [or Zmalas], whose leader, Mustafa-ibn-Ismail, was an enemy of Abd-el-Kader, had had to evacuate their territory to the south of the Sebkha in Oran to take refuge near the city. Lamoricière had taken charge of these two tribes of about 7,800 people, who had been struck by famine. The coulouglis were descendants of Turkish soldiers and Algerian women and formed separate tribes. Those of Wadi Zetoun, which flowed from the left bank of Wadi Isser southwest of Algiers, had been dispersed by Abd-el-Kader. Marshal Valée, Bugeaud's predecessor, had brought back about 1,600 of them and put them in charge of defending the Boudouaou fortress in Mitidja.

14. [See p. 84 below for Tocqueville's development of this argument. —J.P.]

15. Tocqueville may be alluding here to M.-L.-Bonav. Urtis, a lawyer who published his *Opinion émise par M. Urtis, . . . devant la Commission de colonisation de l'Algérie, à la séance du 12 mars 1842* (Paris: P. Dupont, n.d.).

16. The ellipsis is in the manuscript.

17. Monsignor Dupuch and Abd-el-Kader's lieutenant, Muhammad Ben Hamlan, bey of Miliana, met at a farm near Boufarik on 19 May 1841. Adrien-Louis Berbrugger (see n. 31 below) discusses the preparations and the interview itself in *Négociations entre Monseigneur l'évêque d'Alger et Abd el Qader pour l'échange des prisonniers* (Paris: J. Delahaye, 1844). See also Emerit 1954b.

18. [Dupuch is indeed a Gascon name, but the term *gascon* also means "braggart." —J.P.]

19. Alexis Auguste Lepescheux, born in Ambriçeres (Mayenne), had come to Algiers as inspector of public instruction on 1 September 1832. Named inspector of the academy in 1848, and subordinated at that point to a rector, he left the colony to become inspector of the academy in Agen in 1850, a position he kept until his retirement in 1863. His notes present him as a gentle and affable man, but of modest education. Archives nationales F17C1 116 and F17 21156.

20. Justin Laurence (1794–1863), deputy for the Landes from 1831 to 1848, was a member of the 1833–34 committee on Algeria and went there to organize the justice system. He then became director of African affairs in the Ministry of the Interior (July 1837), from which he resigned in 1842.

21. This commission, created in 1839 and placed under the leadership of Colonel Bory Saint-Vincent, included naturalists, archeologists, painters, etc. These included several Saint-Simonians, among them "Père" Enfantin, who had been named as an ethnographer. See Emerit 1941.

22. Tocqueville appears to be referring here to the decree of 18 April 1841 on the granting of lands, rather than to the law of 3 May 1841 on expropriation by reason of eminent domain.

23. Ordinance of 28 February 1841, modifying that of 10 August 1834.

24. Comte Eugène Guyot-Desherbiers, deputy prefect from 1830 to 1837 (finally at Vendôme), was appointed civil subintendant of the province of Constantine in January 1838, director of the interior in Algeria on 31 October 1838, director of the interior and public works in 1845, and director of the interior and of colonization in 1846. Recalled to France because of the elimination of the functions he exercised in September 1847, he was named *receveur particulier* [i.e., tax farmer] in Morlaix. Arch. nat. F80 249.

25. Claude Eugene Henriot (1802–74) was named attorney general of Algiers in March 1840. Arch. nat. BB6II and F80253.

26. Dr. Louis-François Trolliet, chief physician of the civil hospital in Algiers and author of *Mémoire sur la nécessité et sur les avantages de la colonisation d'Alger* (Lyon: J.-M. Barret [1835]), and *Statistique médicale de la province d'Alger, mêlée d'observations agricoles* (Lyon: L. Boitel, 1844).

27. The communal college of Algiers had been founded in 1835 with a course of study like that in the metropole; the course of study particular to Algiers, to which Tocqueville is referring here, had been introduced in 1840.

28. Probably Louis-Jacques Bresnier, who, although a simple typographical worker, attended the courses given at the Collège de France by the famous orientalist Silvestre de Sacy (1758–1838). Bresnier arrived in Algiers in 1836 and devoted himself for thirty-three years to teaching the Arabic language. He published educational texts, including *Anthologie arabe élémentaire* (1852), *Cour pratique et théorique de langue arabe* (1855), and *Chrestomathie arabe* (1857).

29. A blank in the text. There are too many Latin translations of the Koran for us to know which one Tocqueville alludes to here.

30. Savary 1783.

31. Adrien-Louis Berbrugger (1801–69), professor of languages, physician, archeologist, Fourierist, and a friend of the Saint-Simonians, arrived in Algeria in 1833 as secretary to Marshal Clauzel. He returned for good in 1835 and married an Arab woman. Librarian of the Bibliothèque d'Alger, he founded the museum, was a member of the scientific commission of 1839, and later became inspector of historic monuments. In 1850, he explored southern Algeria and Tunisia; in 1862, Morocco. In 1856, he started the *Revue africaine*. See Robert Dournon, *Autour du Tombeau de la Chrétienne, documents pour servir à l'histoire de l'Afrique du Nord* [Lettres d'Adrien Berbrugger à sa fille, 1865–66] (Algiers: Charlot, 1946).

32. The Hadjoutes were a powerful tribe of the area around Miliana; in November

1839, their cavalry had massacred the colonists of the Mitidja. They submitted in June 1842.

33. The so-called Portes de Fer, or Iron Gates, in Kabylia, a defile crossed by the duc d'Orléans, son of King Louis-Philippe and heir to the French throne, on 28 October 1839.

34. Charles Barthélémy Filhon, born in 1797, was named president of the Algiers tribunal in 1834. When Tocqueville met him, he had just been named a judge in Paris (23 April 1841).

35. Two lines are illegible because of a tear in the manuscript.

36. Tocqueville left the next day, 28 May, for Philippeville, which he reached on the 30th, having stopped off at Bougie and Djidjelli on the 29th. On the 31st, he left with a convoy that was to reach Constantine in three days. But he had to be sent back to Philippeville because of illness, and as soon as he was convalescent, he returned to France presumably reaching Toulon on 11 June. See *OC* 14: 429–36, letters to his wife of 28 and 30 May and 12 June 1841.

37. Doubtful transcription.

38. The ellipsis is in the manuscript.

39. Name left blank. Undoubtedly the Wadi Soummam.

40. France had occupied Bougie since October 1833.

41. [Spahis were soldiers in the native cavalry corps in the French army in Algeria. See Second Letter on Algeria (22 August 1837), n. 4, above. — J.P.]

42. The ellipsis is in the manuscipt.

43. General Négrier (1788–1848) had replaced General Galbois in February 1841 in command of Constantine province. He had already occupied the post before Galbois's arrival in 1838, and would continue in it until 1842.

As Tocqueville notes later, Négrier's procedures were heavily criticized. In the Chamber of Deputies, Soult even had to admit the "explosion of illegalities" committed in Constantine province. The polemic between Negrier's and Galbois's partisans can be found in anonymous brochures such as *Coup d'oeil sur l'administration française dans la province de Constantine; par un Constantinien* (Paris: H. Fournier, 1843).

44. Djidjelli was taken on 13 May 1839 by the Salles squadron chief, who had immediately made it defensible. See A. Rétout, *Histoire de Djidjelli* (Algiers: Jules Carbonel, 1927).

45. This commander, who had recently distinguished himself by successfully countering a Kabyle offensive, was Lieutenant Colonel Philippe Picouleau (b. 1798), a member of the expeditionary force that had taken Algiers in 1830.

46. Philippeville was founded in October 1838, on a site sheltered by the Stora harbor, by Marshal Valée, who bought the land from the indigenous people for 150 francs. The name Philippeville was given by a decree that appeared November 17, according to the *Moniteur.* Scholars agree on the rapid development of the town from 1839 to 1842: L.-Ch. Féraud, *Histoire des villes de la province de Constantine* (Algiers: A. Jourdan, 1875), estimates that it had 800 inhabitants at the beginning of 1839 and 4,000 by the second trimester of 1840; this despite fevers that severely afflicted the

civilian population and the garrison. See also E.-V. Fenech, *Histoire de Philippeville* (Philippeville: Le Proust des Ageux, 1852–53); and Louis Bertrand, *Histoire de Philippeville* (Philippeville: Imprimerie administrative et commerciale moderne, 1903).

ESSAY ON ALGERIA (OCTOBER 1841)

1. The date given suggests that the essay, which remained unpublished until 1962, was written after Tocqueville's return from his 1841 trip to Algeria with Gustave de Beaumont. Tocqueville, who had contracted dysentery in Algeria, returned to Toulon on 11 June (see p. 241 n. 36), whence he made his way gradually to Paris, staying there from 21 to 29 June; he finally arrived at the château de Tocqueville on 30 June and was obliged to remain there, in an often precarious state of health, until December. Some letters written during his stay inform us of the nature of this "essay," which appears to be the sketch for a report or a journal article. In a letter to his brother Edouard of 17 October 1841, Tocqueville wrote: "A month ago I had been very ill for some time. During this state of illness, I attempted to put the finishing touches on some writings, among others my notes on Algeria" (see *OC* 14: 224). Two letters to Gustave de Beaumont give further details: "I think as you do, my dear friend, that you could not spend the remaining two months better than in writing about Africa. It is a very great question that we already know enough about to be able to throw many new and true ideas into circulation. To do so would be very useful for the country; very useful for you, and, I would add, for myself, since we cannot separate ourselves on this matter. I cannot encourage you enough to throw yourself *furiously* into this work, since you are quite fortunate that your health allows you transports of this kind. During the past three months, I have fitfully put some ideas about Algeria on paper. I shall send you this *memorial* when you like. It is feebly and slackly written, like all work done in many stints and without any prospect of publication. It lacks exactitude and detail throughout. I have no documents at hand. They all stayed in Paris. It does not teach much, but such as it is, I put it at your disposal. Tell me whether you want me to send it to you or to bring it on my return. In writing these few pages, I felt hampered at each moment by the lack of real knowledge and sufficient facts. I nearly abandoned this thankless task many times. I hope that you will draw from the same subject a book that, first, will give you honor; that will give you great authority in the matter, and that will serve as foundation and preface to everything we shall have occasion to say in session" (letter of 21 October 1841). "My dear friend — Hippolyte, who leaves today for Paris, is taking my memorial, which I would have sent you sooner if I had not been uncertain whether I was taking it myself. I ask only one thing in sending you this piece, which is that you take the trouble to read it, despite the impatience that my detestable writing will provoke. . . . These notes were written with my pen flying, but without the least verve and without art. I don't need to tell you that I didn't write a draft, for you will be able to see that for yourself. I have just reread this work for the first time. There are several ideas in it that seem quite good to me, but almost all are yours or are known to you. They are connected by plenty of useless filler" (letter of 15 November 1841).

Beaumont never wrote the projected work, but instead only a series of anonymous articles in *Le Siècle* under the title *Etat de la question d'Afrique* (26 and 30 November, 3, 7, and 11 December 1842), articles that engaged in a lively polemic against Bugeaud. Bugeaud claimed to have recognized Tocqueville's hand in the anonymous articles, causing Beaumont to acknowledge authorship.

2. These lines were written just after the crisis of 1840, and Tocqueville was hostile to Guizot's policy of appeasement.

3. Captain d'Assigny was captain of the port of Mers-el-Kebir.

4. Tocqueville is referring to the travel notes he took at Mers-el-Kebir (reprinted in this volume, pp. 37–39).

5. In 1830 the port of Algiers was of modest dimensions and had a vulnerable harbor. The engineer Poirel had begun in 1833 to reinforce the Kheir-ed-din Jetty, joining the islet of la Marine to the coast by submerging blocks of concrete that had been poured into 10 m³ boxes. In 1839 he began to build the North Jetty. But in 1840 Raffeneau de Lisle was sent to inspect the works and developed much more ambitious plans to make Algiers into a large military port, which seemed necessary to general opinion because of the international crisis. These projects, constantly put off, were the subject of many discussions, especially in the Chamber of Deputies, where a great debate on the subject took place again in 1847. Despite these plans, only Poirel's plans, somewhat enlarged, were executed.

6. Abd-el-Kader's regular forces (8,000 foot soldiers, 2,000 cavalry, an artillery corps with 20 cannons), trained by European deserters, could not hold out against the French in open country, but they served to keep the tribes in submission.

7. See the reports by Léon Roches and Garcin printed in Emerit 1951, 261–99, on Abd-el-Kader's position and forces. He had trouble subjugating Western Algeria: in addition to the hostility of the Douairs and Smelas [Zmalas], he had to fight the tribal chiefs who formed a true "nobility of the sword" (in General Azan's words), who scorned him as a descendant of marabouts (such as El Gomari, sheikh of the Angads, Kaddour ben Moklifi of the Bordija, and Sidi Larbi in the Chélif region). He encountered adversaries even in his own family. In 1834 his situation was critical: he was recognized neither by the qadi of Arzeu, nor by the garrisons of Tlemcen and Mostaganem, and his taxes were resisted almost everywhere. The aid and munitions sent to him by General Desmichels allowed him to subdue his principal enemies.

8. The ideas developed by Tocqueville are very much like those Bugeaud applied in Algeria; but the latter, from 1843 onward, tended toward more direct government. See Germain 1955, esp. pt. 2, ch. 3, and Sullivan 1983.

9. Bugeaud drew a similar parallel in an article published in the *Moniteur algérien* (25 December 1843):

People have revolted against the razzia in Africa but do not object to bombarding and starving a large town in Europe. What sort of spectacle does a besieged town often present? Bombs and projectiles of all sorts flying through houses, striking women, children, old people, all the innocent victims of war . . . You should know,

244 Notes to Pages 71-78

you excellent philanthropists, that the razzia is a hundred times less cruel. We strike neither women nor children as your bombs do in Europe; we feed and care for those who fall into our hands; we protect them as a guarantee of their tribe's submission; but, when the tribe capitulates, we give back all its people and sometimes part of its herds.

10. See Tocqueville's conversation with Berbrugger, recorded in his journals (pp. 49–50 above).

11. *Sic.* This is undoubtedly a word misunderstood by Tocqueville.

12. The numbers are left blank. A letter to his brother Edouard addressed from Philippeville, 30 May 1841, allows us to complete this passage: "We have *ascertained* this morning through the registers of the civil state that we were shown that last year the civil population, already 4,000 souls strong, had only 158 deaths, while the 3,000 men of the garrison had 800 deaths." [See *OC* 14 for the full text of the letter. — J.P.]

We find similar testimony in a letter written on 28 January 1841 by General Berthois: "In just the area from Philippeville to Harrouch eight leagues away, we have had 1,000 deaths from fever in a garrison of 4,000. These deaths must not be attributed to the climate, however, as much as to the exhaustion these malnourished and truly overwhelmed soldiers are forced to suffer. Besides, how are they to recover their health in hospitals that are nothing but huts built of planks, with plank roofs, and with neither beds nor mattresses!"

13. Tocqueville had known General Louis de Lamoricière, then commander at Oran, since October 1828, through his friend Louis de Kergorlay. He seems to have corresponded with Lamoricière beginning in 1837 at the latest. In any case, he met the general during his trip to Algeria and had several conversations with him at Mostaganem and Oran on 15 May and the days that followed (see pp. 39–40 above).

14. [On these former makhzen tribes, who resented the loss of the privileges they had enjoyed as tax collectors under the Turks and broke with Abd-el-Kader to seek similar arrangements with the French, see Danziger 1977, 114 ff.). — J.P.]

15. Soon after the conquest, Bourmont had accepted the services of indigenous mercenaries, most of whom were Kabyles from Djudjura, from the Zouaoua tribe: this was the origin of the Zouaves. On 1 October 1830, Clauzel formed them into two battalions, led by French officers, into whose ranks other Europeans began to be admitted the following year. Although they for a brief time included cavalry, the Zouaves soon became solely a corps of indigenous infantry, whose leadership brought fame to generals such as Duvivier and Lamoricière. An ordinance of 7 December 1841 organizing the Algerian soldiers, however, turned the Zouaves into a predominantly European regiment; its three battalions of nine companies included only one recruited from among indigenous Algerians. See Jean Delasalle, "Zouaves et tirailleurs algériens," *Revue internationale d'Histoire militaire* (1953).

16. Under the Second Republic, Tocqueville supported General Louis-Eugène Cavaignac's government in the Constituent Assembly and pressed Cavaignac's candidacy for the presidency of the Republic. [Cavaignac had made his reputation in

Algeria and was appointed governor-general there by the republican provisional government in February 1848. He was soon promoted to minister of war, in which capacity he brutally suppressed demonstrations by Paris workers in the Ateliers nationaux that June. Cavaignac was subsequently granted plenary powers as head of the executive, a post he held until he lost the presidential election to Louis-Napoléon Bonaparte in December. He appointed General Lamoricière, another product of Algeria, as his war minister. See Heffernan 1989 for a discussion of Cavaignac's colonization schemes. — J.P.]

17. The most important developments of the general's Algerian career are described in E. Keller, *Le Général de La Moricière: Sa vie militaire, politique et religieuse* (Paris: Dumaine, 1874), vol. 1.

18. [See Heffernan 1989 for a thorough historical account of colonization measures around this time, including discussion of Cavaignac's colonization schemes. — J.P.]

19. Bugeaud disagreed, as Tocqueville's summary of Bugeaud's letter to the governor (26 November 1841) shows: "Before anything else, the military question must be resolved. . . . Colonization can only occur after the war, because the war is necessary for colonizing. Only the army can prepare for colonization. . . . Military colonization: the best way."

20. Tocqueville is alluding to a speech that Laurence (on whom see Notes on the Voyage to Algeria in 1841, n. 20, above) gave before the Chamber on 16 July 1839.

21. The project of European colonization was, however, proposed again in 1847 by Lamoricière. See Christophe-Louis-Léon Juchault de Lamoricière, *Projets de colonisation pour les provinces d'Oran et de Constantine présenté par les lieutenant-généraux de la Moricière et Bedeau* (Paris: Imprimerie royale, 1847).

22. [On Islamic property law and its role in the French colonial administration in Algeria, see Schacht 1964, esp. ch. 14, "Anglo-Muhammadan Law and Droit Musulman Algérien," and Christelow 1985. — J.P.]

23. The treaty of Tafna (30 May 1837), signed by Bugeaud and Abd-el-Kader, bounded the territory occupied by France around Oran with the swamps of Macta, Sig, Rio Salado, and the southern bank of the great Sebkha. To the south of the Sebkha was the territory originally occupied by the Douairs and the Smelas, which they had abandoned to move closer to Oran. [See the treaty's text, with translations of both the French and the Arabic versions of the treaty, in Danziger 1977. — J.P.]

24. The coulougli population of Wadi Zeïtoun, which flowed into the Isser to the east of Algiers, had accepted a caid chosen by the French administration. In January 1838, seeking to demonstrate his power east of Wadi Khadra, which the French wanted to impose as his boundary, Abd-el-Kader attacked them with his regulars. Fleeing from the mountains, the coulouglis succumbed after a desperate defense; the caid named by the French was taunted and decapitated. Governor-General Valée forced Abd-el-Kader to retreat, however, and recovered 1,600 survivors, men, women, and children. Three hundred men organized in companies occupied the stronghold of Boudouaou for France.

25. The "continuous barrier" composed of a trench and a wall four meters high flanked by blockhouses was conceived in France. Three-quarters of it was then built from August to December 1841 by General Berthois. Not only was its construction murderous for the workers (Berthois himself had to be relieved by General Charon), but it did not perform the function expected of it. Berthois's papers regarding this enterprise are housed in the Archives nationales, ser. F80, carton 1132. On General Berthois (1787–1870), see Anatole de Berthois, *Notices sur le colonel de Berthois de la Rousselière et le général baron de Berthois son fils* (Paris: Lahure, 1874). General Lamoricière had also encircled Oran with a trench. See Tocqueville's journal, p. 39, above.

26. Among the many testaments to the unhealthiness of the Mitidja and the south of the Massif, the most striking, perhaps, are those collected in Gautier 1930. See also Bussière 1853.

27. As soon as Algiers was conquered, a swarm of speculators descended on the town to buy land in the surrounding area. The natives, convinced the French would have to leave, offered lands of all sorts: alongside assignable lands, they sold inalienable lands, beylik lands, and lands that were partly or totally nonexistent. Lamoricière calculated in 1847 that the property sold amounted to more than twice the area that existed. The problem of the validity of these sales, in general effected before the qadi, was almost insoluble; the royal commission of 1842–44 was preoccupied with them for a long time (Arch. nat. F80 1129). The decrees of 1 October 1844, 21 July 1845, and 21 July 1846 strove to regulate these difficult problems equitably. See the *Rapport au roi* of 21 July 1846 in Ménerville 1877–81, 1: 559–61.

28. At the beginning of 1842, following a declaration by Laurence to the royal commission on Algeria (Arch. nat. F80 1129), the services could only survey the town of Algiers (excluding the suburbs), Blida, Cherchel, Philippeville, and Mostaganem.

29. Abbé J.-M. Landmann, the parish priest [*curé*] of Constantine, was a disciple of the Christian socialist Philippe Buchez (1796–1865). Under the July Monarchy, he published various writings on the colonization of Algeria (*Les Fermes du Petit Atlas* [1841]; *Mémoires au roi sur la colonisation de l'Algérie* [1845]). On 27 May 1848, Baron de Montreuil proposed to the Constituent Assembly that he be given 300 million francs over ten years to realize his ideas; this proposal was turned over to the Commission on Algeria, which preferred Lamoricière's projects. In 1847, Landmann created the agricultural settlement of Medjez-Amar (in the district of Bône), where he took in foundlings, but he soon had to give up running the settlement (see Baudicour 1856, 307–9). His last writings are dedicated to this problem of agricultural colonies for French orphans. See J.-B. Duroselle, *Les Débuts du catholicisme social en France* (Paris: Presses universitaires de France, 1951).

30. Bugeaud expounded his ideas on colonization in multiple writings, speeches, and articles, in particular *De l'établissement de légion de colons militaires dans les possessions françaises du Nord de l'Afrique* (1838) and *L'Algérie: Des moyens de conserver et d'utiliser cette conquête* (1842). For Tocqueville's discussion of his ideas, see pp. 187 ff. above.

[For the most complete account in English of Bugeaud's political and military activity, see Sullivan 1983. — J.P.]

31. Bugeaud was always sensitive to the objection that he was planning a colonization by bachelors. In response, he granted leave to soldiers intending to become colonists, in order for them to find wives. When, at the end of 1841, he founded the military colony of Ain Fouka, he organized the famous "drumhead marriages" of soldiers with orphan girls from Toulon.

32. Behind this general condemnation, Tocqueville also seems to be targeting Saint-Simonian projects such as described in B.-P. Enfantin's *Colonisation de l'Algérie* (Paris: P. Bertrand, 1843). Cf. Emerit 1941, 114–20.

33. Customs laws for Algeria had been established by the edict of 11 November 1835 (Duvergier 1835, 399). This legislation, more liberal than the preceding laws, allowed the duty-free importation into Algeria of metropolitan goods and foreign merchandise not produced in Algeria or useful for agriculture and construction; other goods were taxed at 15 percent of value; no exit tax was imposed on exports to the metropole, but they faced an entrance tax in France, which the edict of 16 December 1843 reduced by half.

34. Tocqueville returned to this subject in his notes on India; see *OC* 3, pt. 1: 471–72, 528.

35. A blank in the text. A ministerial decree of 1 September 1834 regulated the powers of the governor-general, of the administration leaders placed under his order, and of the administrative council. This was completed by a decree by the minister of war of 2 August 1836. These two decrees can be found in Ménerville 1877–81, 1: 20–34; 2: 281–93. In addition, these underwent modifications as a result of the publication of the decree of 31 October 1838 on Algeria's civil administration (Duvergier 1838, 693–94).

36. See Notes on the Voyage to Algeria in 1841, pp. 57–58 above.

37. Actually the decree of 17 October 1833 concerning expropriation on grounds of eminent domain (Ménerville 1877–81, 1: 337).

38. On this director of the interior, Comte Eugène Guyot-Desherbiers, see Notes on the Voyage to Algeria in 1841, n. 24, above, and *OC* 5, pt. 2: 203 n. 3. Demontès 1918 paints a more flattering picture of Guyot-Desherbiers than Tocqueville does here.

39. The governor-general's decree of 21 April 1841 granted to "troops settled in permanent camps thirty hectares of land suited to production" (Ménerville 1877–81, 1: 307).

40. A blank in the text. Tocqueville is referring to the ordinance of 28 February 1841 (Duvergier 1841, 94–101).

41. Marshal Soult, at that time war minister and president of the Conseil d'Etat, even though a partisan of the occupation of Algeria, avoided declaring it for a long time, either so as not to offend the partisans of abandonment directly or, rather, to accommodate England. Still, in opening the session of the Chambers on 27 December 1841, the king did not hesitate to announce that Algeria was French forever.

42. One should not conclude from Tocqueville's words here that Soult had lost

interest in the Algerian administration. Shortly after appointing Bugeaud governor-general, he reinstated the direct correspondence between the minister and the department heads in Algiers; until his retirement he artfully sought to sideline or thwart his hotheaded subordinate.

43. In a report dated 27 July 1838, Marshal Valée, governor-general of Algeria, had recommended creating a special ministry for Algeria, or at least attaching Algerian affairs to the presidency of the Conseil d'Etat, but only under the Second Empire was a Ministry of Algeria and the Colonies established, albeit ephemerally (1858–60). When later, under the Third Republic, the Gambetta ministry appointed a deputy secretary of state for the colonies, a decree of unification (*rattachements*) (26 August 1881) placed the various Algerian bureaux under the authority of the ministers responsible for the metropole.

44. On Justin Laurence, see Notes on the Voyage to Algeria in 1841, n. 20, above.

45. It was only in 1879 that the first civilian governor-general, Albert Grévy, was appointed.

46. This prohibition was a result of article 26 of the ordinance of 1 October 1844 on the right of property in Algeria (Duvergier 1844, 482 ff.): "No officer of the army or navy, no military official or employee, and no salaried civil official, may, during his service in Algeria, acquire real property, directly or indirectly by himself or through intermediaries, or become a tenant or leaseholder of such property through a lease exceeding nine years, without obtaining special authorization from our minister of war."

47. The Algerian judicial regime was to be modified shortly afterward by the ordinance of 26 September 1842 (Duvergier 1842, 326–34), which brought it somewhat closer to the French system without solving the problems Tocqueville lists here.

INTERVENTION IN THE DEBATE OVER THE
APPROPRIATION OF SPECIAL FUNDING (1846)

1. The vote on the appropriation of special funds proved the occasion for an exceptionally important debate on the Algerian problem in the Chamber of Deputies; Dufaure, the reporter for the committee, had recommended the recasting of the colonial administration, and in the course of the meetings of 8, 9, and 10 June, Corcelle, Tocqueville, de Tracy, Lamartine, and Guizot, then minister of foreign affairs, delivered important speeches. That of Tocqueville, delivered on 9 June (*Moniteur universel*, 1722–24), was not republished until the 1963 Gallimard edition.

2. The day before, General Moline de Saint-Yon, who had replaced Marshal Soult as minister of war on 10 November 1845, had drawn an optimistic portrait of pacification, colonization, the administration, and the public works that had been completed.

3. Tocqueville is probably alluding here to the slitting of French prisoners' throats by Abd-el-Kader's *dā'irah* on 17–18 April, but he seems to have in mind the 1845 insurrection, which, although at first it seemed to threaten Algiers itself, was suppressed fairly easily.

4. [The term *chouannerie* refers to peasant movements of resistance to the French Revolution that involved sporadic guerrilla actions. See Furet and Ozouf 1989, 3–10, and Sutherland 1982. — J.P.]

5. [Francisque de Corcelle, Tocqueville's close friend and parliamentary ally, with whom Tocqueville had traveled in Algeria in 1841. — J.P.]

6. In his speech of the previous day, Corcelle had denounced the "odious maxims against the natives" of the Algiers newspapers and had cited the following example:

Here is an issue of a newspaper from the past May 2. We are directed to an article entitled, "What Are the Signs That Show That a Human Race Is Destined for Destruction by a Providential Decree?"

The author claims that nature moves constantly toward new inspirations by destroying numerous creatures, but that these are healthy inspirations toward more perfect forms of existence. There follows a historical list of all the inferior races that, according to the article, have had to disappear before superior races: Mexicans, Caribbeans, redskins [*peaux-rouges*], etc. . . . Coming to the Arabs of Algeria and Morocco, the author takes no account of their ancient civilization: he declares them to be more or less like the redskins, and announces, without further hesitation, their death warrant. *The extinction of this guilty race,* he says, *is a harmony.* His conclusion, in a word, is that true philanthropists have a humanitarian mission to destroy the races opposed to progress.

Research has failed to identify the newspaper in question.

7. Corcelle had merely underlined the possibility of attracting Arabs to French civilization and of bringing them to participate in colonization.

8. General de la Rue (1795–1872), director of Algeria in the ministry of war from November 1845 to March 1848, carried out important diplomatic missions, in particular to Morocco, and took part, as the king's commissioner, in most of the debates on Algeria at the end of the July Monarchy. On this subject, he appears to have had cordial relations with Tocqueville.

9. It was estimated that out of 100,000 Europeans, only 7,000 made their living in agriculture, and of those 5,000 were market gardeners on the outskirts of the towns.

10. In the course of the debate, this thesis was supported by de Tracy and Desjobert.

11. Recalled to Algiers as soon as he arrived at his estate in the Périgord, Bugeaud had demanded horses in the postal service, in a letter to the prefect of the Dordogne, M. de Marcillac (6 October 1845). He complained bitterly in this letter of his mistreatment by the government. The *Conservateur de la Dordogne*'s publication of this letter, possibly without consulting Bugeaud, provoked protests in the Paris press against the "rebellious pasha." See Guizot, *Mémoires,* vol. 7 (Paris, 1865), 202–7.

12. See Essay on Algeria (1841), n. 43, above.

13. At the previous day's session, Desmousseaux de Givré had called the project an "Algerian revolution."

14. Bugeaud threatened to resign his commission several times in 1844 and 1845 in order to give exposure in France to his ideas on colonization. The last of these threats had occurred, it seems, the previous April. See Guizot, *Mémoires*, vol. 7 (Paris, 1865), 233–34.

FIRST REPORT ON ALGERIA (1847)

1. This report appeared in the *Moniteur,* 1379–86, as an appendix to the proceedings of 24 May 1847. It was reprinted by Beaumont (*OC* [B] 9: 423–84).

2. On 27 February 1847, the government submitted to the Chamber two draft bills, one regarding supplemental credits for Algeria, the other on the creation of military camps in Algeria, according to Marshal Bugeaud's plans.

Following a suggestion by Gustave de Beaumont, the Chamber decided to have a single committee examine the two projects, fearing that otherwise the proposed appropriations of funds would lead to duplications. The government consented, but requested two separate reports. The committee included the following members: Dufaure, Morny, Allard, d'Oraison, de Tracy, de Corcelle, de Lasteyrie, Schneider, Plichon, Oudinot, Tocqueville, Desjobert, de Boblaye, de la Guiche, Béchameil, de Chasselou-Laubat, de Beaumont, and Abraham Dubois; it chose Dufaure as president and appointed Tocqueville reporter, the majority preferring him to Beaumont, who was also a candidate for reporter.

[On Bugeaud's own colonization plans, see Bugeaud de la Piconnerie 1842; Sullivan 1983. — J.P.]

3. [For a summary of the war that France waged against Abd-el-Kader from 1839 to 1847, during which France disabled Algerian resistance and the European civilian population in Algeria grew from 25,000 to 104,000, see Danziger 1977, Epilogue. — J.P.]

4. Tocqueville no doubt refers here to the massacre of French prisoners by Abd-el-Kader's *dā'irah,* or mobile "circle" of followers [see also Intervention in the Debate over the Appropriation of Special Funding (1846), n. 3, above].

[It should be noted that Abd-el-Kader himself deplored the April 1846 massacre of 270 French prisoners by his deputy in Morocco, which took place while Abd-el-Kader himself was campaigning in Algeria, and after Bugeaud had refused a prisoner exchange. See Danziger 1977, 235. — J.P.]

5. [Muhammad b. Abdallah, known as Bu Maza, a Moroccan of the Tayyibiyah Sufi order, had provoked a revolt in Oran and Tittery provinces in April 1845. The French used their most repressive measures against his followers, smoking 500 men, women, and children to death in a cave (see Danziger 1977). He surrendered to Marshal Saint-Arnaud on 13 April 1847 and was sent to France. See Saint-Arnaud, 1855, 2: 132–47. — J.P.]

6. "Monsieur de Tocqueville . . . recognized the truth of many things, especially the governmental power we exercise over the Arabs, which quite astonished him; secondly,

the great works of all sorts that the army made," Bugeaud wrote General de la Rue (21 January 1847) at the time of Tocqueville's second journey to Algeria (Demontès 1918, 241).

7. These advances in knowledge of North Africa were owed largely to the Arab bureaux, created by the decree of 1 February 1844. By this point, there were twenty-one such bureaux, whose officers enthusiastically studied various aspects of Arab society and civilization under the direction of Colonel Daumas. See Emerit 1947; Yacono 1953.

8. The transcriptions of the debates of the 1847 committee on Algeria are housed in the Archives nationales (C 898, 899, 900). But they do not mention the opinions expressed on this question.

9. Petit-Désert was the name given to the high steppes of the province of Tittery, between the Tellian Atlas and the Ouled Naïl.

10. Bugeaud had established a line of outposts at the edges of the steppes and of the Tell, thus controlling the nomads' access to wheat. In addition, each year after 1843, columns left these outposts to march south, going as far as the Sahara. The state of the strategic outposts in the middle of 1847 is described in Guizot's *Memoires,* 7: 532.

11. Tocqueville had direct experience to support this claim: during his journey to Algeria the previous year, he had met at Mouzaïa Pass two Frenchmen who had just returned alone on foot from Médéa to Blida. Several days later, in the Chélif region, the center of the 1845 insurrection, he similarly met two French workers who, alone and unarmed, had walked from Orléansville to Miliana, a journey that took more than two days. See Bussière 1853.

12. The east of the old regency consisted of the province of Constantine, which General Bedeau had ruled since October 1844, aside from a few months in 1845 when he was fighting Abd-el-Kader in the province of Algiers. Bedeau was an active administrator and showed himself to be a partisan of conciliatory methods toward the Arab population. See Perkins 1981. The social structure of eastern Algeria is discussed in Emerit 1951, 237–42.

13. In addition to these 94,000 men, there were about 10,000 indigenous troops.

14. Still, the penetration in the Algerian south had begun, as shown by the state of the occupied outposts cited by Guizot (see n. 10 above). Thus a permanent garrison was established at Biskra.

15. In December 1846, negotiations between Bugeaud and the leaders of western Kabylia had been broached, in particular with Ben-Salem, Abd-el-Kader's former lieutenant, and Ben-Kassem, who came to pay homage to the governor at the end of February 1847. Still, in mid May, when Tocqueville was drafting his report, the governor was leading an expedition into Kabylia. See pp. 168–73 below. A detailed history of the reports of the military authorities and the Kabyles can be found in Colonel Robin, "Notices historique sur la Grande Kabylie de 1838 à 1851," *Revue africaine,* 1902, 1903, 1904.

16. In 1847, following Abd-el-Kader's example, an entire hierarchy of indigenous leaders had been put in place: independent khalifas, bachaghas, and independent aghas,

belonging in general to the high Arab aristocracy, performed the most important liaison functions with the French military authorities; below them, aghas divided into several classes had various military and judicial roles; the qaids who served as their subordinates were mostly administrators and judges; and, finally, ordinary sheikhs carried out decisions at the local level. Officers of the Arab bureaux nonetheless intervened in relations between the leaders and the population. A tendency toward more direct government thus emerged with increasing force.

17. See n. 7 above.

18. An attempt by Marshal Clauzel's government to impose town Moors on the tribes near Algiers as caids failed miserably. During the struggle against Abd-el-Kader, Bugeaud sought with little success to support rivals of lesser origins against the aghas of the great families who had rallied to the enemy, and after the pacification, the governor most often returned power and dignity to those of great family and religious prestige.

19. In 1843, at Bugeaud's request, the Ministry of the Marine first placed a ship at the disposal of pilgrims to Mecca. As for the mosques built by the military authority, most of them replaced mosques that had been destroyed or converted to hospitals or warehouses. Mosques were also built for new towns such as Sétif and Philippeville, but the indigenous people had contributed financially to their construction.

20. The *Annuaire de la Légion d'Honneur* published in 1852 lists 16 officers and 76 cavalrymen of Algerian origin, among whom were 4 officers and 72 cavalrymen given the award before Tocqueville's report was published. Taking account of those who died between 1847 and 1852, the number of indigenous soldiers granted this decoration could not have exceeded 100 in 1847. Among those whose names we have, there are approximately equal numbers of officers, noncommissioned officers, and even simple soldiers, on the one hand, and, on the other, of notables, aghas, caids, and sheikhs.

21. This bias in favor of the indigenous people was sometimes created by the officers of the Arab bureaux, especially Colonel Daumas (cf. Demontès 1918, 520–34).

22. It seems that Tocqueville's report was originally even more severe in regard to these military favors bestowed on native Algerians, and that he had softened it at the request of certain members of the committee (cf. the speech by Chasseloup-Laubat during the session of 7 June 1847).

23. Marcel Emerit (1954a) located the report by Bedeau to which Tocqueville refers in the Archives du ministère de la Guerre (Algérie no. 235). He notes the existence in these archives of a contemporary report by Lepescheux, who had informed Tocqueville of these problems at the time of his visit to Algeria in 1841.

24. Sidi el-Aribi, from a tribe of the lower Chélif and whose family enjoyed a great religious reputation in the Oran area, was a loyal ally of the French. Indeed, his uncle had been taken prisoner by Abd-el-Kader, to whom he refused to submit (1834), and died in captivity at Mascara. Named khalifa in 1842 by Bugeaud, Sidi el-Aribi inflicted a serious defeat on Bou Maza in the Dhara in 1845.

25. In November 1846, Tocqueville had visited the house of the bachagha Bou-Allem. His traveling companion Bussière has left an interesting description of the site,

the house, and the hospitality that Bugeaud and his guests, the deputies visiting Algeria, received there (Bussière 1853).

26. According to Pellissier de Reynaud (1854, 3: 400), Arabs had built 2,241 houses outside the towns by 1850, so the results in this respect might have been greater than Tocqueville suggests.

27. The war of Bou Maza in 1844–45.

28. Tocqueville appears to be referring to ideas current at that time, and which he discussed again when he wrote *The Old Regime and the Revolution:* that the barbarian chiefs who seized lands in the Roman Empire were the ancestors of the feudal lords.

29. Thomas Robert Malthus (1766–1834), economist and author of the *Essay on the Principle of Population* (London, 1798), taught the history of political economy at Haileybury College from 1805 until his death. Sir James Mackintosh, M.P. (1765–1832), who taught at Haileybury from 1818 to 1824, wrote on philosophy, jurisprudence, and history but is perhaps best known for his *Vindiciae Gallicae* (1791), a reply to Burke's *Reflections on the Revolution in France.*

30. The radical M.P. Charles Buller (1806–48) was taken to Canada by Lord Durham as chief of his secretariat when Durham was named governor-general in 1838. Durham's famous *Report on the Affairs of British North America* (1839) was largely drafted by Buller, who in fact knew Tocqueville. When Tocqueville ran the journal *Le Commerce,* Buller contributed unsigned articles on English politics. [For a comparison of Durham's and Tocqueville's "liberal" views on colonization, see Stéphane Dion, "Durham et Tocqueville sur la colonisation libérale," *Journal of Canadian Studies,* 25, no. 1 (1990): 60–78. — J.P.]

31. Two departments, interior and public works, on the one hand, and finances, on the other, were created by an ordinance of 31 October 1838 dealing with the civil administration of Algeria (Duvergier 1838, 693–94), but an ordinance of 22 April 1846 split the first in two, creating a department of public works alongside a department of the interior and colonization (ibid. 1846, 98).

32. Antoine-Philippe-Léon Blondel (b. 1795) was sent to North Africa as director of finance in 1834 and named director general of civil affairs in Algeria by Marshal Soult in May 1845. Confronted with Bugeaud's deep hostility and a coalition of high officials under his orders seeking to free themselves from his control, Blondel quickly found himself in an almost impossible position, and he had to give up his post in July 1846. See Arch. nat. F80 315.

33. The powers of the governor-general, those of the director of civil affairs, and the composition and powers of the superior administrative council of Algeria and the litigation council [*conseil du contentieux*] had been set by the ordinance of 15 April 1845 regarding the reorganization of general administration and of the provinces in Algeria (Duvergier 1845, 83–96).

34. Because Bugeaud spent less time altogether in Algiers than he did on military campaigns or in Paris, where he served as a deputy for the Dordogne.

35. The transcriptions of the committee's meetings do not offer any precision on this point.

36. This principle was stated in article 109 of the constitution of 4 November 1848: "The territory of Algeria is declared French territory and will be ruled by particular laws until a special law places it under the rule of the present constitution."

37. In New Zealand, British colonization was founded on purchases of land from Maori tribes. In 1840, Colonel Wakefield (brother of the famous advocate of colonization), bought twenty million acres on behalf of the New Zealand Company, which were then granted to farmers. This sale was contested by indigenous tribes, and an arbitrator was sent, who, after three years of study, granted the essential justice of the Maoris' claims. Many colonists lost the land they had bought.

Nonetheless, after having prohibited such sales, in 1844 the British government once again authorized land purchases directly from natives. The result was serious disputes over land rights between colonists and Maoris, which led to twenty years of hostilities between the tribes and British authorities. See Keith Sinclair, *A History of New Zealand* (Baltimore: Penguin Books, 1959).

38. See Duvergier 1844, 482–92, for the 1844 ordinance, and ibid. 1846, 320–23, for the 1846 ordinance. These ordinances were clarified or modified by administrative rulings issued on 17 September 1846, 2 November 1846, and 6 March 1847 (Ménerville 1877–81, 1: 591–93).

39. This reform was carried out in the ordinance of 28 September 1847 (Duvergier, 1847, 424).

40. In the course of the discussion, Dufaure pointed out some ridiculous prohibitions by the Algiers censors, such as the prohibition against talking about the defective state of the roads as a result of drought.

41. The transcripts of the committee's meetings give no details on this point.

42. At that time, according to the *Tableau des établissements français dans l'Algérie,* IX (1846–49), there were 53,696 French residents of Algeria, or 51 percent of the Europeans there; and 50,197 foreigners, or 49 percent (about 29 percent Spanish, 6 percent Maltese, 6 percent Italians, and 8 percent of other nationalities).

43. The transcripts of the committee's meetings give no details on this point.

44. See Tocqueville's intervention in the debates, p. 125 above.

45. This proclamation by Bugeaud can be found in the *Moniteur universel,* 16 May 1847, 1189.

46. A series of difficult campaigns were to follow in Kabylia until 1857, when a network of roads and the founding of Fort-National at the heart of the territory assured its subjection by French forces.

47. In 1845, in particular, the committee on special funding for Africa, whose *rapporteur* was Magne, had taken a similar step; shortly thereafter, Magne, who was a government official, received a promotion.

48. [The government appears to have considered direct appeals by letter from parliamentary committees a violation of constitutional law. — J.P.]

49. [The report concludes with a detailed examination of particular allocations, omitted here. See *OC* 3, pt. 1: 363–79. — J.P.]

SECOND REPORT ON ALGERIA (1847)

1. [The bill, rejected by the committee, appears at the end of this report, on pp. 197–98. — J.P.]

2. [European emigration to Algeria had peaked in 1846, when almost 18,000 European colonists arrived; 13,000 of them were from France, while others arrived from Spain, Malta, Italy, and Germany. The pace of emigration slowed in subsequent years, in part because financial crisis in France led to a decrease in capital investment in Algeria; see Heffernan 1989, 380–82. — J.P.]

3. For the list of committee members, see p. 250 n. 2. From the composition of the committee, we can deduce that Desjobert and de Tracy held this opinion.

4. A report to the National Assembly in 1873 estimated that there were 1,500,000 hectares of state land, 300,000 of wasteland, 5,000,000 of *arch* land, and 4,500,000 of *melk* land in the Tell in 1830 (Pouyanne 1900, 223). *Melk* lands were individual property; *arch* lands were lands the indigenous Algerians believed they could not be dispossessed of as long as they cultivated them and paid taxes. Thus the theory of "cantonment," under which they were compensated with absolute title to part of these lands, would seem rather illusory.

5. The first villages settled were often devastated by malaria. The most striking account of their struggle is undoubtedly Gautier 1930.

6. [Colonists succumbed to plague, cholera, and typhus, among other diseases. In the summer of 1849, in a particularly brutal epidemic, over 5,000 inhabitants of the new agricultural colonies, or 65 percent of the population of these villages, fell ill with cholera; a third of these died. The administration attributed much of the suffering to the colonists' laziness and drunkenness; see Heffernan 1989, 398–400. — J.P.]

7. On the economic crisis in Algiers, interesting indicators are provided by the *Tableau des Établissements français dans l'Algérie*, IX (1846–49), 88 ff., and by Lespès 1930. The latter author, too, attributes the crisis to the speculation abuses that emerged after 1840, when it seemed that the total conquest of the country would be undertaken. In 1847, the town of Algiers lost 10,000 inhabitants, the province of Algiers 14,000, whereas in the provinces of Oran and Constantine, the number of Europeans continued to grow.

8. An overview of French colonization in the Algiers region can be found in Franc 1928. Baudicour 1856 also offers many interesting insights.

9. This was the system used by the director of the Algiers interior, Comte Eugène Guyot-Desherbiers.

10. Here Tocqueville undoubtedly alludes to the villages prepared for colonists by military convicts under the direction of Colonel Marengo.

11. An extended discussion of the experiences of Ain Fouka, Mahelma, and Beni-

Mered can be found in Demontès 1918, 274–350. Aïn-Fouka is located in the Sahel between the sea and Coléa, Mahelma on the last crests of the Sahel near Mazafran, and Beni-Mered in the Mitidja plain, a few kilometers from Boufarik.

12. The year before, Tocqueville had carefully visited the colonial villages in the Mitidja and the Sahel, so he is speaking from direct experience. Some of his impressions are discussed in an article by his travel companion, the journalist A. Bussière (Bussière 1853).

13. The center of Saint-Ferdinand in the Sahel had been devoted to colonization by a governor's decree of 5 September 1843. Colonists were offered a house with an area of 60 to 64 square meters, twelve hectares of arable land, of which four were cleared and trees were planted. The colonists could also request the construction of a lean-to for their livestock, and they were promised a church at the state's expense. This work had been performed by Colonel Marengo's military convicts.

14. Cheragas, located, like Saint-Ferdinand, in the Sahel, was founded by Comte Eugène Guyot-Desherbiers.

15. The reports by Lamoricière and Bedeau [see n. 25 below] mention three villages near Oran (La Senia, Sidi-Chamy, and Misserghin), three villages near Philippeville (Valée, Damrémont, and Saint-Antoine), and the center of El-Arrouch. These amounted to little next to the already dense colonization of the Sahel and the Mitidja.

16. On this question, see Hildebert Isnard, "Les Entreprises de fondation de villages dans le Sahel d'Alger," *Revue africaine* 1938, which gives a less optimistic account than Tocqueville's of free colonization.

17. Alexander I founded military colonies in the province of Mohilev, then Novgorod, beginning in 1815. Starting in 1816 he generalized this system by founding many colonies in the provinces of Kharkov, Ekaterinoslav, and Kherson. At the end of his reign, almost a third of his army was made up of soldier-laborers. The soldiers were unhappy and complained that they had been committed to permanent service; the peasants, for their part, saw themselves absorbed by military discipline. The system led to riots that were fiercely repressed.

18. The law of 1 floréal year XI [21 April 1803] *granting plots of territory to veterans of the 20th and 27th military divisions who will settle there* (Duvergier 14: 203–4). Decrees of 26 prairial year XI [15 June 1803] *concerning the formation and organization of veterans camps* and *concerning the formation of the first camp of the 27th military division* (Duvergier 14: 327–31). Decree of 15 floréal year XII [5 May 1804] *concerning the plots of territory granted to married or widowed soldiers with children, and aged between forty and fifty-four years* (Duvergier 14: 551).

19. This account by Vauban (a direct ancestor of Tocqueville's) is reprinted in *Vauban, sa famille et ses écrits, ses oisivités et sa correspondance* (Paris, 1910), 413–40.

20. Desjobert, who was to emphasize in a speech to the Chamber on 7 June the burden the recruitment would place on the poor, was probably one of these members.

21. Bugeaud's primitive projects originally involved legions of veterans organized militarily and working communally. But he had been led to develop his projects in a

more individualist direction (thus, to obtain a better level of production, the soldiers of the Beni-Mered colony had to be "disassociated").

22. On these three villages, see n. 11 above. The preceding autumn, Bugeaud himself had taken several deputies, including Tocqueville, to visit Beni-Mered.

23. On Bugeaud's orders, a report lauding military colonization at Beni-Mered was issued in 1845. See Demontès 1918, 345–48.

24. Chasseloup-Laubat was the author of this project, which was discussed on 14 April, according to the committee minutes.

25. The two projects, presented respectively by the generals commanding these two towns, were addressed to Bugeaud and published in a work entitled *Projets de colonisation pour les provinces d'Oran et de Constantine, présentés par mm. les lieutenants généraux De La Moricière et Bedeau* (Lamoricière 1847). Bugeaud, who had ordered their publication, did not fail, with his usual taste for polemic, to attack them in his very critical observations, thus making the public the judge of the debate.

Tocqueville here outlines what the reports presented by Bugeaud's lieutenants (Lamoricière's had been the work of officers in his entourage, essentially of Lieutenant Colonel de Martimprey) had in common, but there are just as many notable differences.

The Oran plan was concerned to find land for colonization where villages could be founded at the least expense. The state would cede the territory with the site for the village marked by stakes, with a simple Arab path leading to it (no church, school, town hall, or police office). It seems to admit that this territory would, as a general rule, go to enterprises that would liberally repopulate the land with indigenous Algerians.

Bedeau's plan was far more nuanced. Although he excluded colonization by "the poor," he thought that large landowners and more modest colonists should be placed side by side, and he hoped to introduce the indigenous people to the agricultural improvements that would be carried out. Without absolutely excluding the reintroduction of indigenous people, he recommended far greater prudence with respect to them.

26. [See, e.g., B.-P. Enfantin, *Colonisation de l'Algérie* (Paris: P. Bertrand, 1843) for the proposal by Saint-Simon's self-appointed heir; also A. de Montgravier, *Projet de fermes départementales en Algérie appliqué aux enfants trouvés* (1845). For some discussions of these projects, see Emerit 1941 and "L'Idée de colonisation dans les socialismes français," *L'Age nouveau* 24 (1967); and Rouchdi Fakkar, *Reflets de la sociologie prémarxiste dans le monde arabe: Idées progressistes et pratiques industrielles des Saint-Simoniens en Algérie et en Egypte au XIX* siècle (Paris: P. Geuthner, 1974). — J.P.]

THE EMANCIPATION OF SLAVES (1843)

1. These articles were published by the journal *Le Siècle* in the issues of 22 and 28 October, 8 and 21 November, and 6 and 14 December 1843. They were anonymous but preceded by the following note: "A man who owes his pure reputation and his high position in letters and politics entirely to conscientious works has sent us a series of articles on the grave question of the emancipation of slaves, to which we recommend

the full attention of our readers." Beaumont reprinted the articles in his edition of the *Œuvres complètes* (*OC* [B] 9: 265–98).

2. [Here Tocqueville is referring to the aristocrats who fled France during the Revolution. — J.P.]

3. A law of 4 March 1831 had organized the repression of the slave trade (see Duvergier 1831, 92–97). Condemned by the Congress of Vienna, the trade already theoretically had been abolished in France by Napoleon (decree of 29 March 1815) and by Louis XVIII (ordinance of 30 July 1815).

4. Tocqueville appears to refer to the decree of 7 September 1830 stating that "the acts of the civil state of the white population and the free population of color in the colonies will be inscribed in the same registers" (Duvergier 1830, 293). Also the ordinance of 24 February 1830, "abrogating the colonial decrees that restricted the enjoyment of civil rights by free persons of color" (Duvergier 1831, 113).

5. "What is slavery today?" asked the director of the Conseil spécial of Guadeloupe, repeating what according to him had become a proverb in the colony: "It is a state of affairs where the black works for his master as little as he can, five days a week, while the latter dare not say anything to him" (*Questions relatives à l'abolition de l'esclavage*, pt. 2: *Délibération du Conseil spécial de la Guadeloupe* [1843], 128, quoted in [Broglie] 1840–43: 2, 52).

6. Dominique, Grenada, Saint Lucia, Saint Vincent, Tobago, and Mauritius.

7. "Martinique is only eight leagues from St. Lucia, a former French colony, and twelve leagues from Dominique, another colony of the same origin. Guadeloupe is only eleven leagues from Dominique and eight from Antigua; a good wind, the cover of night, and the smallest boat are enough for part or all of a workshop to escape.

"Bourbon [Réunion] is only thirty-five leagues from Mauritius, a French colony until 1815.

"Guyana is a continental territory, at whose borders the blacks of Surinam live in complete freedom" ([Broglie] 1840–43: 2, 55).

8. The same idea was presented in [Broglie] 1840–43: 2, 50–52.

9. The exaggeration here is obvious. In the ten years that preceded 1843, just one state was created in the Mississippi region: Arkansas, in 1836.

10. In 1843, several east-west railway lines — Philadelphia-Pittsburgh, Baltimore-Ohio, Charleston-Ohio, Savannah-Macon — were completed or nearly completed. In just a few years, they would siphon off a large part of the commercial flow that had once used the Mississippi River. Tocqueville, probably relying on his impressions from the 1832 voyage, seems not to have predicted this.

11. Pointe-à-Pitre.

12. Fort-de-France.

13. After the crisis of 1840, Guizot, who had become minister of foreign affairs, pursued a policy of appeasement and concessions toward England. This policy was violently attacked by the liberal opposition as against the national honor. [See Furet 1992, 359–67, for a discussion of Guizot's policies and his relationship with the opposition. — J.P.]

14. The royal commission (see *OC* introduction, 10–11) was convened from 4 June 1840 to 6 March 1843. See [Broglie] 1840–43.

15. This thesis was supported in particular by the duc de Fitz-James in the Chamber of Peers during the debate on the slave trade of 23 July 1827. It was further developed by Jollivet in the Chamber of Deputies on 29 May 1845, on the occasion of the Mackau bill (see, e.g., Cyrille Charles Auguste Bissette, *Du projet Mackau tendant à violer la loi du 24 avril 1833 sur le régime législatif des colonies* [Paris: P. Dupont, 1844]).

16. [The former Dutch colony of Demerara — purchased by the British after the Napoleonic Wars — became part of British Guiana in 1831, which was renamed Guyana after it attained independence in 1966. — J.P.]

17. Maurice d'Argout, *Java, Singapour et Manille* (Paris: Vinchon, 1842), p. 9. Cited in [Broglie] 1840–43: 2, 66–67.

18. William Wilberforce began his struggle against the slave trade in 1787, but despite periodic demands in Parliament, the trade was not prohibited until 1807. During the 1820s, with the help of Thomas Buxton, Wilberforce attacked the problem of slavery itself. In 1823, he founded the Society for Effecting the Abolition of the Slave Trade, more commonly known as the Anti-Slavery Society, whose efforts, despite front-bench opposition in Parliament, especially that of Prime Minister George Canning, resulted in the 1833 act. It was a coalition of evangelicals, led by the Methodists and Baptists, and liberals that led the parliamentary leadership to take radical action despite itself. [The motion declared that "the state of slavery is repugnant to the principles of the British constitution and of the Christian religion" and that it should gradually be abolished "with as much expedition as may be found consistent with a due regard to the well-being of the parties concerned." See Robin Furneaux, *William Wilberforce* (London: Hamilton, 1974), 414. See also Robin Blackburn, *The Overthrow of Colonial Slavery, 1776–1848* (New York: Verso, 1988). — J.P.]

19. In December 1831, the emancipation of crown slaves led to a slave revolt on Jamaica that left the island pillaged. The white militias who reestablished order razed the temples of dissident sects.

20. In fact, the nineteen were the Cape of Good Hope; Mauritius, in the Indian Ocean; and seventeen colonies in the Western Hemisphere: Jamaica, British Honduras [Belize], Trinidad, Tobago, Grenada and its dependencies, Saint Vincent, Barbados, Saint Lucia, Dominica, Saint Christopher, Montserrat, Antigua, Nevis and Anguilla, Tortola and the Virgin Islands, the Bahamas, Bermuda, and British Guiana.

21. A list of documents and works on the emancipation in the British colonies is given in [Broglie] 1840–43, 2: xiii–xv.

22. Chevalier 1958, 32, notes that census-taking for a long time seemed "impious" to the French population, reminding them of the revolutionary and imperial requisitions, and that in 1841, the census still provoked troubles in certain regions.

23. François Guizot's report to King Louis-Philippe on the execution of the law of 28 June 1833 (April 1834) gives school attendance in France, counting only boys, as 1 in 20 inhabitants during the winter, and 1 in 40 during the summer. But this proportion would have to be raised to take account of girls' school attendance. See also Maurice

Gontard, *L'Enseignement primaire en France de la Révolution à la loi Guizot (1789–1833); des petites écoles de la monarchie d'ancien régime aux écoles primaires de la monarchie bourgeoise,* Annales de l'Université de Lyon, 3d ser., Lettres, fasc. 33 (Paris: Belles Lettres, 1959).

24. The details of these annual figures are found in [Broglie] 1840–43: 2, 21. In the first series of years cited by Tocqueville, 1834 is excluded; in the second, 1841 is included.

25. In September 1841, Lord Melbourne's Whig government was replaced by Sir Robert Peel's Tory ministry. Contrary to what Tocqueville indicates, however, the Abolition Act was not passed under Melbourne's administration, but under that of Lord Charles Grey, in 1833, when Lord Edward Stanley, 14th earl of Derby, was colonial secretary, an office he subsequently held again under Peel.

26. See the testimonies in [Broglie] 1840–43: 2, 33–39.

27. Tocqueville here echoes the lively discussions that were produced during the preceding session on the right of visitation and search. A treaty proposal that would have permitted English ships to board French ships to suppress the trade was violently attacked by the liberal opposition and rejected by the Chamber. [See Lawlor 1959, ch. 4, "The Right of Search," for a thorough discussion of these debates. — J.P.]

28. See *Tableaux de population, de cultures, de commerce, de navigation etc., formant pour l'année 1839 la suite des tableaux insérés dans les notices statistique sur les colonies françaises* (1842).

29. Charles de Rémusat, *Rapport fait au nom de la Commission chargé de l'examen de la proposition de M. Passy sur le sort des esclaves dans les colonies françaises* (1838). Rémusat concluded by demanding that the necessity of abolition be proclaimed, and that France should prepare for it by developing religious and primary instruction, reforming regulations on marriages among slaves, legalizing slave property and buying out, and by creating a service to oversee the application of the laws.

30. Achille-Léon-Victor, duc de Broglie (1785–1870).

31. Tocqueville wrote to his friend Beaumont on 9 October 1843: "This work has forced me to read the duc de Broglie's report again. It is a masterpiece. The discussion is confused, however, which explains why the effect it produces is not greater. And this whole work radiates a sincere love of humanity, that great and noble passion that the philanthropists' childishness has managed to make almost ridiculous."

32. The majority had adopted a plan for general and simultaneous emancipation, while the minority preferred a plan for partial and progressive emancipation. The two plans are published in an appendix to [Broglie] 1840–43: 2, 361–75.

33. *Notices statistique sur les colonies françaises* (1840) gives the following figures for cultivated land in 1838: Martinique, 37,565 hectares; Guadeloupe, 44,817 hectares; Guyana, 11,693 hectares; Bourbon [Réunion], 72,926 hectares.

34. Guadeloupe had been struck by an earthquake followed by fire at Pointe-à-Pitre on 8 February, which killed 3,000, and by a new fire on 26 August that devastated Basse-Terre. See Alfred Martineau and L.-Ph. May, *Trois siècles d'histoire antillaise: Martinique et Guadeloupe, de 1635 à nos jours* (Paris: Société de l'histoire des colonies françaises et Librairie Leroux, 1935), 224.

35. On the problem of the price of sugar and of maintaining a balance between colonial sugar and indigenous sugar, see E. Boizard and Henri E. Tardieu, *Histoire de la législation des sucres (1664–1891)* (Paris: Aux bureaux de la Sucrerie indigène et coloniale, 1891).

36. On 7 May 1841 (and not in 1840 as Tocqueville says), the British prime minister, Lord Melbourne, proposed a reduction of import duties on foreign sugar. His project was rebuffed by a coalition of Tories, protectionist Whigs, and abolitionists. He attempted to remain in power, but on 4 June a no-confidence motion introduced by Sir Robert Peel won a majority and forced him to resign.

37. Tocqueville seems to suggest that the king was hostile to abolition. Baron Charles Dupin, the great defender of slavery, wrote on the same subject with regard to Louis-Philippe: "His superior spirit does not allow itself to be abused by any vain utopia" (letter of 26 December 1837, in box 1106 of the Archives de la France d'Outre-Mer, cited in an unpublished study by Louis Bergeron).

38. At the 28 June 1843 session's discussion of the naval budget, Guizot, after having made assurances that the government was committed to resolving the question of slavery, added, "The expense to which the operation will give rise, and that will come to at least 220 or 250 million (*exclamations . . .*), which will come to at least 220 or 250 million, is also a grave fact that it would be impossible for the government not to consider." *Moniteur universel,* 1843, 1594.

39. [Broglie] 1840–43: 2, 279.

SELECT BIBLIOGRAPHY

TOCQUEVILLE'S WRITINGS

Alexis de Tocqueville. 1861–77. *Œuvres complètes*. Edited by Gustave de Beaumont. Paris: Michel Lévy frères, 1861. 9 vols. Cited as *OC* [B] and by volume and page number.

———. 1958–98. *Œuvres complètes*. Edited by J.-P. Mayer. Paris: Gallimard. Cited as *OC* and by volume, part, and page number.

———. 1968. *Tocqueville and Beaumont on Social Reform*. Edited and translated by Seymour Drescher. New York: Harper & Row.

———. 1985. *Selected Letters on Politics and Society*. Translated by James Toupin and Roger Boesche. Edited by Roger Boesche. Berkeley and Los Angeles: University of California Press.

———. 1986. *Recollections: The French Revolution of 1848*. Translated by George Lawrence. Edited by J.-P. Mayer and A. P. Kerr. Introduction by Fernand Braudel. New Brunswick, N.J.: Transaction Books.

———. 1990. *Democracy in America*. Translated by Henry Reeve. 4 vols. 1835–40. Edited by Phillips Bradley. 2 vols. 1945. Reprint, New York: Random House, Vintage Books. Cited as *Democracy*.

———. 1998. *The Old Regime and the Revolution*. Translated by Alan S. Kahan. Edited by François Furet and Françoise Mélonio. Chicago: University of Chicago Press.

OTHER SOURCES

Ageron, Charles-Robert. 1991. *Modern Algeria*. Edited and translated by Michael Brett. Trenton, N.J.: Africa World Press.

Baudet, Henri. 1960. "Tocqueville et la pensée coloniale du XIXᵉ siècle." In *Tocqueville: Livre du Centenaire, 1859–1959*, 121–32. Paris: Centre national de la recherche scientifique.

Baudicour, Louis de. 1856. *La Colonisation de l'Algérie, ses éléments.* Paris: J. Lecoffre.

Beaumont, Gustave de. 1835. *Marie, ou, l'esclavage aux Etats-Unis: Tableau de moeurs americaines.* 2 vols. Paris: C. Gosselin. Translated by Barbara Chapman under the title *Marie, or, Slavery in the United States: A Novel of Jacksonian America* (Baltimore: Johns Hopkins University Press, 1999).

Berlin, Isaiah. 1965. "The Thought of de Tocqueville." Review of *The Social and Political Thought of Alexis de Tocqueville,* by Jack Lively (Oxford: Clarendon Press, 1962, 1965). *History* 50: 199–206.

Blackburn, Robin. 1988. *The Overthrow of Colonial Slavery, 1776–1848.* London: Verso.

Blanc, Louis. 1844–45. *The History of Ten Years, 1830–1840.* 2 vols. London: Chapman & Hall.

Boesche, Roger. 1987. *The Strange Liberalism of Alexis de Tocqueville,* Ithaca, N.Y.: Cornell University Press.

Bouche, Denise. 1991. *Histoire de la colonisation française.* Vol. 2. Paris: Fayard.

Brogan, Hugh. 1973. *Tocqueville.* London: Collins/Fontana.

[Broglie, Achille-Léon-Victor, duc de] Ministère de la marine et des colonies. Commission instituée par decision royale du 26 mai 1840, pour l'examen des questions relatives à l'esclavage et à la constitution politique des colonies. 1840–43. *Rapport sur l'abolition de l'esclavage.* 2 vols. Paris: Imprimerie royale.

Bugeaud de la Piconnerie, Thomas-Robert, duc d'Isly. 1838. *De l'établissement de legions de colons militaires dans les possessions françaises du nord de l'Afrique; suivi d'un projet d'ordonnance adressé au gouvernement et aux chambres.* Paris: Didot Frères.

———. 1842. *L'Algérie: Des moyens de conserver et d'utiliser cette conquête.* Paris: Dentu.

———. 1948. *Par l'épée et par la charrue: Ecrits et discours.* Edited by Paul Azan. Paris: Presses universitaires de France.

Burke, Edmund, III. 1971. "Recent Books on Colonial Algerian History." *Middle Eastern Studies* 7, no. 2: 241–50.

———. 1993. *Struggle and Survival in the Modern Middle East.* Berkeley and Los Angeles: University of California Press.

Burke, Edmund, III, and Ira Lapidus, eds. 1988. *Islam, Politics, and Social Movements.* Berkeley and Los Angeles: University of California Press.

Bussière, A. 1853. "Le Maréchal Bugeaud et la colonisation de l'Algérie: Souvenirs et récits de la vie coloniale en Afrique." *Revue des Deux Mondes* (November).

Chevalier, Louis. *Classes laborieuses et classes dangereuses à Paris pendant la première moitié du XIXe siècle.* Paris: Plon, 1958. Translated by Frank Jellinek under the title *Laboring Classes and Dangerous Classes in Paris during the First Half of the Nineteenth Century* (Princeton, N.J.: Princeton University Press, 1973).

Chevallier, J.-J., and André Jardin. 1963. "Introduction." In *Tocqueville: Œuvres complètes.* Vol. 3, pt. 1: *Écrits et discours politiques,* edited by J.-J. Chevallier and André Jardin. Paris: Gallimard.

Christelow, Allan. 1985. *Muslim Law Courts and the French Colonial State in Algeria.* Princeton: Princeton University Press.

Clancy-Smith, Julia A. 1994. *Rebel and Saint: Muslim Notables, Populist Protest, Colonial*

Encounters: Algeria and Tunisia, 1800–1904. Berkeley and Los Angeles: University of California Press.

Cobban, Alfred. 1961. *A History of Modern France.* 3 vols. Vol. 2: *From the First Empire to the Second Empire.* Baltimore: Penguin Books.

Danziger, Raphael. 1977. *Abd al-Qadir and the Algerians: Resistance to the French and Internal Consolidation.* New York: Holmes & Meier.

Demontès, Victor. 1918. *La Colonisation militaire sous Bugeaud.* Paris: E. Larose.

Desjobert, Amédée. 1837. *La Question d'Alger: Politique, colonisation, commerce.* Paris: Crapelet.

Dion, Stéphane. 1990. "Durham et Tocqueville sur la colonisation libérale." *Journal of Canadian Studies* 25, no. 1: 60–78.

Drescher, Seymour. 1964. *Tocqueville and England.* Cambridge, Mass.: Harvard University Press.

———. 1968. *Dilemmas of Democracy: Tocqueville and Modernization.* Pittsburgh: University of Pittsburgh Press.

Duvergier, J.-B. 1830–1949. *Collection complète des lois, décrets, ordonnances, règlements, avis du Conseil d'état, publiée sur les éditions officielles du Louvre.* Paris.

Emerit, Marcel. 1941. *Les Saint-Simoniens en Algérie.* Paris: Les Belles Lettres.

———. 1947. *Les Bureaux arabes.* Extraits des documents algériens. Série politique, 10 November 1947. Algiers: Cabinet du Gouverneur géneral de l'Algérie.

———, ed. 1949. *La Révolution de 1848 en Algérie.* Paris: Larose.

———. 1951. *L'Algérie à l'époque d'Abd-el-Kader.* Gouvernement général de l'Algérie, Collection de documents inédits sur l'histoire de l'Algérie, 2d ser., Documents divers, vol. 4. Paris: Larose.

——— 1954a. "L'Etat intellectuel et moral de l'Algérie en 1830." *Revue d'histoire moderne et contemporaine,* 199–212.

———. 1954b. "Toustain du Manoir au pays d'Abd-el-Kader [Journal de mon voyage d'Alger au Ghréris, près Mascara, par M. Toustain Du Manoir]." 3d trip, June 1841. *Revue africaine* 98, nos. 440–41.

Esquer, Gabriel. 1923. *Les Commencements d'un Empire: La Prise d'Alger.* Algiers. Rev. ed., Paris: Larose, 1929.

Forment, Carlos. 1996. "Peripheral Peoples and Narrative Identities: Arendtian Reflections on Late Modernity." In *Democracy and Difference: Contesting the Boundaries of the Political,* edited by Seyla Benhabib, 314–30. Princeton: Princeton University Press.

Franc, Julien. 1928. *La Colonisation française de la Mitidja.* Paris: H. Champion.

Furet, François. 1992. *Revolutionary France, 1770–1880.* Oxford: Blackwell.

Furet, François, and Mona Ozouf, eds. 1989. *A Critical Dictionary of the French Revolution.* Translated by Arthur Goldhammer. Cambridge, Mass.: Harvard University Press.

Gargan, Edward T. 1955. *Alexis de Tocqueville: The Critical Years 1848–1851.* Washington, D.C.: Catholic University of America Press.

Gautier, E. F. 1930, *Un Siècle de civilisation au microscope: L'Exemple de Boufarik.* Paris: F. Alcan.

Gellner, Ernest. 1969. *Saints of the Atlas.* London: Weidenfeld & Nicolson.

Germain, Roger. 1955. *La Politique indigène de Bugeaud.* Paris: Larose.

Guizot, François. 1828. *L'Histoire de la civilisation d'Europe.* Paris: Pichon & Didier.

———. 1858–67. *Mémoires pour servir à l'histoire de mon temps.* 8 vols. Paris: Levy frères.

———. 1865. *Memoirs to Illustrate the History of My Time.* 4 vols. London: Richard Bentley.

Heffernan, Michael J. 1989. "The Parisian Poor and the Colonization of Algeria During the Second Republic." *French History* 3, no. 4: 377–403.

Heggoy, Alf A. 1986. *The French Conquest of Algiers, 1830: An Algerian Oral Tradition.* Athens, Ohio: Center for International Studies, Ohio University.

Jardin, André. 1962. "Tocqueville et l'Algérie." *Revue des Travaux de l'Académie des Sciences morales et politiques,* 4th ser., no. 1: 61–74.

———. 1977. "Alexis de Tocqueville, Gustave de Beaumont et le problème de l'inegalité des races." In *L'Idée de race dans la pensée politique française contemporaine,* edited by Pierre Guiral and Emile Temime, 200–219. Paris: Centre national de la recherche scientifique.

———. 1988. *Tocqueville: A Biography.* Translated by Lydia Davis. New York: Farrar Straus Giroux. Originally published as *Alexis de Tocqueville, 1805–1859* (Paris: Hachette littérature, 1984).

Johnson, Douglas. 1976. "The Maghrib." In *The Cambridge History of Africa,* vol. 5: *c. 1790 to c. 1870,* edited by John E. Flint, 99–119. Cambridge: Cambridge University Press.

Julien, Charles-André. 1931. *Histoire de l'Afrique du Nord: Tunisie, Algérie, Maroc.* Paris: Payot.

———. 1964. *Histoire de l'Algérie contemporaine: La Conquête et les débuts de la colonisation, 1827–1871.* Paris: Presses universitaires de France.

Keddie, Hikki R., ed. 1972. *Scholars, Saints, and Sufis: Muslim Religious Institutions since 1500.* Berkeley and Los Angeles: University of California Press.

Kelly, George Armstrong. 1992. *The Humane Comedy: Constant, Tocqueville and French Liberalism.* Cambridge: Cambridge University Press.

Lamoricière, Christophe Louis Léon Juchault de. 1847. *Projets de colonisation pour les provinces d'Oran et de Constantine, présentés par mm. les lieutenants généraux De La Moricière et Bedeau.* Paris: Imprimerie royale.

Lawless, Richard I., comp. 1976. *Algerian Bibliography: English Language Publications, 1830–1973.* London: Bowker for the Centre for Middle Eastern and Islamic Studies of the University of Durham.

Lawlor, Mary. 1959. *Alexis de Tocqueville in the Chamber of Deputies: His Views on Foreign and Colonial Policy.* Washington, D.C.: Catholic University of America Press.

Lespès, Rene. 1930. *Alger: Etude de géographie et d'histoire urbaines.* Paris: F. Alcan.

Letters on American Slavery. 1860. Boston: American Anti-Slavery Society.

Liebersohn, Harry. 1994. "Discovering Indigenous Nobility: Tocqueville, Chamisso, and Romantic Travel Writing." *American Historical Review* 99, no. 3: 746–66.
———. 1998. *Aristocratic Encounters: European Travelers and American Indians.* Cambridge: Cambridge University Press.
Lokke, Carl Ludwig. 1932. *France and the Colonial Question: A Study of Contemporary French Opinion, 1763–1801.* New York: Columbia University Press.
Lorcin, Patricia M. E. 1995. *Imperial Identities: Stereotyping, Prejudice and Race in Colonial Algeria.* New York: I. B. Tauris.
Mayer, J.-P. 1960. *Alexis de Tocqueville: A Biographical Study in Political Science.* New York: Harper & Brothers.
Mehta, Pratap. 1996. "Liberalism, Nation and Empire: The Case of J. S. Mill." Paper presented to the American Political Science Association, San Francisco.
Mehta, Uday S. 1990. "Liberal Strategies of Exclusion." *Politics & Society* 18, no. 4: 427–54.
———. 1999. *Liberalism and Empire: A Study in Nineteenth-Century British Liberal Thought.* Chicago: University of Chicago Press.
Mélonio, Françoise. 1998. *Tocqueville and the French.* Translated by Beth G. Raps. Charlottesville: University Press of Virginia.
Ménerville, Charles-Louis Pinson de. [1867–72] 1877–81. *Dictionnaire de la législation algérienne, code annoté et manuel raisonné des lois, ordonnances, décrets, décisions et arrêtés publiés au « Bulletin officiel des actes du gouvernement ».* 3 vols. Algiers: A. Jourdan. Vol. 1 covers the years 1830–60.
Mill, John Stuart. 1974. *Collected Works.* Edited by J. M. Robson and R. F. McRae. Toronto: University of Toronto Press.
Mitchell, Timothy. 1988. *Colonising Egypt.* New York: Cambridge University Press. Reprint. Berkeley and Los Angeles: University of California Press, 1991.
Naylor, Phillip Chiviges, and Alf Andrew Heggoy. 1994. *The Historical Dictionary of Algeria.* 2d ed. Metuchen, N.J.: Scarecrow Press.
Pagden, Anthony. 1995. *Lords of All the World: Ideologies of Empire in Spain, Britain and France, 1500–1850.* New Haven: Yale University Press.
Parekh, Bhikhu. 1994. "Superior People: The Narrowness of Liberalism from Mill to Rawls." *Times Literary Supplement,* 25 February, 11–13.
Pellissier de Reynaud, E. 1854. *Annales algériennes, nouvelle édition revue, corrigée et continuée jusqu'à la chute d'Abd-el-Kader, avec un appendice contenant le résumé de l'histoire de l'Algérie de 1848 à 1854 et divers mémoires et documents.* 3 vols. Paris: J. Dumaine.
Perkins, Kenneth J. 1981. *Qaids, Captains, and Colons: French Military Administration in the Colonial Maghrib, 1844–1934,* New York: Africana.
Pierson, George Wilson. 1938. *Tocqueville and Beaumont in America.* Oxford: Oxford University Press. Reprinted under the title *Tocqueville in America* (Baltimore: Johns Hopkins University Press, 1996).
Pouyanne, Maurice. 1900. *La Propriété foncière en Algérie.* Algiers: Jourdan.

Prochaska, David. 1990. *Making Algeria French: Colonialism in Bône, 1870–1920*. Cambridge: Cambridge University Press.

Rey-Goldzeiguer, Annie. 1991. "La France coloniale de 1830–1870." In *Histoire de la France coloniale*, edited by Jean Meyer, Jean Tarrade, Annie Rey-Goldzeiguer, and Jacques Thobie. Paris: Colin.

Richter, Melvin. 1963. "Tocqueville on Algeria." *Review of Politics* 25 (July): 362–98.

———. 1988. "Tocqueville, Napoleon, and Bonapartism." In *Reconsidering Tocqueville's Democracy in America*, edited by Abraham Eisenstadt. New Brunswick, N.J.: Rutgers University Press.

Roberts, Stephen H. 1963. *The History of French Colonial Policy, 1870–1925*. London: Frank Cass.

Ruedy, John. 1992. *Modern Algeria: The Origins and Development of a Nation*. Bloomington: Indiana University Press.

Saint-Arnaud, Arnaud-Jacques Leroy de. 1855. *Lettres du Maréchal de Saint-Arnaud, 1832–1854*. 2 vols. Paris: M. Levy frères.

Savary, Claude. 1783. *Le Coran, traduit de l'Arabe, accompagné de notes et précédé d'un abrégé de la vie de Mohammed tiré des ecrivains orientaux les plus estimés*. 2 vols. Paris: Knapen et fils.

Schacht, Joseph. 1964. *An Introduction to Islamic Law*. Oxford: Clarendon Press, 1964. Reprint, 1982.

Schefer, Christian. 1928. *La Politique coloniale de la Monarchie de juillet: L'Algérie et l'évolution de la colonisation française*. Paris: H. Champion.

Sivers, Peter von. 1975. "Insurrection and Accommodation: Indigenous Leadership in Eastern Algeria, 1840–1900." *International Journal of Middle East Studies* 6, no. 3: 259–75.

Soltau, Roger Henry. [1931] 1959. *French Political Thought in the Nineteenth Century*. New York: Russell & Russell.

Stokes, Eric. 1959. *The English Utilitarians and India*. Oxford: Clarendon Press.

Stora, Benjamin. 1991. *Histoire de l'Algérie coloniale, 1830–1954*. Paris: La Découverte.

Sullivan, Antony Thrall. 1983. *Thomas-Robert Bugeaud, France and Algeria, 1784–1849: Politics, Power, and the Good Society*. Hamden, Conn.: Archon Books.

Sutherland, Donald. 1982. *The Chouans: The Social Origins of Popular Counter-Revolution in Upper Brittany, 1770–1796*. Oxford: Clarendon Press.

Tableau des Etablissements français dans l'Algérie (Années 1838–1858). Paris: Imprimerie royale.

Thomson, Ann. 1987. *Barbary and Enlightenment: European Attitudes towards the Maghreb in the Eighteenth Century*. Leiden: E. J. Brill.

Todorov, Tzvetan. 1988. "Tocqueville et la doctrine coloniale." In Alexis de Tocqueville, *De la colonie en Algérie*, edited by Tzvetan Todorov, 9–34. Brussels: Editions Complexe.

———. 1993. *On Human Diversity: Nationalism, Racism, and Exoticism in French Thought*. Translated by Catherine Porter. Cambridge, Mass.: Harvard University Press.

Valensi, Lucette. 1977. *On the Eve of Colonialism: North Africa before the French Conquest.* Translated by K. J. Perkins. New York: Africana.

Valet, René. 1924. *L'Afrique du Nord devant le parlement au XIXᵉ siècle (1828–1838 — 1880–1881): Etude d'histoire parlementaire et de politique coloniale.* Algiers: Imprimerie "La Typo-litho."

Yacono, Xavier. 1953. *Les Bureaux arabes et l'évolution des genres de vie indigènes dans l'Ouest du Tell algérois.* Paris: Larose.

———. 1955. *Peut-on évaluer la population de l'Algérie vers 1830?* Paris: Imprimerie nationale.

INDEX

Abd-el-Kader, xxxvi, 9; character of, 64;
    followers of, 49–50, 87; leadership and
    power of, xix, xxii, 18–19, 22, 39–41,
    62, 65–69, 84; relations with French,
    xxxvi, 43; war with France, 65–72, 84,
    94, 108, 129, 248 n. 3
abolition of slavery, xxix–xxxii, 199–226;
    in Algeria, 146. *See also* slave eman-
    cipation
administration, colonial, xiii, 148, 194
administration, French, in Algeria, xxiii,
    15, 44, 131, 147–68; compared with
    France, 152; cost of, 156–59; oppres-
    sive to Algerians, 144; special colonial
    ministry needed, 107, 126–27; vices of,
    88, 93–105, 123, 147–60, 181. *See also*
    centralization; reform
administration, Turkish, in Algeria, 11
administrative law, excessive scope of, 51,
    104, 109–10
Africa, 216–17; and the African question,
    119, 121, 128, 130, 142; Guinea, 216.
    See also Algeria
agricultural population, European, 175–
    77, 180–83; importance of, 118; as
    source of friction with Algerians, 82
agriculture, in Algeria, 37, 41–43, 54, 87–

88, 118–19, 140, 171, 179; basis of
    colonial prosperity, 178–79; cost of,
    188; and military camps, 174–98; not
    profitable in Algeria, 197; products
    and markets, 124, 196
Ahmad Bey, xxxvi, 18–19, 22, 233 n. 66,
    234 n. 2[b]
Algeria: French knowledge of, 15, 26,
    137; geography of, 5–6, 14, 40, 52–53,
    86, 124, 131–33; history of, xii, xviii,
    xxxv–xxxviii, 16, 175; as part of
    France, xxiv, 110–11, 161
Algerian question, xiii. *See also* Africa
Algerians, indigenous: attitude toward
    French, xxvii, 83, 118, 129, 138, 145;
    correct way to govern, 131, 138–46;
    customs and character of, xxvi, 83;
    French knowledge of, xvii, xxv, 118,
    129–30, 148, 171; French mistreat-
    ment of, 140–41; political organiza-
    tion, xx, 55, 62; towns of, xxii, 72–73.
    See also Arabs; Jews; Kabyles; Moors
Algiers (city), xxxvii, 16; as center of ad-
    ministration, 123, 151–55; conquest of
    (1830), xi, xxxvi, 143, 169; European
    settlements in, 82, 85, 140, 163, 177–
    79; financial crisis in, 151, 177–78; im-

Library of Congress Cataloging-in-Publication Data

Tocqueville, Alexis de, 1805–1859.

[Selections. English. 2001.]

Writings on empire and slavery / Alexis de Tocqueville ; edited
and translated by Jennifer Pitts.

p. cm.

Includes bibliographical references and index.

ISBN 0-8018-6509-3 (hard : alk. paper)

1. Algeria—History—1830–1962.   2. France—Colonies.
3. Slaves—Emancipation—France—Colonies.   I. Pitts, Jennifer A.

II. Title.

DT294 .T63 2001

965'.03—dc21

00-009272

Printed in the United States
1311600004BA/49-129

Made in the USA
Lexington, KY
06 February 2015